The Sociology of Health and Illness Reader

Edited by

Sarah Nettleton and Ulla Gustafsson

polity

First published in 2002 by Polity Press in association with Blackwell Publishers Ltd

Editorial office:
Polity Press
65 Bridge Street
Cambridge CB2 1UR, UK

Marketing and production:
Blackwell Publishers Ltd
108 Cowley Road
Oxford OX4 1JF, UK

ISBN 0–7456–2290–9
ISBN 0–7456–2291–7 (pbk)

A catalogue record for this book is available from the British Library

Typeset in 10 on 12 pt Sabon
by Kolam Information Services Pvt. Ltd., Pondicherry, India
Printed in Great Britain by TJ International, Padstow, Cornwall
This book is printed on acid-free paper.

Contents

Acknowledgements

The editors and publishers wish to thank the following for permission to use copyright material:

E. Annandale, for material from 'Working on the front-line: risk culture and nursing in the new NHS', *Sociological Review* (1996) pp. 416–48, by permission of Blackwell Publishers; D. Armstrong, for material from 'The rise of surveillance medicine', *Sociology of Health and Illness*, 17:3 (1995) pp. 393–403, by permission of Blackwell Publishers; K. Atkin and W. Ahmad, for material from 'Pumping iron: compliance with chelation therapy among young people who have thalassaemia major', *Sociology of Health and Illness*, 22:4 (2000) pp. 500–20, by permission of Blackwell Publishers; P. Atkinson, for material from *Medical Talk and Medical Work* by P. Atkinson (1995) pp. 60–89, by permission of Sage Publications Ltd; S. Cant and U. Sharma, for material from *A New Medical Pluralism* by S. Cant and U. Sharma (1999) pp. 139–55, UCL Press Ltd, by permission of Taylor & Francis Ltd; D. Carricaburu and J. Pierret, for material from 'From biographical disruption to biographical reinforcement: the case of HIV positive men', *Sociology of Health and Illness*, 17:1 (1995) pp. 65–87, by permission of Blackwell Publishers; P. Conrad, for material from 'The mirage of genes', *Sociology of Health and Illness*, 21:2 (1999) pp. 228–40, by permission of Blackwell Publishers; L. Cooper, for material from 'ME and the medical encounter', *Sociology of Health and Illness*, 19:2 (1997) pp. 186–203, by permission of Blackwell Publishers; J. I. Elstad, for material from 'The psycho-social perspective on social inequalities in health', *Sociology of Health and Illness*, 20:5 (1998) pp. 598–611, by permission of Blackwell Publishers; C. Emslie, K. Hunt and G. Watt, for material from 'Invisible women? The importance of gender in lay beliefs about heart problems', *Sociology of Health and Illness*, 23:2 (2001) pp. 203–28, by permission of Blackwell Publishers; E. Ettorre, for material from 'Reproductive genetics, gender and the body: "Please, doctor, may I have a normal baby?"', *Sociology*, 34:3 (2000) pp. 403–17. Copyright © BSA Publications Ltd 2000, by permission of Sage Publications Ltd; S. M. Gifford, for material from 'The meaning of lumps: a case study of the ambiguities of risk' in C. P. Janes, R. Staff and S. M. Gifford, eds, *Anthropology and Epidemiology – Interdisciplinary Approaches to the Study of Health and Disease* (1986) pp. 213–38, by permission of Kluwer Academic Publishers; H. Graham, for material from 'Socioeconomic change and inequalities in men and women's health in the UK' in E. Annandale and K. Hunt, eds, *Gender Inequalities in Health* (2000) pp. 90–116, by permission of Open University Press; J. Green, for material from 'From accidents to risk: public health and preventable injury' in R. Bunton, S. Nettleton and

R. Burrows, eds, *The Sociology of Health Promotion*, Routledge (1995) pp. 116–32, by permission of Taylor & Francis Ltd; L. Griffiths, for material from 'Humour as resistance to professional dominance in community mental health teams', *Sociology of Health and Illness*, 20:6 (1998) pp. 874–93, by permission of Blackwell Publishers; S. Harrison and W. I. U. Ahmad, for material from 'Medical autonomy and the UK state 1975–2025', *Sociology*, 34:1 (2000) pp. 129–42. Copyright © BSA Publications Ltd 2000, by permission of Sage Publications Ltd; E. Heitman, for material from 'Social and ethical aspects of in vitro fertilization', *International Journal of Assessment in Health Care*, 15:1 (1999) pp. 22–32, by permission of Cambridge University Press; J. Lawton, for material from 'Contemporary hospice care: the sequestration of the unbounded body and dirty dying', *Sociology of Health and Illness*, 20:2 (1998) pp. 123–39, by permission of Blackwell Publishers; D. Lupton, for material from 'Your life in their hands: trust in the medical encounter', *Social Science and Medicine*, 45 (1996) pp. 373–81, by permission of Elsevier Science Ltd; S. Macintyre, S. MacIver and A. Sooman, for material from 'Area, class and health: should we be focussing on places or people?', *Journal of Social Policy*, 22:2 (1993) pp. 213–32, by permission of Cambridge University Press; G. Nijhof, for material from 'Parkinson's disease as a problem of shame in public appearance', *Sociology of Health and Illness*, 17:2 (1995) pp. 194–205, by permission of Blackwell Publishers; S. Pavis, S. Cunningham-Burley and A. Amos, for material from 'Health related behavioural change in context: young people in transition', *Social Science and Medicine*, 47 (1998) pp. 1407–17, by permission of Elsevier Science Ltd; L. Prior, P. L. Chun and S. B. Huat, for material from 'Beliefs and accounts of illness: views from two Cantonese-speaking communities in England', *Sociology of Health and Illness*, 22:6 (2000) pp. 815–36, by permission of Blackwell Publishers; L. A. Rhodes et al., for material from 'The power of the visible: the meaning of diagnostic tests in chronic back pain', *Social Science and Medicine*, 48 (1999) pp. 1189–201, by permission of Elsevier Science Ltd; M. A. Sanner, for material from 'Exchanging spare parts or becoming a new person? People's attitudes toward receiving and donating organs', *Social Science and Medicine*, 52 (2001) pp. 1491–8, by permission of Elsevier Science Ltd; D. Smith, N. Chaturvedi, N. Harding, S. Nazroo and R. Williams, for material from 'Ethnic inequalities in health: a review of UK epidemiological evidence', *Critical Public Health*, 10:4 (2000) pp. 375–408, by permission of Taylor & Francis Ltd; D. Webb, for material from 'A revenge on modern times: notes on traumatic brain injury', *Sociology*, 32:3 (1998) pp. 542–55. Copyright © BSA Publications Ltd 1998, by permission of Sage Publications Ltd.

Crown copyright material is reproduced under Class Licence No. C01W0000283 with the permission of the Controller of HMSO and the Queen's Printer for Scotland.

Introduction

'How are you?' 'Fine.' 'Great, never felt better.' 'OK apart from this stinking cold.' Routine, everyday conversations with friends, colleagues and family, where we talk about our health and illness. All of us have experience of health and illness, and our ideas about it are shaped by our social context. We probably all have some notion of what it means to be healthy. Furthermore, anyone who has *never* experienced some sort of illness would be extremely unusual, if not to say, extremely lucky. Everyone reading this book will also have some experience of health *care*. That health care might have been in the guise of 'formal health care', such as visiting their general practitioner, or 'informal health care', such as being cared for by one's father or mother or, indeed, even 'caring' for one's own health. Health and illness are therefore the stuff of everyday life: from the mundane routines of practising self-care, such as cleaning our teeth, to more dramatic experiences, such as being transported to hospital in an ambulance with its lights flashing and sirens blaring.

The subject matter of this book is therefore something that each and every one of us is familiar with, perhaps so much so that we may not have spent a great deal of time reflecting on the academic salience of these day-to-day matters, and may not necessarily have thought through the broader social, economic and cultural ramifications of the topic. Indeed, it is all too easy to assume that our experiences of illness and health are simply the consequences of natural biophysical changes in our bodies, rather than being shaped by our social and cultural context. This assumption is challenged by sociologists of health and illness. For example, they have shown that the way in which we, and indeed doctors, interpret our illness symptoms is very different today from how they would have been interpreted fifty or one hundred years ago (Armstrong, 1993; Atkinson, 1981; Duden, 1991). Disease categories are not neutral, unambiguous descriptions of physiological processes; rather, they are imbued by the language, metaphors and values of the broader social contexts (Martin, 1989; Sontag, 1988). The types of illnesses that we are likely to suffer from have changed between time and place. Health care treatments have also been transformed dramatically.

This is what the sub-discipline – the sociology of health and illness – is about. It draws upon a range of sociological perspectives in order both to *make sense of how health and illness is experienced* and to *critically examine society's response to health, illness and disease*. By society's response we refer to how health care systems are organized and how health and illness are measured and assessed; how informal health care is carried out; and how medical 'experts' and lay people make sense of, and define, various categories of disease. Like any sociological enterprise, the sociology of health and illness is riven with debate; however, the shared premiss of this field of study is that health, illness and disease are fundamentally social concepts, rather than purely biophysical ones. The rest of this chapter will examine this contention further when we juxtapose two models of health and illness: the *biomedical model* and the *social model*. These models represent an analytic distinction between medicine and sociology; in practice, however, the boundaries between the two disciplines are more blurred than these models might suggest. The content and methods of sociology and medicine are, for example, both contingent upon their wider social and historical context – they tend to be interested in the same sorts of issues at the same time. In this Reader we are concerned to restrict our focus to papers which are topical and reflect contemporary developments in sociology, and which have, in turn, sought to make sense of broader social transformations. In particular, our focus is on health and illness within a *late modern context*.

Two models: the biomedical and the social

There has been a tradition within medical sociology of arguing that the *biomedical model* has long formed the dominant paradigm in Western medicine. Arguably this model is based upon a number of assumptions: first, that the mind and the body can be treated separately, an idea sometimes termed *mind–body dualism*; and second, that the body can be repaired in much the same way as a machine can be fixed. Thus medicine adopts a *mechanical metaphor*, presuming that doctors can act like engineers to mend the dysfunctioning body. Solutions to medical problems will therefore be found in technologies such as drugs or machinery which can invade the anatomical frame and put it right, hence the *technological imperative*. This idea is *reductionist* in that explanations of disease and solutions are sought within biological, physical and technological contexts, to the relative neglect of social and psychological factors. Such reductionism has been reinforced by the so-called *doctrine of specific aetiology*, which presumes that diseases are often caused by a specific, identifiable agent – such as a parasite, virus, bacterium or gene (chapter 6). Finally, medical knowledge is presumed to be *objective*, and therefore neutral, based on rational empirical evidence, and thus to be distinct from the social context in which such knowledge is produced.

The *social model*, of course, is very different, and really emerged out of a critique of medicine which drew attention to the assumptions which we have just described. In this respect, it could be said that the biomedical model is *itself* a sociological construct – that is, a 'model' which sociologists created in order to make a claim that they had a privileged view of health and illness (Kelly and Field, 1994). Not surprisingly, therefore, the social model of health and illness is the antithesis of the biomedical one. It challenges the mind–body dualism inherent in medicine, and suggests that such a distinction is at best wrong and at worst pernicious. Humans are embodied – that is, they simultaneously are and have bodies which are experienced (Williams and Bendelow, 1998). Such a view undermines the idea that the physical body can be 'treated' or 'fixed' independently, and instead posits that the whole person should be considered and cared for. This holistic approach to medicine espouses the idea that health, disease and illness are not just related to biophysical changes, but are also influenced and shaped by the wider socio-economic context. For example, patterns of disease almost invariably correspond to the distribution of power and resources throughout society. Thus, to understand health, disease and illness, we must have a clear knowledge of power relations and social inequalities. Finally, medical knowledge can never be objective; like all scientific knowledge, it is contingent upon the context in which it is produced. Medical practitioners, for example, have to be taught how to 'see' the body. What they learn from medical texts, and from within the context of the teaching hospital, is but one of many accounts of how the body might be 'seen' or understood. Thus the body itself – the central object of medical practice – is presumed to be a social construction. As Armstrong (1983, p. xi) noted in the introduction to his influential book *Political Anatomy of the Body*,

> At first it seemed strange to me how the apparent obviousness of disease and its manifestations inside the body had eluded scientific discovery for so long. How had pre-Enlightenment generations failed to see the clearly differentiated organs and tissues of the body? Or failed to link patient symptoms with the existence of localised pathological processes? Or failed to apply the most rudimentary diagnostic techniques of physical examination? My disbelief grew until it occurred to me that perhaps I was asking the wrong questions: the problem was not how something which is so obvious today had remained hidden for so long, but how the body had become so evident in the first place. In dissecting and examining bodies I had come to take for granted that what I saw was obvious. I had thought that medical knowledge simply described the body... [however]...the relationship is more complex...medical knowledge both describes and constructs the body as an invariate biological reality.

Armstrong's work is based on the ideas of Foucault (1976, 1979). Whilst most sociologists of health and illness share the view that medical knowledge is socially constructed (the idea that the creation of knowledge is an outcome of social processes, rather than a neutral, objective scientific endeavour), they differ on the extent to which our ideas about the body are socially influenced. For example, a Foucauldian approach suggests that ideas about the body and disease are simply discursive constructions – they are effects of practices, activities and language (Arney and Bergen, 1984; Bunton and Petersen, 1997). This approach has been criticized by other sociologists of health and illness, who maintain that knowledge of the body, health and illness is often distorted due to the social relations in which that knowledge is created (see Annandale, 1998, pp. 41–5). The most obvious example of this is the way in which medical knowledge about women's bodies and diseases has both reflected and reinforced patriarchal relations (Martin, 1989; Stacey, 1988).

Medicine and sociology – common interests

It is evident from the above discussion that two divergent paradigms have been identified within sociology and medicine. As noted, this dualist approach has been criticized by sociologists. Nevertheless, the models can serve as useful heuristic devices to enable us to identify the scope and limitations of the disciplines. At a more fundamental level, sociology and medicine have much in common. After all, practitioners of sociology and of medicine are both concerned with people, bodies and the 'well-being' of populations, even if at a day-to-day level their focus is different. Medicine obviously has a much longer history than sociology, and some have suggested that sociology emerged within the context of 'modern medicine', and in particular public health and 'surveillance medicine' (chapter 9). As Foucault (1980, p.151) famously put it, in his usual polemical style, 'Countless people have sought the origins of sociology in Montesquieu and Comte. That is a very ignorant enterprise. Sociological knowledge is formed rather in the practices like those of doctors.' What is being referred to here is the copious documentation of the health, environment and living standards of, usually, urban populations. Some of these were drafted by medical personnel, others by engineers (such as Edwin Chadwick), still others by social scientists (such as Charles Booth and Joseph Rowntree). They all produced data on individual bodies and on the body of the population. This is what Foucault called 'disciplinary power' – the practices used by those working within institutions to regulate, monitor, train and come to understand bodies (Lupton, 1995; Turner, 1995). This notion is an important one within contemporary sociology of health and illness, because it helps us to grasp the salience of *risk*. If bodies are perpetually assessed and monitored, this then facilitates our understanding of the likelihood that any given 'type' of person may be at risk of a particular illness. For example, a person who smokes, is overweight, and has high blood pressure according to current data will be at greater 'risk' of suffering from a heart attack.

Smoking, heart attacks, blood pressure and diet are topics which are of interest to both sociologists and medical practitioners working in the twenty-first century. In other words, the two disciplines which are sometimes presumed to be at odds with each other have much in common. Medicine has incorporated social issues, and sociology has in recent decades been keen to 'bring the body back in' (Frank, 1990). This has emerged partly as a result of dialogue between the two disciplines, but also because of changes in the nature of the disease burden. The second half of the twentieth century saw a shift from predominantly acute, life-threatening infections to conditions such as heart disease, cancers, diabetes mellitus and asthma. There was a corresponding shift from intervention to surveillance, and from curing to caring. By definition, chronic conditions are not curable, and medicine is limited to more ameliorative responses. Alternative or complementary therapies are increasingly being used by those who suffer from chronic conditions (Cant and Sharma, 1999), so medicine is increasingly becoming one of a range of health care responses which are 'reflexively' (Giddens, 1991) sought out by patients. Causal models of disease burdens are now more broad, incorporating both social and biomedical factors. Social determinants of disease include lifestyle factors such as smoking, stress and exercise at an individual level and unemployment and poverty at a structural level. In concert with these changes, there have been shifts in the organizational responses to illness and disease, in particular the shift from health care within the locale of the hospital to care within the community.

The advent of the twenty-first century then saw the consolidation of a new paradigm of health, health care and health policy (Nettleton, 1995; Klein, 2001). This is what Armstrong (1993) refers to as a new 'regime of total health'. Within this regime, people are encouraged to monitor and maintain their own health; people are increasingly being cared for in non-institutional environments; and patients and users of health care services are encouraged to voice their views about their health and their health care. The idea that we have consistently to monitor risks, both collectively, at a societal level, and individually, on a personal level, is a feature of contemporary society more generally.

Health and illness in contemporary society

In many countries throughout the world, parents are encouraged to have their children immunized against measles, mumps and rubella (MMR). In the UK the current practice is to use a combined vaccine and so use one 'jab'. Not all parents are confident that this combined vaccine is completely 'safe' (Rogers and Pilgrim, 1995). The British Government and the medical profession are keen to assure parents that there are no side effects. The following extract is taken from a newsgroup on the Internet where this topic has been debated at length.

> My son had the MMR jab when it first became available – he is now 11 years old and has been diabetic for 5 years. There is little or no published evidence of MMR and Insulin Dependent Diabetes Mellitus (Juvenile diabetes) being linked but I believe this could be the cause. It is also a fact that the incidence of IDDM has risen since MMR has been routinely given. My daughter is now three years old and has not been given MMR for this very reason. Several health professionals have asked why Nell has not had the jab and on being told my reasons NONE have questioned me or argued further. I have nothing against jabs – [Daughter] & [Son] have had all the others – and nothing against taking Measles, Mumps and Rubella jabs singularly. [Daughter] will have Rubella jab as she gets older as I am a firm believer in this particular inoculation especially for girls. But I am very opposed to 'cocktails' of jabs. I do not think enough is known about the effects the semulti-doses [*sic*] can have on individuals. This is just my opinion and my experience – your decision should be exactly that – Yours!

This extract is indicative of many of the issues which have come to the fore in contemporary debates on health and illness, to do with risks, technology and the status of both expert and non-expert knowledge.

Before we discuss these further, let us take another example of a debate which was highlighted in the UK media, one that involves the definition of death for the purposes of organ removal for use in transplant surgery. According to one national newspaper, some 'leading' anaesthetists are arguing that anaesthetics should be given routinely to patients who are certified 'brain dead' before they are operated upon to remove their heart, liver and pancreas. They have argued that although patients may be legally brain dead, there is evidence to suggest that they may still experience pain. Definitions of brain death vary between countries, and the British definition is different from that in the USA and in some other European countries. These various definitions of legal death were necessitated by technological developments in transplantation surgery, which needs healthy and functioning organs, but were far from straightforward (Lock, 1997). What is of interest to us here is not the rights and wrongs of the debate, but the very fact of the debate itself. Uncertainty and lack of consensus surround something that might at first sight seem clear-cut – the divide between life and death.

The MMR debate concerns a routine intervention which aims to reduce the prevalence of disease. The life-and-death debate focuses on the possibility that once people are legally 'dead', they may still 'suffer' pain when they are operated upon. Whilst these are two very different examples, they both highlight a number of characteristics of late modern society. First, they both draw our attention to *technological developments*. The combined vaccine is itself an example of a techno-logical development within the context of pharmaceutics. In this example, we also see how the Internet has provided a new forum for the MMR issue to be debated. Information and communication technologies (ICTs) provide new scope and possibilities for information to be sought and exchanged between both lay people and professionals. It also draws attention to changes at the level of health care delivery, where advice may be sought on-line from services such as NHS on-line, rather than at a hospital outpatients' department. Second, our examples highlight the *uncertainties* associated with medical knowledge and med-ical practices. Our life-and-death example reveals how among medical experts decisions are rarely clear-cut and empirical evidence is invariably contentious. Thus a third point is the *contingent nature of medical knowledge*. Debates about scientific medical knowledge are not restricted to medical circles. Non-professional 'experts', or lay people, are also prepared to question and examine scientific knowledge, and do not accept it uncritically. We see here a further issue: the *ambivalence* of ordinary people to medical knowledge and authority, and the changing status of *lay knowledge*. This relates to a fifth point, which is that faith and *trust in a powerful professional group* such as medical personnel is on the decline. This is in a context where the *risks* associated with medical interventions are also evident. For example, making decisions about whether or not to have one's child vaccinated involves the *reflexive* assessment of a complex array of infor-mation.

As noted above, these features are not only pertinent to issues associated with health and illness; they are also characteristics of contemporary late modern society. To understand contemporary health matters further, then, it would be instructive to have an appreciation of the contours of *late modernity*, as it has been described by some contemporary social theorists.

Late modernity – some key concepts

Most social commentators seem to agree that the turn of the twenty-first century is a period characterized by significant social, cultural, economic and technological change. Terms such as post-Fordist (Burrows and Loader, 1994), postmodernity (Harvey, 1989), late modernity (Giddens, 1990), information society (Castells, 2000), disorganized capitalism (Lash and Urry, 1994), reflexive modernization and the risk society (Beck, 1992) have been variously used to try and capture some of these transformations. Of course, the precise reasons for, and contours of, the changes have been discussed extensively, and there is not the space here, or the necessity, to rehearse these debates. Instead we will focus on those aspects of change and those features of contemporary society which we consider to be instructive for our understanding of many contemporary issues in health and illness.

Modernity, or the 'industrial age' in retrospect (and this is probably a good example of retrospective theorizing), was characterized by certainty, stability and security. It had the following features: the growth and dominance of manufacturing industries, clear work patterns, and social hierarchies between 'workers' and 'managers', 'professionals' and 'patients', and 'experts' and 'lay people'. Gendered divisions of labour in both paid and unpaid work were fairly clear-cut. Men worked, women looked after children at home. These traditions pre-patterned one's fate – one grew up, left home, worked and married. Life was certain and, because of this, some suggest it was more secure. There was not only a certainty about one's future, but also a certainty about the development of new and successful technologies and science. For example, there was a confidence that medicine would either conquer or at least treat many more diseases. Of course, the reality of people's lives did not always live up to such stereotypes and was invariably more complex than this brief sketch portrays. Furthermore, people's beliefs were not so uni-dimensional. But this outline does highlight some of the socio-economic factors of modern life, and aims to capture what theorists have suggested were features of modern (as opposed to late modern) living.

By the mid-1970s, it is suggested, things began to change, and it is the more recent *intensification of these changes* that characterizes late modernity. The decline in manufacturing on a large scale and the rise of service sector employment meant that work patterns changed – people now have fixed, short-term contracts; there is more part-time work; there is relatively more work for women (albeit still relatively poorly paid); and men no longer have 'jobs for life' (chapter 19). In terms of our social and personal relationships, marriage often ends in divorce, and women are not getting married and having children! Family forms are becoming more divergent. More uncertainty at these social and economic levels is matched by cultural changes, such as a greater questioning of the merits of developments within science and technology. Perhaps experts didn't have the answers after all. So a sea change has occurred in people's lives at the level of work and home life; faith in science, technology and progress; and in trust in professional experts.

Beck (1998) and Giddens (1999) have reflected upon some of the social and cultural factors (as opposed to the economic and technological factors) which have brought about these changes. First is what they refer to as the *end of nature*. 'The risk society begins where nature ends' (Beck, 1998, p. 10). According to these writers, we have switched from being worried about what nature does to us, to worrying about what we have done to nature. Of course, we can still suffer from the effects of nature, such as floods and hurricanes (although are they due to global warming?). But the point is that there are very few areas of the material environment that have not been affected by human intervention. These writers therefore distinguish between *external* and *manufactured risks*. External risks characterized early and pre-modernity, and manufactured risks late modernity. Manufactured risks, the type of risks in our society, are therefore those that are the consequence of human interventions. They are also less amenable to actuarial calculation. For example, we don't know the levels of risk of global warming, genetically modified foods, or BSE. Indeed, we aren't even sure – or rather, the 'experts' cannot agree – if there *are* risks associated with them. Manufactured risk, it is argued, doesn't just affect nature – it permeates other areas of life, such as our personal relationships. Our *personal* futures are much more open and *flexible* than they were in the past.

A second precipitating factor is what Beck and Giddens call the *end of tradition*. The less we rely on traditional 'certainties', the more risks we have to negotiate (Beck, 1998, p. 10). More risks mean more choices, and therefore more decisions.

Part of the end of traditional social forms is the loss of faith in those traditionally in authority – *detraditionalization*. Experts, doctors, teachers and even medical personnel are subject to increased scrutiny. In modernity, scientific knowledge became a kind of traditional authority (for example, scientific expertise would often override our grandmothers' advice on our children's diet). 'Lay people "took" advice from experts' (Giddens, 1999, p. 4). But now, the more science and technology intrude into our lives, the more people question it. The lay view of science has changed. Scientists, of course, have always changed their ideas and disagreed with each other – that is the nature of knowledge. But that was not how people viewed it. Now, increasingly, so-called expert or scientific knowledge is under inspection, a process which is amplified by the media. More and more people are making their own decisions and *reflexively* assessing complex and often conflicting sources of advice and information on health routines, health interventions and on their experiences of illness. Such activities, it is argued, permeate the psyche, and may impact upon one's notion of self and identity – what Giddens calls the *reflexivity of the self*, a project carried out amid a profusion of reflexive resources: 'therapy and self help manuals of all kinds, television programmes and magazine articles' (Giddens, 1991, p. 30). To these we can add the myriad of virtual resources of cyberspace.

The sociology of health and illness – an empirical enterprise

The above discussion provides a brief overview of some recent theorizing on contemporary social changes. A feature of the sociology of health and illness as a field of study, in stark contrast to some strands of sociological theory, is that it is predominantly empirical. The papers in this Reader reflect this trend, in that they are virtually all empirical papers which make use of the analytic tools that have been developed within sociology. The empirical and applied nature of the sociology of health and illness is what makes this area of study not only so interesting and exciting, but also of value to health care practitioners, lay people and sociologists alike. Those working in the field often concurrently undertake two types of research: that which has been described as 'sociology *in* medicine' and that which is termed 'sociology *of* medicine'. The former refers to social research which seeks to address issues which are of concern to health care practitioners and policy makers. Questions such as: What factors contribute to good-quality health care? Why is it that some patients are more likely to take their prescribed medicines than others? A sociology *of* medicine, by contrast, seeks to explore what is of sociological interest, such as how certain types of knowledge come to be accepted, why certain occupational groups come to dominate the division of labour within health care, and so on. Turner (1995, p. 2) has argued that the sociology *of* medicine can also be useful and contribute to improving health and health care in our society. He notes: 'Ultimately sociology can better serve the practice problems and needs of patients by formulating sociological rather than medical questions.' The empirical papers in this Reader focus on sociological questions which are associated with health, illness, and health and medical care. Notions of risk, reflexivity, uncertainty, flexibility and technological change reappear throughout the five parts, on bodies, health and risk, experiencing illness, social patterning of health and illness and health care work.

References

Annandale, E. (1998) *The Sociology of Health and Medicine*. Cambridge: Polity.

Armstrong, D. (1983) *Political Anatomy of the Body: Medical Knowledge in Britain in the Twentieth Century*. Cambridge: Cambridge University Press.

Armstrong, D. (1993) From Clinical Gaze to a Regime of Total Health. In A. Beattie, M. Gott, L. Jones and L. Sidell (eds), *Health and Wellbeing: A Reader*, London: Macmillan, 55–67.

Arney, W. R. and Bergen, B. (1984) *Medicine and the Management of Living: Taming the Last Great Beast*. London: University of Chicago Press.

Atkinson, P. (1981) *The Clinical Experience: The Construction and Reconstruction of Medical Reality*. Aldershot: Gower.

Beck, U. (1992) *Risk Society: Towards a New Modernity*. London: Sage.

Beck, U. (1998) Politics of Risk Society. In J. Frankin (ed.), *The Politics of Risk Society*, Cambridge: Polity, 9–22.

Bunton, R. and Petersen, A. (eds) (1997) *Foucault, Health and Medicine*. London: Routledge.

Burrows, R. and Loader, B. (1994) *Towards a Post Fordist Welfare State?* London: Routledge.

Cant, S. and Sharma, U. (1999) *A New Medical Pluralism*. London: UCL Press.

Castells, M. (2000) Materials for an Exploratory Theory of the Network Society. *British Journal of Sociology*, 51 (1), 5–24.

Duden, B. (1991) *The Woman Beneath the Skin: A Doctor's Patients in Eighteenth-Century Germany*. London: Harvard University Press.

Foucault, M. (1976) *The Birth of the Clinic: An Archaeology of Medical Perception*. London: Tavistock.

Foucault, M. (1979) *Discipline and Punish, the Birth of the Prison*. Harmondsworth: Peregrine.

Foucault, M. (1980) The Politics of Health in the Eighteenth Century. In C. Gordon (ed.), *Michel Foucault Power/Knowledge: Selected Interviews and Other Writings 1972–1977 by Michel Foucault*, Brighton: Harvester Press, 166–82.

Frank, A. (1990) Bringing Bodies Back In: A Decade Review. *Theory, Culture and Society*, 7 (1), 131–62.

Giddens, A. (1990) *The Consequences of Modernity*. Cambridge: Polity.

Giddens, A. (1991) *Modernity and Self-Identity: Self and Society in the Late Modern Age*. Cambridge: Polity.

Giddens, A. (1999) The Runaway World: The 1999 Reith Lectures. http://news.bbc. co.uk/hi/english/static/events/reith_99/default.htm

Harvey, D. (1989) *The Condition of Postmodernity*. Oxford: Blackwell.

Kelly, M. and Field, O. (1994) Comments on the Rejection of the Biomedical Model in Sociological Discourse. *Medical Sociology News*, 19, 34–7.

Klein, R. (2001) *The New Politics of the NHS*. London: Longman.

Lash, S. and Urry, J. (1994) *Economies of Signs and Space*. London: Sage.

Lock, M. (1997) Displacing Suffering: The Reconstruction of Death in North America and Japan. In A. Kleinman, V. Das and M. Lock (eds), *Social Suffering*, London: University of California Press, 207–44.

Lupton, D. (1995) *The Imperative of Health*. London: Sage.

Martin, E. (1989) *The Woman in the Body: A Cultural Analysis of Reproduction*. Milton Keynes: Open University Press.

Nettleton, S. (1995) Women and the New Paradigm of Health and Medicine. *Critical Social Policy*, 16 (3), 33–53.

Rogers, A. and Pilgrim, D. (1995) The Risk of Resistance: Perspectives on the Mass Childhood Immunisation Programme. In J. Gabe (ed.), *Medicine, Health and Risk*, Oxford: Blackwell, 73–89.

Sontag, S. (1988) *AIDS and its Metaphors*. Harmondsworth: Penguin.
Stacey, M. (1988) *The Sociology of Health and Healing*. London: Unwin Hyman.
Turner, B. S. (1995) *Medical Power and Social Knowledge*. London: Sage.
Williams, S. and Bendelow, G. (1998) *The Lived Body: Sociological Themes, Embodied Issues*. London: Routledge.

Part I

Bodies

Introduction

In the first year of the twenty-first century the Hayward Art Gallery in London mounted an exhibition devoted to the depiction of the body in art entitled *Spectacular Bodies: The Art and Science of the Human Body from Leonardo to Now*. This was perhaps not surprising, because by the year 2000 the body had become a fashionable topic of discussion and debate amongst both academics and producers of popular culture. Sociologists in particular developed a 'sociology of the body' which both draws upon, and contributes to, debates within the sociology of health and illness. Indeed, commenting on these debates, Turner argues that a sociology of the body should form 'an organising principle in medical sociology' (1992, p. 169).

A number of writers have suggested that the reason why we have come to pay so much attention to our bodies in recent times is because they represent a site over which we can exert some control. Whilst our social, economic and environmental contexts may be characterized by insurmountable risks and uncertainties (see Introduction to this volume), our bodies may be more amenable to management and manipulation. As Shilling puts it:

> Investing in the body provides people with a means of self expression and a way of potentially feeling good and increasing the control they have over their bodies. If one feels unable to exert control over an increasingly complex society, at least one can have some effect on the size, shape and appearance of one's body. (1993, p. 7)

In the context of uncertainty, then, the body becomes something of an anchor, a seemingly secure site over which one can have some influence. Giddens (1991) further points out that because the self is 'embodied', the body becomes a medium through which one's biography and self-identity are created and sustained. Thus he observes that people 'reflexively' draw upon a whole array of activities and resources to 'work upon' their 'health, diet, appearance, exercise, lovemaking and many other things' (1991, p. 218). But of course there is an irony here: for as we develop our knowledge, expertise, technologies and activities associated with the body, the more uncertain we become as to what the body actually is. The boundaries between the biological, social and technological body become less clear. Boundaries, such as the distinction between life and death, that once appeared immutable, are no longer clear-cut.

Bodies and medical knowledge

Within the sociology of health and illness, much of the debate about 'bodies' focuses on the ways in which medical knowledge of the body is created or produced. Within a Western context, biomedical discourses of the body tend to predominate, and there is a cherished assumption that medical science understands and describes the 'real' or natural body. We have come to know our bodies through the discourse of medicine, and the way in which biomedicine describes the body is often taken to be the 'true' knowledge of it. Certainly it is often held that current medical knowledge is the correct knowledge, whereas ideas set out in 'old' medical texts are wrong, confused or unenlightened. This assumption is challenged by those who adhere to the social constructionist perspective, which at base argues that *all* medical and scientific knowledge of the body is no different from any other ideas about the body, all of which are produced and established through social interaction and interpretations (Lupton, 2000; Nettleton, 1995). The physical anatomy of the patient came to be the prime focus of medicine towards the end of the eighteenth century. This, according to Foucault (1976), was when the *Clinic* or *Hospital Medicine* was formed (see chapter 9). Foucault describes how at the turn of the eighteenth century doctors carried out examinations of dead bodies (autopsies) within hospital or clinical environments, to find out the true cause and nature of disease. Disease from then on was located within the depths of the anatomical frame, and illness was thereby reduced to a pathological lesion. The patient's body, rather than the patient, was the focus of the *medical gaze* (Foucault, 1976) and so the prime source of knowledge, a feature of the biomedical model.

The social production of medical knowledge within the context of the hospital laboratory is the subject of our first paper, by Atkinson, who discusses the findings of his ethnographic study of haematologists practising in both the USA and the UK. As Atkinson explains, haematologists constitute but one of many specialist or occupational groups, who use various technologies (e.g. ultrasound, magnetic resonance imaging (MRI) and X-rays) to scrutinize the interior frame of the body. Here we see how this group of specialists go about examining blood samples which are sent to the laboratory for investigation. Atkinson illustrates the way in which, in their routine practice, haematologists interpret their observations of blood samples, and how they are schooled in observation. 'Seeing is not straightforward', he argues, because 'there is nothing natural about the haematologists' or pathologists' descriptions, and nothing given about the descriptive categories or their use. On the contrary the language of the pathological gaze is, like any other specialized register, a socially shared collection of conventions.' In the paper we see instances where novice pathologists and haematologists are taught to look for certain shapes, images and fragments. Their shape, size, colour and so on are not readily obvious; they are debated, discussed and negotiated even between trained clinicians.

The use of technologies to scrutinize the interior space of the body is the subject of the next paper in this section. Here Rhodes and her colleagues examine the consequences for patients with back pain of privileging those technologies (such as X-rays, MRI and computed tomography) which aim to provide accurate readings of the anatomy over the lived experience of patients. In those instances where the diagnostic tests were able to locate the source of the pain within the body, there was no problem for patients. However, in other cases, where a range of diagnostic tests failed to identify any visible 'cause' of the pain, patients felt that their pain was not seen as 'legitimate' in the eyes of practitioners, or indeed, their relatives and friends. This, the authors of the paper argue, is because there is a strong historical, cultural as well as medical assumption that 'the inside of the body corresponds to visual images of it'. The findings of this paper resonate with postmodern debates about the body within medicine, which have suggested that the body itself is no longer the prime focus of the medical gaze, but that the *image* of the patient's body now forms the basis of medical practice. Frank, drawing on the work of Baudrillard to develop this argument, states:

> Real diagnostic work takes place away from the patient; bedside is secondary to screen side. For diagnostic and even treatment purposes, the image on the screen becomes the 'true' patient, of which the bedridden body is an imperfect replicant, less worthy of attention. In the screens' simulations of our initial certainty of the real (the body) becomes lost in hyperreal images that are better than the real body. (1992, p. 83)

Better than the real body for clinicians perhaps, but as we see from the views presented in the paper, not necessarily better for the patients. Rhodes and her colleagues conclude their paper on an optimistic note, and cite the work of Martin (1994), who suggests that such rigid notions of the body and the anatomy may be giving way to alternative visions or representations of the human body – a body which is conceptualized as being more flexible and fluid.

The issue of flexibility is also evident in Sanner's paper, which, by way of an empirical analysis of people's views on organ donation, deciphers some underlying conceptualizations of the body. Two dominant images of the body are the 'body as a machine' (akin to the biomedical model outlined in the Introduction to this volume) and the 'influenced body' (the idea that new bodily organs could transfer the donors' qualities). Empirical understandings of these matters are important, as ethical, social and psychological tensions will invariably emerge alongside technological developments associated with the exchange of body parts and other interventions such as those developed in order to 'assist' reproduction. Reproductive technologies form the topic of the following two papers. Heitman examines the social and ethical aspects of *in vitro* fertilization, and Ettorre identifies a number of issues which emerge with the development and application of reproductive genetics. Reproductive genetics, she notes, involves the use of DNA-based technologies in the medical management and supervision of the reproductive process. Common to all these papers is the important fact that people are presented with more and more choices – choices which, prior to the development of these new technologies, did not exist. Of course, to some extent this is true of any technology or treatment – whether to intervene or not presents the provider and the recipient of care with a choice – but choices associated with the creation and modification of life itself do involve more profound social and ethical considerations.

Organ donation and assisted reproductive technologies are examples of technological developments which are associated with transformations of our bodies. Perhaps the technological development which has most captured the popular imagination in recent decades is that associated with the new genetics. Conrad's paper argues that the public discourse on genetics has much in common with the discourse that emerged alongside the germ theory of disease in the nineteenth century. Conrad makes use of Dubos's classic and influential work the *Mirage of Health*, which argued that the germ theory of disease was based on three assumptions which form the basis of the biomedical model: 'the doctrine of specific aetiology; a focus on the internal rather than the external environment; and the metaphor of the body as a machine' (see chapter 6). Conrad then suggests that the popular discourse of genetics, as it occurs in the media, works with a similar, or parallel, set of assumptions. These assumptions make the language of genetics very appealing: for gene theory 'appeals to existing western ideas of individuality and current notions about responsibility for health, and shifts blame for problems from environments and social structures to individuals and biophysiology'.

Embodiment and late modernity

Sociologists of health and illness have been keen to dispel the idea that there is a difference between the physical and the subjective body, sometimes referred to as mind–body dualism, which we discussed in the Introduction. Drawing on phenomenological sociology, some writers have suggested that we might more appropriately develop a *sociology of embodiment* rather than a sociology of the body (Williams and Bendelow, 1998). They argue for a 'lived body' approach, one which recognizes the inextricable interaction or 'oneness' of the mind and body. Consciousness, it is pointed out, is invariably embodied, and humans are embodied social agents. The idea that the self and the body are inseparable is one that has long been recognized by empirical researchers who have studied how people *experience illness* (see Part III).

The problem with much of this literature and its emergent concepts – such as 'the body project' and 'the reflexive self' – is that they all tend to assume a competent mind. David Webb's paper on the impact on families of traumatic brain injury (TBI) draws our attention to the prevalence of this assumption. 'Without the competent mind', he writes, 'there is no sociology of the body. There is too the much wider (and delicate) question about the relationship between subjectivity and our conceptions of "being human".' Traumatic brain injury results in fifteen people (mainly young men) being taken to hospital every hour in the UK, and it has been described as a silent epidemic of our modern times. Webb draws attention to the irony that although the epidemic is a function of modern living – with fast cars, motorbikes, etc. – its victims are unable to participate in one of the defining characteristics of late modernity. As Webb explains:

> Indeed the case here is that with a physiologically damaged brain comes the likelihood of a fractured mind, and that consequently this will have a bearing on the person's capacity to existentially 'live their body' – to reflexively experience it [...] [H]igh modernity revolves around a mentalist discourse in which greater importance is given to the mind than the sociological talk of 'body matters' suggests.

The extent to which sufferers will be able to reflect upon their lives, their past and their future aspirations will therefore depend on their mental capacity to do so. As with most injuries or disabilities, there is a continuum in terms of severity. For some who retain some degree of mental capacity, there may well be a process of reflexivity.

Writing in the *Guardian* (17 August 2000) about his experiences following severe head injuries incurred as a result of a car crash, Nick Munroe described how

> I worked out a structure for my life and lowered my expectations, then gradually came to terms with my limitations by identifying them and working with them. Now I lead a full, rewarding and productive life because I have set different goals to achieve. [...] Yet with the uninitiated in society, the lack of awareness surrounding head injuries tends to invite a negative attitude through ignorance and insensitivity.

Head injuries, and the associated impact on the victim's mental capacity, are something that we prefer to ignore in contemporary society. It is something we do not want to have to acknowledge. This, Webb argues, compromises both our commitment and our capacity to support and care for sufferers of TBI. Health care provision and support for the victims' families, he argues, are relatively underfunded.

Just as society displays an unease with those who suffer from TBI, we also find certain forms of dying particularly difficult to cope with. Julia Lawton's paper on hospice care reveals that we are especially uncomfortable with what she calls 'dirty dying'. By focusing on the body itself, she argues that it is not necessarily death *per se* that we find problematic; it is dying of diseases which result in bodily deterioration and disintegration that we, in Western societies, cannot tolerate. It is in cases where body boundaries are transgressed, or bodily controls are not maintained, that patients are removed from their home environments and placed in a hospice. In her analysis Lawton draws upon the work of anthropologist Mary Douglas and sociologist Norbert Elias, who have both argued that the way in which the social body is perceived finds a correspondence in the way the physical body is perceived. Furthermore, Elias has argued that part of the civilizing process has involved the privatization and removal of many of the 'natural' functions of the body from public view.

Whilst Webb's paper on TBI reminds us that the 'reflexive self' relies on the presence of a competent mind, Lawton's paper demonstrates that the functioning of a competent mind can be undermined by a dysfunctioning physical body. She shows how not being able to control one's body can affect a person's capacity to continue with their life projects or their reflexive self. Based on her observations within a hospice, she describes how patients who had the least control over their bodily functions 'all exhibited behaviour which suggested a total loss of self and social identity once their bodies became severely and irreversibly unbounded'. She illustrates this point by detailing the circumstances and experiences of a number of the patients in the hospice.

The papers by Lawton and Webb both focus on topics which are pertinent to late modern Western society: that is, the sequestration (or removal) of death and dying from public view and the epidemic of head injuries due to fast modern lifestyles. But the findings of these empirically grounded studies challenge some of the central assumptions upon which contemporary theorizing is based. Whilst many people may actively pursue body projects, or take advantage of the growing array of technological interventions to modify their bodies, there are still instances where the possibilities and potential for the self-control of the lived body are constrained by the physical capacity of the body itself.

References

Foucault, M. (1976) *The Birth of the Clinic: An Archaeology of Medical Perception*. London: Tavistock.

Frank, A. (1992) Twin Nightmares of the Medical Simulacrum: Jean Baudrillard and David Cronenberg. In W. Stearns and W. Chaloupka (eds), *Jean Baudrillard: The Disappearance of Art and Politics*, London: Macmillan, 82–97.

Giddens, A. (1991) *Modernity and Self-Identity: Self and Society in the Late Modern Age*. Cambridge: Polity.

Lupton, D. (2000) The Social Construction of Medicine and the Body. In G. L. Albrecht, R. Fitzpatrick and S. C. Scrimshaw (eds), *Handbook of Social Studies in Health and Medicine*, London: Sage, 50–63.

Martin, E. (1994) *Flexible Bodies: The Role of Immunity in American Culture from the Days of Polio to the Age of AIDS*. Boston: Beacon Press.

Nettleton, S. (1995) *The Sociology of Health and Illness*. Cambridge: Polity.

Shilling, C. (1993) *The Body and Social Theory*. London: Sage.

Turner, B. S. (1992) *Regulating Bodies: Essays in Medical Sociology*. London: Routledge.

Williams, S. and Bendelow, G. (1998) *The Lived Body: Sociological Themes, Embodied Issues*. London: Routledge.

1

Reading the Body

Paul Atkinson

The body and the clinic

The cultural history of modern medicine clearly identifies an orientation to the body as a key feature in its emergence (Lupton, 1994). This view is articulated in Foucault's treatment of the birth of the clinic (Foucault, 1973). The epistemological break that marks the foundation of modern medicine is to be identified in the inspection of the patient's body, and the privileged revelation claimed for the *clinical gaze*. This mode of seeing was part and parcel of a technology of surveillance and monitoring. In this political anatomy, the patient's body became legible. Moreover, the observable signs and the patient's symptoms were increasingly matched to the findings of pathological science. A new discipline of pathological anatomy enabled the physician to treat disease in terms of localized lesions and processes. The body in modern medicine is thus constituted as a site for *inspection*. [. . .] The body is thus read as the localized setting for disease processes that are themselves traced to specific organs and systems. As Armstrong summarizes this view of modern political anatomy:

> The modern body of the patient, which has become the unquestioned object of clinical practice, has no social existence prior to those same clinical techniques being exercised upon it. It is as if the medical gaze, in which is encompassed all the techniques, languages and assumptions of modern medicine, establishes by its authority and penetration an observable and analysable space in which is crystalised that apparently solid figure – which has now become as familiar – the discrete human body. (Armstrong, 1983: 2)

[. . .]

It is in this way that the body is rendered legible. It is made to render up its signs by means of a variety of technologies that produce traces, images and enumerations that can be interpreted by physicians and others. The special senses of sight, touch, sound and smell are supplemented by intermediary technologies.

In other words, the body yields its clues by means of a wide range of clinical methods. The modern history of medical technology has furnished the clinic with a powerful armamentarium of investigative machinery. Through that machinery of investigation and description, the body is disaggregated into numerous traces and fragments. Each of them may then be read by competent observers. Each specialist offers his or her special gaze, which in turn may inform the generalized gaze of the primary care physician or team. In other words, the body of modern medicine has entirely ceased to be coterminous with the physical presence of the individual patient. The body may be read and interpreted *in absentia*. The traces and signs of the body's structures and functions may be taken and read elsewhere. [...]

The body is thus transformed into a series of signs and representations, by means of a complex array of technologies of inspection. The technical division of labour within the modern clinic is, in part, a diversity of specialized means for visualizing and enumerating the fragmented body. In this way 'information' about the patient and his/her condition is dispersed in time and space. The physical complexity of the modern hospital, and its equally complex temporal order, provide a matrix in which clinical knowledge is constructed and lodged.

The body is represented in various departments, divisions and laboratories. Each specialty claims expertise in a representational technique and its own organs or systems. The modern body has been appropriated and reconstituted by a diversity of experts. In this system of medical inspection and surveillance, the integrity of the body is dissolved into a series of more or less discrete domains of knowledge and technique. Moreover, as new technologies have developed, as their availability and use has spread, so the body itself may be ever more fully probed, more delicately visualized, and more finely enumerated.

The modern clinic has multifarious means and devices whereby the body's constituents and configurations are rendered visible and legible. Among the most dramatically obvious to the contemporary observer are the various mechanisms for the production of *images*: X-rays; ultrasound; computed tomography; magnetic resonance imaging; nuclear tracing. Each of those imaging techniques reveals differing aspects of space, tissue and motion.

[...]

These various imaging techniques by no means exhaust the means available to render the body visible and legible. There are many other ways to remove and render traces of the body. Many – unlike imaging – depend on the removal of sample tissue and its further preparation and treatment. Many of the techniques employed by clinical pathologists and haematologists depend on the close inspection of small samples of body fluids and tissues.

The haematologist will typically use a number of routine procedures for the examination of blood and other systems or organs. The most obvious is the examination of a smear of peripheral blood under the microscope – which is used to gather a great deal of information about the composition and morphology of the blood and its constituent parts. Equally basic to the haematological investigation is the inspection of a small sample of bone marrow. The latter is important for the reason that bone marrow is the site of manufacture for red blood cells (erythropoesis). Hence the presence or absence of young cells can be detected in the marrow as can abnormality in their maturation.

The haematologist who works with related cancers (such as the lymphomas) will have occasion to work with biopsies taken from tissues suspected or believed to be malignant. The products of a biopsy will be subject to visual inspection, possibly in collaboration or serially with a clinical pathologist. Larger tissues may also be sampled for frozen-section preparation and pathological inspection.

With each of these techniques – and others like them – the haematologist helps to disaggregate the body into finer and finer discriminations. Each is removed from the patient in time and space, and each sample becomes a kind of 'text' which can then be read by competent investigators. Blood, bone marrow, lymph nodes and the like are thus sampled and dispersed. Their information is therefore de-contextualized from the patient, and reconstituted as the object of knowledge in the complex organization of the clinic.

The visible body

In many instances the tissues of the body require preparation before the sample can be read and interpreted. It needs to be fixed and enhanced as a legible text. In some cases, therefore, it needs to be prepared by *staining*. The staining of blood samples is one way in which body tissue is rendered visible to the clinical gaze. Each stain fixes and makes apparent particular haematological features. Each therefore corresponds in a general sense to the sort of image enhancement that has interested sociologists of scientific knowledge. In one sense, microscopy appears to be technology for the direct and detailed inspection of human tissues. And, to a limited extent, that is true. The microscope has, historically, furnished a potent extension of the clinical gaze. It allows the clinician or the pathologist to peer beyond the gross features of structure and function. It permits a close-up view of pathology and an examination of structures not available to the naked eye.

On the other hand, the microscopic gaze is not unmediated. The tissues need to be rendered visible to the microscope's lenses; and the images so yielded need to be interpreted, in the light of the means used to render them legible in the first place. The competent microscope user must, for instance, know about the properties of reflected and refracted light; about the relative thickness of specimens and preparations; about appropriate levels of magnification. Equally, the microscopic gaze is mediated by the conventional methods used to make certain structures or contents visible. The practice of staining microscope slides is an old one. Sometimes the stain's value is primarily in just rendering visible otherwise translucent tissues. Where there is a virtual absence of 'natural' colour, then the addition of artificial colours enhances the visibility of the tissue. Such staining introduces one element of *contrast* – between 'light' and 'dark', or 'opaque' versus 'translucent'. Other modes of staining may introduce further elements of contrast by revealing structures or substances that would not otherwise be visible. In some cases, for instance, the haematologist will need to use a special stain to reveal the presence of iron. The choice of stain, of course, will depend upon what visual information is being sought. [...]

The practised haematologist or pathologist is, therefore, adept at seeing the evidence revealed to microscopic inspection. He or she is familiar with the conventional reading practices used to produce legible traces. The laboratory has available a variety of general and special stains that enhance the visibility of particular features. The laboratory staff use various recipes to produce stains, or use commercially prepared standard preparations. The modern use of microscopy is thoroughly dependent on stains, and it would be virtually impossible without the visual enhancement they allow.

The use of natural dyes to stain microscopic specimens did not become wide-spread until about 1850.

> It is safe to say...that the use of stains revolutionized microscopic technic. The early microscopists were able to make much progress without stains because of their pains-taking diligence. The work without stains must have been extremely difficult, and it is hard on reading some of the old publications to believe that some of the minute structures described were actually seen. Few users of the microscope today would be likely to have either the patience or the eyesight to do the work described in those early days. The fact that the microscope is now being used successfully in the hands of so many students who would not think of comparing themselves with the pioneers in microscopy is due to the use of stains more than to any other factor – although, of course, no one can deny that modern improvements in the microscope have also played a part of great importance. (Conn, 1961: 2)

As Conn indicates the modern habits of scientific vision are virtually 'unthinkable' without the enhancements of histological staining.

[...]

The topic takes us beyond the scope of the present work and into another project altogether, but one must note that the laboratory practices that render the body visible are themselves 'craft' work, often dependent on tacit, embodied know-ledge. The laboratory scientist or technician is routinely engaged in the day-to-day preparation, administration and checking of things like special stains, or the routine inspection of body tissues and samples. The everyday work of the clinical laboratory scientist has been almost totally neglected in sociological investiga-tions of the modern hospital or medical school. Yet their backroom work – for all that it takes place in the backstage regions of the clinic – is of fundamental importance to the social organization of modern medicine. The visibility of the disaggregated body depends on a technical division of labour, whereby the practices of 'revealing' and 'seeing', 'counting' and 'classifying' are socially and spatially distributed.

Seeing is not straightforward. Whether or not the smears and traces have been prepared in special ways, the specimen does not automatically and self-evidently yield its clues to the scientist or clinician. Competent observation is predicated on tacit, embodied knowledge of how to 'see' and 'what to look for'. These implicit competences are also supplemented by external sources of reference. In particular, the haematologist (or laboratory scientist) can refer to the illustrations in textbooks or 'atlases' of haematology. This includes various kinds of printed representation against which observed instances can be compared. These atlas representations provide especially important reference-points for students and less experienced practitioners.

[...]

These representations are useful for the practitioner who needs to recognize and classify features of a given specimen. The exemplars in printed representations may be used as a point of reference, or as a set of templates, against which 'reality' is contrasted and composed. The representations of the textbook or atlas are actual types (such as photographs of particularly clear examples) or ideal types (such as diagrams constructed to illustrate 'classic' forms). Whether or not they are constructed or reproduced, such illustrations 'simplify' in various ways. Since even photographic illustrations are carefully made and carefully selected, they normally contrast with the complexities and ambiguities of what is 'actually' seen under the microscope. [...]

[...] The anatomical or histological atlas can direct the gaze towards the most appropriate kinds of distinctive features. It encodes and reproduces its implicit theory of knowledge. [...] The haematologist's manual [...] inscribes a theory of types of phenomena such as blood cells. [...] The presence and distribution of key types of blood cells in turn helps to allocate the blood itself to a type, which may imply a diagnosis (in turn dependent on another theory of disease types).

The haematologist therefore uses the atlas (from time to time) to produce descriptions and categorizations of phenomena such as blood-cell types. His or her concerns include the capacity to perform the following perceptual and cognitive tasks: identify the shape, colour and relative size of blood cells; use appropriate linguistic categories to generate descriptions of those phenomena: categorize and classify those cells into types (developmental lines); estimate relative frequencies of cell types; produce accurate counts of cell types.

In these ways – as in many other areas of clinical medicine and pathology – the expert (primary physician, specialist, laboratory scientist) acts as a practical phenomenologist. He or she is concerned, as a matter of everyday work, with the nature of *appearances* and the production of *descriptions*. Those descriptions need to be adequate for the practical purposes of sharing and recording biomedical observations. They need to be sufficiently delicate to capture sometimes subtle variations in the appearance of tissues and traces. Equally, they draw on a register of occupationally given vocabularies that are a socially shared medium of description.

These matters are by no means confined to the work of haematologists. All medical work is dependent on the use of the senses, and the observation of the patient's body is grounded in the construction of medically relevant descriptions. I have, for instance, documented elsewhere some of the problems encountered by junior medical students in their attempts to produce descriptions of patients and their bodies that are regarded as adequate and accurate by their clinical teachers. The novice does not immediately see a pertinent description of, say, a patient's complexion. It was apparent during my earlier fieldwork with Scottish medical students that confronted by an instruction to 'observe' a patient they could easily flounder (Atkinson, 1988). They could not always produce satisfactory descriptions of the clinical signs – even the most apparently obvious kind. (Obvious, that is, to the teaching clinicians.) Observations are not self-evident to the 'uninitiated'. In the absence of a conceptual framework and a descriptive vocabulary there is no socially shared 'observation': there is no agreement as to a stable world of phenomena. Hence, even agreement to describe a patient as 'pale' or 'jaundiced', or 'tanned' or the like is dependent on the situated vocabularies of clinical medicine.

In precisely the same way, the haematologist or clinical pathologist assembles descriptions of potentially significant phenomena out of a common stock of descriptive categories. At first sight, the shared vocabulary of the clinical laboratory may seem unremarkable – no more nor less than a technical, neutral language of scientific description. In practice, however, there is nothing natural about the haematologists' or pathologists' descriptions, and nothing given about the descriptive categories or their use. On the contrary the language of the pathological gaze is, like any other such specialized register, a socially shared collection of conventions. The linguistically defined categories of medical description provide the cultural resources for the production of facts. The trained clinician or pathologist draws on a vast repertory of descriptors in order to generate accounts of what has been seen, what has been noticed or observed. Many of those terms are in common usage – not restricted to clinical or laboratory settings. Others are far more domain-specific, and characteristic of pathology discourse.

The choice of an appropriate description has implications for how phenomena are categorized, and hence for possible differential diagnoses. The following exchange between clinicians (in this case a fellow (F) and an attending (At)) and a pathologist (P) is illustrative [see Appendix]:

F: Yeah, there weren't that much then when we went back and looked we were more impressed with it, so it would be good if you could review it and see if it is atypical
At: Because the thing that we were noticing, you know, when you see the Wright stain of the lymphocytes, quite often the cleft is right down straight and deep, right through the middle.
P: Yeah
At: Well a lot of these cleftings looked more like circumferential cleftings.
P: Mm

Pathologist and clinicians go on discussing the tests they want to carry out on the tissue. Later in the interaction, looking now under the microscope, they return to the issue of 'cleft' cells:

At: Those are clefts. There's a cleft
P: A *notch!*
F: Hahehh
At: Hehnhnhum huhuhm
P: Well, I'd hate to have to make it on this. I think the *bone* marrow's very suspicious
At: There *were* some there

What is at stake here is whether the cells that have been seen, and are not being scrutinized by the pathologist, can properly be described as 'clefts'. The clinicians are in some difficulty in establishing a diagnosis concerning this patient, on the basis of a wide range of information, and the evidence of the microscope and of the laboratory remains equivocal in their eyes. It is puzzling enough a picture. Here, as we can see, it remains obscure. The clinicians want to describe the presence of 'clefts' in the lymphocytes, even though they do not seem to claim them as straightfor-wardly present. On the other hand, the pathologist – to whom appeal has been made for a more definitive opinion – remains equivocal as to the general characterization of the specimen. Moreover, the pathologist challenges the clinicians' description of what they all 'see' under magnification. The description 'notch' is preferred to 'cleft', with unstated but implied consequences of undermining further the clinicians' attempts to characterize the case.

The identification of distinctive features, such as clefts or notches, in the samples of bone marrow or blood cells, is one major task for the clinical pathologist or clinical haematologist. The observer needs to be able to characterize sizes, shapes, colours, degree of symmetry, texture and internal morphology of cells. These characteristics, of course, constitute the 'normal' types and lines of cell maturation. Equally, they are used to construct 'abnormal', sometimes pathognomonic, cell types. (It must be borne in mind that while deviations from the normal may be described as 'atypical' cells, their descriptions are – from one point of view – equally typified, and often associated with ideal-typical disease entities.) Likewise, other tissue samples (lymph nodes, for example) require the same sort of histological description. The following exchange illustrates the point. It also demonstrates a further issue in the clinical division of labour – the privileged gaze of the clinical pathologist:

At: We will find you another node
P: Only if you can find yourself another pathologist! [*Laughter*]
F: If you don't like it we'll change it.
P: But I don't think anybody could get around this node. It's full of germinal centres.
At: The nodules of nodular lymphoma would be bigger than that?
P: Well, no they would be this size, but they don't have this very nice mix of cell types with a lot of mitosis.
At: Mitosis suggests reactivity, do you reckon on that?
P: Yeah, I mean, that's *soft*, but the very high mitotic rate tends to suggest reactivity. . . .
F: [*to the pathologist*] You know, Carol, it was a very *large* node, so you know the node *clini*cally was pathological you know, so I don't think we just missed and got a bad node or something 'cos it was a pa*thol*ogically large node.
P: It's *strik*ingly granulomous, isn't it?
F: There's granulomas with *giant* cells, lots and lots of giant cells.
P: Well there're more *giant* cells and fewer regular peculiar cells than you normally see . . .

In this and similar sequences, then, the clinicians and the pathologist together seek to negotiate an acceptable description of the specimen itself (the product of a biopsy). The vocabulary of pathological description (for example, granuloma, giant cells, mitosis) provides a framework for the shared perception of the tissue, and out of that vocabulary emerges descriptions that will fit other, relevant descriptive frameworks. In this way, the description of the node can be used by the clinicians and the pathologist to enter it into possible disease categories. For instance, the sequence quoted above continues:

P: . . . Um and there *is* no ne*crosis* and you usually see necrosis in well-established Fletcher granulomas.
F: So it doesn't look like TB
P: It wouldn't be your first choice . . .

In the course of the fieldwork with the haematologists it became apparent that the clinical pathologist quoted above held an especially privileged position in the technical and moral division of labour locally. Pathologists in general have special rights in adjudicating on the presence and character of disease processes or entities in the body's organs and cells. They have a special place in the discourse of the clinico-pathological conference at which different specialists contribute their distinctive perspective on a given case. Not all are granted equal powers of observation and adjudication by their clinical colleagues, however. The pathologist just referred to, Carol Greene, however, was strikingly revered by her colleagues. She was granted special powers of vision, and was appealed to to render pathological judgements when clinicians or other pathologists were in a quandary and unable to arrive at a mutually acceptable description. By the same token, if Carol Greene decided that a given specimen of tissues such as a bone marrow aspirate or biopsy, could *not* be adjudicated on unequivocally, then the degree of uncertainty was treated as the definitive state of understanding concerning that particular case, pending further investigation or further clinical developments. The privilege granted to that one individual pathologist suggested that over and above the shared competence of practitioners, there was a personal element whereby particular individuals had a 'gift' or an 'eye' for recognition and description.

The development of a vocabulary of haematology or of clinical pathology is reminiscent of the shared vocabulary of, say, wine buffs and experts. As Lehrer (1983) has documented, the taste and the bouquet of wine are recognized and marshalled in accordance with a vocabulary of sensory categories and analogies. The wine taster, whether professional or lay, selects from an enormous repertoire of everyday descriptors in order to convey to others the elusive character of taste. Many such terms, though used in a particular way in the domain of wine tasting, consist of everyday descriptive and evaluative terms that are extended into wine usage. They are thus transformed into more esoteric terms within the register of wine. In just the same way, the haematologist needs to be able to describe blood, its constituents and traces. These registers of practical recognition are learned and reinforced through the shared talk of instruction and rounds. They are organized socially through the vocabularies and imagery that are shared among physicians and scientists. Medical work and medical science, indeed, are striking for their rich array of descriptive terms. The production of images is accompanied by descriptive languages for their interpretations. Since images and specimens cannot speak for themselves, physicians must draw on shared descriptive resources. [...]

In the second half of this chapter, therefore, I look more closely at the linguistic organization of visual perception and the production of clinical descriptions. I concentrate in particular on the work of the haematologists in inspecting samples of blood and bone marrow under the microscope.

Seeing and talking

[...] There is ample evidence in the haematology data of how the student or junior doctor is guided in seeing. There were, for instance, several occasions when I was able to locate the tape-recorder immediately below the microscope that was used during morning rounds. The microscope had four sets of eye-pieces: consequently, if there were three or two participants it was also possible for me to look at the slide too. If there were four that was not possible, though a helpful student might give me the chance to take a peek through his or her lens. The detailed talk about the specimen is often preceded or accompanied by talk and instruction about the skills and mechanics associated with the manipulation of the microscope itself.

The following example also begins with comment about the press of bodies around the microscope. One must imagine four heads bent close together, arms and elbows touching. The discussion takes place while the participants are looking down the microscope, and they are examining a blood smear. The ethnographer on this occasion was able to have his own eye-piece.

At: Do you want me to drive?

F: Go right ahead

At: Okay, I'll just try and get my elbows clear here.

St: Huhm

At: Okay, I'll get my right elbow farther over. [*to the student*] I'm sure Hale [*the fellow*] has told you that whenever you look at a smear the first thing you do is you look under low power

St: Yuh

At: You do that for several reasons. Can you give me a few?

St: Well, first of all just to get a general you know an overall look at it. Then you also um

At: Yeah whaddaya get from the overall look *for*?

St: Oh the ratio cells you know the red blood cells to you know white cells to um just get the per*centages* of each you know just a general look at it mm?

At: Well let's take each in turn

St: Okay

At: What am I looking for in the red cells?

St: Red cells, you're looking for uniformity of size and whether they're hypochromic or hyperchromic and

At: = Right you can make some *guess*timates at low power

St: Right

At: On those issues but you're not gonna be…

St: You'd really get a better look under high power

At: Anything else?

St: As far as the red blood cells?

At: Yeah

St: Umm

At: Something very simple and obvious

St: How many of them there are?

At: *No*. That hehehm

St: Alright, simple and obvious

At: Well what can we achi*eve* at this power? What if we free associate once, how's that?

St: Okay

At: I'm cruising along here and several things are registering in my head consciously and unconsciously. The most important thing I'm looking for at this stage is the staining quality of the smear and where I can go down under under oil.

St: Yuh okay

At: You know I've had arguments with Henry Kretschmer who never uses oil immersion and I've proved him wrong on several occasions. See oil immersion, I never use high dry as a power, a pathologist uses high dry but I go for low to oil.

St: Mhm

At: And as haematologists we need this. So I'm basically looking, I'm making some overall judgement of the quality of the smear.

St: Mhm

At: And my judgement on this on a scale of *ten* is and I'm gonna give this smear at least an eight. It looks like a beautifully spread and beautifully stained smear.

St: Mhm

At: With automation this is this is great praise from me. You can get garbage you know slipping through ah not uncommonly.

PAA: D'you get a lot of problems with the stains?

At: Well these are automated now

PAA: Mm

At: And a lotta times the screening process fails. Technicians will accept it rather than band smearing or make another one. Okay, so I'm looking, number one on that. Number two, I'm looking to see whether the red cells in addition to being nicely stained and nicely spread are there any abnormalities are there – is there any malformation?

St: Mhm

At: The answer is no

St: Mhm

At: You know, there's no clumping at all and from this long distance away there does not appear to be any significant degree of microcytosis that I can see, it may be a little anisocytosis *and* from this distance these cells may be a tad hypochromic. I can't be sure. But that's a *call* we make under a higher power from immersion, and then while I'm cruising al*ong* obviously I'm seeing all the *white* cells.

St: Mhm

At: And I'm looking to see for heterogeneity or monotony. All these decisions on all these cells that I'll be making at a higher power. And what I see is heterogeneity and I see the yeah segmented neutrophils being the most prominent cells, which is what we want it to be.

St: Mhm

At: And at this power you can see plaques that see platelets but again that's something that we'll get down to later on. Okay this is pretty much what *I'm* looking for at this power we *can* recognize nucleated reds we *can* recognize homogeneity in a white cell population suggesting you know a leukaemia.

St: Mhm

At: Ah and also we can see if there's a fair amount of anisocytosis evident, we can see sickle cells uh oh why not play the ball game on our own home field and let's get down to *thou*sand power rather than hundred power.

St: = Mhm

At: Hale, do you wanna add anything at least at this power?

F: No, I –

At: Pretty much you're looking for an area on which you wanna go down on

St: Mhm

At: And this is such a nice smear we can go down anywhere

St: Mhm

At: Some areas you get a lot of *artifact* and some will look hypochromic, others will look normochromic

St: Hhm

At: This smear we have to say is *superb* . . .

   . . .

At: Is this in focus for everybody?

St: Mhm

At: And now we get down to the red cells at this time now we see platelets and we see them. You don't have to look hard to see them, they're in every field. And my guesstimate at the moment I'll hold back on, because I want to see how things are here . . . but I do know right now there's no thrombocytopenia with certainty because you wouldn't be seeing platelets of this number you know on survey.

St: Mhm

At: Now that cell in the middle is what?

St: Erm a lymphocyte? Hm?

At: Ex*actly*

St: Okay hhe hh

At: Would you say that's a typical lymphocyte or an *a*typical lymphocyte? Is that the way it looks seen on the drawing board or is it

St: = It's a little atypical isn't it. Or is it totally atypical?

At: Now wait, what's atypical about it?

St: Well does it have a little more cytoplasm that might make it

At: = Well I would think the cytoplasm and nucleus

St: = Is right
       [   ]
At: is quite right

St: = Good okay

At: = for a lymphocyte. That's all right, but there are at least two atypical features

St: Okay

At: that I can see

St: But the nu

At: = Maybe *three*
       [   ]
St: clues

At: And they're all, I'm gonna make this distinction. If you look at a *normal* smear and you apply rigorous criteria you will find a small percentage of atypical lymphocytes

St: Hhm

At: That's good, and baggage, that's the *substrate*. That's, whenever you look at a smear expanding your range of normality so that you don't go hopping and say this has to be that because you see one cell

St: Mhm

At: This is atypical for a few reasons. One is it has vacuoles in its cytoplasm. Secondly it has some serration, you know it's like the corona radiata round the sun

St: Hhm

At: Of the cytoplasm. And third is the little indentation in that nucleus

St: = Right

At: And the nuclear chromatic may not be *quite* as closely packed as you'd expect

St: Okay

At: So there are three criteria for atypicality

St: Mhm

At: That doesn't mean this should automatically trigger in our differential diagnosis all the things that cause atypical *lymphs*

St: Mhm

At: Um what I'm looking for really is a *typical* lymph because Oh look at this, that comes down the pike. Now my head's beginning to trigger. What do you think, now what's *that*?

St: That's also a lymphocyte

At: Well it – er

St: Uh?

At: Yeah, I admire your frank –, your zeroing in on it. Exactly

St: Well that – that also has that kind of a corona radiata thing the other one does. And um doesn't really have any indentations but it's not, it's like the other one it's not condensed, as condensed as you'd expect it to be

At: Right, and *also* there's a nucleolus in that

St: = That looks like right there in the

At: = Right, lower left

St: = lower left corner that there is

At: It's lower left for me, is it lower left for everybody?

St: = Yeah lower left for me

At: = about seven o'clock

St: Uh I have a nucleolus

At: Okay, so NOW I'm saying what the hell's going *on* here

St: Mhm

At: What I'm really looking for is a typical lymphocyte that all of us will agree on which will be one marker because *that* nucleus would give us the diameter, baseline for to assess whether these cells are microcytic or not. Certainly on the basis of those two cells we have to say all the red in these microcytic but here's, now they're getting a little better

St: Mhm

At: Okay? So there's a typically typical lymphocyte and not being too *picky* both of those would be you know

St: Mhm

At: = with our X-ray vision we could see maybe vacularization of the cytoplasm

St: Mhm

At: and now with *that* there as a *marker* we can say that the *red* cells … we can make a better judgement that the reds approximate a mild degree of anisocytosis while over *here* is a small cell right in the centre

St: Mhm mhm

At: And there's a little cytosis, this cell *here*.   Can hedge on that very nicely by saying Dr Lollard [*the attending*] got it smudged so I really can't commit myself.

St: Mhhm

At: And I'll have to *accept* that, but you could also could try to *guess*timate …

St: I'm not sure if it er I'm not sure

At: Well we know it's not a lymphocyte

St: Right

At: We know it's not a neutrophil. We know it's not an eo*sino*phil. We know it's

St: = Like a mast?

At: = not a basophil

St: hehehm
F: Can't be a mast
At: It can't be a circulating mast. You don't get circulating *mast* cells
St: = Yeah huhm Ahm
At: = And that leaves us with one other denizen of the peripheral *blood*
St: Peripheral blood Umm
At: Like a monocyte, right?
St: = Monocyte
At: Okay?
St: Okay
At: It has the size, it has the tinctorial qualities it has the nucleus and the cytoplasm
of a typical monocyte
St: = Okay
At: A monocyte that's been squashed
        . . .
At: Is that typical lymphocyte?
St: Well, it looks like there might be a little bit of nucleolus left in the
At: = That's hard to tell, yeah
St: That's hard to tell 'cos of the stain
At: Right
St: Um I think it looks *pretty* typical
At: It's not *bad*, but there are so many vacularizations in the cytoplasm

This extended extract displays the oral transmission of the craft skill of recognition. [. . .] I make little or no apology for imposing such a lengthy extract from the
data on the reader. It is rare to encounter such a sustained sequence preserved in
which instructions in 'how to see' are explicated. It is a microcosmic interaction, in
that it represents a myriad of similar occasions when experienced practitioners
coach their juniors in ways of seeing and describing. This particular extract from
the field data is especially useful in one sense: the student involved is not very
confident in her responses to the attending physician, and the latter engages in a
good deal of prompting, correcting and repair. While one may enter no claim as to
the typicality of such an exchange, therefore, it is a particularly useful one. The
student's reticence and lack of skill prompts the senior physician himself to articulate
his own activities at some length. He seeks to explicate some of his normally tacit
knowledge in talking through the smear with the novice student.

What is noticeable is how the act of visual recognition is achieved through speech
acts. As the participants share a single microscope with multiple eye-pieces, they can
operate with the practical assumption that they see the same field. As practical
phenomenologists, they operate with the sort of assumptions identified by Schutz
(1967). That is, they may assume, for all practical purposes, that they inhabit a
world of shared objects. They simultaneously scan the same sectors of the blood
smear, and the same cells are visible to each of them simultaneously.

[. . .]

The purely physical visual field may be assumed to be a shared one, and the
arrangement of objects to be recognizably the same. Yet they cannot be held to

constitute identical objects in any meaningful fashion. In the absence of a shared frame of reference, and a shared language of special descriptions, then even physical objects themselves may not be discerned in the same way.

In this sense, therefore, the shared visual field of the microscope may ensure that in a purely physical sense the same phenomena are under inspection. On the other hand, as we have seen in this data extract, that does *not* mean that the same things will be seen. Expert vision depends on the capacity to recognize and to describe. These capacities are socially – that is, culturally and linguistically – organized. The competent practitioner will be able to discriminate and to describe phenomena using complex series of categories and descriptors that are not available to the lay person or to the novice. [...]

The physician or medical student – in common with practitioners in other fields of expertise – faces repeated problems of practical phenomenology. The objects of the clinical gaze repeatedly present problems and puzzles of description and recognition. The haematologist, as we have seen, has his or her special set of signs and fields that must be scanned, read and decoded. [...] [T]he haematologist reads the patient's body – its gross features and its local manifestations of deviations from normality – in order to render professionally adequate descriptions. [...]

[...]

Body work

This [...] chapter [has] attempted to provide a preliminary account of how members of one medical specialty set about the assessment of the body. This descriptive account of haematological work illustrates a number of fundamental issues. First, it highlights the importance of the principle of 'symmetry' in the sociological treatment of the body in medical knowledge. We have now become accustomed to historical accounts that demonstrate the understanding and representation of the body in past periods. It is a commonplace to note that 'the body' has not been a stable, fixed entity. Historical distance undoubtedly helps us to appreciate the social and culture specificity of bodies and their representation (Gilman, 1988; Lupton, 1994; Stafford, 1991). One must not, however, pay attention primarily to the 'other' bodies of history, while neglecting the socially constructed bodies of our own specialized knowledge. The body (or, more properly, the bodies) of contemporary biomedicine are just as much social products as those of, say, Tudor obstetrics, seventeenth-century anatomy, eighteenth-century surgery or nineteenth-century pathology.

Secondly, it draws attention to some of the processes and procedures whereby the body is surveyed within the framework of a rationalized technical division of labour. The glimpses of haematology and clinical pathology afforded by the fieldwork and recordings illuminate some of the socially organized practices whereby the body is dispersed within that division of labour. Bucher and Strauss (1961) outlined the distinctive Chicago-school view of the professions by stressing the extent of *segmentation* within elite occupations like medicine. They emphasized – in contrast to sociological perspectives that stressed a homogeneous professional 'community' – that occupations like medicine could be thought of as coalitions of interest-groups and specialisms. Each segment identified itself, in contradistinction to other segments, in terms of its distinctive mission, its knowledge-base and its characteristic approach to work. In just the same way, one can think of the body as being segmented into shards and fragments, tissues and traces. The fragmentation of the body directly mirrors the segmentation of the modern medical setting. Each professional group, each segment, lays claim to its distinctive knowledge; each lays claim to particular bits of the body. The haematologist, of course, claims the blood, the bone marrow and the lymph nodes. Elsewhere, the other specialists ply their trade with their own body framework. Furthermore, this division of labour rests upon a further collection of specialist workers – the laboratory scientists and technicians who transform the body's tissues and products into values and readings.

Thirdly, therefore, we must recognize that this work goes into rendering the body legible and visible in various ways. The body of the modern clinic is not merely fragmented and dispersed: it is manipulated, transformed and fixed into a series of representations and enumerations. The surveillance of the body is thus intimately connected to the existence, location and use of medical and scientific laboratory technologies. As yet we lack a thoroughgoing sociology of medical technology and instrumentation. It is, however, abundantly clear that the possibilities and limitations of a medical understanding of the body are coterminous with the limits and possibilities of the technologies and techniques that render the body's traces readable, visible, recordable and countable.

[...] [W]e have a few excellent studies of the means whereby the body is rendered into images. The history of X-ray imaging and the recent history of the other imaging techniques have been explored, and they are among the most striking examples of how the body is rendered as an object of expert knowledge and scrutiny. They are indicative of how the modern body is transfigured into shadows, shapes, spaces and traces. There are, however, many other techniques and methods whereby the body may be inspected, its manifestations indexed and permanently recorded. We have already encountered methods of inspecting and counting features of the blood, and the methods used to make the blood or bone marrow visible. The body of the modern clinic, therefore, is to be thought of – at least in part – as a series of representations. Those representations are themselves dispersed in time and space within the complex organization of the clinic. They are inspected, interpreted and reported by different cadres of specialized personnel. In a paradoxical manner, therefore, one should think of the modern clinic as producing a disembodied body. That is, a body – as an object of medical scrutiny – that is divorced from the body of the patient. The body may therefore be read at different sites. The bedside itself is one such locale, of course, and the patient's own body is always available for surveillance. It is, however, one among many possible versions of the body that may be assembled in the modern clinic. The patient thus may have a multiple existence within the clinic. [...]

Appendix: use of transcription conventions

As I have explained in the text, the tape-recordings of rounds, conferences and other interactions were transcribed delicately, using the full range of typographical conventions that are now standard for the purposes of conversation analysis. Such transcripts are intended to capture a variety of the features of spoken action, such as pauses (timed), false starts and interruptions, stress, relative amplitude, audible intakes of breath or exhalations, noticeable lengthening of sounds and syllables. In preparing data extracts for publication and commentary here I have deliberately simplified the transcripts. The interaction has, therefore, been rendered in a more readable fashion. This has involved the removal of some of the slight hesitations, repetitions, incomplete words and other common aspects of speech that are inessential to the kind of commentary I have offered here.

I have retained some of the normal conventions, and they are listed and explained here.

(word)	parentheses round a word or words indicate uncertainty about the transcription
( )	empty parentheses indicate failure to transcribe a word or part of an utterance
[ ]	brackets indicate onset and end of simultaneous talk
=	equals sign indicates 'latching' of utterances with no intervening silence
,.?	punctuation indicates intonation contours, not grammatical categories
wor-	word cut off abruptly
word	italics indicate emphasis
WORD	upper case indicates increased loudness
<word>	noticeable slowing of speech tempo
>word<	noticeable increase in speech tempo
...	omission of portion of transcript

References

Armstrong, D. (1983) *Political Anatomy of the Body: Medical Knowledge in Britain in the Twentieth Century*. Cambridge: Cambridge University Press.

Atkinson, P. (1988) 'Discourse, descriptions and diagnoses', in M. Lock and D. Gordon (eds), *Biomedicine Examined*. Dordrecht: Kluwer.

Bucher, R. and Strauss, A. L. (1961) 'Professions in process', *American Journal of Sociology*, 66: 325–54.

Conn, H. J. (1961) *Biological Stains: A Handbook on the Nature and Uses of the Dyes Used in the Biological Laboratory*, 7th edn. Baltimore: Williams and Wilkins.

Foucault, M. (1973) *The Birth of the Clinic*. London: Tavistock.

Gilman, S. L. (1988) *Disease and Representation: Images of Illness from Madness to AIDS*. Ithaca, NY: Cornell University Press.

Lehrer, A. (1983) *Wine and Conversation*. Bloomington: Indiana University Press.

Lupton, D. (1994) *Medicine as Culture: Illness, Disease and the Body in Western Societies*. London: Sage.

Schutz, A. (1967) *The Phenomenology of the Social World*. Evanston, Ill.: Northwestern University Press.

Stafford, B. M. (1991) *Body Criticism: Imaging the Unseen in Enlightenment Art and Medicine*. Cambridge, Mass.: MIT Press.

2

The Power of the Visible: The Meaning of Diagnostic Tests in Chronic Back Pain

Lorna A. Rhodes, Carol A. McPhillips-Tangum, Christine Markham and Rebecca Klenk

Introduction

In this article we explore the meaning of diagnostic tests for people with chronic back pain. Drawing on interviews from a study of chronic back pain patients' attitudes toward treatment, we argue that testing constitutes an important element in the legitimation of illness for these patients. To understand the relationship between testing and the legitimation of illness we explore connections between cultural and historical assumptions about the anatomical body and patients' accounts of their experiences of the process of diagnostic testing. We show that visual objectification of the body plays a strong part in the power of tests to provide either positive experiences, which encourage patients to align with their medical providers or, on the other hand, negative experiences of disconfirmation, which lead to alienation and a continued search for resolution. [...]

This article is based on the results of a study in which we interviewed patients with chronic lower back problems to answer the question: 'What motivates patients with these problems to return again and again for medical care, even when conventional treatment offers them little relief from their pain?' Virtually all of our respondents said that they were driven by difficulties in performing their daily activities to seek the cause of their pain (McPhillips-Tangum et al., 1998). For a significant subset of our sample, diagnostic testing was an important aspect of this search. These patients gave highly charged descriptions of being tested and asserted that testing had either confirmed or delegitimized their pain. [...]

Methods

Our study explored chronic back pain patients' experiences of pain, self-care and medical treatment. The study was carried out in Atlanta, Dallas and Seattle; in each city participants were enrollees of a managed health care plan at the time of the interview. [...]

Seventy patients agreed to be interviewed (McPhillips-Tangum et al., 1998). Of these, 16 are excluded from our discussion because they spoke primarily of experience with chiropractors and there is evidence that patients who visit chiropractors differ significantly from patients who visit medical doctors (Shekelle et al., 1995; cf. Coulehan, 1985). Of the 54 remaining participants discussed here, 20 were men and 34 women. Their age range was 26–65, with a mean age of 47. The majority were white (72%), married (72%) and employed (69%). [...]

Diagnostic testing and the invisibility of back pain

[...] A number of imaging tests are used to locate the source of acute or chronic back pain, including plain radiography (X-ray), computed tomography (CT) and magnetic resonance imaging (MRI). [...] While the biomedical model holds out hope that diagnostic tests can provide accurate diagnosis, effective (often surgical) treatment and permanent resolution of pain, this finding suggests that their meaning is far more ambiguous. [...]

The issues of testing, legitimation and visibility are tightly linked in interviews in which they are mentioned together. This comment is typical and touches on many of the themes we will be addressing.

> ...people have a problem talking to their doctors. Because they (doctors) just don't pay them much attention. They don't, they're not listening to what you say...[they] try to tell you back aches are psychosomatic and your back couldn't be hurting, [that] there's nothing, no reason for it to hurt. X-rays don't show anything and you don't really have a back ache. Oh yes I do, yes I do...but back aches are hard to see. Unless there's something that's a visible thing, it's kind of your word against who's looking.

As another patient said, 'I'm so healthy, and [people] look at me and they don't understand the severity of this problem I have'. In this situation patients must depend on words, on their ability to speak effectively to disbelief. As Jackson puts it in her ethnography of a pain clinic, '[Clinic] patients...were sometimes not accorded the social recognition provided by the sick role...communicating [the pain] to others can be as intractable and baffling a problem as the pain itself' (Jackson, n.d., p. 6).

[...]

These patients describe a situation always slipping toward disbelief and delegitimation, one that they have to actively – if sometimes ineffectively – protest if they are to retain a sense of the integrity of their own experience.

[...]

We will show that it is in this context of delegitimation that testing gains meaning as a visual representation of the truth of pain. We turn first to a discussion of the historical and cultural context that informs the connection between diagnostic tests and the legitimation of illness. [...]

The anatomical body and the body in pain

Recent work in history and anthropology suggests the historical specificity of modern images of the body (Foucault, 1975; Armstrong, 1983; Romanyshyn, 1989). An extensive discussion is beyond the scope of this paper, but we draw on this literature to suggest that the concern with the visual representation of illness expressed by the participants in our study has roots in biomedical and popular attitudes that privilege this form of representation. Prior to the seventeenth century, and despite the existence of dissection and some anatomical understanding, medicine was not primarily a study of the inside structures of the body. However, with the development of modern anatomical science, clinic-based medical care, modern surgery and modern visual perspective, the body came increasingly to be understood as a 'specimen', an object with an interior space knowable through [primarily] visual means (Foucault, 1975; Romanyshyn, 1989). Good (1994, pp. 72–3) describes the visual training experienced by medical students learning to see the body in this way. 'As the skin is drawn back, a different "interior" emerges... [A] "whole other world" becomes the paramount reality in the anatomy lab'. Dissection, the X-ray and recent more sophisticated tools for visual diagnosis all create an 'inside' body, another world that can be seen, accurately represented through drawings, photographs and computer images, and, ultimately, manipulated through surgical and medical intervention.

In a study of an eighteenth century German doctor, Duden (1991, p. 106) shows that he and his patients shared a vivid language that embedded suffering in narratives in the context of an impenetrable body. For the German doctor and his patients:

> The body is opaque. It is a place of hidden activities. As long as a person was alive, his body could not be opened, his inside could not be deciphered. People could speculate about its inside only with the help of signs that appeared on the body or emanated from it.

Prominent among these signs were the patient's own words (Foucault, 1975). In contrast, modern visual representations, from anatomy texts to advertisements, have fostered a common understanding of the body as an inner space, a container in which organs and structures operate somewhat like the engine in a car. A true representation of the situation inside this space cannot be trusted to words alone. One of our informants explicitly made this point.

> My back hurt. And you know, I tell [the doctor] what's up. And he still won't examine me to see if I'm telling the truth or not. I [don't] understand... sitting across the room and telling [you] [you're] not hurting. You know, you've got to put your hands on somebody... you can't fix a car by looking at it!

The anatomical understanding of the body depends on two related assumptions that inform both medical and lay understanding.

1   The inside of the body corresponds to visual images of it. The body is 'filled' with organs that can be made visible in the same way that a landscape is visible through a window (cf. Romanyshyn, 1989, p. 128). This 'view' is objective, showing the body as it 'really' is.

2   The variations in people's bodies can be measured against norms – objective standards – that show what is typical and what is deviant. This process can reveal how an individual manifestation of disease is both specific and an instance of a general type (Foucault, 1975).

[...] The physician showing test results to a patient provides a visual representation of the body as a 'site of disease' (Good, 1994). These representations are taken for granted as simple representations: while an expert is needed to read them, their correlation to the body seems nothing more than common sense. However, the patient who sees an image of the inside of her own body while, at the same time, experiencing her pain 'from the inside', is, in fact, faced with a uniquely modern task. Writing about the use of ultrasound imaging for pregnant women in Greece, Georges (1996) notes the sensuous, compelling nature of the image which pulls the women into a valued form of 'contact' with their fetuses. The images seen by pain patients, while negative in their connotations, offer a similar sensuousness and concreteness. They call on the patient to align herself with their reality, demanding to be read as factual evidence of a match between the inside of the body as 'specimen' and the inside of the body as the private and incontrovertible ground of experience.

We have discussed three elements that combine to make testing an arena of concern for patients: a strong historical connection between visual images and the medicalization of the interior of the body, a set of cultural assumptions that make seeing into the body central to confirming and normalizing patients' symptoms and the sensuousness of diagnostic images themselves. This potent convergence of elements forms the background of the interview material that follows.

Seeing it in black and white: patterns of alignment or alienation

When participants in our study were asked to describe their experience of back pain, most told a story that included when and how it started and what they had done to resolve it. Diagnostic testing was embedded in these stories both as something done to them by the medical system – something over which they had little control – and as something they actively sought, interpreted, accepted or rejected. [...]

For some patients, diagnostic tests produce results in which the visual image seems to correspond exactly to the experience of pain. When this happens, the visible deviation inside the body is described as satisfyingly concrete.[...]

I felt relieved. I felt like, well, here's proof. It's not just me going crazy or complaining. It's black and white and anybody can see it.

[The doctor] showed me and ... he showed me where it hurt. He said, your disc is kinda bulging out there, just kinda laying on this nerve.

Patients for whom something 'shows' on tests emphasize a feeling of justification, of not being 'crazy'. Tests 'show where it hurts' and confirm the reality of pain; in fact, patients repeatedly use the word *real* to describe this confirmation and remark that what 'shows' is 'obvious' and 'concrete' (see Jackson (1992), p. 143 for a typology of 'unreal' forms of pain).

> The first CT scan [was] almost two years ago and that's when it was really concrete. It came back, yeah, it's just a bulging disc...degenerative disc disease. So that's when it was more of a reality and it's like, see, I told you. But you know it was solid proof, it wasn't just aches and pains anymore.

[...] What is proved here is that what has been experienced corresponds to what is represented by the test. The sensuousness of the image, its black and white concreteness, provides not only a meaningful diagnosis, but evidence that the pain itself is meaningful: it points to something beyond itself that can, perhaps, be remedied.

[...]

As they share the results of tests, physicians seem to provide patients with a moment in which they are both examining the body 'abstractly'; for a moment both are on the same side of the 'window' into the body that the test represents. This quote shows how the sense of reality induced in these moments can reverse a patient's sense of delegitimation and affirm her suffering.

> I'm sure he thought that there was something wrong with the spine but nothing really serious. And they had done a CT scan which had turned up nothing. And they had done a normal X-ray which turned up nothing...And he kept telling me, we're just not finding anything. And I said, well, you can't hurt this bad and there not be something wrong...So finally, I think because I was insistent about it, he decided to do a myelogram...and I was laying on the table...and the technician said 'Oh my gosh!' and I knew he had found it. And he called one of the doctors in.

In an instant this patient goes from feeling disbelieved – that she has to 'insist' in the face of repeated disappointment – to an intense feeling of relief, despite the fact that what has been found means that she faces surgery. What she had been saying to her doctor could not be heard until, to her joy, it could be seen. Patients who describe events like this express satisfaction even when the diagnosis itself does not suggest imminent or even eventual relief.

> It was wonderful...he showed me on the X-ray the nerves that were pinched.

What happens when this 'wonderful' alignment does not occur? Intractable pain may not 'show up' on any test, nor do test abnormalities necessarily correspond to the cause of pain (Jensen et al., 1994). Patients whose findings are negative or inconclusive must face a disjunction between their inner experience of the reality of a body that has become an ongoing negative and constraining influence in their lives and the 'normality' of their test results. Like the patients quoted above, they are caught in trying to find legitimation for what they say, but without the resolution offered by tests they remain in an alienated position, seeking but not finding a sense of alignment with their providers.

> I told my doctor once that I felt like, my back hurt so bad I felt like I had a large grapefruit down about the curve of the back . . . Course there's not a grapefruit there and they X-rayed me and there's nothing there.

The 'nothing' found on tests suggests that there is no reason, and therefore perhaps no justification, for the pain. And without justification for it, what is its status? As we have seen, to be 'real' is to 'show up' visually. To anticipate the words of a patient whose story we will report at greater length in the next section: 'The doctors . . . left me with the impression [my pain] was not real'.

Our study does not tell us what doctors actually said to patients, but what patients believe they heard. Many heard an enthusiasm for psychological explanation in the face of negative test results. As Jackson (1992, p. 142, emphasis in original) notes, 'Even though a psychologically minded physician may try to reassure the patient that he or she is *not* suggesting that "your pain is imaginary" . . . the patient will very likely see the physician as suggesting just that'. An assumption of psychological causation is entirely consonant with the cultural underpinnings of the anatomical body: if pain is not 'in' the body, where can it be but in the mind?

> And then you've got the doctors for four years telling you, 'Well, we can't find anything wrong. It's all in your head'. And you're going, 'no, it's right here. My head ain't down here'.

> . . . and that's where I got into the problem where they would give you those tests and tell you, 'You don't have a problem'. And you know you got a problem!

Here, the apparent transparency and simplicity of testing – its promise to reveal the inside body – betrays the patient who finds herself with subjective certainty but no proof. [. . .]

The patient in this situation faces a choice between disavowing pain (and thereby denying what Good (1994, p. 121) calls the 'subtle sentient quality of . . . suffering') or turning away from medicine. The majority of the patients in our study who described negative experiences of testing turned away from medicine to some extent, expressing anger or resignation about its failure to help them.

> Why does it have to be black and white in front of their face before they believe there's a problem?

> I found that every so often these guys would want to run another battery of these expensive tests, and I've been through 'em twice already . . . just to get back to the same place I'm in.

> . . . who's to say what they find? Because, you know, each time you go they come up with something else . . . who's to tell who's right and who's wrong?

Doubtfulness about tests shades into questions about whether diagnosis itself means much.

I think there can be several different diagnoses, all of which may have some validity, none of which may have some validity. I even hesitate to tell people exactly what is going on with my back as far as those hard findings because it seems so vague...I think it's a particularly difficult kind of thing. It's not like saying the bone's broken or the bone's not broken.

This patient's language is suggestive of a long history of confusion and disappointment. He struggles with the 'vagueness' of what he can say to others, as though in the absence of something 'hard', his own words about his experience are tainted. The experience of delegitimation in the absence of 'hard findings' and as a result of such histories – what one patient called 'the redundancy of the situation' – takes shape both as a sense of doubt about the self and as a struggle with the issue of being heard. [...]

Our interviews show that patients for whom testing can point to effective treatment find themselves in alignment with a basic premise of medicine, that the patient is 'a translucent screen through which we peer to find a diagnostic entity within' (Coulehan, 1985, p. 371). When this premise fails, either because no diagnostic entity can be found or because what is found cannot be treated, our participants described themselves as alienated, yet driven by pain into repeated attempts to gain relief from medicine (cf. McPhillips-Tangum et al., 1998). We turn now to the embeddedness of these attempts in individual histories.

Narratives of testing for chronic back pain

[...] The two patients whose stories we present experienced testing differently at different times in their illness. Both went through periods of pain in which nothing could be found on tests and experiences of satisfaction at seeing a concrete result. Our first participant, Pamela Lloyd, eventually undergoes successful surgery while our second, Stan Diermyer, fails to find a resolution and remains alienated from his providers.

Both of these narratives begin with a trivial action that seems to mark the start of years of pain. Like patients described by Good (1992), Delvecchio Good (1994), Garro (1992, 1994) and Kleinman (1988), these patients experienced an unmaking (Scarry, 1985) of their taken for granted life-world. Because we asked them for stories about treatment, we do not have the rich description of this unmaking available in other accounts. What follows rather are descriptions by these patients of how the process of testing offers them a changing and often ambiguous object-body and contributes to a shifting and highly charged relationship to medicine. We give each history primarily in the patient's own words, then discuss them together.

First case history: Pamela Lloyd

Pamela Lloyd is in her mid-forties, white, divorced and living in the southern US. She describes the onset of her experience with lower back pain.

The very first time I was mid-twenties. I was getting ready to go to work, I was in the bathtub, taking a hot bath. I could not get out of the tub. I went to a medical doctor, took muscle relaxants, heating pads, stayed in bed.

Off and on from '85 when I had my back surgery, I would have spells of it...The last time I knew it was different...So I went first to my primary care physician and they did X-rays and he said that I had a stenosis thing...So then he sent me to Dr. S., an outstanding orthopedic man. They did another X-ray and...he showed me, on the diagrams, and he said it was complicated by arthritis, but no big deal. And that we could treat this. I did traction. I did spinal injections of steroids. I did everything, heating pads and ice, you know, back and forth. Everything they said to do. No results, nothing.

I know in my heart of hearts that at least three of these [doctors] felt that I wasn't really in the kind of pain that I said I was in. They couldn't understand why I kept on hurting, when all these things indicated that I should be better. Well, the reason is because it didn't show up on all of their tests.

Frustrated with the mounting 'proof' that the pain was not real, Pamela began to question her own feelings.

When you don't feel well you tend to react emotionally...And they probably thought, well, this ditzy woman. I mean, you can almost see it, when they're thinking that...And then it causes you to doubt yourself: is this all in my mind? Maybe they're right, maybe this is a ditzy broad [with no] idea what's going on. That's the pain, it clouds everything. It clouds your emotions.

The day I drew the line, was [the day] they sent me to a doctor, a chronic pain doctor, who told me he could teach me to live with this. And I said, 'But I don't want to live with this'. I mean, it hurt to walk. It hurt to move...I was living on codeine and Tyleno...and tranquilizers...So I called Dr. S's office. [But] since I was referred to him, he couldn't refer me to another specialist. I had to go back to my primary care person. Well, my primary care person was not very anxious to help me. So I...got names of different back people and I called, every one of them said, you have to have an MRI before we can see you. [N]obody wanted to give me an MRI so finally I called member services... I was just bawling, because I hurt so bad and nobody wanted to help me. And [they] said, 'Your primary care physician will be calling you back...' It wasn't fifteen minutes later that he called back and I was scheduled for an MRI the next morning. And they told me that whatever specialist I wanted to see there would be a referral for.

I went to see Dr. K...He told me he could help me. And [he] explained again pretty much the same thing...And he said, 'Basically, your back is worn out'. So he said, I want you to go in for a myelogram. And we're going to do...this fusion and we're going to leave these two metal bars and these screws in place and...it'll be better. At this point, I was ready to agree to anything.

So I go for the myelogram because he doesn't want any surprises when he gets into surgery. He tells me in two and a half hours he can be in and out, it will be clean and quick, no problems. He's got the X-ray, the MRI, and the myelo-gram. He's got his maps of what he's going to do. [But] the surgery took five hours. When he got in they discovered that I had a ruptured disc that did not show up on the X-ray, the MRI, or the myelogram. That's why I never responded to any of the treatments.

It surprised him, he wasn't above saying that it shocked him. And he couldn't understand why it didn't show up anywhere. It should have shown up on the very first X-ray. It for sure should have shown up on the myelogram, or the MRI. It didn't show up on any of those things. But it was there . . . where it was pressing on the nerve, the blinding kind of pain was a direct result from something nobody could find.

Pamela considered herself fortunate to eventually find a physician who was willing to work with her, and she felt that the surgery was successful.

The difference was he was willing to look, he was willing to try and fix it and everybody else was not. They weren't looking any further. You can't just stop right there, with the pain still there. There's got to be another answer and at least he was willing to look for it.

It's not their [physicians'] fault. And I'm not saying that it is, but I'm saying that they need to be more tuned in. I just believe that there is too much technology, too much knowledge [so] that people shouldn't have to live with that much pain on a regular basis.

Second case history: Stan Diermyer

Stan is in his early forties, white, married and living in the Pacific Northwest. He describes the onset of his experience with lower back pain.

The incident with the back started four years ago. I was just recovering from the flu . . . and everybody else in the family came down with it. I was cooking dinner because I was the only healthy one in the family, and I dropped a can of beans on the floor, unopened. I bent down and there was this burning sensation that shot through my lower back . . . By the next morning I could hardly move and they had to wheelchair me into the clinic. And the doctor put me in the hospital, saying, 'Your back is out'. So I was in the hospital for about a week and they sent me home.

Since that time Stan has experienced 'constant pain' with no diagnostic closure.

[Y]ou've got doctors for the first four years telling you, 'Well, we can't find anything wrong. It's all in your head' . . . If they can't find it within their parameter of discipline it's got to be psychosomatic. Which one doctor told me, an intern doctor said, 'It's got to be in your head'. Just point blank told me that. I said, 'Thanks, doc. You just helped a whole bunch'. And he said, 'Well, look at the tests'. I said, 'But you haven't run all of the tests because it's still hurting and it's still very real. And I am not psychosomatically inclined'.

And the doctors, up until some final test, kind of left me with the impression that it was not real. Because up to a certain point they weren't able to ascertain [the problem]. [The disc] bulges like normal discs bulge. What mine does is . . . when it flares, it expands and contracts up and down, not in and out . . . So until just recently the concept of it going up and down didn't dawn on them. Until they started to do a couple of X-rays and they said, 'You've got a big gap there'. . . . [A]nd I say, 'Could that cause my pain?' 'Oh yes. Most definitely'.

For four years I've been living with, except for my one physician, 'It's all in your head'. Until I saw on the X-ray the swollen disc, and I'm going, thank you, Lord, at last I saw something that says, there's something wrong.

For Stan, a test that revealed a problem did not lead to relief. He had to learn how to deal with the pain himself, using medication and other self-management techniques. Sometimes the pain flared up despite these efforts.

There's a very central core spot in the lower part of the spinal cord itself and it starts as a burning sensation. Like somebody took a hot iron and is just putting it right next to your back bone. And as it begins to develop it turns from a burning sensation to a cold ice knife feeling. Like somebody just took a knife and just went like this and started to turn it. And it starts boring into my left hip. Then it shoots down into the knee and into the ankle and the bones feel like they're ice cold . . . If I don't stop it then it goes to the point where even to lie in bed is painful. To move, to roll, to have somebody touch the bed. Because if you touch my bed I'm going to scream or cry. It's that much.

In addition to this physical suffering, the pain has had a great emotional impact on Stan's life. He has been forced to rethink what he calls the 'normalcy' of his life and to come to terms with a new image of himself, including feelings of guilt and frustration in his relationship with his physician and family.

You feel like you're letting the doctor down because you're not in control . . . You sense the doctor is frustrated because he's got a patient that really hurts and there's times when I've had to come in on an emergency basis so it screws up their scheduling . . . There's a whole lot of dynamics . . . As the patient, you're the focal point and you feel guilty internally and externally.

I did a lot of hiking. I did a lot of camping. I did a lot of wrestling with the kids. And when the back injury happened a lot of that was taken away. And the kids for a long time resented it. Resented me.

Stan felt that most of his physicians were unwilling to question test results or to continue searching until they found a satisfactory diagnosis.

I guess I'm a little frustrated at the medical profession because I've [been forced] to find the answers and the solutions to the problems, instead of them being willing to roll up their sleeves and help me find the answers and the solutions.

The medical profession is forgetting how to research and practice and realize that we're going into the 21st century. There's a whole new set of rules and we're going to have to learn how to play the game...by exploring different things and not being afraid to say, 'I don't know. Let's find out'.

Discussion

Returning now to the historical and cultural assumptions we discussed earlier, we can see how they are implicated in the way Pam and Stan and our other informants talk about their experience.

1   The inside of the body corresponds to visual images of it. Both Pam and Stan assume that this correspondence must exist, and they continue searching until they find evidence that it does. Both emphasize that the role of the doctor is to *look*. Pam describes her doctor as 'willing to look' and Stan expresses frustration that his does not look further. In Pam's case, it is her doctor's faith that her pain must indicate a need for surgery that leads to the discovery, in surgery, of the ruptured disc that had failed to show up on any test. Pam's description of her emotion as repeated tests come up negative expresses the fraught quality of this absence. Negative findings threaten to trap her in the failure of her body to conform to the expectations of anatomical medicine. Stan, on the other hand, experiences a satisfying moment of alignment as X-rays finally reveal the 'gap' that indexes his pain; however, without effective treatment this conclusion is ultimately frustrating to him. He persists in believing that his doctors *can not* have run all the tests if his back still hurts.

2   The body can be measured against objective norms and standards. Pam and Stan find themselves struggling to deal with this assumption. Diagnostic testing holds out the possibility that they can *see* where deviation occurs and despite their expressions of hostility, they live in the same universe of explanation as their doctors. They fully expect that deviation from normal should show up and should be susceptible to repair. Pam finds, instead, that her tests inexplicably fail to reveal what is wrong. Sam turns to the idea that his deviation is not just from the norm, but from the norm of deviance – *his* disc bulges in an atypical way that makes it hard for his doctors to see. Sam's feeling that he is 'letting the doctor down' suggests that the body that fails to conform falls short in a very personal way ('you feel guilty internally and externally').

The medical management of back pain carries the implicit promise that doctors can 'roll up their sleeves' and find the answer. These patients are both enmeshed with and estranged from this promise (cf. Good, 1992; Jackson, 1992). They are highly critical of specialists who seem to lack the necessary knowledge; Pamela stresses that her doctors 'couldn't understand', while for Stan, his pain seemed not to fit 'within the parameter of their discipline'. On the other hand, both Pamela and Stan, with most of our patients, *believe* in the medical model. They want their doctors to 'realize we're going into the 21st century' to be 'more tuned in'.

[...]

Conclusion

[...] The hope invested in testing is a two-edge sword. When physicians cannot locate the problem, or express doubt about the possibility of solution, patients feel that their pain is disconfirmed. To feel 'delegitimized' is, in fact to experience a series of negative consequences, from not being seen, to not being heard, to a sense of deficiency and shame. We have suggested that for these patients betrayal occurs at a deeper level than the merely personal. Faced with the disjunction between the cultural model of the visible body and the private – and problematically 'quiet' – experience of pain, patients are alienated not only from individual physicians but from an important aspect of the symbolic world of medicine. They find themselves in the position of the seventeenth century patients described by Duden (1991) for whom the body was opaque, but without the cultural expectation of a shared language of suffering that was, historically, the complement to that opacity.

What these patients suggest, and what studies confirm (e.g. Deyo, 1983; Jensen et al., 1994) is that diagnostic imaging tests often fail to provide a solution – or even a meaningful diagnosis – for chronic back pain. Our work suggests that we might consider looking elsewhere for sources of satisfaction and meaning for these patients. One possibility might be the exploration of creative ways to develop the potentially healing gesture of 'looking at results together'. Perhaps the visual orientation of medicine could be enlisted to produce individualized representations of the body that legitimize pain without the expense and ambiguity of current forms of testing. Another possibility would be to actively engage patients' desire for agency and self authorship in the exploration of alternative solutions. As Coulehan (1985) points out, the success of chiropractic rests partly on its ability to mobilize the patient's resources. Finally, recent work by Martin (1994) suggests that new images of the body are replacing the old anatomical version in areas such as immunology; we may have entered a new era in which the image of the body is becoming more open and flexible. Perhaps current research on chronic pain can provide new images that will allow for a more fluid, less localized understanding of pain and a greater sense of legitimacy for back pain patients.

Acknowledgements

We gratefully acknowledge the participation of the patients we interviewed for this study and express our appreciation for their willingness to share their stories. We are also grateful for the participation in this research of Daniel Cherkin, Tracy Scott, Barbara Tunney, Toyia Arrington and Janet Street. Thanks are due to David Jesse Peters, Mark Sullivan, Daniel Cherkin, Richard Deyo and two anonymous reviewers for helpful comments on earlier versions of this paper. An earlier version of this work was presented at the University of Washington Pain Clinic Didactics Series; we thank the audience for their comments. The research on which this paper is based was supported by the Prudential Center for Health Care Research.

References

Armstrong, D., 1983. *The Political Anatomy of the Body: Medical Knowledge in Britain in the Twentieth Century.* Cambridge University Press, Cambridge.

Coulehan, J. L., 1985. Adjustment, the hands and healing. *Culture, Medicine and Psychiatry* 9, 353–82.

Delvecchio Good, M.-J., 1994. Work as a haven from pain. In: Delvecchio Good, M.-J., Brodwin, P., Good, B., Kleinman, A. (Eds.), *Pain as Human Experience: an Anthropological Perspective.* University of California Press, Berkeley.

Deyo, R.A., 1983. Conservative therapy for low back pain: distinguishing useful from useless therapy. *Journal of the American Medical Association* 250, 1057–62.

Duden, B., 1991. *The Woman Beneath the Skin: a Doctor's Patients in Eighteenth-Century Germany.* Harvard University Press, Cambridge.

Foucault, M., 1975. *The Birth of the Clinic: an Archaeology of Medical Perception.* Vintage Books, New York.

Garro, L. C., 1992. Chronic illness and the construction of narratives. In: Delvecchio Good, M.-J., Brodwin, P., Good, B., Kleinman, A. (Eds.), *Pain as Human Experience: an Anthropological Perspective.* University of California Press. Berkeley.

Garro, L. C., 1994. Narrative representations of chronic illness experience: cultural models of illness, mind and body in stories concerning the temporomandibular joint (TMJ). *Social Science and Medicine* 38 (6), 775–88.

Georges, E., 1996. Fetal ultrasound imaging and the production of authoritative knowledge in Greece. *Medical Anthropology Quarterly* 10 (2), 157–75.

Good, B. J., 1992. A body in pain: the making of a world of chronic pain. In: Delvecchio Good, M.-J., Brodwin, P., Good, B., Kleinman, A. (Eds.), *Pain as Human Experience: an Anthropological Perspective.* University of California Press, Berkeley.

Good, B. J., 1994. *Medicine, Rationality and Experience: an Anthropological Perspective.* Cambridge University Press, Cambridge.

Jackson, J. E., 1992. After a while no one believes you: real and unreal pain. In: Delvecchio Good, M. -J., Brodwin, P., Good, B., and Kleinman, A. (Eds.), *Pain as Human Experience: an Anthropological Perspective.* University of California Press, Berkeley.

Jackson, J. E., n.d. Camp pain. Unpublished manuscript.

Jensen, M. C., Brant-Zawadzki, M., Obuchowski, N., Modic, M., Malkasian, D., Ross, J., 1994. Magnetic resonance imaging of the lumbar spine in people without back pain. *New England Journal of Medicine* 331 (2), 69–73.

Kleinman, A., 1992. Pain and resistance: the delegitimation and relegitimation of local worlds. In: Delvecchio Good, M.-J., Brodwin, P., Good, B., Kleinman, A. (Eds.), *Pain as Human Experience: an Anthropological Perspective.* University of California Press, Berkeley.

McPhillips-Tangum, C. A., Cherkin, D. C., Rhodes L. A., Markham, C., 1998. Reasons for repeated medical visits among patients with chronic back pain. *Journal of General Internal Medicine* 13, 289–95.

Martin, E., 1994. *Flexible Bodies: Tracking Immunity in American Culture from the Days of Polio to the Age of AIDS.* Beacon Press, Boston.

Romanyshyn, R., 1989. *Technology as Symptom and Dream.* Routledge, London.

Scarry, E., 1985. *The Body in Pain: the Making and Unmaking of the World.* Oxford University Press, Oxford.

Shekelle, P. G., Markovich, M., Louie, R., 1995. Factors associated with choosing a chiropractor for episodes of back pain care. *Medical Care* 33, 842–50.

3

Exchanging Spare Parts or Becoming a New Person? People's Attitudes toward Receiving and Donating Organs

Margareta A. Sanner

Introduction

Transplantation surgery has been successful in prolonging life for people with life-threatening diseases, and new cadres of recipients are continuously included in the projects. However, the expansion of the activity is hampered by the lack of donors (i.e. people who have developed a state of brain death during respirator treatment, who are medically suited to become donors, and who have themselves or via relatives agreed on/not refused organ donation). Efforts to expand the donor population are inclusions of older donors, extended use of living donors for kidney, liver and lung transplantation, and use of non-heart-beating cadaver donors. There are also attempts to make xenotransplantation become reality.

Even this short description of the state of the transplantation enterprise gives rise to several intriguing questions, i.e. the meaning of death, the constitution of human identity, the borders between individuals and between species, the differences between nature and culture, and the kind of medical and biological science that our society develops. The conception of these questions forms the opinion on the transplantation enterprise and have bearing on the willingness not only to donate organs but also to receive organs, which surprisingly is a rather neglected research area.

There seems to have been a tacit assumption that to donate organs is controversial but to receive transplants goes without saying. [...]

The present study explored the public's feelings and ideas about *receiving* organs, and how this influenced their attitudes toward accepting a transplant themselves. Also the willingness to *donate* was examined in order to provide a complementary perspective. The main aim was to identify consistent attitude patterns that would include attitudes toward both receiving and donating organs and the motives behind this. The body is fundamental in the development of our identity, and the knowledge of the way we think about bodily changes (in this case, removing and adding an organ) will have something to do with the way we construct and reconstruct this identity. It is important to know how people react in an unprovoked situation, i.e. when there is no immediate need of a transplant. People with a lethal disease probably cannot afford feelings of uneasiness about the offered organ if, for instance, a xenotransplant might be their only remedy. Consequently they might suppress such feelings. However, the reactions with which a patient enters the transplantation procedure may influence the outcome. Feelings and ideas are essential in the process of integrating a transplant physically and mentally. [...]

Method

Sample

The first step was a survey of representative samples of the public, registered bone-marrow donors, and blood donors. The mailed questionnaires included items about receiving and donating organs and tissues. The questionnaire to the public also included a special question about receiving organs of different origins (viz. from a deceased, a close relative, an animal, and artificial organs). Departing from these three surveys it was possible to invite respondents with varying sociodemographic background to in-depth interviews. The participants of the interviews were selected also to represent varying willingness to receive and donate organs. Also people with varying readiness to receive organs of different origins (a relative, a deceased, an animal, and artificial organs) were invited. In these ways the interviewees formed a strategic, or purposive, sample (Patton, 1990).

The design of the study is displayed in Table 1.

Thirty-one registered bone-marrow donors, 17 blood donors and 21 individuals from the general public participated in the interviews. Eight persons who were invited to the interviews did not participate for different reasons. They were replaced by other persons with similar characteristics with regard to sociodemographic background and willingness to receive and donate organs. In Table 2, the 69 participants are presented together with the characteristics that made them fit in this strategic sample. As can be seen, the number of individuals that were negative to receive organs was small, which reflects the fact that people in general would accept at least one kind of transplant if their life is at stake (Sanner, 1998).

[...]

Results

Seven typical attitude patterns

Willingness both to receive and to give   One of the attitude patterns was characterized by the perspective of the body as a machine where the parts could be easily

Table 1   The design of the study

Population	Representative sample for the questionnaires	Strategic sample for the interviews
The public	1500 persons	21 persons
Registered bone-marrow donors	460 persons	31 persons
Blood donors	800 persons	17 persons

Table 2 Background characteristics and attitudes toward organ donation and reception of the informants (according to statements in the questionnaires)

	The public	Blood donors	BM-donors	Total	%
Age					
18–29 yr	4	3	11	18	26
30–59 yr	11	12	20	43	62
60–69 yr	6	2	0	8	12
Sex					
Men	10	9	18	37	54
Women	11	8	13	32	46
Education					
< 10 yr	3	2	7	12	17
10–12 yr	8	1	7	16	23
> 12 yr	10	14	17	41	60
Attitudes toward organ donation					
Positive	10	10	24	44	64
Negative	11	3	7	21	30
Undecided	0	4	0	4	6
Attitudes toward reception of organs[a]					
Positive	15	13	25	53	77
Negative	3	2	0	5	7
Undecided	3	2	6	11	16

[a]In the questionnaire to the public was included also an item on attitudes toward receiving organs of different origins. Twelve of the informants accepted an organ from a relative, eight an organ from a deceased, four an organ from an animal, nine an artificial organ, and four all kind of organs.

exchanged. The main worry was about the function: 'An organ from a fresh animal is better than a worn-out human kidney.' 'I would trust a living organ more than an apparatus. With living organs you know that they've been utilized and function well.' There was an implicit belief that the mind, personality, self and so on, were not situated in the organs: 'If you receive a new heart, it will become your own.' 'What is me, is not depending on whose kidney I have received.' Rather these entities were located in the brain. These individuals had a very relaxed view on giving blood and bone marrow as well as donating their own and their relatives' organs for transplantation and their whole body for training purposes. They might have made these attitudes manifest in blood-giving, registering in a registry of anonymous bone-marrow donors, and signing a donor card. In these acts they evidently had a very clear image of the body as an object; of *possessing* a body more than *being* a body. They seemed to cathexe (i.e. charge with emotional energy) their bodies less than others and by this it was easier to give up body parts. It might also be easier to accept foreign material in one's own body if one regarded them as mere spare-parts: 'Cynically speaking, it's machine parts, in principle nothing strange.' Or as a well known, established treatment: 'A kind of treatment simply, like drugs.' They found it 'natural' that the human body can be a composite of different materials. Another characteristic of this attitude pattern was weak death anxiety, which was explored in the interviews. The strength of death anxiety seems to be an important factor in people's acceptance of operations on their dead bodies. Individuals with weak death anxiety usually find it easier to accept such operations, than those who have strong anxiety. This seems to interfere with the latter's understanding that a corpse is really dead. [...]

Willingness to receive but not to give   On the other hand, people typical of one of the other attitude patterns had strong death anxiety, according to their own evaluation. Just like the individuals belonging to the first attitude pattern they accepted receiving all kinds of organs, which was quite logical, as they were the very people who take every chance to outwit death. Their ambition was to survive at any price. 'If you are so ill as when you need a new organ, you will be glad whatever help you can get.' 'Surviving is most important of all. I would do anything.' However, as they had strong death anxiety they did not want to donate their own and relatives' organs, even if this was felt as a moral dilemma in accordance with the principle of reciprocity ('You must give, if you want to receive'). They were prepared to exchange body parts as soon as these did not function, and their only question about a possible transplant regarded its function. They did not admit any uneasiness toward receiving any kind of organs. Evidently their death anxiety took over all other feelings of uneasiness. Indeed, they might not be able to afford feelings of uneasiness about a treatment that would give them a chance to live on.

Willingness neither to receive nor to give; Nature's order   A third attitude pattern indicated a special view of the borders of nature and the risk of trespassing these borders. In its extreme form this meant that breaching the boundaries even between two human beings was against nature. To cross species' boundaries was completely unacceptable and led to transhuman bodies. If we created transgenic animals for organ transplantation this might result in chaos and disaster in the end, i.e. nature's revenge: 'The desire to play God that many doctors have is really dangerous. In the end they will breach the borders that nature has determined.' 'We try to do things we shouldn't.' This idea is well known from mythology, as for instance the myth of Adam and Eve, Prometheus, Faust, and Dr Frankenstein, which illustrate that knowledge and scientific experiments are dangerous. In extreme cases of this attitude pattern there was – besides a refusal to receive organs – also a consistent refusal to donate organs. One did not want to contribute to such an unnatural activity as transplantation: 'Transplantation is a manipulation of life itself.' Blood transfusion would be acceptable because blood is renewable. 'Blood is *not mine* for a short time only, while a kidney will always be foreign.' A less-extreme attitude pattern set the limits between what was natural and unnatural, allowed and not allowed, between the species: 'I feel instinctively that it's wrong to mix different species, it would go wrong.' 'My body would let me know that an animal organ didn't fit. It's contrary to nature.' 'It's unnatural to move body parts between species.' Thus, people with such beliefs accepted transplantation between humans but not xeno-transplantation. They were also positive toward donating their own organs.

Willingness neither to receive nor to give; the influencing organ   Another attitude pattern focused on changes of identity if one received a transplant from another person or even more so from an animal. There was a conviction that personality, behaviour, or appearance would be influenced by the new organ, that would transfer the qualities of the donor: 'At least 5% of me would become animal.' 'I would perhaps look more piggish with a pig's kidney.' 'Would I become half a pig, if I got an organ from a pig?' 'What if I would start grunting?' People with this attitude pattern refused to have a transplant and also to donate their own organs as they did not want to become part of an unknown individual, which was thought to be just as frightening as receiving an organ. They strongly cathexed their bodies and even more certain organs such as eyes, skin and heart. The latter were felt as more personal and having more identity, because they could be seen and sensed (more than the kidneys or the liver, which were felt as more anonymous), and were therefore the most difficult to donate: 'Everything is in the heart; I neither want to give it nor take it.' 'A kidney is more of another person than blood and bone marrow.' Compared to the third attitude pattern this one stressed changes of personal identity and what such changes would mean for a special individual, while the third attitude pattern focused on the principle of changing nature in a broad sense.

Willingness neither to receive nor to give; the reincarnated body   A fifth attitude pattern demonstrated a special philosophy of life and a concrete view on reincarnation and direct resurrection of the earthly body: every molecule of the body would be needed in the next existence; one could not start a new life with a transplantation if some organs were donated when one died. Besides, there would be no need for transplants, as death would not be the end but just a border to your next life in this world: 'Death is not the end. You will be reborn with a brand new and healthy body. So you don't need any new organs.' This view was not in correspondence to any established religion or world view and did not reflect a coherent philosophy of life but was rather a home-made mixture of elements including both wishful thinking and quasi-scientific ideas. It corresponded to what Thomas Luckmann calls 'the invisible religion': these individuals choose various components of world views that are available to them and combine these elements to a more or less consistent system (Luckmann, 1967). [...]

Mixed feelings initially to receive; willingness to give, preferably to family members   Still another attitude pattern was characterized by mixed feelings toward receiving organs, even if, in the end, there usually was an acceptance of most kinds of organs. The uneasiness was mostly not very strong but seemed to be of an initial character. There was an ambivalence depending on the simultaneous wish to survive and a vague feeling of the risk of becoming influenced in some unforeseeable way by the transplant: 'What if it comes from a sinful man? Then God has to clean my new heart.' 'A member of the family would be the safest.' 'If the organ were rejected you would wonder if the rightful owner really wanted you to have it.' 'Artificial organs are more dead than anything else.' There might also be a feeling of disgust to have another person's intimate belongings or something connected with food and eating inside one's own body, i.e. being contaminated by such material: 'To get a transplant would be felt as having another person's dirty underwear on.' 'The whole pig nature just feels like a big *no*.' 'I use to buy pig liver prepacked at the supermarket. To have it inside me – well, it feels a bit disgusting.' 'I wouldn't like to have an organ from a dead animal inside me and it's the same thing with a dead person.' 'Disgusting to have an old rotten thing from a deceased.' This disgust might involve associations to cannibalism with regard to human organs: 'No, I would never accept an organ from a human. I'm no cannibal.' 'You don't eat people, but you eat pigs so it would be better to have an animal organ.' 'A wish to survive, then you can accept even cannibalism and receiving human organs.' In these cases animal organs were preferred. People with this attitude pattern of (initial) ambivalence were mostly willing to donate their own organs and tissues (but they would prefer to do so to their close relatives).

Mixed feelings initially to receive; willingness to give   Finally there was an attitude pattern that focused on the body image and how changes of the body would be perceived. There was a feeling of uncertainty concerning the perception of the body image if a transplantation was performed: 'A plastic thing would feel unnatural.' 'How would my body image change if much of me would be exchanged?' 'The mere knowledge that I'll go around with a pig's kidney is horrifying.' Would one recognize oneself? The emphasis was on the disturbance of a well-balanced identity and a feeling that any modification would call for strenuous work to adjust to the new 'composition'. Thus, there was an ambivalence that originated from a holistic view of the body. There was also a fear of people becoming unrecognizable in an increasingly science-fiction-like world. There might not be any human beings any longer, only 'cyborgs', i.e. a fusion between man and machine, and transhumans. However, one was aware of the relative rapidity with which people adapt to new inventions and procedures: 'Animals are already used in medicine making; transplantation will make no difference.' 'We are used to eating animals but not yet to having their organs inside us in this way.' 'Today you put a lot of things in the body, nails and joints and so on. That's OK.' 'A pacemaker is totally accepted today. It will probably be the same with other artifical implants or transplants.' 'You will have to get used to it, it will be accepted as time goes by.' People holding this reaction would eventually accept to receive organs. Most of them were positive to organ donation; a few were undecided.

Discussion

[...]

Two different conceptions

In this section I would like to discuss the two radically different conceptions of the body that were revealed in some of the attitude patterns, the 'body-as-machine' and 'the influenced body'. [...]

The body-as-machine   The first conception was held by those who easily objectified their bodies and conceived of them as machine-like, not expressing their personal identity or self. In this context some words must be said about the inevitable dualism of body perspectives – the phenomenon of both having and being a body. Thoombs excellently describes the shifting of perspectives in her book 'The meaning of illness' (Thoombs, 1993). If focus is on the lived body, i.e. the body experienced at the pre-reflective level in a non-objective way, we *are* our bodies, and there is no separation between body and self. On the other hand, if we focus on the objective or physiological body, i.e. the body apprehended at the reflective level as a material object among others within the world, then we definitely *have* or possess a body. However, we explicitly recognize these bodies as *our* bodies. Still, we apprehend the body as 'Other-than-me'. The act of reflection is needed to make the body stand out as *body*, i.e. to turn our lived bodies into objects for us as subjects.

There are different needs to objectify the body in different contexts. In order to be able to consider procedures with our bodies, we must focus on the body as a 'physico-biological thing'. People seem to vary in the easiness with which they shift perspective from the lived body to the body as an object. There are also differences in how people usually cathexe their body, that is, how much emotional energy they concentrate on their body and body parts, and how much their body in that way becomes central to their self (Belk, 1990). This helps to explain why it is harder to donate eyes, skin, and heart, that are felt as 'more myself' than the kidneys or the pancreas, that are apprehended as more anonymous (cf. Sanner, 1994). People who hold the first conception evidently belong to those who cathexe their body very little and who easily shift perspectives from the lived body to the objectified body.

Several anthropologists have drawn attention to how the biomedical tradition reinforces the objectification of the body (Featherstone, 1982; Featherstone & Turner, 1995; Helman, 1994; Williams, 1997). The reductionism inherent in this tradition has led to a fragmentation of the body into a series of body parts followed by a focus on progressively smaller areas, ending with the cell itself. This paradigm has been extremely successful in diagnosing and treating diseases. Many contemporary concepts of the body's structure and function are borrowed from technology, and machines provide the models in terms of which people conceptualize and explain the structure and workings of the body (Helman, 1994). This machine metaphor paves the way for the understanding that parts of the body may fail and even need to be replaced by spare parts. Transplantation surgery, the use of pacemakers, implants of titan and plastic reinforce the idea of the body as a repairable machine. By creating bodies which are 'partly machine', medical technology has profoundly influenced the contemporary body image.

The influenced body   The second conception was held by those who believed or suspected that a new organ would transfer the donor's qualities, that is, influence the identity of the recipient. How this transmission would happen was not clear and not even reflected on. This belief has probably a multifactorial base. One factor seems to be the empirical fact that substances that are mixed with each other usually show traits from all parts involved, the bigger or more important or impressive, the more impact on the resulting blend. This seems to be one reason why the heart is considered so special, both because it is symbolically charged and because it is conceived to be crucial for life. Another factor might be the obvious parallel to other kinds of treatment, especially drugs, by which patients' behaviour, appearance, and personality in some cases are intentionally changed. It is also well known that non-intentional side effects on behaviour, appearance, and personality sometimes do occur. These factors represent a kind of 'analogy thinking' which constitutes a fundamental pattern of everyday reasoning and is a rational way of thinking even if the analogies sometimes prove to be false. Implicitly this way of thinking means that the body parts are conceived as segments of the whole and also express the being in its totality.

An alternative or additional explanatory factor would be a kind of magical thinking. (Magic presupposes that an object or a person can be influenced by supernatural forces, not only by natural laws.) Magical patterns of thought are common even in our high-tech Western world where it exists more or less beneath the surface of our 'scientific' thinking. Superstition is one example. People are often not aware of it, and it may even contrast with their explicit beliefs but it nonetheless influences them (Nemeroff & Rozin, 1989). [...]

In the context of organ transplantation, which is a concrete form of incorporation, the association to food (oral incorporation) and ingestion is near at hand. Belief in 'You are what you eat', in the sense of acquiring the attributes of ingested foods, is not unusual. This has the same intuitive appeal as in the analogy thinking discussed above. However, it might also be an example of sympathetic magic and 'the law of contagion' (Rozin, Millman, & Nemeroff, 1986). This law states that things that have been in contact with each other or have belonged together may influence each other through transfer of some of their properties via an 'essence'. Such a contamination remains after the physical contact has ceased and may be permanent. The rule is 'once in contact, always in contact'. 'You are what you eat' can be considered as a derivative of 'the law of contagion'. It is easy to understand that to receive an organ from another person or an animal may evoke the same ideas and feelings. Some of the informants associated to cannibalism when thinking of receiving human organs, while others expressed disgust at receiving animal organs, which are obvious associations to oral incorporation. Also in this magical thinking the body parts are conceived as representatives of the whole. With regard to animal organs there are (beside rational deliberations on compatibility, infections, and function) also the ancient human concerns of distinguishing oneself from other animals. When accepting an animal organ as a transplant this challenges one's humanity. [...]

Certainly, it should be easier to accept a transplant of any kind for those who embrace the idea of the body as a machine with interchangeable parts, than for those who believe that their personality will be influenced by the donor's characteristics. Magical thinking as delineated by contagion may, when extreme, result in maladaptive or irrational behaviour. However, the great majority of people probably fall somewhere between these extremes. [...]

It should also be pointed out that those who have adopted the machine model of the body should be encouraged to supplement this with a more holistic view in a transplantation situation. Apart from the two conceptions already discussed there are also traces of a third conception which emphasizes another kind of influence on the recipient than the second conception, and which is based on another tradition. This tradition stresses the interdependence of all body parts as well as body and mind, and organism and environment. In this frame of reference it is self-evident that a transplant will definitely influence the receiving organism in toto. However, this does not imply that characteristics of the donor are transferred, rather that the individual has to restructure his/her identity depending on the illness, the special experiences in connection with the transplantation, and the adjustments of life that will be necessary afterwards.

Acknowledgements

This study was funded by the Swedish Council for Social Research and the Vardalstiftelsen.

References

Belk, R. W. (1990). Me and thee versus mine and thine: How perceptions of the body influence organ donation and transplantation. In J. Shanteau, A. Jackson, & R. Harris, *Organ donation and transplantation: Psychological and behavioral factors* (pp. 139–49). New York: American Psychological Association.

Featherstone, M. (1982). The body in consumer culture. *Theory, Culture, and Society, 1,* 18–33.

Featherstone, M., & Turner, B. S. (1995). Body and society: An introduction. *Body and Society, 1,* 1–12.

Helman, C. G. (1994). *Culture, health and illness.* (pp. 2–36). Oxford: Butterworth & Heinemann.

Luckmann, T. (1967). *The invisible religion. The problem of religion in modern society.* New York: Macmillan.

Nemeroff, C., & Rozin, P. (1989). 'You are what you eat': Applying the demand-free 'impressions' technique to an unacknowledged belief. *Ethos: The Journal of Psychological Anthropology, 17,* 50–69.

Patton, M. Q. (1990). *Qualitative evaluation and research methods.* London: Sage.

Rozin, P., Millman, L., & Nemeroff, C. (1986). Operation of the laws of sympathetic magic in disgust and other domains. *Journal of Personality and Social Psychology, 50,* 703–12.

Sanner, M. A. (1994). Attitudes toward organ donation and transplantation. A model for understanding reactions to medical procedures after death. *Social Science & Medicine, 38,* 1141–52.

Sanner, M. A. (1998). Giving and taking – to whom and from whom?. Peoples attitudes toward transplantation of organs and tissue from different sources. *Clinical Transplantation, 12,* 530–7.

Thoombs, S. K. (1993). *The meaning of illness.* (pp. 51–88). Dordrecht, The Netherlands: Kluwer Academic Publishers.

Williams, S. J. (1997). Modern medicine and the 'uncertain body': From corporeality to hyperreality? *Social Science & Medicine, 45,* 1041–9.

4

Social and Ethical Aspects of in vitro Fertilization

Elizabeth Heitman

[...]

The medicalization of infertility

[In vitro fertilization (IVF)] took the public consciousness by storm in 1978, with the internationally publicized birth of Louise Brown in England. Familiar to many from Aldous Huxley's novel *Brave New World* (17) as a futuristic means of social control, IVF epitomized both the miraculous ability of medical technology to redefine the boundaries of life and its tendency to move intimate human activities out of the private realm and into the control of experts and institutions. Dire predictions about the use and misuse of IVF were swift in coming.

[...] By the early 1980s, the availability of IVF had prompted a shift in both lay and professional interpretations of childlessness, away from a social and religious framework to a medical model that stressed clinical diagnosis and an expanding array of treatment options.

[...]

The perception that infertility is a serious and growing health problem is due largely to the high profile of ART [assisted reproductive technologies] – particularly IVF – among medical professionals, policy makers, and lay people, and to the subsequent growing demand for reproductive technologies. By the end of the 1980s, the increased ability to diagnose individual cases of infertility, increased availability of medical and surgical intervention for infertility, and increased expectation of technologic success had medicalized the experience of involuntary childlessness for many couples. Medicalization is a complex phenomenon that may result from a number of factors (10, 39). When a physical or social condition results in suffering, there may be considerable moral and practical appeal to identifying a specific physical cause. In its classification of various infirmities and deviant conditions as diseases, medical science offers sufferers a logical cause for the unwanted condition, and often holds out the possibility of controlling or eliminating it through concrete medical interventions.

Medicalization also provides a morally neutral explanation for stigmatized conditions; rather than someone whose affliction is a justly deserved punishment or sign of immorality, the affected individual becomes an unfortunate victim who deserves others' compassion and assistance (14). The victim's moral responsibility shifts from repentance to being a 'good' patient and making a good faith effort to get well by taking advantage of available treatments.

Medicalization may also result from the exercise of power by physicians and others who seek to assume control over a particular experience or condition (10, 18, 39). In many cases, medicalization brings marked financial advantage to physicians, medically oriented institutions, and the pharmaceutical and medical device industries. However, medicalization may also confer authority on groups of individuals who seek to promote a particular ideology or political or moral agenda.

Infertility was a prime candidate for medicalization when early researchers offered the possibility of technologic intervention. Reproduction is an essential human activity, both biologically and socially, and infertility has been a source of suffering throughout history. In both western and nonwestern cultures, childlessness has traditionally been interpreted as a punishment or sign of divine disfavor that has long been a source of shame; infertile women have traditionally been subject to social judgment, rejection, and isolation (15). In many nonwestern societies infertility still carries considerable moral stigma (28). The medical model of infertility offered couples both an organic theory that relieved them of personal responsibility for the deviance of childlessness and an active, practical response to the problem. As patients, the infertile couple could find not only a possible solution to their problem, but also a social role that made their childlessness more socially acceptable.

Medicalization also promised enormous rewards to the medical researchers and clinicians who pioneered fertility treatments and the pharmaceutical companies that produce drugs essential to ART. Today the medical treatment of infertility is a multibillion dollar industry worldwide, with IVF as the mainstay of countless fertility clinics (6, 11). Physicians in ART have made tremendous personal gains not only in terms of wealth and prestige, but also in the less tangible power that they hold over the creation of life and the control that they wield in the lives of their patients (34).

IVF was initially developed to treat a narrow set of indications, most importantly occlusion of the fallopian tubes that was not amenable to surgery. However, in a classic example of the technologic imperative (13), the very availability of IVF created a 'need' for its use that extends far beyond the initial indications. In a clinical context, any diagnosis of infertility implies a disease state that, for medical reasons, should be treated (26); any available treatment that is not contraindicated may seem to offer a chance of benefit.

By the mid-1980s, IVF had become the fallback treatment for a wide range of infertile couples who had not had a baby after treatment with drugs and/or surgery (1, 12). In the 1990s, IVF became the intervention of choice when doctors or prospective parents wanted to limit the many uncertainties associated with natural conception (12). Two increasingly common procedures, oocyte donation (OD) and intracytoplasmic sperm injection (ICSI), require IVF (8, 27).

Feminist scholars in sociology and ethics recognized in the 1980s that many infertile couples would do almost anything to have a baby of their own, and that the appeal of kinship made ART much more attractive than adoption, the traditional social response to infertility (33–6). While infertility specialists hailed IVF as offering infertile couples new options, critics pointed out that IVF typically foreclosed the choice not to undergo treatment. Because both patients and clinicians are often more willing to risk the failure or harmful effects of intervention than they are to accept the failure to try 'everything possible' (38), even a slim hope of pregnancy drove many couples to multiple rounds of IVF. The limits of IVF and its imperative character have received popular attention in the 1990s (5, 6, 16), but the promises of IVF still seem irresistible to many for as long as they can afford it. For such couples, it is harder to stop unsuccessful fertility treatment than it is to keep trying in the face of almost insurmountable odds (5).

IVF with donor oocytes has also created a new need for infertility treatment among older women by redefining the traditional biological boundaries on reproductive age. IVF with donor oocytes has extended the time in which women may become pregnant from the traditional period of age 15 to 44 into the early 60s. OD was originally developed to compensate for premature ovarian failure, surgical removal of the ovaries, or impaired ovarian function (3). But OD's ability to reverse the natural decrease in women's fertility (37), combined with the medicalization of menopause already under way in much of the industrialized world (30), soon led to demand for OD among postmenopausal women. Despite higher morbidity among older pregnant women and their infants, researchers intrigued by the challenge of postmenopausal fertility found the clinical possibilities exciting (29).

[...]

The medicalization of infertility has reduced the moral stigma once associated with childlessness and has resulted in the birth of many healthy babies. However, IVF does not result in a baby for the majority who undergo it, and many couples, and particularly women, experience unsuccessful IVF as a personal failure that carries much of the old moral stigma of punishment (5, 33–5). The profound despair that follows unsuccessful IVF can be as overwhelming as the unrealistically high hope that preceded it. Moreover, medicalization has imposed a new social stigma on the couples for whom IVF is not effective. Because the treatment is still widely assumed to be a solution to infertility, couples who do not achieve pregnancy following IVF may be blamed for not having done the right thing; in the medical vernacular, they 'fail the treatment' rather than the treatment failing them. [...]

Shifting definitions of parenthood and family

One of the recognized ethical effects of medical technology is its ability to transform simple questions into complex problems. The creation of extracorporeal embryos through IVF quickly confounded the once straightforward meanings of mother and father by separating the biological and relational aspects of parenthood. Moreover, by introducing professional and institutional brokers into the once private areas of conception and birth, the medicalization of procreation generally has legalized our understanding of parenthood and blurred the social definitions of mother, father, and child in detailed legal exceptions and intricate reinterpretations of traditional law (4, 25).

[...]

In many ways, the institutionalized practice of AI [artificial insemination] simply made public age-old, private anxieties about the uncertainty of paternity and legal exceptions intended to preserve family unity. IVF, however, revolutionized the definition of parenthood by separating motherhood from pregnancy and childbirth. In addition to the two potential fathers, IVF may involve as many as three women who could claim the status of mother: the genetic mother, who provides the ovum; the gestating mother, who carries the developing child and gives birth; and the mother who may have arranged for the conception and who rears the child after delivery. The growing demand for IVF, and the subsequent development of and demand for OD and embryo transfer (ET), quickly demonstrated the conflicts possible between these claims and the need for legal clarity. As predicted by U.S. medical-legal analyst George Annas (4), the growth of IVF soon made private legal contracts indispensable to the treatment of infertility. [...]

Would-be parents, gamete donors, infertility specialists, medical institutions, and the state all have interests to protect in the creation of a child, whose own interests may be viewed quite differently by these parties. The ultimate value of contractual parenthood and a case-based legal definition of the status of parents and children would appear to be the attention that can be given to the special characteristics and needs of the 'family' and child, and protection of the child's interests. However, conflicts over surrogacy contracts, and even over traditional adoptions, have demonstrated the limits of contracts in predicting the parties' emotional responses to the resulting child. Moreover, the adversarial nature of legal procedures may hinder the sort of trusting social relationships upon which families have traditionally depended.

The ultimate inability of contracts and the courts to protect a child of IVF can be seen in the case of John and Luanne Buzzanca (7), who contracted with a surrogate to gestate an embryo conceived from anonymous donor gametes, agreeing to adopt the resulting child at birth. After the surrogate became pregnant, the couple separated; Luanne Buzzanca accepted the child at birth, but her husband denied paternity and refused to pay child support. In October 1997, a California family court judge agreed that John Buzzanca was not legally responsible for the then 2-year-old child whom he had intentionally arranged to have conceived; the ruling further held that Luanne Buzzanca was the child's temporary custodian, not her legal mother. In 1998 the appeals court concluded that the Buzzancas *were* the child's legal parents because they had initiated and consented to the medical procedure that had resulted in her procreation (7). Nonetheless, the child's interests may well have been compromised by the prolonged uncertainty of her legal status and the anxiety and financial consequences to her legalized mother, as well as by the ongoing contractual denial of access to her other 'parents'.

Whereas the interests of the children of IVF have been difficult to safeguard, the interests and appropriate protection of embryos conceived through IVF have been almost impossible to define. Since the 1960s, debate over the moral legitimacy of abortion and efforts to regulate the practice have demonstrated the impossibility of achieving social and legal consensus on the status of embryos or fetuses in utero. In most western countries the fetus is accorded rights proportional to its viability: notwithstanding the stance of the Roman Catholic Church and other religious traditions that maintain that personal life begins at conception (9), legal scholars have concluded that extracorporeal embryos have neither rights to nor interests in being born (31).

While the law has largely concluded that extracorporeal embryos are not persons, there is still significant debate about the nature of the legal relationship between would-be parents and the embryos that they conceive through IVF (32). A number of highly publicized divorce proceedings involving the disposition of frozen embryos have raised the question of custodial rights versus property rights to frozen embryos that the couple once hoped would become babies.

[...]

Recent experience has demonstrated that, even more important than provisions for divorce, it is essential for IVF contracts to address the abandonment of frozen embryos by the couples who stored them for future use. One of the earliest publicized dilemmas over abandoned embryos involved the accidental death of Elsa and Mario Rios, who died in a plane crash in 1983 after storing two embryos at an IVF clinic in Melbourne. International debates over the disposition of the embryos were complicated by the question of their status as heirs to the Rios' large estate, offers from a number of women to gestate them, and the insistence of religious groups that the embryos were orphans who deserved the state's protection (22).

Planning and contractual arrangements for the disposition of stored embryos in the event of death is likely to be difficult for some couples, as many people prefer to ignore their own mortality. Remarkably, however, most embryos are not abandoned as a result of death, but rather as the result of the withdrawal of infertile couples from treatment. In the United States alone, an estimated 10,000 frozen embryos are stored indefinitely each year (20), many on behalf of infertile couples who simply disappear from clinic rolls or do not respond to the clinic's attempts to contact them.

[...]

The United Kingdom's limitation on storing frozen embryos was enacted primarily out of concern about the effects of long-term freezing on the health of children that might result from implantation. However, the requirement that 5-year-old embryos not be implanted, donated, or subjected to research turns on the difficult moral assumption that respect for the potential personhood of an embryo demands its destruction after a certain period of time. Because the naturally occurring rate of nonimplantation, combined with the loss of pregnancy after implantation, is between 40% and 70% of all conceptions (2, 23), it is difficult to argue that either the nonimplantation or destruction of extracorporeal embryos is inherently disrespectful. Nonetheless, in August 1996, when infertility clinics across the United Kingdom were legally compelled to destroy over 3,300 unclaimed frozen embryos (19), clinic workers and the public at large seemed unpersuaded that the embryos' destruction served everyone's interests.

Just as infertile couples have a mixed response to their embryos, there is tension in the attitude of fertility specialists and their staff toward the embryos that they create and store. Fertility specialists insist that they take precautions in their handling of embryos that reflect concern for them as 'viable, developing babies' (21). Yet alongside the commitment to 'the human person integrally and adequately considered' (2), the standard practice of IVF is clearly shaped by clinics' commercial interests and the commodification of embryos (15). In extreme cases, these forces have led to profit-driven scandals in which neither infertility patients nor their embryos were treated with respect (24).

Recently larger infertility clinics in the United States have added a new twist to the tension inherent in the extracorporeal embryo as a potential child: rather than discarding surplus donor eggs, some have fertilized them with donor sperm, offering the resulting embryos for 'adoption' (21). Unlike ET, in which the parental rights of the donors are typically addressed by contract after conception, the embryos offered for 'adoption' are created from donor gametes that are legally unrelated to anyone; the clinic is their sole 'guardian.' Some of these embryos have been custom-made to provide a specific ethnic or national ancestry, raising renewed charges of their commodification. However, calling the process of transferring these embryos to unrelated prospective parents 'adoption' emphasizes the person that the embryo may become in the future; similarly, using the term 'adoption' harkens back to the social response to infertility that preceded ART.

Whether this euphemism came into use because of its marketing value or because it reflects infertility specialists' deeper convictions about the microscopic entities with which they work, the term 'embryo adoption' captures the ambiguity of society's response to the technologically created child. As with many other aspects of life that have been profoundly affected by technology, it will be virtually impossible to resolve the ambiguity that IVF has raised, except as we find and create new meanings for vital concepts, and experience allows us to integrate them into new interpretations of our social and ethical worldviews.

[...]

References

1   Alberta Heritage Foundation for Medical Research. *In vitro fertilization and embryo transfer as a treatment for infertility.* Edmonton, AB: AHFMR, 1997.

2   American Fertility Society. Ethical considerations of the new reproductive technologies. *Fertility and Sterility,* 1990, 53 (suppl. 2), 17S.

3   American Fertility Society. Guidelines for gamete donation: 1993. *Fertility and Sterility,* 1993, 59 (suppl. 1), 1–9S.

4   Annas, G. J. Redefining parenthood and protecting embryos: Why we need new laws. *Hastings Center Report,* 1984, 14 (Oct.), 50–2.

5   Begley, S. The baby myth. *Newsweek,* 1995 (Sept. 4), 38–47.

6   Brownlee, S. The baby chase. *U.S. News and World Report,* 1994, 117 (Dec. 5), 84–92.

7   *Buzzanca v. Buzzanca,* 61 Cal. App. 4th 1410 (1998).

8   Cohen, C. (ed.). *New ways of making babies: Oocyte donation.* Bloomington, IN: Indiana University Press, 1996.

9   Congregation for the Doctrine of the Faith. *Instruction on respect for human life in its origin and on the dignity of procreation: Replies to certain questions of the day.* English version reprinted by the Pope John XXII Medical Moral Research and Education Center, Braintree, MA, 1987.

10 Conrad, P., & Schneider, J. *Deviance and medicalization: From badness to sickness.* Columbus, OH: Merrill Publishing Co., 1985.

11 DeWitt, P. M. In pursuit of pregnancy. *American Demographics,* 1993, 15 (5), 48–54.

12 Elmer-Dewitt, P. Making babies. *Time*, 1991 (Sept. 30), 57–63.

13 Fuchs, V. *Who shall live? Health, economics, and social choice*. New York: Basic Books, 1974.

14 Heitman, E. The influence of values and culture in responses to suffering. In P. Stark & J. P. McGovern (eds.), *The hidden dimension of illness: Human suffering*. New York: National League for Nursing, 1992, 81–103.

15 Heitman, E., & Schlachtenhaufen, M. The differential effects of race, ethnicity, and socio-economic status on infertility and its treatment: Ethical and policy issues for oocyte donation. In C. Cohen (ed.), *New ways of making babies: Oocyte donation*. Bloomington, IN: Indiana University Press, 1996, 188–212.

16 Herman, R. Dying to conceive. *Mirabella*, 1994 (July), 124–5.

17 Huxley, A. *Brave new world*. New York: Perennial Library, 1969.

18 Illich, I. *Medical nemesis: The expropriation of health*. New York: Pantheon Books, 1976.

19 Johnson, M. British scientists destroy thousands of embryos. *Houston Chronicle*, 1996 (Aug. 2), 20A.

20 Kolata, G. Medicine's troubling bonus: Surplus of human embryos. *New York Times*, 1997 (Mar. 16), 1, 32.

21 Kolata, G. Clinics selling embryos made for 'adoption': Couples can even pick ancestry, for $2,750. *New York Times*, 1997 (Nov. 23), 1, 18.

22 Lieber, J. A piece of yourself in the world. *Atlantic Monthly*, 1989 (June), 76–80.

23 Little, A. B. There's many a slip 'twixt implantation and the crib. *New England Journal of Medicine*, 1988, 319, 241–2.

24 Lovitt, J. T., & Price, R. Reproductive clinic, doctors ran amok, ex-employee claims. *USA Today*, 1995 (June 15), 3A.

25 Maklin, R. Artificial means of reproduction and our understanding of the family. *Hastings Center Report*, 1991 (Jan.–Feb.), 5–11.

26 Mosher, W. D., & Pratt, W. F. Fecundity and infertility in the United States: Incidence and trends. *Fertility and Sterility*, 1991, 56, 192–3.

27 Palermo, G. D., Cohen, J., Alikani, M., Adler, A., & Rosenwaks, A. Intracytoplasmic sperm injection: A novel treatment for all forms of male factor infertility. *Fertility and Sterility*, 1995, 63, 1231–40.

28 Pandit, R. D. Ethics in infertility management: Asian aspects. *Asia-Oceania Journal of Obstetrics and Gynaecology*, 1989, 15, 79–85.

29 Quigley, M. M. The new frontier of reproductive age (editorial). *JAMA*, 1992, 268, 1320–1.

30 Ratliff, K. S. Health technology for women: Whose health? Whose technology? In K. S. Ratliff (ed.), *Healing technology: Feminist perspectives*. Ann Arbor, MI: University of Michigan Press, 1989, 173–98.

31 Robertson, J. A. Resolving disputes over frozen embryos. *Hastings Center Report*, 1989, 19 (6), 7–12.

32 Robertson, J. A. Legal troublespots in assisted reproduction. *Fertility and Sterility*, 1996, 65, 11–12.

33 Rothman, B. K. The meanings of choice in reproductive technology. In R. Arditti, R. D. Klein, & S. Minden (eds.), *Test-tube women: What future for motherhood*. London: Pandora Press, 1984, 23–33.

34 Rowland, R. Technology and motherhood: Reproductive choice reconsidered. *Signs: Journal of Women in Culture and Society*, 1987, 12, 512–29.

35 Sandelowski, M. The color gray: Ambiguity and infertility. *Image: Journal of Nursing Scholarship*, 1987, 19, 70–4.

36 Sandelowski, M., & Pollock, C. Women's experiences of infertility. *Image: Journal of Nursing Scholarship*, 1986, 18 (4), 140–4.

37 Sauer, M. V., Paulson, R. J., & Lobo, R. A. Reversing the natural decline in human fertility: An extended clinical trial of oocyte donation to women of advanced reproductive age. *JAMA*, 1992, 268, 1275–9.

38 Tymstra, T. The imperative character of medical technology and the meaning of 'anticipated decision regret.' *International Journal of Technology Assessment in Health Care*, 1989, 5, 207–13.

39 Williams, S. J., & Calnan, M. The limits of medicalization? Modern medicine and the lay populace in 'late' modernity. *Social Science and Medicine*, 1996, 42, 1609–20.

5

Reproductive Genetics, Gender and the Body: 'Please Doctor, may I have a Normal Baby?'

Elizabeth Ettorre

The purpose of this paper is to highlight key sociological issues which become visible when 'the body' becomes a theoretical site in reproductive genetics. [...] Reproductive genetics is defined as the utilisation of DNA based technologies in the medical management and supervision of the reproductive process. This term suggests that complex social and cultural processes are involved in the organisation and use of genetic tests for prenatal diagnosis. [...]

By positioning the body as a central feature in sociological analyses of reproductive genetics, the paper: (1) describes how a mechanistic view of the body is privileged in this discourse and the effects of this view; (2) examines how through reproductive genetics limits are practised on the gendered body through a feminised regime of reproductive asceticism and involvement in a discourse on shame; and (3) explores the social effects and limitations of reproductive genetics in relation to disability as a cultural representation of impaired bodies. Framed by a social constructionist view of the body (Shilling 1993), the central assumption of this paper is that the science of reproductive genetics appears within surveillance medicine (Armstrong 1995) as part of a disciplinary process in society's creation of a genetic moral order. [...]

Methodology

The source of empirical data presented in this paper is a qualitative study on experts' accounts of the use of prenatal genetic screening in four European countries: UK, Finland, The Netherlands and Greece.

[...]

Experts were asked their views on genetic testing and screening in prenatal diagnosis. The interview questions revolved around their attitudes on the use of these techniques; their perceptions of the prevailing state of knowledge on legal, medical and ethical aspects; social effects; and policy priorities on local and national levels. [...]

[...] In this paper, the focus is mainly on similarities in experts as a group and their attitudes towards reproductive genetics.

The body as machine: dangerous genes and fetal containers

The language of reproductive genetics tends to privilege an individualistic, mechanistic view of a gendered body with the effect that the full significance of reproductive processes tends to be lost. Of course, this view, modelled on the workings of an inanimate object (i.e. a machine) is not new in medicine. Within this paradigm, the body is treated as a machine and it is the doctor, the mechanic, who fixes it (Martin 1992). [...]

Treating the body as a machine is consistent with the belief that genes can be manipulated, undergo therapy or be altered. We have the idea that bad or defective genes can be weeded out from the good ones and replaced. Conrad (1997) notes this sort of 'gene talk' functions to over-simplify very complex issues. In the end, problems arise as attempts are made to make hard and fast distinctions between good and bad genes – as one can with, say, a good and bad car. A clinical geneticist claimed that one effect of making this distinction between good and bad genes was where to draw the line:

> We are wanting to go [in] ... that direction that we are selecting for the good genes and selecting against the bad genes. Where is the limit between good and bad genes? That is the question. Because there are examples where this limit is really hard to draw. (Clinical geneticist FIN4[1])

Within this body as a machine paradigm, the body is also viewed as a container of genes – a carrier of genetic material. This idea perpetuates the belief that genetic disease is not only something terrible that someone has but something someone is (Steinberg 1997: 117). If genes are diseased, someone is diseased and this someone's body can be perceived as carrying dangerous material. In this context, one expert says:

> I think that very often people get afraid. They think they are carrying something which is very dangerous and at the same time, people ... don't understand that we all have genes which are more or less diseased or which might get a disease ... (Lawyer FIN15)

[...]

The pregnant body, reproductive asceticism and genetic capital

The language of genetics tends to set reproductive limits both upon the inner body and the outer body in our modern consumerist culture with the result that women's more than men's bodies are restrained. In short, the science of genetics becomes an ideal way of bringing together what Turner (1992: 58–9) has referred to as external problems of representation (i.e. commodification) and regulation and the interior ones of restraint (i.e. control of desire, passion and need) and reproduction. What does this mean? Simply, through reproductive genetics the pregnant body will experience self-imposed restraint through a type of *reproductive asceticism*. [...] It has been argued that as it is diffused into society, prenatal diagnosis in the form of prenatal genetic testing may become a need (Beaulieu and Lippman 1995), a lifestyle or even an addiction (Lippman 1994) in our consumerist culture. For example, as these technologies become routinised, pregnant women, as consumers, 'crave' these technologies. Significantly, consumers are attracted to these technologies and begin to accept prenatal genetic testing and screening under the rubric of older non-controversial medical practices and routine prenatal care (Press and Browner 1997). In this context, one clinical geneticist explains how trust, as a part and parcel of a patient's experience of traditional medical practice, will support her (i.e. the patient's) acceptance of new technologies (i.e. prenatal screening for Down's) even though the patient may have difficulties understanding the results of these technologies:

> ...If I go to a doctor and the doctor says well your gall bladder should be operated..., it is very rare that I go for a second opinion....I believe the first one. He's the doctor and he told me to go for an operation so I go. So all of this [screening] is the same thing.... – that we have the trust. I don't know what the level of information [is] and how well people really do understand the ideas...the philosophy behind these different screenings [which are] totally different. So...for instance Down's screening is a very complicated screening that practically no one really understands. Because you screen to find a group that has a higher risk...So actually if I am pregnant and I go to a screening...they can't tell me whether I will have a Down's syndrome child or not. But, they will tell me something about my risk of having Down's syndrome...According to that, I decide whether to take the test [amniocentesis] or not. It is actually very complicated because even if I get very good results in the screening, I still may carry a Down's child. Also...even if I get the worst results...it is rather likely that the child is healthy. (Clinical geneticist FIN5)

Nevertheless, another expert suggests that because the technology 'is there', women's choices are shaped by pressures from others and the technology itself. Regardless that the information learned through these technologies may be 'too much', women want them:

> If you are [developing] a technology, it is going further and further...I see that many people...don't choose any more. They are only going with it because it is there...[As the technology] goes further and further, then I think it will be...common to do [these] things and then [I think] 'Because everyone does it, I have to do it'...It is not [only] pressure from....others but...also pressure from the technology and all its possibilities that [makes me] want more. But there is so much that I have to make a decision about. That's too much for me...There is too much information, there is too much technology...(Midwife NL8)

When pregnant bodies undergo these invasive tests, this austere self-disciplining of reproductive asceticism can be viewed and experienced as necessary for the overall, external regulation of 'fit' populations in consumer culture. In this regime, the female body emerges as a reproductive resource. Drawing on Bourdieu's work, Shilling (1993: 127) notes that in contemporary society, the body has become a more comprehensive form of physical capital, a possessor of power, status and distinctive symbolic forms – integral to the accumulation of resources. In reproductive genetics, the female body can be seen as women's physical capital. In turn, women's physical capital becomes inexorably linked with their genetic capital (i.e. genes or genetic make up), as they encounter the regulatory practices of prenatal genetics. In this feminised regimen, women enact a morality of the body which upholds the external population's standard – the desire for conventional (i.e. non-diseased, genetically normal) offspring and the need for citizens who are fit to be born. Genetic capital not only determines whether or not a particular woman's body should be viewed as a reproductive resource but also is central to constructing a genetic moral order.

Thus, when physicians speak of 'affected offspring' or 'risk' and utilise technologies to rid wombs of 'non-viable fetuses', they are actively supporting the population's assumed desire and society's supposed need for fit bodies as well as firmly establishing the link between physical and genetic capital. In this context, one scholar Hubbard (1985) suggests that it is not so different to abort a fetus who is a girl in China and a Down's Syndrome one in the USA – both decisions are deeply embedded in social pressures. In a related context, the same author (Hubbard 1986) refers to these pressurised decisions as 'obscene choices', confronting pregnant women. One clinical geneticist contextualises the pressures and the lack of freedom people have:

> If the society is discriminating against . . . handicapped people then it reflects on the individual, personal and familial level too – that people who otherwise would and should be free to make their choices about their children – for example, if they want to have a handicapped child, they do not feel free to make their choice if the general attitude in society is that we are trying to get rid of the handicapped people and they are just useless people and that it is better not to have handicapped people. (Clinical geneticist FIN4)

Coinciding with society's standard for reproducing able bodied citizens, there exists a powerful representation of the female body as a vehicle for women to achieve motherhood or a reproductive life style. An extreme version of reproductive asceticism not only upholds the body as machine view but also represents the female body as a commodity (Corea 1985) and 'children' themselves as consumer objects – subject to quality control.

The pregnant body and the discourse on shame

As a powerful way of injecting biology and hierarchy into social relationships, reproductive genetics constructs the idea that genetic capital, pedigree (i.e. 'pure' breeding) and ultimately, social fitness can be ranked. But, of course, this ranking is carried out in already unequal social contexts in which gender and disability are devalued. Caught between bodies ranked according to their pure breeding potential and those ranked according to stable systems of inequality (i.e. class, race, gender, etc.), pregnant bodies can be disciplined further by a discourse on shame. Here, shame is about an awareness of some serious flaw or mistake in oneself – one is guilty because one has committed a wrongdoing. Shame always needs 'the Other' – an audience (Bartky 1990).

[...]

[...] Women are divided into two opposite types of bodies/fetal containers on the basis of how well they reproduce. There are those women who are good reproducers with sound wombs capable of breeding well and with healthy genes. They should reproduce children and make babies. On the other hand, there is a group of women who are bad reproducers with problematic wombs not capable of breeding well and with faulty genes (Finger 1990). These women have the potential to reproduce genetic mistakes. They should not reproduce or make babies.

[...] This is an unintended social consequence of reproductive genetics – the division of women into good and bad reproducers.

[...] [W]omen who are bad reproducers inevitably experience psychic distress (Farrant 1985). One leading expert in the field discussed this type of anxiety by referring to a recent headline:

> *Screening test designed to allay anxiety has reverse effect.* What does that headline tell us? Is the screening test designed to allay anxiety? That journalist didn't stop to think. Of course, he [*sic*] didn't. A screening test creates anxiety in a sense, it's deliberately doing that. So I am going to tap you on the shoulder and give you bad news. You are going to be extremely distressed by that bad news. But there is an important consequence in the news that I gave you and you have a number of options that you can take – some of which you may wish to take recognizing that you are going to be quite upset. What's important is that people have a choice as to whether to get into that situation in the first place. But, once they are in that situation, they will either be more or less where they were before, that's of having no news.... screening negative does not mean you won't have bad news. That's another question. It means that you have got a lower risk of Down's. (Epidemiologist UK6)

For women with 'bad news' and reproducing genetically bad children, shame becomes linked up with the production of individuals not fit to be born (Dragonas 1999). In this context, a new type of social wrongdoing or transgression becomes visible for women – the bad reproducer. If this bad reproducer decides to continue with a pregnancy with a 'bad result', she may experience further shame as one who decides to reproduce badly.

[...]

Reproductive genetics and disability

The final discussion in the paper illustrates the social effects and limitations of reproductive genetics in relation to disability as a cultural representation of impaired bodies. [...] Within the social model of disability, two notions, disability and disabilism, have been defined by Thomas (1997: 623) and are illuminating in this context:

Disability is not the condition or functional consequence of being physically or mentally impaired. Rather, dis-ability refers to the disadvantaging affects – referred to by many – as the 'social barriers' – faced by people with impairments flowing from disablism: the ideological antipathy to what is considered to be undesirable physical, sensory or mentally-related difference or 'abnormality' in western culture.

Inherent in the concept of disability and the process of disablism is the idea that a pervasive medically describable paradigm of human, physical ability or mastery of the body is possible (Wendell 1992). As Shakespeare (1995: 24) aptly states, 'people are disabled not by their bodies but by society'. From a similar viewpoint, Wendell (1992: 70) notes that 'the oppression of disabled people is the oppression of everyone's real body' – meaning that regardless of the fact that bodies are tremendously 'diverse in size, shape, colour, texture, structure, function, range and habits of movement, and development', this is not reflected in our culture. Wendell contends that even though physical ideals change over time, we idealise the human body. Cultural ideals are not just about appearance, images or looks, but also these ideals are about human comportment. Cultural ideals on the body are concerned with how well bodies confront and conform to delineated social spaces.

Disabled bodies, disablism and reproductive genetics

[...] DNA based prenatal technologies (i.e. chorionic villous screening and amniocentesis) are used 'on bodies' to detect fetal abnormalities with the effect that the reproductive process is medicalised further (Birke *et al.* 1992: 154). As genes and bodies are being culturally shaped, pregnant and disabled bodies are meant to fall outside of the paradigm of health or well-being as well as the universal, medically describable paradigm of human physical ability. The cultural message (i.e. to have 'perfect' children) directed towards women during pregnancy is employed strategically by the medical profession to engage them in a disablist discourse. Most, if not all pregnant women are meant to have an 'antipathy' to what is considered to be undesirable physical, sensory or mentally-related difference or 'abnormality' in 'their bodies' in Western culture. Two experts mirrored this view:

> [When] I think always [of] pregnant women, there [is] no pregnant woman who wants to have a handicapped child. They all want to have a healthy child... (Gynaecologist NL6)

and

> If you say to a woman that your baby is a Downs, what do you think? Do you think that she is going to terminate the pregnancy or not? In Greece, she is going to terminate the pregnancy. (Obstetrician GR3)

Another expert, a gynaecologist, exposed his own discomfort for disabled bodies when he said bluntly:

> Setting out to have an accident is different from preventing it. (Gynaecologist NL2)

In a related context, one medical geneticist's wants reflected what appeared to be the wants of pregnant women (i.e. to have a healthy child):

> Personally, of course, I am against [interrupting] a pregnancy except if the child is going to be a handicapped child. (Medical geneticist GR5)

Another expert (a lawyer) extended these wants to the wider society:

> For the general public, ... they want healthy babies and [want to] get rid of [the] disabled. (Lawyer GR9)

[...]

Disabilism: from State benefits to benevolent technologies

In a real sense, society attempts to place disabled bodies in social spaces marked by isolation, separation and exclusion. This process tends to be legitimated by the fact that the disabled, as a group of non-aesthetic citizens, are seen to benefit from the benevolence of the Welfare State. Implicit here is a type of 'state sponsored model of disability', promoting individual failing above any attention to environmental or social factors (Shildrick 1997: 57). In reproductive genetics, the existing logic is that the genetic moral order (i.e. improving genetic capital and ultimately bodies) and its attendant technologies are able to proliferate in society as long as the State provides a certain 'high' standard of disability benefits (i.e. taking good care of the disabled). The following excerpts from two experts reflect this type of logic:

> What is good in the whole of Western Europe is that at the same time we are developing the testing and the screening for genetic diseases, we are providing genetic services. We are improving the race ... and in a way, we are also taking quite good care of handicapped people ... this shows that our society has a moral[ity] which is still good ... As long as we are taking good care of those with diseases and [the] handicapped, then we can trust that it [technology] is not misused. But, ... I am afraid that it is possible to discriminate [against] more and more sick people and handicapped people. It is quite obvious that it is happening already. (Clinical geneticist FIN4)

and

> ... I think, that if we are going to have prenatal or genetic screening generally, it is important at the same time to have a commitment to continue services for people who are disabled, because otherwise ... they will have less rights. (Policy maker UK8)

Nevertheless, as disabled bodies become progressively de-valued and disabilism shapes the dominant discourse on the body in reproductive genetics, benevolence in the form of benefits from the State will be transformed to benefits received from the technologies themselves. Simply, technologies used to abort, for example,

Down's fetuses will be increasingly viewed as helping the 'potential' disabled and/or their 'relatives'. One expert expressed the idea that the technologies themselves are helping relatives to be (i.e. parents) and that this 'benevolent' process is not new:

> I do not know much about the opinions within the group of handicapped people, but I know there is some discussion about prenatal screening because it would mean, we do not accept any longer handicapped people. I don't think that's the case, because it's not a denial of handicapped people. The only thing you want to reach with prenatal screening is to in fact . . . to help parents to be of handicapped people. . . . Some of them don't want to have a handicapped child. I don't think that's much different now [than] from the techniques we had [from] 30 years ago. Then . . . we had some techniques to look at the unborn child and now . . . the techniques changed, but not . . . what we think about and what people think about. (Gynaecologist NL6)

Another gynaecologist expressed a similar view, but suggested how this type of medical benevolence was welcomed by the disabled themselves:

> I always find it . . . [with] people with neural tube defects . . . they come themselves to [me to] have anionic fluid tested for alpha beta protein because they want to know if their baby will have a neural tube defect or not. So these people might be the strongest advocates against prenatal diagnosis but, no, they are often the strongest supporters. . . . We . . . have our chairman of the (Local Disabled Society) . . . she has a child herself and she is our strongest supporter for prenatal testing. (Gynaecologist NL2)

Uncomfortable ethics and disabilism as the dominant morality of the body

Regardless of the fact that these technologies are also seen as benevolent and improving the condition of the disabled, reduction of birth incidence of genetically flawed individuals may place society on an uncomfortable ethical landscape (Davison *et al.* 1994, Ettorre 1997). Some experts were keenly aware of the ethical dilemmas involved in prenatal screening and they wanted to share their views:

> the more instruments you have in hand to prevent disability, the less you come to accept it. I mean it's something that can be avoided. . . . Well, it's a sort of preventive medicine but you don't know how far it will go. Because you do all this testing in order to prevent disabled babies being born with some defects. And . . . we will want to [see] whether this will turn to [be] a sort of eugenics or not in the long run. (Lawyer GR7)

and

> It is rather unethical to ask someone who is disabled to – what he thinks about prenatal diagnosis. (Gynaecologist NL2)

But, the State will more than likely continue to uphold disabilism as its dominant morality of the body in order to serve the interests of scientists, the medical profession and the general public. While the State may need these self same genetics experts (i.e. reporting here) to guide government and society in decision making about the new genetics (Kerr *et al.* 1997), the State also needs able bodied citizens as mothers, workers and warriors. The State also has clear economic concerns, as expressed by the views of the following expert:

[...]

The child may need extra care. Down's children often need extra [care] and they need lots of day care systems and things which cost money. And we have the recession ... and we have this less and less tolerant climate ... I mean, it has happened already in a number of countries at least it is happening in [Finland] and I think it probably has in the [USA], [It's] about people actually ... pressurized not to give birth to children with disability because it will be costly. And pressurized in a way that they then have to pay the cost themselves, if they want to give birth to this child although they know it's going to be handicapped. (Clinical geneticist FIN17)

Conclusion: 'Please doctor, may I have a normal baby?'

[...] Bodies, constructed by reproductive genetics, play down the importance of human agency. Bodies are ranked according to genetic capital – how well they conform to being and doing in a genetic moral order. Furthermore, society disciplines those 'potential' and 'real' bodies, believed to 'contain' 'defective' genes more severely than those 'containing' 'normal' genes. This disciplinary process tends to offer a somewhat limited view of bodies' potential and shadows the fact that what may appear as 'defective genes' is in fact a result of the body's interaction not only with the environment but also gendered social practices. In this matrix, bodies appear to lack embodied agency, a quality which should be protected, valued and preserved in our contemporary society (Shilling 1997).

In future, more and more women, as female embodiments of the genetic moral order, may ask, 'Please doctor, may I have a normal baby?' If so, we need to provide an atmosphere in which an understanding of the social complexities and implications of asking that specific question becomes possible. In reproductive genetics, women's active agency and an awareness of bodies, inscribed by difference, need to replace the medical and social empowerment of prenatal technologies as strategic engagements in the disabilist discourse.

Acknowledgement

This work emerges from a research project, 'The development of prenatal screening in Europe: the past, the present and the future', funded by the European Commission DGXII BIOMED2 (Contract Number BMH4-CT96-0740) from June 1996–June 1999. This project was coordinated by the author, who is a Docent in the Department of Sociology, University of Helsinki, where this work was carried out.

Note

1   All interviews are numbered in chronological order. FIN stands for Finland, UK for United
    Kingdom, GR for Greece and NL for The Netherlands. For example, UK1 means the first
    interview carried out in the UK.

References

Armstrong, D. 1995. 'The Rise of Surveillance Medicine'. *Sociology of Health and Illness* 17:
    393–404.
Bartky, S. L. 1990. *Femininity and Domination*. New York: Routledge.
Beaulieu, A. and Lippman, A. 1995. 'Everything You Need to Know: How Women's Maga-
    zines Structure Prenatal Diagnosis for Women over 35'. *Women and Health* 23: 59–74.
Birke, L., Himmelweit, S. and Vines, G. 1992. 'Detecting Genetic Diseases: Prenatal Screening
    and Its Problems', in G. Kirup and L. Smith Keller (eds.), *Inventing Women: Science,
    Technology and Gender*. Cambridge: Polity in association with Open University Press.
Conrad, P. 1997. 'Public Eyes and Private Genes: Historical Frames, New Constructions and
    Social Problems'. *Social Problems* 44: 139–54.
Corea, G. 1985. *The Mother Machine*. London: The Women's Press.
Davison, C., Macintyre, S. and Davey Smith, G. 1994. 'The Potential Social Impact of
    Predictive Genetic Testing for Susceptibility to Common Chronic Diseases: A Review and
    Proposed Research Agenda.' *Sociology of Health and Illness* 16: 340–71.
Dragonas, T. 1999. '"Whose Fault Is It?" Shame and Guilt for the Genetic Defect', in
    E. Ettorre, A. Adams, P. Alderson, A. Aro, T. Dragonas, E. Hemminki, T. Tymstra, and
    W. Van de Hueval (eds.), *Final Report of the European Union Project on the Development
    of Prenatal Screening in Europe: The Past, the Present and the Future*. Finland: University
    of Helsinki.
Ettorre, E. 1997. 'The Complexities of Genetic Technologies: Unintended Consequences and
    Responsible Ethics'. *Sosiaalilääketieteelinen Aikakauslehti (Journal of Finnish Social Medi-
    cine)* 34: 257–67.
Farrant, W. 1985. 'Who's for Amniocentesis? The Politics of Prenatal Screening', in H.
    Homans (ed.), *The Sexual Politics of Reproduction*. Aldershot: Gower.
Finger, A. 1990. *Past Due: A Story of Disability, Pregnancy and Birth*. London: The Women's
    Press.
Haraway, D. 1991. *Simians, Cyborgs and Women*. New York: Routledge.
Hubbard, R. 1985. 'Genomania and Health'. *American Scientist* 83: 8–10.
Hubbard, R. 1986. 'Eugenics and Prenatal Testing'. *International Journal of Health Services*
    16: 227–42.
Kerr, A., Cunningham-Burley, S. and Amos, A. 1997. 'The New Genetics: Professionals'
    Discursive Boundaries'. *Sociological Review* 45: 297–303.
Lippman, A. 1994. 'The Genetic Construction of Prenatal Testing', in K. Rothenberg and E. J.
    Thomson (eds.), *Women and Prenatal Testing: Facing the Challenges of Genetic Testing*.
    Columbus: Ohio State University Press.
Press, N. and Browner, C. H. 1997. 'Why Women Say Yes to Prenatal Diagnosis'. *Social
    Science and Medicine* 45: 979–89.
Shakespeare, T. 1995. 'Back to the Future? New Genetics and Disabled People'. *Critical Social
    Policy* 15: 22–35.
Shildrick, M. 1997. *Leaky Bodies and Boundaries: Feminism, Postmodernism and (Bio)eth-
    ics*. London: Routledge.

Shilling, C. 1993. *The Body and Social Theory.* London: Sage.

Shilling, C. 1997. 'The Undersocialised Conception of the (Embodied) Agent in Modern Sociology'. *Sociology* 31: 737–54.

Steinberg, D. L. 1997. *Bodies in Glass. Genetics, Eugenics, Embryo Ethics.* Manchester: Manchester University Press.

Thomas, C. 1997. 'The Baby and the Bath Water: Disabled Women and Motherhood in Social Context'. *Sociology of Health and Illness* 19: 622–43.

Turner, B. 1992. *Regulating Bodies: Essays in Medical Sociology.* London: Routledge.

Wendell, S. 1992. 'Toward a Feminist Theory of Disability', in H. B. Holmes and L. Purdy (eds.) *Feminist Perspectives in Medical Ethics.* Bloomington: Indiana University Press.

6

A Mirage of Genes

Peter Conrad

Introduction

In his classic book *Mirage of Health*, René Dubos (1959) contends that the ultimate conquest of disease is illusory and that what constitutes health is fundamentally humans adapting to their environments. Because environments continually change, an inevitable amount of maladaptation results, often manifested as disease. Since health consists of adaptation to changing environments, the existence of something approaching a perfect state of health is a mirage.

Dubos' writings have influenced generations of medical sociologists and public health thinkers, and his analysis provided the theoretical underpinnings of the important empirical research of McKeown (1971) and McKinlay and McKinlay (1977). Dubos' work is still prominently cited in textbooks for its seminal contributions to medical sociological thinking.

He was sceptical about the predominant germ theory explanations of the conquest of infectious disease and was among the first to observe that the decrease in incidence of most infectious diseases occurred before the introduction of vaccines and antibiotics. He hypothesised that the reforms inspired by the Sanitation Movement and a rising standard of living were more critical for the reduction of disease mortality in society than the advent of germ theory.[1]

Dubos had studied the history of tuberculosis and observed that mortality rates from the disease were declining prior to the discovery of the TB bacillus and long before the availability of any form of biomedical intervention. He was critical of the belief that germs *cause* disease; they may be necessary but not sufficient causes of most diseases. He noted, for example, that many individuals harboured the TB microbe but did not have tuberculosis. Germ theory as a causal model was too simplistic, and narrowed our vision about disease aetiology. In particular cases, like TB, it was restricting, misleading and at times mistaken. But Dubos' thesis is not widely known outside the medical social science and public health worlds; in many circles germ-theory-based interventions alone are credited with 'conquering' infectious diseases.

In the 20th century, germ theory – the notion that microbes cause disease – became the dominant popular explanation of disease causation. While the germ theory model is still prevalent, its dominance has been challenged, complemented and supplemented by environmental theories, lifestyle perspectives, alternative medicine and other explanatory frameworks (*cf.* Tesh 1988). Emily Martin (1994) has recently proposed the flexible body with its immune system as another emergent model.

In the past three decades new genetic models have come to the forefront of medical thinking and have become the cutting edge of much research on disease and behaviour. In this paper I build upon Dubos' depiction of germ theory to assess why genetic explanations have been so readily accepted in medicine and the public discourse, even when the evidence in many cases is limited. Moreover, I want to suggest that some of the illusions Dubos pointed out for germ theory have their parallels with genetic explanations. My concern here is the popular image and discourse about genes, essentially how we talk about genes and genetic causation. My interest focuses on the viability of genetic conceptions rather than the validity of particular genetic associations.

[...] The goal of this paper is [...] to outline some general features about how genetics is conceptualised in the press and in popular discourse. I use the news media as a vehicle for understanding the public discourse around genetics; I make no claim that this discourse by itself represents 'popular thinking' about genetics. But the news medium is the major avenue by which genetic findings and theories get infused into the culture, so it is likely to have a significant impact on popular conceptions of genetics.

The germ theory model and the acceptance of genetics

Germ theory is the basis of the clinical medical model that underlies medical and public thinking about disease. This perspective provides an overall lens for seeing and treating disease in modern society. Dubos articulated the structure of the germ theory model as consisting of three interrelated and fundamental assumptions: the doctrine of specific aetiology; a focus on the internal rather than the external environment; and the metaphor of the body as a machine.

The doctrine of specific aetiology contends that every disease has a specific and knowable causal agent. Based on the laboratory work of giants like Koch and Pasteur, the belief is that each disease is caused by a specific microorganism such as a germ or virus. This was not only limited to infectious diseases:

> From the field of infection the doctrine of specific etiology spread rapidly to other areas of medicine ... Microbial agents, disturbances in essential metabolic processes, deficiencies in growth factors or hormones, and physiological stresses are now regarded as specific causes of disease. (Dubos 1959: 101–2)

Dubos recognised that the doctrine of specific aetiology was a very constructive approach in medical research, but emphasised that 'few are the cases in which it has provided a complete account of the causation of disease' (1959: 102). We still see the objective of specific aetiology embraced in various forms in medicine, such as medicine's continual search for *the* cause of cancer.

The second assumption of germ theory is a focus on the internal environment. As Dubos (1959: 101) and others have noted, until the late 19th century, disease had been widely looked upon as an imbalance or disharmony between the sick person and the environment. Thus the aetiological search typically included the environment and disturbances in the individual's relation to it. With the advent of germ theory, however, the clinical focus shifted entirely to the internal environment: How do the microbes affect cells, organs and tissues to produce disease? In the clinical realm, the external environment became largely superfluous for understanding the causes of disease.

The final germ theory assumption, conceptualising the body as a machine, is less explicit in Dubos' writing. This assumption is mechanistic in orientation; that the body is made up of repairable and replaceable parts where problematic functioning can be identified and remedied. Dubos touched on this in his discussion of medicine's pursuit of 'magic bullets' to eradicate disease-producing microbes. The machine metaphor is manifested in other clinical interventions including organ transplants, joint replacements, hormone substitutes (*e.g.* insulin for diabetes), supplements for biochemical processes (*e.g.* serotonin levels), or seeking technologies like the artificial heart. I do not mean to suggest that these interventions are not effective; indeed, many are. But the metaphor suggests that by treating the body as a machine we will solve the problem. Frequently the underlying difficulty remains and new problems are created. My point here, however, brackets effectiveness; I simply want to indicate that the dominant model in clinical medicine conceptualises the body as a machine that can be repaired.

My claim is that the public depiction of the new genetics aligns perfectly with the old germ theory model and, independent of scientific validity, fuels the acceptance of genetics in medicine and society. Genetics in the public discourse carries similar and familiar assumptions that are already present in germ theory. I shall briefly outline how the three assumptions of germ theory pertain to the new genetics.

We increasingly hear about discoveries of genes for disease and behaviours; reading the news, it often seems as if announcements of new discoveries appear as frequently as a 'gene of the week'. The popular conception is really a monogenic model of specific aetiology: a gene or genetic mutation determines a disease or behaviour. While some well-known cases of monogenic causation have been identified, such as cystic fibrosis or Huntington's disease, these are unusual. More typically genes may play a role in aetiology, but are not determinative (Strohman 1993). Single-gene disorders are the exception, yet the model of gene specificity is common, creating an OGOD assumption: one gene, one disease. This is manifested in talking about finding a gene 'for' a particular trait or in terming genetic findings as 'the breast cancer gene', 'the gay gene', or 'the obesity gene'.

By focusing on genetics, we home in on the internal environment, primarily on the level of DNA. When we talk about discovering a gene for a particular trait or disease, we often make the assumption that the internal environment is the primary causative factor. A gene for alcoholism is more significant than cultural meanings of drinking; a gene for schizophrenia is deemed more primary than family environment. Nature trumps nurture. Rarely is the talk about how genes can be expressed in different environments; the assumption is that genes, like microbes, can be determinant apart from context.

Genes are often pictured as the blueprint for the body as machine. We can see the mechanistic metaphor when genes are depicted as the coding device which determines how some bodily feature or function will be manifested. Genetic testing can sometimes ascertain whether an individual has a faulty part that may lead to disease or debility. The metaphor is evidenced when we talk about gene therapy in terms of replacing faulty genes or selecting particular genes for human enhancement. Change the gene and fix the problem. The field of genetic engineering is based on this assumption. The recent discourse on human cloning reflects the metaphor as well; the assumption that a cloned offspring would grow up virtually identical to its 'parent', dispensing with all life experience and effects of social context.

In my view, the close fit between germ theory and gene theory is one of the chief reasons that genetic explanations have been so readily accepted in medicine and the popular discourse. At least on the level of assumptions and structure, gene theory does not challenge common conceptions of aetiology but rather shifts its focus. In this sense at least, genetics is a complementary rather than a challenging paradigm in medicine (see Strohman 1997). Many of Dubos' caveats and criticisms about germ theory similarly pertain to genetics. In the next section I shall examine some of the pitfalls and illusions in the popular conceptions of genetics.

Pitfalls and illusions

Based on the characteristics of germ theory he identified, Dubos outlined some of their pitfalls and limitations in understanding disease causation. We can see some remarkable parallels with genetics.

The illusion of specific aetiology

In scientific announcements, news reports and popular discourse we frequently hear of specific disease or behaviour genes. The image is that this newly discovered gene – its presence or absence – causes a particular trait. The OGOD (one gene, one disease) assumption is the image of specific aetiology.

Until recently human genetics was not interested in particular genes, focusing rather on how traits were heritable. Adoption and twin studies produced heritability estimates and relied on concordance among relatives to measure genetic influence. With the maturation of molecular biology in the last three decades, scientists have begun to identify specific genes associated with human traits and disorders (Billings *et al.* 1992).

Some of the early discoveries were very impressive. Scientists identified specific genes for disorders like cystic fibrosis, Huntington's disease, Duchenne muscular dystrophy, and Fragile X Syndrome. For all practical purposes, in these cases we have specific aetiology. But such single gene disorders are relatively rare; they constitute only 2 per cent of disease morbidity. Yet discourse about genetics slides almost seamlessly from monogenic disorders to any case of genetic association. It is as if a classic Mendelian model of genetics prevails in the popular discourse.

Over the past decade front page news stories announced the discovery of the 'gay gene', 'breast cancer gene' and 'obesity gene'. The imagery of the language suggested that a specific gene had been identified. In each instance, such an interpretation was at best misleading, if not downright wrong. When Dean Hamer identified the Xq28 marker for male homosexuality (Hamer *et al.* 1993), we soon saw depictions and discussions of the implications of discovering a gay gene. What Hamer found, however, was a 'marker' associated with male homosexuality – designating an area on the X chromosome containing perhaps hundreds of genes. Thus there was no gene for homosexuality. For breast cancer, scientists did indeed identify a specific gene, BRCA1 (and soon followed by BRCA2) that is associated with breast cancer

(Miki *et al.* 1994). Initial reports suggested women with this gene had a 50 per cent chance of developing breast cancer by the age of 50 and an 80 per cent chance by 70 (these estimates have since been reduced). But even here, this could not rightly be termed *the* breast cancer gene, but *a* breast cancer gene. Roughly 5–10 per cent of all breast cancer is hereditary; the BRCA genes did not appear related to 90 per cent of breast cancer. While identifying a specific gene for breast cancer is surely a great breakthrough, it does not mean that most breast cancer is genetic. News about the obesity gene (cutely named by scientists the ob gene or tubby gene) appeared in most major newspapers and magazines. Hope for those struggling with overweight may have been kindled, but the only obesity gene scientists so far have found produces fat mice. The obesity gene, whatever validity it has for mice, has yet to be demonstrated relevant for humans. Moreover, important conceptual and aetiological differences exist between diseases and behaviours, which are subsumed and ignored by depictions of 'the' gene for a particular problem.

Rather than specific aetiology, in the great majority of cases, genes are not directly deterministic, if we mean that if the gene is present an individual will inevitably get the disorder (Rutter and Plomin 1997). For most diseases (*e.g.* hypertension, diabetes, asthma, coronary heart disease), genes are a probabilistic rather than deterministic cause. The language of specific aetiology 'disarticulates complex properties of individuals into isolated lumps of biology' (Rose 1995: 381). Dubos' (1959: 102) observations seem suitable for genetics:

> In reality, however, the search for *the* cause may be a hopeless pursuit because most disease is an indirect outcome of a constellation of circumstances rather than a direct result of a single determinant factor.

Beyond the internal environment

As with germ theory, genetics focuses the medical gaze on the internal environment. But with genetics, the issue often is framed in terms of nature versus nurture. Most geneticists acknowledge that for many diseases and most behaviours, the issue is nature *and* nurture (Rutter and Plomin 1997), but the question is how much weight to give to each. In the popular discourse genetics is often privileged (Nelkin and Lindee 1995, Conrad 1997), and genes are presented as if they operated independently of their environment.

On one level, we know what DNA does; it codes for proteins. What is frequently unclear are the mechanisms by which genes are implicated with diseases or traits. It is certainly a long way from producing a protein to causing a specific human behaviour. But even with diseases like cystic fibrosis we don't know how the gene works in relation to the manifestation of the disorder (Marks 1996). What is important is how genes are expressed in environments.

In Kitcher's (1996) terms, genes are associated with particular traits in the context of a 'standard environment'. When geneticists say that people carrying a gene (or more accurately, an 'allele') will develop a particular trait, they mean it will be manifested in a standard environment, not necessarily in all environments. For example, in cases like phenylketonuria (PKU) the genetic propensity for the disease is not manifested under a specific dietary environment. Particular environments may be as necessary as genes, but neither geneticists nor the public talk about an environment for this or that condition.

With behaviour, it is usually clear that the external (social) environment is significant in how genes are expressed. If there were a gene associated with alcoholism, how could we imagine its expression? Would it be a gene that causes an individual to open a bottle and imbibe the drink? How would such a gene fare in a Muslim culture? With homosexuality, studies of identical twins show over a 50 per cent concordance among gay siblings; but what about the other 50 per cent? Even with siblings who had the Xq28 marker associated with homosexuality, more than a third were not gay. Genetics without an external environment is an incomplete explanation.

There is evidence that genes can create environments. Certain characteristics in children (at least partly genetically influenced) can evoke negative responses from family members which in turn affect the children (Patterson 1982, cited in Rutter and Plomin 1997). In this case, nature modifies nurture which may affect how genetic propensities are expressed. Moreover, people's own characteristics play a significant role in selecting and shaping their external environments (Jencks 1980). Attractive or athletic children may receive more attention than awkward or plain children. Children who are bright may be attracted to books; aggressive children may have aggressive friends. At the very least, internal and external environments are interactive. As geneticist Richard C. Lewontin (1991: 30) points out:

> Environmental variation and genetic variation are not independent causal pathways. Genes affect how sensitive one is to the environment and environment affects how relevant one's genetic differences may be.

The environment also can be critical to 'turning on and off' genes; for example, the adoption of new exercise regimens can turn on genes that regulate muscle building.

But the focus of the news stories and public discourse is squarely on the internal environment. The BRCA1 gene provides an interesting example. BRCA1 is a tumour suppresser gene. Most women are born with two copies of the gene and have no problem. Those with the inherited BRCA1 mutation have only a single copy. A single copy is sufficient for tumour suppression until, for some reason, it is 'knocked out' and a woman is left without the gene. Then she becomes extremely vulnerable to breast or ovarian cancer. The lack of the BRCA1 allele is seen as the cause of breast cancer. Yet could we not also ask, what caused the second copy of the gene to get knocked out? Could not environmental risk factors like a woman's past exposure to radiation be critical in understanding how the mutation leads to cancer?

As Dubos (1959: 128) noted:

> ...the internal environment is constantly responding to the external environment, and history – racial, social, as well as individual – conditions the manner of response just as much as does the intrinsic nature of the stimulus.

Does it make sense to talk about genes causing particular traits without explicating how they are expressed in the external environment?

Chinks in the body as a machine metaphor

Faulty genes are depicted as causes of disease or behaviour. Fix the gene and the problem will be solved. It is as if genes were a thing that can be separated from the system in which they operate. Such a mechanistic view is an oversimplistic rendition of how genes affect most human traits.

Most geneticists recognise that genetic influences are usually polygenic – traits are determined by many genes acting together – or epigenetic, which involves single-gene or multiple-gene interaction with the environment.

> Epigenesis implies a level of complexity beyond gene-gene interaction and extends to interaction between genes, between genes and gene products (proteins), and between all these and environmental signals, including, of course, individual organismal experience. (Strohman 1993: 114)

The complexity of genetic action belies the scientific utility of the machine metaphor. A single gene may have multiple sites for a mutation.

> A typical gene consists of thousands of base pairs, any one of which is subject to a mutation. In some cases, different mutations in the same gene can lead to very different manifestations of disease. (Alper 1997)

For example, with cystic fibrosis (CF) genes, over 350 mutations are known. This makes genetic testing for CF alleles much more difficult, illustrating that even clearly identified genes are subject to complex interactions. Some forms of CF are so mild that individuals are never aware of it until they undergo genetic testing.

Recent discussions of 'shadow syndromes' (Ratey and Johnson 1997) contend that quirky behaviours may actually be mild mental illnesses. Numerous life problems could be included in this model. The brilliant computer geek who can't make conversation has low level autism; the extremely tidy housekeeper has a mild form of obsessive compulsive disorder; the assertive but disorganised salesman has a touch of attention deficit disorder. These alleged shadow syndromes have been tied to genes. This is an additive model; one or two genes give you a little disorder; perhaps three or four creates a serious personality problem; and seven gives you a full-blown illness. Illness and behaviours are seen on a continuum; the arithmetic genetic loading affects the manifestation of the problem. A couple of genes might make one a bit impulsive; a few more leads to a difficulty in controlling impulses; a dozen could make someone into an out-of-control risk seeker. Genes are deemed causative, with their effects incumbent on their cumulative nature. As one psychiatrist noted, genes may be responsible for shadow syndromes, 'But as you increase the number of genes you pass over a threshold to a clinical syndrome' (quoted in Bagley 1998: 53). While such an arithmetic model could modify the assumptions of specific aetiology, at the same time it extends the focus on the internal environment and mechanistic metaphor, expanding the conceptual influence of genes.

Discovering genes is of course not the goal of medicine. Medicine is concerned with preventing and treating diseases. As Dubos (1959: 153) notes, medicine's 'most important task . . . is to discover some magic bullet capable of reaching and destroying the responsible demon within the body . . .'. The promise of magic bullets for genetic disorders is gene therapy. The clinical strategy here is straightforward: identify the bad copy of a gene and replace it with good copy; knock out problem genes and insert new genes. Simple enough in theory, although gene therapy has yet to be accomplished for human ailments.

The discovery of a specific gene does not necessarily lead to successful treatments. Identifying a Huntington's gene or BRCA1 may result in changing individual reproductive or preventative actions, but as yet we have no magic bullets for treatment. It is unclear what future treatments for epigenetic problems might be, given the complexity of causation.

This highlights an interesting difference in comparison to the acceptance of germ theory. Germ theory achieved broad credibility *after* the advent of vaccines and antibiotics. By contrast, it appears genetic explanations have come to be routinely accepted in the absence of gene therapies. While there is yet no 'magic bullet', faith in the genetic model remains undimmed.

One disturbing implication of the pervasiveness of the machine metaphor is reductionism (*e.g.* see Rose 1995). This is especially true in the behavioural realm, where complex behaviours are deemed determined by genes. As Richard Horton, the editor of *Lancet*, points out, there exists a

> ... popular rhetoric of DNA, which supposes an irreducible and immutable unit of the human self. The correlation between potentially active genes and a behaviour pattern is assumed to indicate cause and effect. (Horton 1995: 38)

The scientific and public discourse are replete with instances of talking about genes 'for' particular traits, such as genes for breast and colon cancer, homosexuality, schizophrenia and even bed-wetting. As Kitcher notes, 'genetalk' reflects an image

> of human bodies as built up of DNA laborers, each making an isolated contribution: Here 'the gene for eye color' goes to work injecting a special pigment, there 'the gene for muscles' assembles a host of cells. (1996: 239)

Virtually an army of industrious genes are working to create all variations of human traits.

The machine metaphor helps to sustain the notion that genetics is the primary cause of a phenomenon, which may not be the case. It reinforces ideas of 'genetic essentialism' (Nelkin and Lindee 1995), seeing humans as fundamentally products of their DNA. In its extreme, this can become a type of 'genetic fatalism', whereby genetic associations to behaviours or conditions are deemed to be deterministic and unchangeable (Alper and Beckwith 1995).

Genetic determinism and susceptibility

In much scientific and public discourse the complexity of genetics is ignored and genes are represented as if they were the causes of diseases and behaviours. This has spawned a naive form of genetic determinism that assumes (in language at least) that there are specific genes for specific traits under all circumstances.

While undoubtedly genes exert important influences on human life, for the most part they are not deterministic. We would be better served if we consciously recast genetic influence as 'genetic susceptibility'. This suggests that individuals may have a 'genetic loading' for a particular trait, but does not assume determinism. It reflects an understanding that there is a genetic component, but is agnostic about the weight to assign to genetic action. I prefer susceptibility to 'predisposition', where the latter reflects more the imagery of a built in mechanism ready to manifest itself, and sounds uncomfortably close to predestination. Susceptibility, like risk, implies probability and interaction, with genes as a contributing rather than determinative factor.

In his discussion of germ theory, Dubos (1959: 66) noted that microbes are not good or bad in themselves yet have a bad reputation for producing disease in humans. He points out, for example, how important micro-organisms are for human digestion or for culturing yoghurt. So it may be with some genetic mutations; particular genetic mutations may actually be beneficial to humans in some environments. It has long been known that the sickle cell trait, common among those with African ancestry, provides a resistance for the carrier to malaria. It has been recently reported that a defective CF gene is likely to benefit the carrier with better resistance to typhoid fever. In both cases disease risk occurs in the offspring of two carriers, but the genetic mutation itself may be protective and evolutionarily adaptive.

Virtually everyone has some genes that make them susceptible to diseases or traits we might find problematic. All of us are genetically liable to some human trouble, be it allergies, nearsightedness, baldness, depression, or forms of heart disease or cancer. The trick is to understand how these susceptibilities interact with particular environments to produce or not produce human traits or disorders. This should be intriguing territory for sociologists interested in genetics and the production of disease (see Richards 1993).

The allure of specificity and a mirage of genes

Given the growing sophistication of molecular biology and the attendant rising genetic paradigm, it is not surprising that an increasing number of human problems are attributed to the workings of genes. But despite the complexity of human behaviour and disease, the public discourse frequently ascribes undue causal power to genes. It is not that genes have no influence; indeed, often their influence is substantial. Rather, we see a privileging of genetic explanations in the media and public discourse.

A significant attraction of genetic explanations is the allure of specificity. Biological theories of human problems have long been popular (Gould 1981) but genetics has allowed a new focus on the particular. With genes we have a tangible causal agent, a strip of DNA we can point to, rather than messy and slippery epidemiological or social factors. Genes seem to be real 'things', with a physical presence. We can have a gene on the short arm of the X chromosome or identified as BRCA1, not 'merely' risk factors like radiation exposure or diet, much less intangibles like social class or stress. There is also an aesthetic elegance and simplicity to gene theory. One molecular biologist put it well:

The theory of the gene is complete and wonderfully so; it is beautiful and magnificent in its utter simplicity. A child could understand it and millions of children now do. But if you mistakenly ask them what it means in terms of function you have shamed them. (Strohman 1997: 196)

In the public discourse, simple aetiologies are communicated easily. Too many qualifications and complexities may confuse and undermine an explanation. While genetic causation like germ theory is not as specific as it appears, the appearance of specificity enhances the acceptance of genetic explanations, independent of the validity of scientific findings.

In the next decade, with the completion of the Human Genome Project, we are likely to see an acceleration in discoveries of genes 'for' human traits, behaviours and diseases. As Dubos cautioned us for germ theory, we need to be alert that what at first seems to be so clear turns out to be a mirage when we look at it more closely.

The news reporting of genetics and behaviour can create a media version of a mirage of genes. In the past decade there have been numerous announcements by scientists of the discovery of a new gene associated with behaviour – alcoholism, schizophrenia, bipolar illness, thrill-seeking – only to be retracted when the research cannot be replicated by others, or the association disappears upon closer examination. When the genes are found the news is trumpeted on page one, but when the findings cannot be confirmed the stories are buried as a small item in the back pages, if noted at all (Conrad 1997, 2000). These 'disconfirmations' are common in science, but it is difficult for the news and public discourse to keep up. The result amplifies finding genes and mutes their subsequent loss, giving the public a false sense of continuous genetic discovery.

I have argued that the cultural resonance with germ theory facilitates the public acceptance and rise of the genetic paradigm. This is not the only sociological reason why genetics has become more popular. As others have pointed out, gene theory also appeals to existing western ideas of individuality and current notions about responsibility for health, and shifts blame for problems from environments and social structures to individuals and biophysiology (Nelkin and Lindee 1995). The huge investment in biomedical funding for genetics and the vast international scientific industry which it supports creates an apparatus continually producing new genetic findings. Professional collaborations between scientists, industry and physicians have put genetics on the cutting edge of medical-scientific thinking. But the pitfalls Dubos identified 40 years ago may point to directions where sociologists can provide an intellectual balance and critique of geneticisation (see Conrad 1997).

Perhaps the fate of genetic explanations will parallel that of germ theory; decontextualising aetiological processes, underrepresenting the role of environments, producing some stunning medical interventions, revealing little about the fate of populations, and becoming the most popular explanation for what ails us. The rising influence and ubiquity of the genetic paradigm is already evident in medicine and popular discourse. It is our challenge to continue to explicate the social realities of illness and behaviour in the midst of an enticing and widening genetic mirage.

Acknowledgements

My thanks to Charles Bosk, Phil Brown, Steven Epstein, Lisa Geller and the anonymous reviewers for comments on an earlier draft of this paper. This research was supported in part by a grant for the section on Ethical, Legal and Social Implications of the Human Genome Project of the National Institutes of Health (1 R55 HGO0849–01A1).

Note

1 Nearly two decades after *Mirage of Health* was published, McKeown (1971) and McKinlay and McKinlay (1977) empirically demonstrated Dubos' thesis and applied it to other infectious diseases as well.

References

Alper, J. S. (1997) Complexity. Unpublished paper.

Alper, J. S. and Beckwith, J. (1995) Genetic fatalism and social policy: the implications of behavior genetics research, *Yale Journal of Biology and Medicine*, 66, 511–24.

Bagley, S. (1998) Is everybody crazy? *Newsweek*, 5 January, 50–5.

Billings, P. R., Beckwith, J. and Alper, J. S. (1992) The genetic analysis of human behavior: a new era? *Social Science and Medicine*, 35, 227–38.

Conrad, P. (1997) Public eyes and private genes: historical frames, news constructions, and social problems, *Social Problems*, 44, 139–54.

Conrad, P. (2000) Media images, genetics and culture: potential impacts of reporting scientific findings on bioethics. In Hoffmaster, B. (ed.), *Bioethics in Context*. Philadelphia: Temple University Press.

Dubos, R. (1959) *Mirage of Health*. New York: Harper and Row.

Gould, S. J. (1981) *The Mismeasure of Man*. New York: Norton.

Hamer, D., Hu, S., Magnuson, V. L., Hu, N. and Pattatucci, A. M. L. (1993) A linkage between DNA markers on the X chromosome and male sexual orientation, *Science*, 261, 321–7.

Horton, R. (1995) Is homosexuality inherited? *New York Review of Books*, 13 July, 36–41.

Jencks, C. (1980) Heredity, environment and public policy reconsidered, *American Sociological Review*, 45, 723–36.

Kitcher, P. (1996) *The Lives to Come: the Genetic Revolution and Human Possibilities*. New York: Simon and Schuster.

Lewontin, R. C. (1991) *Biology as Ideology: the Doctrine of DNA*. New York: Harper Perennial.

Marks, J. (1996) Skepticism about behavioral genetics. In Frankel, M. S. (ed.), *Exploring Public Policy Issues in Genetics*. American Association for the Advancement of Science.

Martin, E. (1994) *Flexible Bodies: Tracking Immunity in American Culture from the Days of Polio to the Age of AIDS*. Boston: Beacon Press.

McKeown, T. (1971) A historical appraisal of the medical task. In McLachlan, G. and McKeown, T. *Medical History and Medical Care: a Symposium of Perspectives*. New York: Oxford.

McKinlay, J. B. and McKinlay, S. K. (1977) The questionable contribution of medical measures to the decline of mortality in the United States, *Milbank Memorial Fund Quarterly/Heath and Society*, 55, 205–28.

Miki, Y., Swanson, J., Shattuck, D., Futreal, P. A. *et al.* (1994) A strong candidate for breast and ovarian cancer susceptibility gene BRCA1, *Science*, 266, 66–71.

Nelkin, D. and Lindee, M. S. (1995) *The DNA Mystique: the Gene as a Cultural Icon*. New York: W. H. Freeman.

Patterson, G. R. (1982) *Coercive Family Process*. Eugene, OR: Castalia Publishing Company.

Ratey, J. and Johnson, C. (1997) *Shadow Syndromes*. New York: Pantheon.

Richards, M. P. M. (1993) The new genetics-issues for social scientists, *Sociology of Health and Illness*, 15, 567–86.

Rose, S. (1995) The rise of neurogenetic determinism, *Nature*, 373, 380–2.

Rutter, M. and Plomin, R. (1997) Opportunities for psychiatry from genetic findings, *British Journal of Psychiatry*, 171, 209–19.

Strohman, R. C. (1993) Ancient genomes, wise bodies, unhealthy people: limits of a genetic paradigm in biology and medicine, *Perspectives in Biology and Medicine*, 37, 112–45.

Strohman, R. C. (1997) The coming Kuhnian revolution in biology, *Nature Biotechnology*, 15, 194–200.

Tesh, S. N. (1988) *Hidden Arguments: Political Ideology and Disease Prevention*. New Brunswick, NJ: Rutgers University Press.

7

A 'Revenge' on Modern Times: Notes on Traumatic Brain Injury

David Webb

A 'condition' – and its social context

A Traumatic Brain Injury (TBI)[1] arises from cerebral damage caused by a blow to the head, arising for example from a road traffic accident. TBI can be distinguished from Acquired Brain Injury brought about by medical or congenital conditions, such as Alzheimer's disease or cerebral palsy. In view of its contemporary prevalence head injury has been characterised as the silent epidemic of modern times (Brock *et al*. 1995); in Britain about fifteen people are taken to hospital every hour with a head injury and every two hours one of these will die. Estimates indicate that by the year 2000 there will be in the region of 135,000 people with TBI in the United Kingdom, with a severity that varies from total recovery, to mild impairment through to a completely vegetative state. Causes are primarily, though not exclusively, attributable to accidents involving motor vehicles, with motor cyclists forming a sizeable proportion of those affected. About a third of TBI incidents are the result of falls or assaults, with sports and playground injuries being other typical examples of how traumatic brain injury can happen. A majority – three quarters – of those who are traumatically brain injured are young men, usually aged between 16 and 25 (Higham *et al*. 1996).

Over and above the rather obvious sociological and economic causes for an increase in head injury – prosperity, mobility and the (particularly masculinist) cultural adulation of speed, cars and motorbikes – the principal reason for this increase in the prevalence of TBI is cruelly ironic. Medical intervention in life expectancy as well as design improvements that give greater driver and passenger safety to motor vehicles mean that there is now a far greater chance of surviving those accidents which in the past would have resulted in death.

[...]

The paradox of traumatic brain injury is that survival, or even seemingly full physical recovery (and 90 per cent of head injured people do in fact make reasonably good progress in this regard), can merely add to the nature of the catastrophe. The triumph of the body is poor compensation for the sequestration of the mind, where memory loss, impairment of attention, slowness in processing information and reduced speed of thought are all common. Further difficulties often also occur in perceptual, language and reasoning skills and in the awareness of self and others

(Higham *et al.* 1996: 14), all of which lead to challenges in the effective management of intersubjectivity.

The head injured person may well be apparently 'normal' with a post-accident recovery of their bodily appearance. In this case, disability cannot simply be read off from the conventional empirical markers of 'what is seen'. The difficulties of being without the dramatic announcement of disability that comes with physical impairment – the stigmatising inscription on the body (Fox 1993: 32) – means that the person who is TBI may well disadvantageously pass for normal in their dealings with significant others (Shakespeare 1994). In fact, managing the invisibility of disability that is frequently associated with head injury is a theme in a number of the interviews with carers of TBI people (Higham *et al.* 1996), as they look for ways to ease the passage of the TBI person to a world that might scale down its expectations. 'Passing for normal' is ironically no asset for those to whom the hidden nature of their disability is especially disabling, where prejudice against the 'mentally incompetent' and the vernacular disdains of everyday life reflect the wider structural and ideological eugenicist-cum-mentalist discourse of modernity. [. . .]

Traumatic Brain Injury, with its typical sufferer being a young man injured in some way or another following a car or motor bike accident, stands quintessentially as a disabling condition (both in its causes and in its consequences for carers) with which we are culturally ill equipped to deal. The individual who is incapacitated through brain injury is unable to overcome their difficulties with the mechanical aids and cybernetic micro-processors which announce the prowess of the technological fix for the person who is physically disabled (Stone 1995).

[. . .]

[. . .] The emphasis in this paper is principally with giving some consideration to mapping the constituent social reactions to Traumatic Brain Injury, from how it is constructed within the discourse of mentalist ideology, to the psychodynamics that typically characterise the family within which the head injured person is cared for. And all this is set within the context of how the mind and the body are sites for certain sorts of meanings within modernity.[2]

The mind, the brain and the body

[. . .]

[. . .] The sociology of the body announces the complete sovereignty of the mind over the corporeal, and it assumes this more or less unproblematically. Without the competent mind there is no sociology of the body. There is too the much wider (and delicate) question about the relationship between subjectivity and our conceptions of 'being human', which run around (and are implicit within) both the sociology of the body and some facets of disability studies. Confronting sociologically the consequences of head injury therefore touches on our discipline's reliance on the brain-mind-self propositional infrastructure. [. . .]

[. . .] Indeed the case here is that with a physiologically damaged brain comes the likelihood of a fractured mind, and that consequently this will have a bearing on the person's capacity to existentially 'live their body' – to reflexively experience it. When the brain is damaged, and where as a result this has an impact on the way in which the body is subjectively apprehended, then we need to consider the issues that arise about the 'lived body' and its possibilities, or what Turner (1992) refers to as its 'phenomenological domains'. The existence of the head injured person is, to a greater or lesser extent primarily corporeal, their essential reflexivity thereby compromised or otherwise diminished.

High modernity and the perfect mind

An analysis that focuses on physical disability is [...] unlikely to open up an account of the specific social constructions that are employed in the case of those who are traumatically brain injured. More or less implicit mentalist assumptions about the nature of disability as a generic category in effect neglect the specifics of disabling head injury and simply replicate the convention that it is all simply a case of 'body matters'. Oliver (1990: 85), who takes a radically constructionist stand on disability ('dependency is not an intrinsic feature of their impairment but is socially created by a disabling and disablist society'), barely mentions what might come under the generic heading of 'learning difficulties' in a book which – ironically in the light of the above – is titled *The Politics of Disablement* (1990). His approach to impairment is an exclusively embodied one, since it is defined as 'lacking part or all of a limb, having a defective limb, organism or mechanism of the body'. Consequently Oliver's concern with the social creation of disability is analytically focused on a critique of a 'contemporary social organisation which takes no or little account of people who have *physical* impairments' (1990: 10, emphasis added).

[...] In high modernity the body has a diminishing *productive* significance, and it becomes increasingly a site more of recreational indulgence than labour power as such. In this context, it is catastrophic to be denied the opportunity to participate in the identity constituting reflexivity of late modernity (Giddens 1990). In so far as brain injury has as one of its sequelae the loss of memory – and very often it does – then being a competent social agent is further thwarted by the incapacity to generate a coherent personal narrative or biography [...]

Brain injury, although the prospect of remission may be tantalisingly offered, often presents the TBI person and their carers with the termination of life projects. More than this particular ending of progress, it almost invariably leads to a reversal of attainments so far achieved. The mind and with it the chance to have command over the future may well have been permanently endangered. The everyday, taken-for-granted prospect – even if it is never realised in practice – is that within the future-oriented culture of modernity promise is always yet to be fulfilled, and head injury compromises that opportunity. This is particularly significant for younger head injured people for whom the reflexivity of planning and the structuring of 'what is to be' has to be set aside. Despairing of this participation in the contemporary importance of 'time to come', one of the head injured respondents in our study remarked: 'life is now and I see nothing there for me. This is what I have' (Higham *et al.* 1996: 182). Another (ibid.: 180) put it in a more concrete, less existential way: 'Well, I have no pressures now as such but, if you like I would like the pressures of having a house, having a wife, having a normal life if you like.'

Brain injury and social exclusion

It is something of a refrain in this discussion that high modernity revolves around a mentalist discourse in which greater importance is given to the mind than the sociological talk of 'body matters' suggests. Whilst there may be an increasing celebration of the plurality of physiology as a contemporary counter-culture repudiates particular norms of appearance or physical attractiveness, there is no such tolerance of those whose waywardness is mental. Perhaps a little controversially [...] the proposition here is that those who are head injured have a greater propensity to be socially excluded than do the potentially more productive group of people who are physically disabled. In locating this differential 'expulsion' within the culture of high modernity where its influence is exerted over individuals through the mentalist domain of what Donzelot (1980) called the 'psy complex', we can note the social favouring of an intact mind over an intact body when it comes to the gradual and reluctant admitting of outsiders to the fold of utility.

The reliability and capacity of mind is accordingly imperative, but because this is not similarly amenable to electro-mechanical alleviation as is physical disability, those who are mind impaired are consigned to the wastelands of social exclusion. This is not just a case of analytical excess inspired by Foucault. A telling empirical index of the subdued social acknowledgement of TBI emerges from a very brief excursion into the social distribution of health care. McMillan and Greenwood (1991) point out that head injury rehabilitation is the poor relation of major surgical technology. In manifest contrast to the existence of a network of National Health Service centres for the rehabilitation of spinal injury patients, there is a more or less complete absence of comparable services for victims of TBI, even though the incidence of head injury to spinal injury is marked by a ratio of about ten to one.

[...] Traumatic Brain Injury is, however, occasioned by modernity itself, the very culture in which so many have invested so much. Head injury is somehow a consequence of what we have done (and the 'we' here is because of our tacit subscription to the 'dysfunctions' as well as the virtues of our society). In this way TBI becomes a particularly powerful source of uneasy collective trauma and guilt. There is, in short, no clarity about the categorisation of those who are head injured. The person becomes 'someone else', an everyday recognition that it is the mind (more than the body) which signifies what it is to be a person. If the mind itself is seriously impaired then it is no longer able to mobilise the body to create the *physical capital* which might compensate for the run on *mental capital* occasioned through head injury (Shilling 1991). Again parents recognised the bankruptcy to identity brought about by this liminal state in which the biological condition to existence is virtually exhausted: 'The only thing we thought', said a mother of her head-injured son, 'was that we were grateful he was still alive. But then we've sat back and thought, for what? What is his life? At times I feel so fed up I wish he hadn't lived' (Higham *et al.* 1996: 183).

The re-awakening of childhood and the psychodynamics of care

[...]

Traumatic Brain Injury [...] disturbs our sense of time and order – what was once going to happen will not now do so, and the various relationships that it was earlier presumed would unfold in a more or less predetermined fashion are also brought to a halt. Underlying this domain of the cognitive is the psychodynamic, where the complex emotional merging and detachment that mark the acquisition of adulthood are gradually revisited. Once the elation of physical survival is absorbed, signifying thereby the medical triumph of delivering a life, the newly dependent person with TBI calls forth from the psyche of their family carers memories of emotions that lay buried in the subconscious, memories that it was assumed could comfortably be left there as the child became an adult. The infantilising of adults with disabilities is a product not only of the physiological dependence they have on their parent-carers (Hubert 1995), but it is also an expression of the return to earlier dynamics within the deep psyche of family relationships – what Fox (1993: 117) refers to as the 'oedipalisation of care'.

The ambivalences that mark the tussle between labour and love as the imperative to parenting are reawakened with a vengeance as what was once seen to have been finished becomes a new and unexpected moral obligation. Another mother's observations about the consequences of her son's injury reveal this complex set of obligations and emotions in which the past, the present and the future are collapsed in a radically revised assumptive world: 'it was like having a baby back in the house, but a baby that isn't going to grow up...he's never going to be independent of me, he's always going to be dependent on someone looking after him...I'm always going to be here as a carer...you know for a fact that you are going to die before he is' (Higham *et al.* 1996: 185). [...]

Not surprisingly, being left with an adult child who will never grow up to lead a 'normal' independent life is exceptionally challenging, since it introduces unanticipated demands on the management of the emotions – of the carer and of the care-recipient. There are none of the readily available stocks of knowledge, or recipes which serve as reference points as happens with the routinised care of children whose developmental sequence is 'normal'. Neither can these children be comfortably regarded as inhabiting the twilight of their lives, as it might be existentially feasible to sustain in the case of a dependent parent with Alzheimer's for example. This domain of acceptance and adjustment exemplifies the aspect of care that is called 'emotional labour' (Thomas 1993: 663) – and it can be hard emotional labour at that. A mother explained to us that caring for her daughter 'breaks my heart. When I'm all right I can cope, but if I get run down then it gets to me and things upset me. Sometimes she will look at me and that look in her eyes goes straight in there. It is horrible because there is nothing you can do. She looks at me as if to say, why me? All I can do is keep a brave face and just keep doing the best I can' (Higham *et al.* 1995: 173).

A cautionary tale

[...] What has been written about here is something tragic within the lives of people who have been disabled through head injury. It is tragedy because the cultural saliency of the mind (or its sociological derivative, the reflexive self) makes it extremely difficult to render Traumatic Brain Injury in terms other than the sorrowfully dramatic. This gloominess is further prompted by the uneasy recognition that we are all to a greater or lesser extent caught up in modernity's endorsement of much that 'causes' head injury, something that is particularly true for those of us who, through a host of everyday practices, routinely and unreflexively construct the iconic supremacy of fast cars and fast bikes. At the same time there is the lingering, and decidedly pre-modern, fear of being touched by some sort of awful retributive force, as hubris wreaks its corporeal violence as well as bringing irreversible mutations to the psychodynamics of our parent–child relations.

Acknowledgement

Three anonymous assessors gave much useful advice and I have drawn extensively on this in revising the paper. Their thoughtful observations were very welcome. Graham Bowpitt encouraged my writing this paper in the first instance. This, and his subsequent comments on earlier drafts, proved indispensable.

Notes

1   The technical term is Traumatic Brain Injury – known by its initials TBI, though often the more easily understood term 'head injury' is adopted in the literature. 'Traumatic Brain Injury', 'TBI' and 'head injury' are all used interchangeably in this paper, with no variation in meaning.
2   The study was commissioned by Headway, the National Head Injuries Association, and was funded by the Tudor Trust. The brief for the research was to assess the long-term residential care needs of people with TBI. The research was undertaken in three different settings of care – the generic residential care home, the residential home dedicated to those with head injury, and the community care setting. Fifteen head injured people, their carers and their families were interviewed, generating life history narratives as well as judgements about the appropriateness of various ways in which TBI people are supported (see Higham *et al.* 1996). There were thirteen men and two women with an age range of twenty-six to seventy. Interviewees consisted of head-injured people, their family and carers. In five of the fifteen cases the head-injured person was not interviewed. The interview transcripts generated data on life history; results and effects of the head injury; needs and quality of life; services received; services wanted; future hopes and fears.

References

Brock, M. D., Schody, W. and Coyne, M. J. 1995. *Living with Head Injury.* Manchester: Manchester University Press.

Donzelot, J. 1980. *The Policing of Families*. London: Hutchinson.

Fox, N. J. 1993. *Postmodernism, Sociology and Health*. Buckingham: Open University Press.

Giddens, A. 1990. *Modernity and Self-Identity*. Cambridge: Polity.

Higham, P., Phelps, K., Bowpitt, G., Webb, D., Mansfield, J., Briggs, P. and Regel, S. 1996. *Assessing the Long Term Needs of People with Traumatic Brain Injury*. Nottingham: York House Publications.

Hubert, J. 1995. *Life After Head Injury*. London: Avebury.

McMillan, T. and Greenwood, R. 1991. *Rehabilitation Programmes for the Brain Injured Adult: Current Practice and Future Options in the UK*. London: Department of Health.

Oliver, M. 1990. *The Politics of Disablement*. London: Macmillan.

Shakespeare, T. 1994. 'Cultural Representation of Disabled People: Dustbins for Disavowal'. *Disability and Society* 9: 283–301.

Shilling, C. 1991. 'Educating the Body: Physical Capital and the Production of Social Inequalities'. *Sociology* 25: 653–72.

Stone, S. D. 1995. 'The Myth of Bodily Perfection'. *Disability and Society* 10: 413–25.

Thomas, C. 1993. 'De-constructing Concepts of Care'. *Sociology* 27: 649–69.

Turner, B. 1992. *Regulating Bodies*. London: Routledge.

8

Contemporary Hospice Care: The Sequestration of the Unbounded Body and 'Dirty Dying'

Julia Lawton

[...]

This paper begins with a detailed description of the observations made directly within [a] hospice. However, the ethnography will be used in a later section as a platform for addressing broader theoretical concerns. Drawing upon the work of Elias and Douglas, together with other anthropological and cross-cultural material, I will examine why an intolerance of the disintegrating, decaying body appears to have become such a marked feature of the contemporary West; an intolerance which has led to the removal of such a body from mainstream social life.

[...]

Case study – Annie

Annie was 67 when she was first admitted to the hospice on 12th April 1995. Prior to her admission she was living at home with her retired husband and recently divorced son. She also had a married daughter living locally.

Annie had been diagnosed as having cancer of the cervix in April 1994. Following surgery and post-operative radiotherapy it was believed that she had made a full recovery. However, in February 1995 a smear test revealed a large recurrence which was subsequently found to have spread to her pelvic wall. Annie was informed by her doctor that there was little further that could be done for her because her cancer was too far advanced. She was referred to a Macmillan nurse for palliative care in March.

Initially, Annie managed at home with regular medical and emotional support from her District and Macmillan nurses. At this stage, her greatest problem stemmed from the development of severe oedema in both of her legs which had caused her to become bed-bound.[1] She found it difficult to relinquish her 'housewife' duties to her husband and son, and was still trying to manage the household from her bed.

Annie's mobility improved a little after she received lymphoedema treatment at home. She became sufficiently ambulant to take herself independently to the

A revised version of this chapter has also been published in J. Lawton, *The Dying Process: Patients' Experience of Palliative Care*. Routledge, London and New York, 2000.

bathroom, but she remained largely bed-bound. With the encouragement and support of her Macmillan nurse, she began to tie up some of her 'loose ends', such as writing her will. Her nurse reported that Annie and her family were 'terrified' about what the future held in store for them.

At the beginning of April, Annie's condition began to deteriorate. She developed a recto-vaginal fistula, which meant that her urine and faeces started coming out through the same passageway. Problems of faecal leakage precipitated her admission to the hospice for symptom control.

Originally, Annie had been very anxious about the possibility of being admitted to the hospice. As she explained about one week into her stay: 'Initially I didn't want to come in here because I didn't think I'd get out again'. In fact, when recurrence of cancer was first diagnosed, Annie made her family promise they would do everything possible to enable her to stay at home. It is highly relevant, therefore, that it was Annie herself who finally requested admission to the hospice. Her rationale was twofold. First, she was concerned about how exhausted her husband had become: 'I could see him crumbling in front of me'. Second, she felt she could not get enough privacy at home to attend to her personal hygiene. Annie had become semi-incontinent and was also suffering from periodic bouts of diarrhoea, which she found deeply distressing and embarrassing. She did not want her family to witness her bodily degradation first hand.

Following her admission to the hospice, Annie was placed on one of the communal wards. Initially, she was sufficiently mobile to take herself independently to the toilet and bathroom, and she remained stubbornly 'self-caring' even though she had to spend up to one hour cleaning herself up after using the toilet. Whilst, superficially, Annie seemed like a bright and cheerful person, the night staff reported a very different picture. Annie was frequently heard sobbing quietly to herself whilst locked inside the toilet.

About ten days into her admission, Annie deteriorated further. Her fistula enlarged substantially and, as a result, every time she attempted to get out of bed and stand up, diarrhoea would pour straight out of her body. Consequently, Annie had to start using a commode on the ward rather than walking to the toilet. She also started passing blood. In addition, she contracted a bladder infection which caused her urine to develop a 'very offensive' smell.

It was around this time that Annie's bodily degradation began to have a significant impact upon the hospice as a whole. Whenever she used the commode on the ward, the smell would penetrate right through the building to the main entrance. The staff burnt aromatherapy oils around her bed, but, generally, these did little to mask the odour. The other patients complained that sometimes the smell made them want to vomit.

Annie became increasingly anxious about the possibility of being discharged home. She felt that she had lost all her dignity. She also stressed that there would be insufficient privacy at home to mask the smell and her degradation from her family. At the multi-disciplinary team meeting to discuss her case, the Senior Consultant argued that it would be 'cruel and futile' to press for a discharge. None of the other staff members challenged his decision in spite of the economic pressures to free Annie's bed. There was no further talk of discharge and Annie and her family were promised that she could remain in the hospice until she died.

Throughout April, Annie continued to deteriorate. She 'rotted away below' (as the nurses put it) and lost all control over her bowel and bladder functions. As a consequence, she suffered from continuous bouts of incontinence. It proved impossible to keep her clean and her sheets fresh. On several occasions when the nurses came to attend to her they found her covered to her shoulders in her own urine and excreta.

By this stage, the smell resulting from her incontinence had become a perpetual problem, and the staff became increasingly concerned about the impact Annie's bodily deterioration was having upon the other patients on her ward. They suggested that she might prefer the privacy of a side room, but Annie remained adamant that she wanted 'to stay with the ladies'. Like a number of working class patients I encountered in the hospice, Annie was worried that she would get lonely if placed in a room on her own. Annie also appeared to have become more or less oblivious to her own smell. Whilst she was lucid on some occasions, she was also suffering from increased bouts of tiredness and confusion.

As Annie had made it clear that she did not want to be moved to a side room, the staff were left with the problem of what to do with the other patients on her ward. Whilst none of them were actually moved out of the ward because of Annie's presence, I did observe that when a patient died or was discharged their bed was not refilled. By the time I became closely involved with Annie's case (which was about three weeks into her stay in the hospice) only two other women remained on her ward. Paula had brain secondaries and was admitted to the hospice for terminal care. She remained uncommunicative and unaware of her environment until she died. Doris, however, was fully lucid and became deeply upset by Annie's deterioration; she requested her own discharge, pointing to 'the terrible smell' and Annie's distress as the main precipitating factors. She made it very clear that under no circumstances did she ever want to return to the hospice. Doris needed a lot of reassurance that her own death was unlikely to be as undignified and distressing as Annie's.

The morning that Doris was discharged Annie became very tearful and afraid. I was instructed by one of the senior nurses to go and comfort her until her husband and the hospice chaplain arrived. Annie was convinced that she was being punished for all the wrongs in her life; she suggested that she must have committed some terrible sin in the past for God to inflict such a cruel exit upon her. She was also upset that her husband had written her a romantic card the previous day telling her how much he loved her. She wanted to know why he was saying this to her now, when he had never done so in the past. Annie complained of feeling worthless and the object of other people's pity.

As the morning went on, Annie became increasingly agitated and afraid. Her diarrhoea escalated, and at lunch time she asked to be sedated. The staff fulfilled her request after she repeated it several further times. This was the last time I spoke to Annie; she remained heavily sedated and unconscious until she died approximately two weeks later.

The day after Annie was first sedated, Paula, the other woman remaining on her ward, died. Once Paula's body had been removed from the ward, the staff felt they had no option but to move Annie to a side room. They approached her family and explained that they could not really admit any patients to Annie's ward because of the smell. The family readily gave their consent for Annie to be moved. Both her husband and son expressed their embarrassment that Annie had been 'stinking out' the ward for so long.

Once Annie had been settled into her side room, visits from her family dropped off rapidly. They could not see any point, they said, in keeping a vigil around her bed when Annie was almost certainly oblivious to their presence. The stench of incontinence and decaying flesh was also considerably stronger in the side room than it had been on the ward.

In the final days of her life, the staff kept Annie very comfortable by increasing her doses of diamorphine. Annie did not actually die until the early hours of 16th May, which was approximately six weeks after she was first admitted to the hospice. None of her family was present at the time of her death.

Outside : inside :: boundedness : unboundedness – hospice care and the unbounded body

Annie's case will be referred to at various points in this paper because of the rich and complex issues it brings to the fore. However, the one theme I want to focus upon at this stage concerns the way in which the development and spread of her cervical cancer affected the boundedness of her body. One of the main factors which precipitated Annie's admission to the hospice for symptom control was the development of a fistula which resulted in faecal leakage. As the fistula enlarged, Annie ceased to have any control over her bowel and bladder functions. Because the management of the effects of this breakdown of bodily control ceased to be effective, all plans for a discharge were abandoned.

In this respect, Annie's case is far from atypical. During the course of my fieldwork, the most common reason for a patient to be admitted to the hospice was for the control of symptoms, a phenomenon which became especially marked after the number of beds was cut. In a study conducted to identify the factors influencing the admission of patients to St. Christopher's hospice in London, Woodhall similarly found that 'the major cause of admission is either "poor symptom control" or "good to fairly good symptom control" which subsequently fails' (1986: 32). As I will illustrate further below, what most of the symptoms requiring control shared in common was that they caused the surfaces of the patient's body to rupture and break down. As a consequence, fluids and matter normally contained within the patient's body were leaked and emitted to the outside, often in an uncontrolled and *ad hoc* fashion. Staff often employed metaphors such as 'falling apart at the seams' when referring to such patients who were 'rotting inside' and 'being eaten away by their cancer'. Patients requiring symptom control thus had bodies which I will term here as 'unbounded'.

Symptom control encompassed a wide range of bodily ailments and their side-effects. Amongst the most common were incontinence of urine and faeces, uncontrolled vomiting (including faecal vomit), fungating tumours (the rotting away of a tumour site on the surface of the skin) and weeping limbs which resulted from the development of gross oedema in the patient's legs and/or arms. As a result, the patient's limbs would swell to such an extent that the skin burst and lymph fluid continuously seeped out.

Other symptoms, though less common, were equally pertinent. For example, several emergency admissions occurred after a patient started coughing up large amounts of blood at home. In another instance a patient, Tony, was admitted after he developed a facial tumour. Apart from causing a gross distortion of his features (Tony's left eye was gradually being pushed sideways and out of its socket), the expanding tumour was also causing the arteries in his nasal area to break down. As a result, Tony suffered from continuous nose bleeds. He had to have a bolus of cloth permanently attached beneath his nose to absorb the frequent outpourings of blood and mucus. The doctors predicted that Tony's death could be caused at any time by a 'catastrophic nose bleed', and for this reason were very reluctant to consider a discharge. [...]

On a number of occasions patients' symptoms could be successfully treated or controlled by the medical staff, and the boundedness of their bodies could thus be reinstated. For example, several patients were admitted with incontinence of urine, and were able to return home once they had been catheterised. Other symptoms such as violent and repeated vomiting and diarrhoea could often be treated through changes in diet and medication, and weeping limbs and fungating tumours through application of dressings and bandages. Having had their bodies successfully 're-bounded', it was then possible, and common, for the patient to be discharged. In this respect, the hospice could be understood as a mediator between the unbounded and the bounded body, with patients being moved into the hospice when the surfaces of their bodies ruptured and broke down, and moved out again when their bodily boundedness and integrity were subsequently restored.

A number of patients, however, like Annie, had symptoms which escalated following their admission to the hospice and, as a consequence, their deterioration was such that the boundedness of their bodies was impossible to reinstate. These patients, who will form the focus of the following ethnography and discussions, were the ones most likely to remain within the hospice until they died. What was striking about this sub-group of patients was that they all exhibited behaviour which suggested a total loss of self and social identity once their bodies became severely and irreversibly unbounded.

Annie was one of several patients admitted with recto-vaginal fistulas during my fieldwork. Another woman, Deborah, experienced a similar trajectory of deterioration and decline. She was originally admitted for a blood transfusion with a view to being discharged within a couple of days, but a developing fistula, coupled with periodic bouts of confusion (possibly caused by the spread of cancer to her brain), kept her in the hospice until she died.

The staff considered Deborah a very difficult patient to look after. One night the nurses were kept occupied for several hours after she disappeared from her side room. She was eventually found in the staff toilets totally covered in excreta. The walls and floor of the toilet were also splattered with her faeces. Deborah had by then recovered from her temporarily confused state and was very upset and embarrassed. The staff decided to move Deborah onto one of the wards so that it would be easier to keep an eye on her. Around this time Deborah's deterioration began to escalate and her incontinence became more or less continuous. The staff were having to change her pads at least four times at night.

When Deborah's bodily deterioration escalated, I observed that she had suddenly become a lot more withdrawn. After she had been on the ward for a couple of days she started asking for the curtains to be drawn around her bed to give her more privacy. A day or so later she stopped talking altogether, unless it was really necessary (to ask for the commode, for example), even when her family and other visitors were present. Deborah spent the remaining ten days of her life either sleeping or staring blankly into space. She refused all food and drink. The staff also noticed this 'strange' behaviour.

One of the hospice doctors concluded that 'for all intents and purposes she [had] shut herself off in a frustrated and irreversible silence'. Deborah was moved back into a side room and died there a couple of days later.

I spoke to Deborah's daughter about a month after she had died and she reflected very frankly and openly upon her mother's death. She felt she had actually said her 'good-byes' to Deborah about a week before she died (*i.e.* around the time Deborah became very withdrawn): 'After that she really wasn't there anymore . . . she wasn't my mother'.

What Deborah appears to have done was to 'disengage' and 'switch herself off' before her physical cessation. This type of withdrawal was common amongst 'unbounded' patients. Another patient, Dolly, had cancer of the colon and was admitted after becoming chronically incontinent at home. Her husband informed me that every time she had a severe bout of diarrhoea she begged him to help her take her own life. Dolly's requests for euthanasia continued during the first week of her stay in the hospice. The staff were unable to get her diarrhoea under control. In addition, she went into obstruction. The tumour mass expanded and blocked her colon and, as a consequence, digested food would reach her lower gut and then come back up as faecal vomit. Around the time Dolly went into total obstruction the staff observed a notable change in her behaviour. Dolly stopped requesting euthanasia; in fact she stopped talking altogether. When the nurses came to turn her in bed or to attend to her care she would close her eyes and totally ignore them. As one nurse observed: 'it's as if she's shut the outside world out and herself off in the process'.

This type of 'switching off' has been identified in other settings such as the Holocaust. Pines points to instances in which women 'overwhelmed by physical and emotional helplessness and despair, almost reached a state of psychic death' (1993: 185, see also Langer 1996). Pines uses Lifton's concept of 'psychic closing off' to indicate the total loss of self that occurred (1993: 180). This form of mental shut-down is clearly a lot more fundamental and radical than experiences of 'fragmentation of the self' observed by Martin amongst women suffering temporary – and reversible – bodily trauma and disruption such as may occur during menstruation, child birth and caesarean section (1989: 86). [. . .] It is, indeed, reasonable to suggest that 'mental shut-down' expresses, and reflects, a total loss of selfhood if one accepts Giddens' argument that the contemporary Western 'self' is an eminently social and relational entity, reflexively constituted through processes connecting the 'personal' to the 'social' (1991: 33, see also Rose 1990).

Other patients, like Annie, attempted to 'switch themselves off' by requesting heavy sedation. Kath, for example, requested that she was moved to a side room and given a large dose of analgesics after commenting, on repeated occasions, that 'you wouldn't put a dog through this'. Her message was clear and simple: it would be much more compassionate if the staff put her out of her misery. Some patients, like Deborah, refused to eat or drink, thereby accelerating their own demise; others, like Dolly, made more explicit requests for euthanasia. Stan, a patient with cancer of the prostate, began suffering from chronic diarrhoea about a week into his admission. He also had problems with his catheter which frequently became blocked because bits of tumour were being secreted in his urine. On a number of occasions he would wake up 'covered in my own dirt and wetness'. Stan repeatedly asked the staff to help him to die.

What all these examples serve to highlight is that once a patient's body fell severely and irreversibly apart, she or he exhibited behaviour which suggests a loss of sense of self. This loss of self was reflected in the tendency of some to switch themselves off and to disengage from the events and relationships taking place around them (hence Deborah's daughter's comment that her mother had already 'gone' once she became withdrawn).

[...] My observations [...] provide interesting insights into the relationship between the body, self and the person in the contemporary Western context. My findings suggest that the identity and selfhood of the contemporary Western person is fundamentally dependent upon the possession of a physically bounded body, since I have indicated something of the impossibility of being a person whilst having a body without boundaries [...]. Thus, it could be argued that hospices served on one level as 'fringe'/'liminal' spaces within which these 'non-persons', wavering 'between two worlds', remain buffered (Van Gennep 1972: 18).

[...]

The sequestration of the unbounded body: an ethnographic and theoretical discussion

One obvious question clearly remains to be addressed: namely, why the sequestration of the unbounded body is deemed both appropriate, and necessary, within the contemporary Western context. This section will be used to demonstrate that contemporary marginalising practices should be understood as a culturally and historically specific response to bodily unboundedness.

When carers discussed their reasons for wanting a patient to come into the hospice, their comments highlighted a common theme. Carers were not explicitly concerned about the fact that the patient was dying, rather, the primary reason they suggested for wanting the patient to be admitted was because they felt repelled by the patient being incontinent, vomiting, and/or emitting other bodily fluids within their own homes. As the wife of one patient put it:

> He started having a lot of problems with vomiting. You just never knew when it was going to happen. All of a sudden it would just come pouring out. It went everywhere... all over his bed, all over the carpet. It was disgusting.

[...]

Carers' perceptions were also shared by the patients themselves. As Annie's case study serves to highlight, patients often felt that home did not afford an appropriate space in which their bodily disintegration should occur.

The breakdown of the body's boundedness, furthermore, was often accompanied by the emission of smells. It quickly came to my attention that the odours released from patients' disintegrating bodies not only precipitated their admission to the hospice, but, in addition, often brought about a further marginalisation within the building itself. I observed that smell created a boundary around the patient, shunting others away. [...]

Sometimes, staff attempted to manage problems of smell by transferring a patient to a side room, thereby enabling the odours emitted from their body to be contained within a more bounded space. Annie is a good case in point. Another patient, Ron, was moved after it was reported that 'he smelt like dog shit'. One of the nurses added that 'you couldn't go into his ward this morning without squirting lemon aerosol in front of your nose'. Other patients were admitted directly to side rooms because of anticipated problems with odour. Sydney, for instance, was placed in a single room because he had a fungating tumour. The smell proved to be so repellent that his wife refused to go into his room from the time of his admission until his death six days later.

The negative reaction which carers and other participants within the hospice exhibited towards unbounded patients can perhaps be understood in terms of the capacity of the unbounded body to breach and percolate their own body boundaries. The smells, and other fluids and matter emitted from the unbounded body, extended the boundaries of the patient's corporeality, such that the patient's body 'seeped' into the boundaries and spaces of other persons and other places. Hence, strategies such as avoidance and/or the removal of a patient to a side room were employed in cases where the *effects* of the patient's unboundedness could not be contained or controlled. In effect, the other participants in the hospice were trying to maintain the integrity of their own selves, by avoiding having their body boundaries breached by the corrosive effects of the sick person's bodily disintegration.

Douglas, in her analysis of pollution concepts and taboos, argues for a symbolic classificatory approach to culturally embedded ideas of defilement and disorder. Concepts of 'dirt', she suggests, emerge in situations where a set of ordered relations and classificatory schema are directly contravened. Hence, pollution behaviour 'is the reaction which condemns any object or idea likely to confuse or contradict cherished classifications' (1984: 35). Douglas's approach, I suggest, can be usefully applied to provide insights into why intolerance of bodily emissions and smells has become such a marked feature of the contemporary 'deodorised' West. Whilst the carers observed in my study expressed revulsion towards unbounded patients, both Classen *et al.* (1994) and Corbin (1986) have provided rich accounts which demonstrate that historically (especially in the Medieval period) mainstream European social life was pervaded by the smells of bodies, bodily emissions and other pungent odours. [. . .] The hospice, I suggest, served to impose order upon disorder through enclosing and containing the odours emitted from patients' disintegrating bodies within a bounded space. It requires little further imagination to argue that the walls of the hospice served as the boundaries of the patient's body in situations where the patient lacked the corporeal capacity for self-containment.

Yet, as the following discussion will serve to make evident, the current Western intolerance of bodily disintegration and bodily emissions can also be related to contemporary individualistic constructions of the person as a stable, bounded and autonomous entity.

[. . .] Whilst the body can act as a 'model for society' by affording 'a source of symbols for other complex structures' ([Douglas] 1984: 115), Douglas also suggests that the 'social body constrains the way the physical body is perceived' (1970: 65). Hence, it is through the body, and the way in which the body is deployed and modified that socially appropriate self-understandings are created and reproduced. [. . .]

The work of the above academics can be fed into, and used to support, Elias's argument that contemporary Western constructions of the body as a 'peculiarly intimate and private thing' are neither natural nor innate, but rather the product of a long, gradual and historically specific 'civilising process' (1994). This process, which extended over many centuries, involved the gradual elaboration and internalisation – in the form of self controls – of a whole series of taboos and precepts regulating such things as bodily functions and bodily exposure. As a consequence, a number of 'natural functions' such as defecating, urinating and spitting which had previously been public acts were eliminated from social life and displaced 'behind the scenes' (1994: 114). As Elias further suggests, the privatisation of bodily functions did not occur uniformly across society. Bodily taboos and affect controls first became commonplace amongst the upper classes in Western Europe, and slowly filtered down to, and became established amongst, the bourgeoisie, followed later by the lower social classes.

Elias thus traces a gradual historical transition from an 'open', 'incomplete body', to a body with clearly defined boundaries, isolated, alone, and fenced off from other bodies (1994: 56, Fontaine 1978: 245). What is particularly pertinent in Elias's historical account is the relationship that can be drawn between the emergence of the bounded body as central to contemporary Western concepts of the person and the rise of individualism. Crawford, for example, stresses the interrelationship between the ascetic individualism of the Protestant Reformation and the construction of the body as 'healthy', 'enclosed', and 'disciplined'. He suggests that the 'Protestant temperament' of austerity, coupled with a 'work ethic' that has inculcated a predisposition towards applied entrepreneurial activity and disciplined saving, has led to an emphasis upon personal discipline, autonomy, and self-responsibility (1994:1349, see also Foucault 1991: 138). Crawford's argument thus closely parallels Douglas's assertion that the body can act as a 'text' which reflects and reproduces the concerns, values and preoccupations of the particular culture within which it is located. Self-control, in effect, has become mapped onto, and experienced within, the physical body as *self-containment*.

[...]

[...] Indeed, as Corbin has emphasised, the contemporary Western perception of body odours and body substances as 'filth' (*i.e.* something to be avoided and disposed of) must be understood as stemming from a new 'spatiality of the body', which has developed in parallel with the emergence of the concept of the individual (1986: 61). It is highly significant, as Corbin further notes, that 'hygiene reforms' geared to 'privatising human waste' and 'deodorising' public and private spaces predated Pasteur's germ theory of disease, but occurred concurrently with the early stages of the historical development of individualism. Much the same observation is, of course, made by Elias who suggests that the closure of the body, achieved through the isolation of natural functions from public life, was originally grounded in 'moral' concerns, and only later came to be understood as necessary for 'hygienic' reasons (1994: 123). In other words, advances in science and medicine cannot be accorded a deterministic role in the development of modern Western 'hygiene sensibilities'; instead we should understand these sensibilities as being essentially symbolic in nature, stemming, in the first instance, from the construction of the person, and the body, as self-contained, bounded entities.

It is now possible to understand why unbounded patients were sequestered within the hospice. As the above analysis serves to demonstrate, within the context of contemporary Western paradigms, the unbounded body is perceived symbolically both as a locus and a source of 'dirt'; as 'matter out of place' (Douglas 1984: 35).

[...]

Discussion

A substantial literature argues that death and dying are one of our main cultural taboos within contemporary Western society (Aries 1974, 1983, Gorer 1965, Moller 1996). Within this framework the contemporary hospice movement, despite its own overt goal of humanising the dying process, is frequently understood as a further exemplar of the widespread social desire to sequester and hide the processes of death and dying from the mainstream of social life (see, for instance, Aries 1974, Mellor 1993, Hockey 1990: 156, Feifel 1959). My analysis, however, suggests this interpretation is far from adequate since, [...] hospices do not veil the dying process *per se*; rather they have come to sequester a particular type of dying and a particular category of patient; namely, one who is disintegrating and has a body which is unbounded.

Note

1   Oedema occurs when a patient's lymphatic system becomes blocked. Lymph fluid accumulates in the limbs causing them to become very heavy and swollen.

Acknowledgements

I am very grateful to Susan Benson, Sarah Green, Charlotte Carr, Catherine Alexander and Geoffrey Woodcock for their comments on earlier versions of this paper. I am also indebted to New Hall, Cambridge, for funding the doctoral research upon which this paper is based.

References

Aries, P. (1974) *Western Attitudes towards Death*. Baltimore: John Hopkins University Press.
Aries, P. (1983) *The Hour of Our Death*. Harmondsworth: Penguin Books.
Classen, C., Howes, D. and Synott, A. (1994) *Aroma: the Cultural History of Smell*. London: Routledge.
Corbin, A. (1986) *The Foul and the Fragrant: Odor and the French Social Imagination*. New York: Berg.
Crawford, R. (1994) The boundaries of the self and the unhealthy other: reflections on health, culture and AIDS, *Social Science and Medicine*, 38, 1347–65.
Douglas, M. (1970) *Natural Symbols: Explorations in Cosmology*. London: Barries and Rockliffe.

Douglas, M. (1984) *Purity and Danger: an Analysis of the Concepts of Pollution and Taboo.* London: Ark.

Elias, N. (1994) *The Civilising Process: the History of Manners and State Formation and Civilisation.* (Trans. E. Jephcott). Oxford: Blackwell.

Feifel, H. (1959) *The Meaning of Death.* New York: McGraw-Hill.

Fontaine, N. (1978) The civilizing process revisited: interview with Norbert Elias, *Theory and Society,* 5, 243–53.

Foucault, M. (1991) *Discipline and Punish: the Birth of the Prison.* Harmondsworth: Penguin Books.

Giddens, A. (1991) *Modernity and Self-Identity: Self and Society in the Late Modern Age.* Cambridge: Polity.

Gorer, G. (1965) *Death, Grief and Mourning.* New York: Routledge.

Hockey, J. (1990). *Experiences of Death: an Anthropological Account.* Edinburgh: Edinburgh University Press.

Langer, L. (1996) The alarmed vision: social suffering and the Holocaust atrocity, *Daedalus: Journal of the American Academy of Arts and Sciences, Social Suffering.* Issued as vol. 125.

Martin, E. (1989). *The Woman in the Body: a Cultural Analysis of Reproduction.* Milton Keynes: Open University Press.

Mellor, P. (1993) Death in high modernity: the contemporary presence and absence of death. In Clark, D. (ed), *The Sociology of Death.* Oxford: Blackwell.

Moller, D. (1996) *Confronting Death: Values, Institutions and Human Mortality.* Oxford: Oxford University Press.

Pines, D. (1993) *A Woman's Unconscious Use of her Body: a Psychoanalytical Perspective.* London: Virago Press.

Rose, N. (1990) *Governing the Soul: the Shaping of the Private Self.* London: Routledge.

Van Gennep, A. (1972) *The Rites of Passage.* Chicago: University of Chicago Press.

Woodhall, C. (1986). Care of the dying: a family concern, *Nursing Times,* Oct. 22, 31–3.

Part II

Health and Risk

Introduction

The concept of health has been interrogated by sociologists. How do people define health? What kinds of things place good health at risk? Who should be responsible for maintaining the health of individuals? There is a significant literature which provides answers to these kinds of questions, as well as another sociological question, which is: Why did sociologists, and indeed medical practitioners, become interested in health in the first place?

Armstrong's paper on the rise of 'Surveillance Medicine' provides clues to this puzzle. He makes a distinction between what he calls 'Hospital Medicine' and 'Surveillance Medicine'. Whereas the medical procedures of the former were typified by the clinical examination of the diseased patient, the medical procedures of the latter comprised the examination, or rather the observation, of everyone. Armstrong argues that around the early twentieth century the 'gaze' of medicine looked beyond the walls of the hospital and rested upon the community. The socio-medical survey was but one example of a number of surveillance mechanisms which were used to collate and assess information about the population. With the aid of statistical information it was possible for practitioners to assess 'normal' or average indicators of physical and mental health. Thus problematic health status was 'delineated not by the absolute categories of physiology and pathology, but by the characteristics of the normal population'. A consequence of 'Surveillance Medicine' is the formation of the contingent concept of 'risk'. Illness symptoms (e.g. high blood pressure) may not merely be problems in and of themselves; they may be risk factors associated with other conditions (e.g. stroke). The incorporation of the 'social' into the medical gaze has meant that risk factors are not restricted to physical symptoms, but also include people's behaviours, lifestyles and social circumstances. Indeed, within the context of promoting good health there has been a veritable 'epidemic' of risk factors (Skolbekken, 1995) which are subjected to social and medical scrutiny.

Alcohol, smoking and accidents are three examples of risks to health which are evident in the health discourse of late modern society and form the topics of our next two papers. Pavis, Cunningham-Burley and Amos set out to discern whether or not it is possible to identify any structural correlates to the smoking and drinking habits of young people during their transition from school to employment, training or further education. As the authors point out, a number of influential contemporary social theorists have suggested that in our era of rapid social and economic change, structural constraints such as 'social class' and 'gender' are less useful in understanding or explaining people's life chances or choices. The quantitative analysis of young

people's behaviours presented in this paper, however, suggests that structural location does in fact still constrain individual action. The analysis shows that drinking
and smoking behaviours are strongly associated with the behaviours of friends, use
of leisure time and changes in disposable income. This leads them to conclude that
'[t]he subjective experience of late modernity does not appear to be one of disembeddedness'. The papers in Part IV of this Reader lend support to the view that
health behaviours and health status are associated with structural factors, such as
age, gender, social class and ethnicity. They provide evidence that health, illness and
disease are still clearly socially patterned, and that poor health is associated with
material and social disadvantage.

As Green points out, accidents are another risk factor which is socially patterned.
For example, male children from social classes IV and V are many times more likely
to be killed or to suffer serious injury than are middle-class girls (Acheson, 1998).
But this is not the prime focus of her paper; rather, the very existence of an
epidemiology, or the social mapping, of accidents forms the starting point of her
analysis. If accidents are patterned and therefore predictable, they cannot occur by
chance or at random. What, then, actually constitutes an accident? Green analyses
the responses of both children and professionals to this question, and finds that their
responses have much in common. The defining characteristics of an 'ideal' accident,
it seems, are unpredictability and blamelessness; yet, when describing specific accidents, both children and professionals invariably begin to talk about causes, culpability and precipitating factors. Thus, under closer scrutiny, the notion of an event
actually being an 'accident' begins to evaporate. A theme running throughout this
paper is that while events can be explained statistically at a collective level, such
explanations do not provide adequate answers for the occurrence of individual
events. Green concludes: 'There is perhaps a search for meaning for all misfortune
at the individual level, where a statistical explanation of risk factors will not suffice.'

The juxtaposition of statistical and individual explanations of risks forms a key
theme in the paper by Emslie, Hunt and Watt on lay beliefs about heart disease. Here
the work by Davison and his colleagues (1991) is described and then developed by
incorporating the missing dimension of gender. Following their analysis of beliefs
about heart disease, Davison et al. (1991) developed the concept of 'coronary
candidacy'. This concept captures the fact that in general people identify those
individuals who are at greater risk of having a heart attack. They would be men
who smoke a lot, don't exercise, are overweight, have a bad diet, and worry a lot.
This observation is summed up in the colloquialism 'a heart attack waiting to
happen'. Yet people could see that many 'coronary candidates' do not have heart
attacks. Indeed, most people seemed to have an 'Uncle Norman' – that is, they knew
of a man, who smoked 40 cigarettes a day and had an 'unhealthy' lifestyle, yet lived
to a very old age. To account for this discrepancy between statistical risk and
individual events, many people invoked notions of luck, fate or destiny. Emslie,
Hunt and Watt draw on fresh data on health beliefs, and find that women were
'invisible' in the discourses about heart disease, even though heart disease is one of
the main causes of death among women in the UK.

While Emslie, Hunt and Watt purport to examine health 'beliefs', other sociologists
have argued that people's articulations of health and illness are not simply expressions
of their beliefs on the topic, but might better be understood as 'accounts' which are
imbued with broader social and ideological discourses (Radley and Billig, 1996).

This argument is developed in the next paper by Prior, Chun and Huat, who examine the accounts of health and illness provided by people living in Cantonese-speaking communities in England. By focusing on 'accounts' rather than beliefs, the authors argue that they avoid any suggestion that they might be representing people's subjective interpretations, but capture instead people's views, which are made publicly available and are verifiable. This is an important distinction, because whereas psychologists may seek to uncover what people inwardly believe or know, sociologists are more likely to want to understand the ways in which people's interpretations of situations and events are shaped by, and imbued with, prevailing public discourses. The analysis of the accounts reveals how the study participants drew upon various agents such as traditional Chinese medicine, demons, spirits, food and the weather to explain their physical and mental health.

References

Acheson, O. (1998) *Independent Inquiry into Inequalities in Health: Report*. London: Stationery Office.

Davison, C., Frankel, S. and Davey Smith, G. (1991) Lay Epidemiology and the Prevention Paradox: The Implications of Coronary Candidacy for Health Education. *Sociology of Health and Illness*, 13 (1), 1–19.

Radley, A. and Billig, M. (1996) Accounts of Health and Illness, Dilemmas and Representations. *Sociology of Health and Illness*, 18 (2), 220–40.

Skolbekken, J. (1995) The Risk Epidemic in Medical Journals. *Social Science and Medicine*, 40 (3), 291–305.

9

The Rise of Surveillance Medicine

David Armstrong

Introduction

Perhaps the most important contribution for understanding the advent of modern medicine has been the work of the medical historian Ackerknecht (1967), who described the emergence of a number of distinct medical perspectives during the early and late eighteenth century. In brief, he identified an earlier phase of Library Medicine in which the classical learning of the physician seemed more important than any specific knowledge of illness. This gave way to Bedside Medicine when physicians began to address the problems of the practical management of illness, particularly in terms of the classification of the patient's symptoms. In its turn Bedside Medicine was replaced by Hospital Medicine with the advent of hospitals in Paris at the end of the eighteenth century.

Hospital Medicine was clearly an important revolution in medical thinking. Also known as the Clinic, pathological medicine, Western medicine and biomedicine, it has survived and extended itself over the last two centuries to become the dominant model of medicine in the modern world. Even so, a significant alternative model of medicine can be discerned as materialising during the twentieth century around the observation of seemingly healthy populations.

Medical spaces

The commanding medical framework of Hospital Medicine first emerged at the turn of the eighteenth century with the appearance of the now familiar medical procedures of the clinical examination, the post-mortem, and hospitalisation. Foucault (1973) has described these changes in terms of a new 'spatialisation' of illness.

[...]

[...] Under Bedside Medicine, illness was best identified in the natural space of the patient's own home; in Hospital Medicine it required the 'neutral' space of the hospital so that the indicators of the underlying lesion might be properly identified without the contaminants of extraneous 'noise'. This facet of the new medicine was marked by the subsequent dominance of the clinic as the prime centre for health care provision as hospitals were rapidly built throughout Europe.

The novel spatialisation of illness that marked the new pathological alignment of Hospital Medicine came to dominate the nineteenth century and has succeeded in maintaining its ascendancy in the twentieth. To be sure, the techniques for identifying the hidden lesions of the body have grown more sophisticated. Indeed, Jewson (1976) has argued that the addition of laboratory investigations to the repertoire of clinical indicators of disease towards the end of the nineteenth century marked yet another medical model that he called Laboratory Medicine, not least because the body of the patient became even more objectified and the identity of the 'sick man' further lost. But, while clinical investigations in the form of X-rays, pathology reports, blood analyses, etc. marked an extension of the technical apparatus of medical procedures it did not challenge the underlying spatialisation of illness nor the logic of clinical practice: experience and illness were still linked through surface and depth, inference of the true nature of the lesion still dominated medical thinking, and the hospital still – indeed even more so – remained the centre of health care activity.

Despite the clear hegemony of Hospital Medicine over the last two centuries, it is the contention of this paper that a new medicine based on the surveillance of normal populations can be identified as beginning to emerge early in the twentieth century. This new Surveillance Medicine involves a fundamental remapping of the spaces of illness. Not only is the relationship between symptom, sign and illness redrawn but the very nature of illness is reconstrued. And illness begins to leave the three-dimensional confine of the volume of the human body to inhabit a novel extracorporal space.

Problematisation of the normal

Hospital Medicine was only concerned with the ill patient in whom a lesion might be identified, but a cardinal feature of Surveillance Medicine is its targeting of everyone. Surveillance Medicine requires the dissolution of the distinct clinical categories of healthy and ill as it attempts to bring everyone within its network of visibility. Therefore one of the earliest expressions of Surveillance Medicine – and a vital precondition for its continuing proliferation – was the problematisation of the normal.

[. . .] It was the child in the twentieth century that became the first target of the full deployment of the concept. The significance of the child was that it underwent growth and development: there was therefore a constant threat that proper stages might not be negotiated that in its turn justified close medical observation. The establishment and wide provision of antenatal care, birth notification, baby clinics, milk depots, infant welfare clinics, day nurseries, health visiting and nursery schools ensured that the early years of child development could be closely monitored (Armstrong 1983). For example, the School Medical (later Health) Service not only provided a traditional 'treatment' clinic, but also provided an 'inspection' clinic that screened all school children at varying times for both incipient and manifest disease, and enabled visits to children's homes by the school nurse to report on conditions and monitor progress (HMSO 1975).

In parallel with the intensive surveillance of the body of the infant during the early twentieth century, the new medical gaze also turned to focus on the unformed mind of the child. As with physical development, psychological growth was construed as inherently problematic, precariously normal. The initial solution was for psycho-logical well-being to be monitored and its abnormal forms identified. (The contemporary work of Freud that located adult psychopathology in early childhood experience can be seen as part of this approach.) The nervous child, the delicate child, the eneuretic child, the neuropathic child, the maladjusted child, the difficult child, the neurotic child, the over-sensitive child, the unstable child and the solitary child, all emerged as a new way of seeing a potentially hazardous normal childhood (Armstrong 1983, Rose 1985, 1990).

If there is one image that captures the nature of the machinery of observation that surrounded the child in those early decades of the twentieth century, it might well be the height and weight growth chart. Such charts contain a series of gently curving lines, each one representing the growth trajectory of a population of children. Each line marked the 'normal' experience of a child who started his or her development at the beginning of the line. Thus, every child could be assigned a place on the chart and, with successive plots, given a personal trajectory. But the individual trajectory only existed in a context of general population trajectories: the child was unique yet uniqueness could only be read from a composition which summed the unique features of all children. A test of normal growth assumed the possibility of abnormal growth, yet how, from knowledge of other children's growth, could the boundaries of normality be identified? When was a single point on the growth and weight chart, to which the sick child was reduced, to be interpreted as abnormal? Abnormality was a relative phenomenon. A child was abnormal with reference to other children, and even then only by degrees. In effect, the growth charts were significant for distributing the body of the child in a field delineated not by the absolute categories of physiology and pathology, but by the characteristics of the normal population.

The socio-medical survey, first introduced during World War II to assess the perceived health status of the population, represented the recruitment to medicine of an efficient technical tool that both measured and reaffirmed the extensiveness of morbidity. The survey revealed the ubiquity of illness, that health was simply a precarious state. The post-war fascination with the weakening person-patient interface – such as in the notion of the clinical iceberg which revealed that most illness lay outside of health care provision (Last 1963), or of illness behaviour which showed that people experience symptoms most days of their lives yet very few were taken to the doctor (Mechanic and Volkart 1960) – was evidence that the patient was inseparable from the person because all persons were becoming patients.

The survey also demanded alternative ways of measuring illness that would encompass nuances of variation from some community-based idea of the normal. Hence the development of health profile questionnaires, subjective health measures, and other survey instruments with which to identify the proto-illness and its sub-clinical manifestations, and latterly the increasing importance of qualitative methodologies that best capture illness as an experience rather than as a lesion (Fitzpatrick *et al.* 1984).

The results of the socio-medical survey threw into relief the important distinction between the biomedical model's binary separation of health and disease, and the survey's continuous distribution of variables throughout the population. The survey classified bodies on a continuum: there were no inherent distinctions between a body at one end and one at the other, their only differences were the spaces that separated them.

[...]

Dissemination of intervention

The blurring of the distinction between health and illness, between the normal and the pathological, meant that health care intervention could no longer focus almost exclusively on the body of the patient in the hospital bed. Medical surveillance would have to leave the hospital and penetrate into the wider population.

The new 'social' diseases of the early twentieth century – tuberculosis, venereal disease, problems of childhood, the neuroses, etc. – were the initial targets for novel forms of health care, but the main expansion in the techniques of monitoring occurred after World War II when an emphasis on comprehensive health care, and primary and community care, underpinned the deployment of explicit surveillance services such as screening and health promotion. But these later radiations out into the community were prefigured by two important inter-war experiments in Britain and the United States that demonstrated the practicality of monitoring precarious normality in a whole population.

The British innovation was the Pioneer Health Centre at Peckham in south London (Pearse and Crocker 1943). The Centre offered ambulatory health care to local families that chose to register – but the care placed special emphasis on continuous observation. From the design of its buildings that permitted clear lines of sight to its social club that facilitated silent observation of patients' spontaneous activity, every development within the Peckham Centre was a conscious attempt to make visible the web of human relations. Perhaps the Peckham key summarises the dream of this new surveillance apparatus. The key and its accompanying locks were designed (though never fully installed) to give access to the building and its facilities for each individual of every enrolled family. But as well as giving freedom of access, the key enabled a precise record of all movement within the building. 'Suppose the scientist should wish to know what individuals are using the swimming bath or consuming milk, the records made by the use of the key give him this information' (Pearse and Crocker 1943: 76–7).

Only 7 per cent of those attending the Peckham Centre were found to be truly healthy; and if everyone had pathology then everyone would need observing. An important mechanism for operationalising this insight was the introduction of extensive screening programmes in the decades following World War II. However, screening, whether individual, population, multi-phasic, or opportunistic, represented a bid by Hospital Medicine to reach out beyond its confines – with all its accompanying limitations. First, it was too focused on the body. It meant that screening still confronted the localised lesion (or, more commonly, proto-lesion) within the body and ignored the newly emerging mobile threats that were insinuated throughout the community, constantly reforming into new dangers. Second, techniques to screen the population have always had to confront points of resistance, particularly the unwillingness of many to participate in these new procedures. The solution to these difficulties had already begun to emerge earlier in the twentieth century with the development of a strategy that involved giving responsibility for surveillance to patients themselves. A strategy of health promotion could potentially circumvent the problems inherent in illness screening.

The process through which the older techniques of hygiene were transformed into the newer strategy of health promotion occurred over several decades during the twentieth century. But perhaps one of the earliest experiments that attempted the transition was the collaborative venture between the city of Fargo in North Dakota and the Commonwealth Fund in 1923. The nominal objective of the project was the incorporation of child health services into the permanent programme of the health department and public school system (Brown 1929) and an essential component of this plan was the introduction of health education in Fargo's schools, supervised by Maud Brown. Brown's campaign was, she wrote, 'an attempt to secure the instant adoption by every child of a completely adequate program of health behaviour' (Brown, 1929: 19).

Prior to 1923 the state had required that elements of personal hygiene be taught in Fargo's schools 'but there was no other deliberately planned link between the study of physical well-being and the realization of physical well-being'. The Commonwealth Fund project was a two pronged strategy. While the classroom was the focus for a systematic campaign of health behaviour, a periodic medical and dental examination both justified and monitored the educational intervention. In effect 'health teaching, health supervision and their effective coordination' were linked together. In Fargo 'health teaching departed from the hygiene textbook, and after a vitalizing change, found its way back to the textbook' (Brown 1929: 19). From its insistence on four hours of physical exercises a day – two of them outdoors – to its concern with the mental maturation of the child, Fargo represented the realisation of a new public health dream of surveillance in which everyone is brought into the vision of the benevolent eye of medicine through the medicalisation of everyday life.

After World War II this approach began to be deployed with more vigour in terms of a strategy of health promotion. Concerns with diet, exercise, stress, sex, etc. become the vehicles for encouraging the community to survey itself. The ultimate triumph of Surveillance Medicine would be its internalisation by all the population.

The tactics of Hospital Medicine have been those of exile and enclosure. The lesion marked out those who were different in a great binary system of illness and health, and processed them (in the hospital) in an attempt to rejoin them to the healthy. The tactics of the new Surveillance Medicine, on the other hand, have been pathologisation and vigilance. The techniques of health promotion recognise that health no longer exists in a strict binary relationship to illness, rather health and illness belong to an ordinal scale in which the healthy can become healthier, and health can co-exist with illness; there is now nothing incongruous in having cancer yet believing oneself to be essentially healthy (Kagawa-Singer 1993). But such a trajectory towards the healthy state can only be achieved if the whole population comes within the purview of surveillance: a world in which everything is normal and at the same time precariously abnormal, and in which a future that can be transformed remains a constant possibility.

Spatialisation of risk factors

The extension of a medical eye over all the population is the outward manifestation of the new framework of Surveillance Medicine. But more fundamentally there is a concomitant shift in the primary spatialisation of illness as the relationship between symptom, sign and illness are reconfigured. From a linkage based on surface and depth, all become components in a more general arrangement of predictive factors.

A symptom or sign for Hospital Medicine was produced by the lesion and consequently could be used to infer the existence and exact nature of the disease. Surveillance Medicine takes these discrete elements of symptom, sign and disease and subsumes them under a more general category of 'factor' that points to, though does not necessarily produce, some future illness. Such inherent contingency is embraced by the novel and pivotal medical concept of *risk*. It is no longer the symptom or sign pointing tantalisingly at the hidden pathological truth of disease, but the risk factor opening up a space of future illness potential.

Symptoms and signs are only important for Surveillance Medicine to the extent that they can be re-read as risk factors. Equally, the illness in the form of the disease or lesion that had been the end-point of clinical inference under Hospital Medicine is also deciphered as a risk factor in as much as one illness becomes a risk factor for another. Symptom, sign, investigation and disease thereby become conflated into an infinite chain of risks. A headache may be a risk factor for high blood pressure (hypertension), but high blood pressure is simply a risk factor for another illness (stroke). And whereas symptoms, signs and diseases were located in the body, the risk factor encompasses any state or event from which a probability of illness can be calculated. This means that Surveillance Medicine turns increasingly to an extracorporal space – often represented by the notion of 'lifestyle' – to identify the precursors of future illness. Lack of exercise and a high fat diet therefore can be joined with angina, high blood cholesterol and diabetes as risk factors for heart disease. Symptoms, signs, illnesses, and health behaviours. Each illness of Hospital Medicine existed as the discrete endpoint in the chain of clinical discovery: in Surveillance Medicine each illness is simply a nodal point in a network of health status monitoring. The problem is less illness *per se* but the semi-pathological pre-illness at-risk state.

[...]

[...] Risk factors, above all else, are pointers to a potential, yet unformed, eventuality. For example, the abnormal cells discovered in cervical cytology screening do not in themselves signify the existence of disease, but only indicate its future possibility. The techniques of Surveillance Medicine – screening, surveys, and public health campaigns – would all address this problem in terms of searching for temporal regularities, offering anticipatory care, and attempting to transform the future by changing the health attitudes and health behaviours of the present. [...]

Reconfiguration of identity

The advent of Hospital Medicine not only signified a new way of thinking about and dealing with illness, it also marked out the three-dimensional outline of the familiar passive and analysable human body.

[...]

The rise of a major new form of medicine during the twentieth century that offers a fundamental reformulation of the epistemological, cognitive and physical map of illness – and, it might be added, its very close alliance with social sciences – merits recognition. But its real significance lies in the way in which a surveillance machinery deployed throughout a population to monitor precarious normality delineates a new temporalised risk identity.

Acknowledgement

I am grateful to Jane Ogden for helpful comments on earlier drafts of this paper.

References

Ackerknecht, E. (1967) *Medicine at the Paris Hospital 1774–1848*. Baltimore: Johns Hopkins.

Armstrong, D. (1983) *Political Anatomy of the Body: Medical Knowledge in Britain in the Twentieth Century*. Cambridge: Cambridge University Press.

Brown, M. A. (1929) *Teaching Health in Fargo*. New York: Commonwealth Fund.

Fitzpatrick, R. Hinton, J., Newman, S., Scambler, G. and Thompson, J. (1984) *The Experience of Illness*. London: Tavistock.

Foucault, M. (1973) *The Birth of the Clinic: An Archaeology of Medical Perception*. London: Tavistock.

HMSO (1975) *The School Health Service: 1908–74*. London.

Jewson, N. (1976) The disappearance of the sick-man from medical cosmologies: 1770–1870, *Sociology*, 10, 225–44.

Kagawa-Singer, M. (1993) Redefining health: living with cancer, *Social Science and Medicine*, 37, 295–304.

Last, J. M. (1963) The clinical iceberg, *Lancet*, 2, 28–30.

Mechanic, D. and Volkart, E. H. (1960) Illness behaviour and medical diagnoses, *Journal of Health and Human Behaviour*, 1, 86–90.

Pearse, I. H. and Crocker, L. H. (1943) *The Peckham Experiment: A Study in the Living Structure of Society*. London: George Allen and Unwin.

Rose, N. (1985) *The Psychological Complex*. London: Routledge and Kegan Paul.

Rose, N. (1990) *Governing the Soul: The Shaping of the Private Self*. London: Routledge.

10

Health Related Behavioural Change in Context: Young People in Transition

Stephen Pavis, Sarah Cunningham-Burley and Amanda Amos

Introduction

In Britain, recent decades have seen numerous changes which affect the lives of young people. The recession which occurred through the early 1980s led to high levels of teenage unemployment (Bartley, 1994) and paid employment was increasingly replaced by various kinds of youth training and further education (Lee, 1990). State benefits for 16–18 year olds were reduced in real terms and closely tied to participation in youth training schemes (DSS, 1993; Coles, 1995). The last 20 years have also seen youth wages fall relative to those of adult workers (Irwin, 1995). In response to these changes young people have begun to stay on at school in ever increasing numbers (Furlong and Cartmel, 1997) and successive cohorts have deferred the timing of marriage and the onset of parenthood (Irwin, 1995; Morrow and Richards, 1996). [...]

At the same time the teenage years are commonly seen as a time of peak physical functioning and as being marked by a low incidence of illness. However, this view can be challenged in at least two ways. First, there is increasing evidence that adolescents' physical and mental health is related to the structure of their family, own educational attainment, current economic position and personal disposable income (West, 1988; Macintyre and West, 1991; Hendry *et al.*, 1993; Winefield *et al.*, 1993; Sweeting and West, 1995; West and Sweeting, 1996; Dennehy *et al.*, 1997; Furlong and Cartmel, 1997). Second, adolescence is a key time when many young people experiment with behaviours that if continued long term are likely to be detrimental to their health. In Scotland, at age 15, around 20% of males and 23% of females smoke regularly (> 1 cigarette per week) (Diamond and Goddard, 1995) and at the same age Millar and Plant (1996) recently found that 48% of Scottish females and 52% of males had consumed more than five alcoholic drinks in a row during the previous 30 days. Millar and Plant (1996) also found that by age 15–16, 80% of females and 81% of males claimed to have been intoxicated at some point in the past.

[...]

[...] Developments and debates within social theory have raised questions regarding the relative importance of and inter-relationships between structure, culture and individual agency in explaining behaviours. At one extreme, some postmodern theorists have suggested that traditional structural analyses are no longer valid and argued that grand theory which privileges structure over agency is unable to predict either lifestyles or behaviours. Concepts such as class and gender, which were once central to sociological theory are said to have lost their explanatory power and the social world is portrayed as having become a less solid place (Lyotard, 1984; Baudrillard, 1988).

Others such as Beck (1992), Giddens (1990; 1991) and Lash (1992) have taken a less extreme position and whilst supporting the importance of rapid social change, the resultant weakening of class identities and the increasing individualisation of lifestyles, they have questioned the epochal nature of these transformations. Beck, in particular, notes the persistence of inequalities and more recently has argued that 'individual decisions are heavily dependent on outside influences' (Beck and Beck-Gernsheim, 1995).

However, an emphasis on individualisation and reflexivity, where the self is often portrayed as disembedded from social structures, remains powerful in current social theory. Risk and uncertainty are cast as central if not defining aspects of late modernity (Giddens, 1990, 1991; Beck, 1992). Agency, where people themselves are central in reflexively constructing their identities and biographies from a diverse range of experiences and opportunities, is prioritised and a sense of disembeddedness assumed to be reflected in subjective experience. Because traditional indicators of structural location have been eroded, for example, through a lessening of class or collective action, an assumption is made that individuals operate without social constraint and/or without a sense of their own social embeddedness.

In relation to understanding young people's health relevant behaviours, this has led some to focus strongly on agency and the active role that individuals play in the construction of self. Consumption (and indeed risk) are noted as having symbolic significance in the process of defining lifestyles and identities. Gray *et al.* (1996) for example, in attempting to provide a theoretical link between style and teenage smoking have argued that:

> In a world where there is an increasing number of commodities available to act as props, identity becomes more than ever a matter of creating and maintaining self-image through selecting and consuming products or behaviours which embody values, analogous with or desirable to a person's own. (p. 216)

Bunton and Burrows (1995) similarly support a link between lifestyle choice, identity and health related behaviours. They argue that the success of the *Death* brand of cigarettes in Britain with their black packet and skull and crossbones emblem, only makes sense because cigarettes are consumed as cultural objects. In relation to alcohol, the recent growth in white ciders like Diamond White, White Lightening, K, Ice Dragon and TNT and 'alcopops' such as 20/20, Thickhead and Maddog might also be of seen as evidence of the importance of 'brands' in symbolic consumption. McKeganey *et al.* (1996), for example, highlight the ways these strong alcoholic drinks are marketed at teenagers through a combination of image and a sweet 'pop' like taste. The names of these new drinks are also often close to the street names of elicit drugs; so for example, White Diamond is a common name for Ecstasy and 'Special K' a slang term for the Ecstasy substitute Ketamine (Kwatra and Brown, 1996).

At the same time, as Furlong and Cartmel (1997) point out,

> ... changing leisure patterns and lifestyles also highlight the extent to which preferences have been manufactured through mass marketing techniques. In other words, lifestyles are increasingly shaped by the market and therefore should not be viewed as an expression of individual choice.

In sum, the preceding literature points to the need to understand teenagers' health relevant behaviours within the structural locations which bound subjective experience, while at the same time exploring the diverse routes through which young people make the transitions towards adulthood in this time of rapid social and economic change. It is through empirical investigation which embraces an analysis both at the level of structure and individual experience that the conditions of late modernity can be more thoroughly understood.

In this paper we report on research which explicitly sought to focus on young people as they made key decisions regarding whether or not to leave school, seek employment, training or undertake some form of further education. We explore the accounts of a sample of 106 Scottish young people at two points in time (ages 15/16 and 16/17 years) in order to understand their experiences of and explanations for changes in the key health related behaviours of smoking and drinking. We explicitly attempt to use research techniques which tap both subjective experience and social location, so as to situate respondents' health related behaviours within the context of the wider transitions taking place in their lives. After outlining the methods used, the paper considers tobacco and alcohol consumption, describing changes in behaviour and the reasons respondents gave for their behaviours. Friendship emerges as an important mediator between structural factors relating to transitions and health related behaviours. In our conclusions we return to a discussion of the conditions of late modernity, the nature of subjective experience and the relevance of social structure. We point to some of the ways that our respondents' lifestyle choices were constrained by their concrete social contexts and highlight the ways that decisions made at one point in time either constrain or open up future possibilities.

Research Design

Our study cohort was recruited through two state comprehensive schools on the east coast of Scotland. The schools were selected on the basis that they were co-educational, had achieved average examination results in the academic year preceding the study, had a catchment area that covered a broad range of socio-economic groupings and included both rural and urban areas. [...] [The] total sample size [was] of 106 young people (female $n = 49$: male $n = 57$): a response rate of 34.5% of all S4[1] pupils in both schools.

Table 1 presents information on the day-time occupations of our sample in November 1995. As is apparent, the study cohort covered the full range of post 16 destinations: school, full-time employment, youth training, work-based apprenticeships, Further Education colleges and unemployment. [...]

Table 1 Day-time occupations of the sample in November 1995

	Males	Females	Overall
School	33	37	70
Work	9	3	12
YT	1	3	4
Other training	3	0	3
FE college	4	2	6
Unemployed	1	0	1
Other	1	1	2
Total	52	46	98

[...]

Research methods and data analysis

The research design entailed the use of both quantitative and qualitative techniques. Respondents were interviewed twice, once in February/March 1995 and again in November/December 1995. A structured questionnaire and a semi-structured interview were used during both rounds of data collection and in the same interviewer/ respondent session. [...] The primary aim of the questionnaire was to gather data that could be easily quantified, including information on: the respondent's current day-time occupation (e.g. school, work, YT, Further Education (FE) college, school); anticipated school leaving date and examinations being taken (where appropriate); respondent's work/educational plans for the next year; weekly income; main leisure activities; the number of evenings meeting with friends during an average week; health behaviours (i.e. amount of weekly exercise, tobacco and alcohol consumption); and household composition. [...]

The semi-structured interview took between 20 and 50 min. [...] The interview schedule covered the topics and issues raised in the questionnaire but sought to obtain a greater level of depth and degree of understanding of the respondents' lives and to locate their health behaviours within their social and cultural contexts. Particular attention was paid to the explanations and meanings that respondents attached to their health related behaviours.

Results

Tobacco and alcohol consumption at interview rounds 1 and 2

Table 2 presents the reported alcohol consumption patterns at interview rounds 1 and 2. The proportion of respondents who reported drinking regularly (at least fortnightly) rose. At the same time the percentage of those who had never drunk alcohol or who only drank very occasionally fell. Table 3 presents similar information in relation to tobacco consumption. Again the smoking rate was higher at round 2 than round 1 and this relationship held for both males and females. The percentage of respondents who reported smoking regularly rose, while the proportion of those who had never tried a cigarette fell.

Table 2   Respondents' reported consumption of alcohol: a comparison of behaviours at rounds 1 and 2

	Males		Females		Overall	
	Rd 1	*Rd 2*	*Rd 1*	*Rd 2*	*Rd 1*	*Rd 2*
Never drunk	4 (7)	1 (2)	4 (8)	2 (4)	8 (8)	3 (3)
Drinks very occasionally	13 (23)	8 (15)	19 (39)	8 (17)	32 (30)	16 (16)
Drinks occasionally	20 (35)	12 (23)	14 (29)	15 (33)	34 (32)	27 (28)
Drinks regularly	20 (35)	31 (60)	12 (24)	21 (46)	32 (30)	52 (53)
Total	57 (100)	52 (100)	49 (100)	46 (100)	106 (100)	98 (100)

Percentage in parentheses.

Tables 2 and 3 describe increases in both alcohol and tobacco consumption during the nine months between the first and second round interviews. It must be borne in mind, however, that these are reported rather than observed behaviours. It is possible that, with the majority of our sample having reached 16 yr by the second round, they may have been more prepared to admit to their use of tobacco and/or alcohol. Similarly, the fact that our respondents were interviewed twice may have meant that there was a higher level of interviewer/respondent rapport and trust at the second round of interviews (Backett, 1992). [...]

In order to address and unpack these issues it is necessary to look beyond reported prevalence and to examine the young people's recognition of and explanations for, their changing behaviours. In the analysis which follows we report both young people's accounts of their behaviours and the structural factors which were statistically related to increases in smoking and drinking, as revealed by our quantitative data analysis. Under the structural factors we concentrate on the influence of gender, day-time occupation, income and the reported behaviour of friendship groups. In this way we present a grounded and contextualised account of the young people's health related behaviours during this period of social transition.

What types of alcohol did the respondents drink?

In the questionnaire we asked respondents which types of alcoholic drink they preferred. This was an open question so as not to restrict choice or bias responses

Table 3   Respondents' reported smoking rates at round 1 and 2

	Males		Females		Overall	
	Rd 1	*Rd 2*	*Rd 1*	*Rd 2*	*Rd 1*	*Rd 2*
Never smoked	24 (42)	10 (19)	20 (41)	15 (33)	44 (41)	25 (26)
Tried once	15 (26)	17 (32)	8 (16)	8 (17)	23 (22)	25 (26)
Used to smoke	6 (11)	1 (2)	9 (18)	4 (9)	15 (14)	5 (5)
Smokes sometimes	4 (7)	7 (13)	3 (6)	5 (11)	7 (7)	12 (12)
Smokes regularly	8 (14)	17 (33)	9 (18)	14 (30)	17 (16)	31 (32)
Total	57 (100)	52 (100)	49 (100)	46 (100)	106 (100)	98 (100)

Percentages in parentheses.
NB 'smokes sometimes' =< 1 cigarette per week; "smokes regularly" => 1 cigarette per week.

by suggesting certain types of drink. The question revealed respondents to hold traditional preferences. At both the first and second round of interviews those who drank regularly (Rd1 $n = 32$: Rd2 $n = 52$) most commonly cited *cider* (Rd1 $n = 6$, Rd2 $n = 12$), *beer* (Rd1 $n = 3$, Rd2 $n = 8$) and *lager* (Rd1 $n = 3$, Rd2 $n = 8$) as their preferred drinks. Only five of the regular drinkers at round one and three at round two cited the new 'alcopops' or white ciders, i.e. *Diamond White* (Rd1 $n = 3$, Rd2 $n = 0$), *20/20* (Rd1 $n = 2$, Rd2 $n = 1$), *Hooch* (Rd1 $n = 0$, Rd2 $n = 1$) and *Moscow Mule* (Rd1 $n = 0$, Rd2 $n = 1$). The sample also reported 'traditional' gender patterns to their drinking, with males preferring beer and lager and females opting for cider or spirits (the most popular being Vodka and Southern Comfort).

Where did the respondents drink?

[. . .] At round 1 respondents who drank alcohol regularly did so in a variety of social settings: at home, in pubs, clubs and discos and on the streets, including local parks and nearby beaches or at friends' houses (Pavis *et al.*, 1997). The vast majority of alcohol consumption, however, took place either on the streets or in friends' houses (while parents or guardians were out or away). A gender distinction was noted, with street drinking being more popular with males (at age 15) and females preferring to drink at friends' houses. In contrast, at the second interview we found that large numbers of respondents had moved to drinking regularly in pubs and clubs; in fact this was now the most popular venue. Of the 32 respondents who drank regularly at the first interview, only 6 reported that they drank in pubs or clubs; 12 cited streets, parks or beaches; 8 cited friends' homes; 5 their own home. At the second interview 52 respondents drank regularly and 31 cited pubs or clubs as their main drinking venue, even though the legal age for buying alcohol in Britain is 18 yrs. There was a slight gender difference with females ($n = 15$) being slightly more likely than males ($n = 17$) to report pubs and clubs as their main drinking venue. Street drinking remained more popular with males ($n = 8$) than females ($n = 1$) although the numbers involved had dropped considerably. [. . .]

[. . .] Respondents offered multiple reasons for drinking alcohol [. . .] We found that these could be grouped together under the four headings of social facilitation, peer influence/pressure, mood alteration and personal solace. However, as the following quotations from respondent 055 illustrate, some young people reported drinking for multiple reasons. At the same time the most often cited explanations were social facilitation and peer influence. The second round of interviews revealed that all four of the reasons for alcohol use remained and social facilitation and peer influence were again the most often reported. The following interview extracts are given as examples of the four 'reasons for drinking alcohol' categories.

Drinking for social facilitation

Interviewer: What is it about drinking that you like? Can you explain?
Respondent: It gives you a better feeling, makes you more friendly and talk to more people . . . just talk to people who normally, like you might not talk to . . . make more friends easily. (m004 Rd 2)

Drinking because of peer influence/pressure

Interviewer: Are you aware of situations that you might be in that you drink more than others?
Respondent: It just depends when I am out, how much I feel like drinking, how much money I've got. I mean like if everyone else is like come on get drunk tonight, come on or something like that, I am just, I will say, all right then, go on then. (f055 Rd 2)

Drinking in order to influence mood

Interviewer: And what do you like about drink in general?
Respondent: Just it makes me feel happy ... It just makes me feel good ... They say that it is a depressant but I do not think it is. (f055 Rd 2)

Drinking for solace

Interviewer: Are there any factors do you think that lead you to drink more or less?
Respondent: If I am depressed I will drink, like with life and all that, hassles, I just cannot be bothered so I will just drink.
Interviewer: Can you give me an example?
Respondent: (pause) Well the first time I split up with my girlfriend, that is when I, I really had a drink there ... she dumped me so I just had a drink.
Interviewer: Was that on your own?
Respondent: Yes. (m005 Rd 2)

Which brands of cigarettes did the respondents smoke?

Regal was by far the most popular brand of cigarettes at both rounds of interview and there were no significant differences by gender. When asked why they smoked this brand most respondents explained their choice either in terms of it being what everyone else smoked or as it being the brand that they started with, again because it was what their peers smoked. These findings are similar to those of Barnard and Forsyth (1996) who in their study of 11–15 yr olds in Dundee also found Regal to be the most popular brand of cigarettes. They argued that the predominance of this brand was not random nor due to expediency or cost (Regal is not the cheapest brand) but rather was one of the ways by which young people sought 'acceptance, kudos and integration' among their friends. In other words young people are unlikely to want to appear different from their friends by smoking a different brand. It is therefore interesting to note that in our study, between rounds 1 and 2 four regular smokers changed their preferred brand, possibly reflecting changes in their peer groups.

Where did the respondents smoke tobacco?

During our first round of interviews we found that respondents smoked in many social settings including: on the way to school (on the bus); during school in the toilets, at break and lunch times; on the way home; in their homes; at youth clubs and community centres; in pubs and while 'hanging out' during the evening on street corners and in local parks (Pavis *et al.*, 1996). Again, examples of all of these consumption contexts were found during the second round of interviews. Additionally, however, by the second interviews some of the young people had left school and moved to work, college, training or unemployment. These new social situations provided new smoking contexts. Some respondents now smoked with work colleagues during breaks, at college with new friends or at home when unemployed. This is explored further below.

The reasons for smoking

We have previously argued (Pavis *et al.*, 1996) that the 'regular smokers' in our study (i.e. those consuming more than one cigarette per week) actually comprised at least three sub-groupings. First, there were those who smoked solely with one group of friends and in one social setting. These smokers tended to smoke least and described their behaviour in terms of 'being sociable' or 'being part of the group'. The second group smoked with various friendship groups and in different social situations. These respondents tended to smoke more heavily but still talked of smoking as a social activity that they did with their friends. The final groups of regular smokers smoked in groups with friends but also when alone. These smokers displayed more adult patterns to their tobacco consumption. They smoked at regular intervals and often used tobacco to punctuate their day. All of these sub-groupings of regular smokers were found at the second interview. As the following quotation shows, movement between these groups is socially complex and by no means always progressive or unidirectional (see also Goddard's 1990 work on younger adolescents).

Interviewer: So when are you smoking then?
Respondent: I was smoking quite often, like a couple of months ago but then it was just a waste of money I thought and it was not as though I was addicted . . . I do not buy any anymore but it is like if someone offers, I will take one. (f076 Rd 2)

[. . .] To summarise, the reasons which the young people offered for consuming alcohol and tobacco remained similar at rounds 1 and 2. For the vast majority, alcohol and tobacco use were social activities that they undertook with their friends. At the same time, however and as noted above, the young people reported considerable increases in their smoking and drinking behaviours. Moreover, there were also certain reported changes in the social contexts of both drinking and smoking, with pub going becoming more popular and some respondents smoking at work, training or college. In the light of these observations we now turn to look at the wider transitions which took place in the respondents' lives between the first and second round of interviews.

Post 16 destination and changes in smoking and drinking

Although the number of our respondents who left school between the first and second interview was quite small, those who were in full-time employment were more likely to be regular smokers (school, regular smoking $n = 22$ (31%); work, regular smoking $n = 6$ (50%): FE college, regular smokers $n = 2$ (33%). Those on

Youth Training or work based apprenticeships were least likely to smoke $n = 1$ (25%). For male respondents, those in full-time work $n = 7$ (77%), on apprenticeships $n = 3$ (100%) or unemployed $n = 1$ (100%), were more likely to drink regularly than those still at school $n = 17$ (33%). This pattern did not hold for females where 46% of those at school reported drinking regularly, compared to 33% ($n = 1$) at youth training; 33% (n=1) at work; and 50% ($n = 1$) at FE college. An analysis of respondents' movements along our smoking and drinking continua revealed similar patterns although not at statistically significant levels.

In the qualitative interviews some respondents commented that their occupational shift had resulted in changes in their health related actions. For some, the movement to a work or college environment, where many people smoked and/or drank, seemed to influence their own behaviour and was indeed described as doing so. This was particularly so for those respondents who had previously experimented with smoking.

Interviewer: The last time that you were interviewed you classed yourself as an ex-smoker...So what prompted you to start again?
Respondent: Just with working and people at my work and that. There is not anybody that does not smoke and just being in the staff-room and just sitting beside smokers. (f055 Rd 2)

[...] For other respondents, however, it was not so much that their new colleagues smoked or drank that was important but rather that they now had more money to spend with their friends. Their social life may or may not have involved new friends made through work, training, college or school.

[...]

No respondents reported that they had reduced smoking because of their new day-time occupation. Conversely, several respondents reported that starting work or staying on at school had meant less frequent drinking. [...]

Interviewer: Last time you spoke to us you said that you were going out every night of the week and now you are only going out at the weekends. How has that change come about?
Respondent: I think its really just the group I used to go about with, we don't really go about any more. And, like everybody's too tired and it is too cold...So I think that's got a lot to do with it. I think folk are working now so they're too tired. (f074 Rd 2)

During the nine months between the first and second round of interviews 35 males and 30 females increased their weekly income. For some this was because they obtained full or part time employment, for others it was related to beginning some form of training or college course and for others it was due to an increase in pocket money or weekly allowances. Regular smoking and weekly income were significantly associated. Of the 31 regular smokers at round 2, 30 (males $n = 16$: females $n = 14$) had more than £10 per week to spend and one less than £10 per week. Conversely, of the 67 respondents who smoked less than weekly 16 had a weekly income of less than £10 ($\chi^2 = 4.94$, df $= 1$, $p =< 0.05$). This trend between income and behaviour was also apparent with regard to regular drinking, but not at statistical significant levels.

Table 4 presents the changes in smoking and drinking behaviours of those who experienced an increase in income between interview rounds 1 and 2. Of these 66 respondents, 33 (males $n = 18$: females $n = 15$) moved at least one place up our drinking continuum and 29 (males $n = 10$: females $n = 19$) moved at least one place up the smoking continuum. Twenty-six (males $n = 16$: females $n = 10$) respondents whose weekly income had risen did not alter their drinking behaviour and 35 respondents (males $n = 20$: females $n = 15$) did not alter their smoking behaviour. However, here it is important to note that 15 of the respondents described as not having changed their drinking behaviour were already at the top of our continuum at round 1 and remained there at round 2 (i.e. they were regular drinkers at both points in time). Similarly 9 of the respondents described as not having changed their smoking behaviours were at the top of the continuum at round 1 and remained there at round 2 (i.e. they were regular smokers at both points). By way of contrast, of the 31 respondents whose income did not increase, only 3 increased both alcohol and tobacco use and 10 reported no change in tobacco or alcohol consumption.

The impact of friendship change and changes in health behaviours

As a result of occupational and educational transitions, respondents faced new social situations and relationships. New work colleagues were potential sources of friendship and often facilitated young people's movement into new and varied social activities. However, respondents who stayed on at school also often experienced changes in their social networks because of the ways that the schools reconstituted classes and/or because respondents started new academic subjects. It was also relatively common for young people who stayed on at school to lose contact with those who had left. The lives of these two groups of young people appeared to diverge remarkably quickly.

The relationship between respondents' smoking and/or drinking and having friends who smoked and/or drank regularly was statistically significant (drinking $\chi^2 = 25.92$, df = 1, $p = < 0.0005$; smoking $\chi^2 = 28.53$, df = 1, $p = < 0.0005$) and in line with the findings of previous research (Chassin et al., 1986; Conrad et al., 1992; Ary et al., 1993; Bahr et al., 1995). Our data also contained some gender differences with the association between having friends who drank and drinking oneself being stronger for males ($\chi^2 = 18.59$, df = 1, $p = < 0.0005$) than for females ($\chi^2 = 6.40$, df = 1, $p = < 0.05$), while conversely the association between having friends who smoked and smoking oneself was stronger for females ($\chi^2 = 18.87$, df = 1, $p = < 0.0005$) than for males ($\chi^2 = 8.60$, df = 1, $p = < 0.005$).

When asked, during the qualitative interviews, about the reasons for changes in drinking and smoking behaviours, many respondents spontaneously cited a link

Table 4 Movements on the drinking and smoking continua for those whose income rose between rounds 1 and 2 (n = 66)

Alcohol use	Tobacco use		
	Increased	No change	Decreased
Increased	19 (28.7)	14 (21.2)	0
No Change	9 (13.6)	16 (24.2)	1 (1.5)
Decreased	1 (1.5)	6 (9.0)	0

Percentage of those who increased income in parentheses.

between changes in their friendship networks and/or their social activities on the one hand and their smoking and drinking behaviours, on the other. Greater alcohol and/or tobacco consumption was most frequently facilitated by a movement into a new social situation or taking part in a social activity where many other people smoked or drank. This was particularly true when respondents started to spend more of their leisure time in pubs and clubs. [. . .]

Discussion

[. . .] When explaining changes in their health related behaviours, respondents contextualised their actions, emphasising their social contexts and the changes taking place in their lives.

In relation to recent developments in social theory regarding individualisation and reflexivity, the period between 15 and 16 yr is of particular interest and importance. If the central tenets of these concepts are correct then this should be a time when individuals devote considerable energy and attention to the careful construction of their identities and actively choose their cultural affiliations and lifestyles. Consumption patterns, leisure activities and health-related behaviours should all form part of the available repertoires which young people draw upon to actively construct their personal and social identities. In the transition to adulthood this is a key period because young people must decide whether or not to continue in education and/or consider their possible career options. For some young people it is a time of looking for paid employment or of applying to colleges or for training places. As a result young people often find themselves in new social settings and they meet new people. Parents also tend to give their children greater autonomy, particularly if the young person becomes economically independent.

In examining this period of the lifecourse, we suggest that our respondents were far from 'disembedded' from the social structure. They were indeed making important decisions but within a specific socio-historical and economic context. For example, when considering whether or not to leave school at 16, respondents did so in the context of the U.K.'s benefit structure which effectively excludes young people from an independent income (at 16 and 17 yr) unless they are on a Youth Training scheme or fulfil other very specific criteria (DSS, 1993; Lothian Region, 1996; Poverty Alliance, 1996). For respondents, the reputation of Youth Training schemes, together with the lack of full-time employment opportunities, were also important. In the geographical region covered by our study the proportion of young people leaving school and going straight on to a Youth Training scheme at 16 fell from 32% in 1987 to only 22% in 1993. While strictly speaking the young people did make choices as to whether or not to stay on at school their decisions were heavily influenced by their perceptions and the reality of the available alternatives, as well as their previous educational experiences and levels of achievement.

[. . .]

Our respondents' smoking and drinking behaviours were strongly associated with the behaviours of friends, the use of leisure time and changes in disposable income. It was those young people whose core friendship group smoked and/or drank regularly, whose social life revolved around pubs or clubs and whose income had risen who were most likely to have increased tobacco or alcohol consumption. These findings support those of previous studies (Plant *et al.*, 1990; Plant and Plant, 1992; Conrad *et al.*, 1992; Diamond and Goddard, 1995). The majority of respondents smoked a specific brand of cigarettes (Regal) and drank along quite traditional gender lines (males drinking beers and lagers, females cider and spirits). However, our respondents only very rarely cited brand labels or the so called 'alco-pops' as their preferred drinks. The single most often cited explanation for drinking and smoking were that these were social activities conducted with friends. Such behaviours may be seen as forming a part of some young people's lifestyles, but these lifestyles did not occur in a social vacuum or reflect unconstrained individual choices. Friendships themselves were at least partially contingent on other significant factors, such as staying on at school or starting a job. Respondents were aware of the intermeshing of structural, cultural and individual factors, as evidenced in their accounts of their own behaviours. The subjective experience of late modernity does not appear to be one of disembeddedness. On the contrary, we would argue that the process of reflecting on one's actions and choices which the research interview demanded elicited a strong sense that respondents were deeply aware of the structural limitations on their choices, both in terms of lifestyle and economic activity.

Acknowledgements

The study was funded by the Chief Scientist Office, Department of Health (Ref K/OPR/17/7). The Research Unit in Health and Behavioural Change is funded by the Chief Scientist Office of the Scottish Office Department of Health (SODoH) and the Health Education Board for Scotland (HEBS). However, the opinions expressed in this paper are those of the authors, not of HEBS or SODoH.

Note

1   Under the Scottish education system secondary four (S4) is the final year of compulsory education. Secondary five (S5) is the first year of post compulsory schooling (i.e. 16–17 year olds). In Scotland school leaving patterns are also more complex than in England and nearly 30% of pupils are too young to leave at the end of secondary four. These pupils have to stay on until the Christmas after their fourth year ends. Standard grades are the final year compulsory examinations in Scotland.

References

Ary, D., Tildesley, E., Hops, H. and Andrews, J. (1993) The Influence of Parent, Sibling and Peer Modelling and Attitudes on Adolescent Use of Alcohol. *International Journal of Addiction* 28, 853–80.

Backett, K. (1992) The Construction of Health Knowledge in Middle Class Families. *Health Education Research* 7, 497–507.

Bahr, S., Marcos, A. and Maughan S. (1995) Family, Educational and Peer Influences on the Alcohol Use of Female and Male Adolescents. *Journal of Studies on Alcohol*, July, 457–69.

Barnard, M. and Forsyth, A. (1996) The Social Context of Under-age Smoking: A Qualitative Study of Cigarette Brand Preference. *Health Education Journal* 55, 175–84.

Bartley, M. (1994) Unemployment and Ill Health: Understanding the Relationship. *Journal of Epidemiology and Community Health* 48, 333–7.

Baudrillard, J. (1988) *Selected Writings*. Oxford University Press, Oxford.

Beck, U. (1992) *Risk Society: Towards a New Modernity*. Sage, London.

Beck, U. and Beck-Gernsheim, E. (1995) *The Normal Chaos of Love*. Polity, Cambridge.

Bunton, R. and Burrows, R. (1995) Consumption and Health in the Epidemiological Clinic of Late Modern Medicine. In *The Sociology of Health Promotion: Critical Analyses of Consumption, Lifestyle and Risk*, eds. Bunton R., Nettleton S., Burrows R., Routledge, London.

Chassin, L., Presson, C., Sherman, S., Montello, O. and McGrew, J. (1986) Changes in Peer and Parent Influence during Adolescence: Longitudinal versus Cross-sectional perspectives on smoking initiation. *Developmental Psychology* 22, 327–34.

Coles, B. (1995) *Youth and Social Policy: Youth Citizenship and Young Careers*. UCL Press, London.

Conrad, K., Flay, B. and Hill, D. (1992) Why do Children Start Smoking Cigarettes: Predictors of Onset? *British Journal of Addiction* 87, 1711–24.

Dennehy, A., Smith, L., Harker, P. and *et al.* (1997) *Young People, Poverty and Health*. CPAG, London.

Diamond, A. and Goddard, E. (1995) *Smoking Among Secondary School Children in 1994 Office of Population Censuses and Surveys Social Survey Division*. HMSO, London.

DSS (1993) *Income Support if you are 16 or 17*. Benefits Agency and Executive Agency of the Department of Social Security, London.

Furlong, A. and Cartmel, F. (1997) *Young People and Social Change*. Open University Press, Buckingham.

Giddens, A. (1990) *The Consequences of Modernity*. Polity, Cambridge.

Giddens, A. (1991) *Modernity and Self-Identity. Self and Society in the Late Modern Age*. Polity, Cambridge.

Goddard, E. (1990) *Why Children Start Smoking*. HMSO, London.

Gray, D., Amos, A. and Currie, C. (1996) Decoding the Image-Consumption, Young People, Magazines and Smoking: An Exploration of Theoretical and Methodological Issues. *Health Education Research* 11, 215–30.

Hendry, L., Shucksmith, J., Love, J. and Glendinning, A. (1993) *Young People's Leisure and Lifestyles*. Routledge, London.

Irwin, S. (1995) *Rights of Passage: Social Change and the Transition from Youth to Adulthood*. UCL Press Limited, London.

Kwatra, A. and Brown, J. (1996) New look for Thickhead Press Association 5/9/96.

Lash, S. (1992) *Modernity and Identity*. Blackwell, Oxford.

Lee, D. (1990) Surrogate Employment, Surrogate Labour Markets and the Development of Training Policies. In *Youth in Transition: the Sociology of Youth and Youth Policy in the Eighties*, eds. Wallace, C. and Cross, M., Falmer Press, London.

Lothian Region (1996) *Welfare Benefits Quick Guide 1995–6*. Lothian Region Department of Social Work Welfare Rights Team, Edinburgh.

Lyotard, J. (1984) *The Post-modern Condition: a Report on Knowledge*. University of Minneapolis Press, Minneapolis.

Macintyre, S. and West, P. (1991) Lack of Class Variation in Health in Adolescence: An Artefact of an Occupational Measure of Social Class. *Social Science and Medicine* 32, 395–402.

McKeganey, N., Forsyth, A., Barnard, M. and Hay, G. (1996) Designer Drinks and Drunkenness Amongst a Sample of Scottish Schoolchildren. *BMJ* 313, 401.

Millar, M. and Plant, M. (1996) Drinking, Smoking and Illicit Drug Use among 15 and 16 yr olds in the United Kingdom. *BMJ* 313, 394–7.

Morrow, V. and Richards, M. (1996) *Transitions to Adulthood: A Family Matter?* Joseph Rowntree Foundation, York.

Pavis, S., Cunningham-Burley, S. and Amos, A. (1996) Young People and Smoking: Exploring Meaning and Social Context. *Social Science in Health: the International Journal of Research and Practice* 2, 228–43.

Pavis, S., Cunningham-Burley, S. and Amos, A. (1997) Alcohol Consumption and Young People: Exploring Meaning and Context. *Health Education Research: Theory and Practice* 12 (3), 311–22.

Plant, M. and Plant, M. (1992) *Risk-takers: Alcohol, Drugs, Sex and Youth.* Routledge, London.

Plant, M., Bagnall, G., Foster, J. and Sales, J. (1990) Young People and Drinking: Results of an English National Survey. *Alcohol and Alcoholism* 25 (6), 685–90.

Poverty Alliance (1996) *Benefits for 16-17 Yr: the Story of Stacey and the Hypocrites.* The Poverty Alliance, Glasgow.

Sweeting, H. and West, P. (1995) Family Life and Health in Adolescence: A Role for Culture in the Health Inequalities Debate? *Social Science and Medicine* 40, 163–75.

Warde, A. (1992) Notes on the Relationship between Production and Consumption. In *Consumption and Class: Divisions and Change*, eds. Burrows, R. and Marsh, C.. Macmillan, London.

West, P. and Sweeting, H. (1996) Nae Job, Nae Future: Young People and Health in a Context of Unemployment. *Health and Social Care in the Community* 4, 50–62.

West, P. (1988) Inequalities? Social Class Differentials in Health in British Youth. *Social Science and Medicine* 27, 291–6.

Winefield, A., Tiggermann, M. and Winefield, H. (1993) *Growing Up with Unemployment: A Longitudinal Study of its Psychological Impact.* Routledge, London.

11

Accidents and the Risk Society: Some Problems with Prevention

Judith Green

Introduction

[...]

Risk has become somewhat of an obsession in sociology of late, and calculation of risk has been seen as a key characteristic of modern life. In his analysis of the implications of modern high risk technologies, for instance, Beck (1992a, 1992b) claims that we are no longer primarily divided by access to wealth, but by our relative susceptibility to risk. For Giddens risk is the dominant organising principle in contemporary culture: 'To live in the universe of high modernity is to live in an environment of chance and risk... Fate and destiny have no part to play in such a system' (Giddens, 1991: 109).

Castel further argues that discourses of risk have emerged as the technique by which prevention has been made possible as a strategy (Castel, 1991). This focus on the role of risk calculation and its implications for how we perceive fate and destiny seems a useful point of departure for an analysis of current policy in accident prevention. If we can take Giddens' statement as a workable summary of aspects of contemporary discourse, or at least the cluster of beliefs that relate to causality and legitimate ways of imputing it, we find that the accident, as it is conventionally constructed by accident prevention literature, has no place.

What are accidents? In everyday usage, the label 'accident' is used for a large and seemingly disparate range of events. A list of such events might include an industrial injury, an unintended pregnancy, incontinence in children, a broken plate and a car crash. Little unites the outcomes of these events, but they are grouped together by assumptions about their cause. An accident, ideally, is characterised by lack of intention (no one meant it to happen) and by unpredictability (no one knew it was going to happen just then). An accident is apparently something that happens 'out of the blue' that no one can be blamed for.

Health promotion is largely concerned with a particular subset of the misfortunes we label as accidental: those that result in a recognisable injury. These injuries cause a considerable amount of death, disability and distress and the risk factors for them have been the subject of increasing study since the middle of the twentieth century. In recent years national and international policy initiatives have encouraged research into accident rates and interventions to try to reduce those rates. [...] Health promotion operates within a discourse of risk and its management in which the accident, as a random misfortune over which one can have no control, has no obvious place. The accident becomes something other than the unforeseen outcome of coincidence or fate. As epidemiology maps an ever-increasing range of risk factors for accidental injury and their social distribution becomes more exactly known, the accident becomes patterned and predictable. Having an accident results no longer from fate but from ignorance, miscalculation or the deliberate negligence of known risks. Accidents, in short, should no longer happen.

Mountain accidents – an example

The annual statistics produced by the Lake District Search and Mountain Rescue Association (LDSAMRA, 1992) provide an initial example of this contemporary view of accidents as constructed through an analysis of risks. The annual report describes 255 cases of 'Mountain accidents' which occurred in 1991. For each case, details of the type, site and outcomes of the accident, prevailing weather conditions and the time of the call-out are listed. In addition details relating to the victim are given: demographic information, the type of clothing they were wearing, the equipment they carried, and an assessment of their experience. Examples include falls while walking and climbing as well as rescues of those suffering from hypothermia after becoming lost or benighted.

One implication of these data is that there are two levels of cause for each of these misfortunes. First is the immediate cause, for instance, slipping on a wet path or collapse. But before this were the conditions that made such an event more likely, such as the environmental and other factors that can be used to predict 'an accident waiting to happen'. Thus the inadequacy of a walker's clothing is noted, or their lack of experience. Victims miscalculate risks by underestimating the weather; they flout safety by wearing inappropriate shoes and clothing and they display ignorance of risks in their lack of experience. Interestingly, responsibility is not inferred from any causal link between the miscalculation of specific risk and the particular injury sustained. Ignoring or miscalculating risks such as weather or inadequate clothing implies somehow a more general culpability. In one case, for instance, a man suffers spinal injuries and a fractured scapula in circumstances that do not appear to require any particular precautions. His accident happens thus: 'On walk from car park to pose for a photograph, fell backwards over a boulder' (LDSAMRA, 1992: Case 208). It is still noted that his clothing consisted of 'canvas shoes, town clothes' and that his experience was 'doubtful'.

Luck, it seems, has been evaporated in this environment of known (or at least knowable) risks. Indeed it is mentioned only in the context of avoiding the consequences of negligent action. In one case (LDSAMRA, 1992: Case 24), for instance, a man who was solo climbing fell 500 feet and sustained a sprained neck and lacerations to scalp and nose. The outcome was described as 'very lucky' in parentheses, which it may well have been, but there is no suggestion that any of those who suffered accidents may have been 'unlucky' in that it happened to them. Indeed the public information at the end of the report (see Figure 1) explicitly holds the victim responsible. 'British mountains can be killers', it notes, 'if proper care is not taken' (LDSAMRA, 1992: 66). If proper care is taken (a daunting prospect involving predicting not only the weather and the physical environment but also protecting against what the recommendations call 'plain damned carelessness') accidents should not happen.

Health promotion: the reported conflict between lay and professional views

These two strands of risk and preventability resonate with the key concerns of contemporary health promotion. There is a professional voice in the literature on accident prevention that constructs as a foil a contrasting 'lay' voice. The professional construction of accidents (as predictable from known risk factors) engages in a constant dialogue with an off-stage 'lay' construction, which is reported to stress fate and therefore unpredictability. The lay view is presented as only looking at the individual event. This leads, it is implied, to a misguided and anachronistic view of accidents as unpredictable and therefore unpreventable. For health promotion, these lay beliefs form a barrier to be overcome in the campaign to reduce accidents. This can only be achieved if the individual misfortunes that we call 'accidents' are seen as part of a rate – as part of a larger pattern which makes sense.

Here are just a few examples of how this debate is presented in the literature:

> Accidents are not totally random events striking innocent victims like bolts from the blue, although they are often described in this way. Accidents have a natural history in which predisposing factors converge to produce an accidental event. (Stone, 1991: 61)

> It is vital to counter the view of accidents as random events due to bad luck. (Henwood, 1992: 26)

[...] There is, then, a professional orthodoxy that all accidents are preventable, and that it is necessary to educate the public to abandon fatalistic views which hold them to be otherwise. Given that accidents are constructed as essentially preventable events, it may be useful to look at the range of strategies proposed to prevent them before examining the success of these strategies.

Conventionally, the main accident prevention strategies are divided into the '3 Es': education, engineering and enforcement (see, for instance, Cliff (1984)). Education involves raising awareness of risks and how to avoid them. Examples might include road safety training for children or leaflets about hazards in the home. Engineering refers to changing the environment to either reduce the risk of an accident happening or to reduce the damage of an accident that does happen. The development of flameproof material for nightdresses and child-resistant aspirin tops are engineering interventions. Enforcement involves introducing legal sanctions against behaviour likely to either cause accidents or increase the risk of damage from accidents, such as legislation making wearing helmets compulsory for riding a motorbike.

[...] There is some evidence that both engineering and enforcement strategies can reduce the mortality rates from specific hazards. The introduction of legislation to enforce seat belt use for drivers and front seat passengers in Britain in 1983 is one example of an 'enforcement' strategy that achieved the aim of reducing mortality and serious injury to drivers (Department of Transport, 1985). Engineering approaches have also had some documented successes. The introduction of flameproof

British mountains can be killers if proper care is not taken. The following notes cover the <u>minimum</u> precautions if you want to avoid getting hurt or lost, and so inconveniencing or endangering others as well as yourselves.

Clothing
This could be colourful, warm, windproof and waterproof. Wear boots with nails or moulded rubber soles, <u>not</u> shoes, plimsols, or gumboots. Take a woollen cap and a spare jersey; it is always colder on the tops.

Food
<u>In addition</u> to the usual sandwiches, take chocolate, dates, mint cake or similar sweet things which restore energy quickly. If you don't need them yourself, someone else may.

Equipment
This <u>must</u> include map, compass, and at least one reliable watch in the party. A whistle, torch and spare batteries and bulbs (six blasts or flashes repeated at minute intervals signal an emergency), and, in winter conditions, an ice-axe and survival bag are <u>essential</u>. Climbers are all urged to wear helmets.

Company
Don't go alone, and make sure party leaders are experienced. Take special care of the youngest and weakest in dangerous places.

Emergencies
Don't press on if conditions are against you – turn back even if it upsets your plan. Learn first aid, and keep injured or exhausted people warm until help reaches you. Get a message to the Police for help as soon as possible, and report changes of route or time-table to them if someone is expecting you. The Police will do the rest.

Dangers Which Can Always Be Avoided
and should be until you know how to cope with them:
Precipices
  Slopes of ice,
    or steep snow,
      or very steep grass (especially frozen),
        or unstable boulders.
Gullies and stream beds.
  Streams in spate.
    Snow cornices on ridges or gully tops.
      Over-ambition.
        Plain damned carelessness.

Dangers Which May Surprise You
and should be guarded against:
Weather changes – mist, gale, rain or snow.

  Get forecasts, and watch the sky in all quarters.

Ice on paths

  Carry an ice-axe and crampons know how to use them.
Excessive cold or heat.

  Dress sensibly, and take a spare jersey.
Incipient exhaustion.

  Know the signs; rest and keep warm.
Accident or illness.

  Don't panic. If you send for help, make sure that the rescuers know exactly where to come.
Flight of time.

  Learn your own pace. Plan your walk. Allow double time in winter conditions.

It is no disgrace to turn back if you are not certain. A party must be governed by the capabilities of the weakest member.

Figure 1 Live a little longer
Source: Lake District Search and Rescue Association, 1992

material for nightdresses and the child-resistant pill bottle tops reduced mortality rates in childhood from burns and poisoning respectively (Croft and Sibert, 1992) and changes to road layouts to separate pedestrians from motorised traffic have been shown to reduce childhood road traffic accidents (Sutherland, 1992). [...]

In contrast, there has been paltry evidence that educational interventions affect accident rates (Croft and Sibert, 1992). [...]

Research provides few grounds for optimism about the likely success of such approaches. One study of accidents to children (Carter and Jones, 1993), for instance, found no significant differences in either knowledge about safety or even in ownership of safety equipment between parents of children who had had accidents and those who had not. The authors still concluded that what was needed was 'more education', opportunistically at the child health surveillance clinic and during home visits. [...]

Despite such findings, education continues to be offered as a universal panacea for reducing the number of accidents. [...]

In [...] epidemiological research, the implication is that the failure of educational initiatives and prevention policies (or at least their lack of documented success) is attributable to the persistence of lay beliefs that hold accidents to be unpredictable and therefore unpreventable. Sociology has been more concerned with the structural barriers to prevention.

Roberts and her co-workers (Roberts *et al.*, 1992, 1993), for instance, in their work on safety on a Glasgow housing estate, suggested a structural critique of accident prevention strategies. They found that although professionals adopted a model which held accidents to be caused by negligence and believed that more education was needed, parents were actually well aware of risks, in fact more aware of specific local dangers than professionals. They took a considerable range of actions, both individually and as campaigners, to keep their children safe, and of course managed to do so almost all of the time. Education aimed at increasing awareness of dangers merely tends to increase maternal anxiety as hazards were often environmental ones that little could be done about by individual carers: sockets with no on/off switches, balcony railings which toddlers could crawl under and unguarded holes left by workers. In addition to the physical dangers of the environment, the sheer cost of providing all the recommended safety equipment to prevent home accidents was prohibitive for families on low incomes.

Such a structural critique implies one explanation for the persistence of educational strategies despite their lack of success: that they focus attention away from the structural inequalities which pattern accident rates and utilise what Crawford (1986) has called a 'victim blaming' ideology. [...]

Is there a difference between lay and professional perspectives?

Such structural critiques offer a convincing account of the persistence of education as the key strategy of health promotion, despite the lack of demonstrated success. Here, I would like to argue that there is perhaps a more fundamental tension at the heart of the idea of accident prevention that makes failure predictable. This tension is not, as has been suggested by the literature, between 'lay' and 'professional' beliefs, but rather lies within our ideas of the accidental itself. First, although lay beliefs are presented as being about the unpredictability and lack of blame-worthiness of accidents, even the most cursory look at what people say about accidents reflects more ambiguity than this, as is apparent in colloquialisms such as 'it was an accident waiting to happen', 'accidents will happen' and the ironic 'we could arrange for you to have an accident'. Such folk wisdom implicitly acknowledges that accidents are both random, unpredictable events on an individual level, but patterned and predictable at a statistical level. The remainder of this chapter explores this tension using some data from a pilot study on how accidents are constructed as a category of misfortune. The way in which accidental happenings are described and debated suggests far more complexity in our ideas about accidents than the mere persistence of beliefs in fate and luck.

The data used are from interviews with people chosen for their expertise on some aspect of accidents. Many people in modern life have some formal or legitimate role in the monitoring, analysis or prevention of accidents. Six of these interviews were with people who identified themselves as having some professional concern with accidents or their prevention. They were an actuary, an astrologer (with a particular interest in the astrology of accidents), an RAF doctor, two Home Accident clerks (who are the people responsible for collecting statistics as part of the Department of Trade and Industry's Home Accident Surveillance System) and a health visitor. Five interviews were with groups of children aged between 5 and 11, who are the major subjects of much accident prevention, and thus key 'lay' people. All interviews were audio-taped and transcribed. The following is based on an analysis of these transcripts.

What people say about accidents

First, all of those interviewed, whether 'lay' people, like the children, or 'professionals', like the actuary whose work perhaps epitomises the modern mapping of risk, readily identified the kind of event that they would label 'an accident'. They provided definitions which appeared to coincide with the 'lay view' that emerged from the accident prevention literature. They all, in summary, could provide a general definition of an accident which stressed the unpredictability or the blamelessness of the act:

> An accident is something that goes wrong . . . by accident that actually hurts you. (Amelia, age 8)

> Things like electrocuted yourself by accident . . . you can't predict that. (Actuary)

> An accident for me is a bodily mishap that happens to people without any intention of hurt, either on the part of the sufferer or the agent. (Astrologer)

> It's people falling down the stairs, breaking plates in the sink . . . half the time when you ask a question how they done it, they've just tripped for no apparent reason. (Home Accident Clerk 1)

> It's a coincidence, like. Some people get accidents and some don't. (Leroy, age 10)

However, it soon becomes clear that these initial working definitions only serve for ideal or hypothetical cases. When people begin to talk about actual events, they described accidents as neither unambiguously unpredictable nor unambiguously morally neutral.

Unpredictability

First, specific accidents may not be unpredictable: some may appear to be inevitable, as Amelia and Jessica note:

Amelia (age 8):   Some of them are going to happen anyway.
Jessica (age 6):   Yeah, because there might be a bomb and it's got to blow up.

The actuary talked about accidents first as specific events, which could not be predicted and which would, as he put it, 'come out as a sort of blip' in the statistics. But in this respect they were like any of the other uncertainties that he dealt with, and would be averaged out:

> They [life assurance firms] might look at the stats on accidental death and say 'are they significant?' If . . . they were getting a significant number of accidental deaths they would have to [load the premiums] but typically it's the case that things even themselves out. (Actuary)

For him, however carefully the rates of events (be they accidents or any other misfortune) were mapped, you could still not predict any individual event:

> This guy . . . might look as healthy as can be, a good risk, and then he just pops his clogs. (Actuary)

This contrast between the predictable and unpredictable is presented in epidemiological terms by this professional: the argument that population statistics are not very useful for predicting what is going to happen to a particular individual. Other respondents also made a distinction between the predictable and the unpredictable, though, even if not in these epidemiological terms. They talked about different classes of event rather than different levels of measurement.

One of the home accident clerks, for instance, thought that accidents could be divided into two kinds, those that could be prevented because the causes were known:

> I mean most of it is carelessness, but if people could be made more aware perhaps they would, you know, like they've got curly flexes for kettles and so on (Home Accident Clerk 1)

and those about which nothing could be done because they were genuinely random occurrences that were not predictable:

> Some, as I say, I suppose what I call the sensible accidents can be helped. But as I say the children falling from swings, you'll never stop will you? (Home Accident Clerk 1)

Her colleague likewise initially attributed half of the accidents she saw to:

> Stupidity really, carelessness, which half of the accidents come from (Home Accident Clerk 2)

and the other half as 'proper' accidents, which could not be prevented: 'They just happen' (Home Accident Clerk 2). Even these remaining 'ideal' accidents were not, though, purely random occurrences. First, the idea of the 'accident prone' individual serves to reduce the unpredictability:

> My eldest one is always falling down the stairs, always rushing about. I bet she falls down the stairs once a week, honestly. 'Cause she's erratic mainly. There's

nothing wrong with the stair carpet, it doesn't matter whether she's got boots or slippers on. (Home Accident Clerk 2)

Second, other agents, such as local councils who failed to maintain uneven pavements, or the unsafe conditions of local bed and breakfast accommodation for young families, were mentioned as contributing to the conditions that made such accidents more likely. Such agents, as well as the victim, may also be held culpable in the final analysis of the event. Blamelessness, like unpredictability, only described accidents in general. Particular accidents were the subject of considerable moral enquiry.

Moral neutrality

The label 'accident' is awarded only provisionally, and seems to designate an event within the legitimate arena of moral negotiation. It is also a label which is constructed through a process of such negotiation. This negotiation is reported to first be with oneself, for negligence:

> When [daughter] caught her finger in the train door, I thought 'why did we sit in that part of the carriage' – the door slammed and that was her finger... you do feel quite guilty and that – I really thought it was my fault I'd sat her there. (Home Accident Clerk 2)

> I was on a step ladder and thought I was on a stool... and went to step off and I was four feet in the air instead of two feet... It was my fault – stupid, careless! (Home Accident Clerk 1)

Although one might refer to such events as 'accidents' they are clearly not purely blameless events. Only accidents in general could be described as 'no one's fault' and most specific instances could be traced to particular causes, with blame potentially attaching either to the victim or another for negligence. The actuary, for instance, suggested Acts of God as classic accidents, but when asked to think of instances, could only identify being struck by lightning:

> being hit by lightning or something like that, or being drowned at sea would count – or it might do... but it wouldn't be an act of God, it would be an act of negligence on the part of the ship's captain. (Actuary)

Similarly, he said, most traffic accidents would involve some human agency:

> they're a crap driver [or] if their brakes fail, it's the fault of the mechanic who serviced their car. (Actuary)

It is apparent that there are no events that are unambiguously accidental in terms of the definitions first suggested – the term emerges as a provisional category only, and one which is open to negotiation. Indeed, in conversations with children, it seems that stories about accidents serve specifically to organise and debate ideas about moral responsibility:

Maria (age 8): We was sliding down the stairs and I was on her lap and then suddenly I fell down and she fell on top of me.
Anja (age 6): And I bumped my head and it really hurt!
JG: And was that an accident?
Maria: Well it was an accident 'cause we were never told that it would hurt us.

The following excerpt refers to an incident that was related to me by several of the children. The incident involved a boy (whose identity changed in the different performances of the story) who falls from a pole in the playground, injuring himself seriously enough to need hospital attention. Amelia is telling the story with Jessica's help:

Amelia (age 8): People go round that pole sometimes and lots of people climb up and he climbed the pole and he slipped . . . but I wouldn't really say that was an accident.
JG: You wouldn't? Why not?
Amelia: Well, I don't think it was his actual fault because someone had done it before I think, and told him to do it – said like 'I dare you'. I don't think it was his fault, but . . .
Jessica (age 6): . . . he shouldn't have done it.
Amelia: He shouldn't have done it, anyway.

Children of course learn early on how to manipulate these ambiguities over responsibility and blame. This can be simply to avoid blame, as Anja confesses: 'I hit Zara once, but I said "it was an accident"' (Anja, age 6), but also for humorous effect. Richard is one of a group of boys who were busy squashing ants with their fists on the table as I talked to them:

> Like that was an accident – I just tried to stop Leroy killing one, and then my hand accidentally went 'crash'! (Richard, age 8)

Adults who did not seem to recognise the ambiguities of culpability and responsibility could be frustrating, as Jessica notes:

Jessica (age 6): Once Hanifa [class teacher] was chatting with Yesim, because she [Yesim] had hurt her hand, it was cut right there . . . and she was saying 'was it an accident or was it on purpose?' and Yesim said 'I don't know' and Hanifa said 'You must know if it was an accident or on purpose' and Yesim said 'I don't know' and Hanifa said 'just tell me'.
JG: Do you think you always do know whether . . .
Jessica: No, but Hanifa thought you must . . .

Sometimes these ambiguities were followed through to their logical conclusion, and respondents could not think of any actual events that would count as ideal, blameless accidents. The RAF doctor, asked what kind of accidents might happen in training, points to the difficulty of finding a specific event that matches the ideal definition of an accident:

> Let me think of a case. You fly into a hill in cloud, which is always down to pilot error really because he didn't recognise the weather was bad and abort early enough and get up to a higher level. (RAF doctor)

All such events would be investigated by a board.

JG: Does the board ever find it was an accident? Do accidents ever happen?
RAF doctor: I mean basically it can be a mechanical error or a pilot error. There's only two things that can go wrong really, I suppose. The aeroplane or the pilot.

We might suppose that even if such an event had to be officially designated a 'cause' then it would still be unofficially described as a tragic accident. However, the doctor went on to describe a mess room ritual that would happen in the event of a pilot dying in such a crash. This involves, among other things, a ritualistic rubbishing of the dead pilot's professional reputation:

> People start talking about memories of him, and the memories tend to be, 'oh well, he always did take risks', you know, 'you know what he was like he always pushed it'. (RAF doctor)

The notion that an accident could happen to any one in mid-air is perhaps too much for anyone expected to get into a plane every day and fly to cope with. Such misfortunes have to be explained as predictable – and therefore preventable – events.

Prevention

If this group of people, both in their professional and lay roles, agreed that accidents could, at least in theory, be prevented, how did they think this could be done? When I asked children about if and how we can stop accidents happening, they could repeat safety advice they had learnt at school, often as a kind of mantra:

JG: Some of you had some ideas about how you could stop accidents happening...
All in chorus (six boys aged 6 to 11): Look, listen, learn...
Matthew (age 6): Stay in your bedroom...
Several [laughs, loud noises of protest]: Stupid!
JG: So how do you stop accidents happening?
Amelia (age 8): Be very, very, careful.

The adults provided advice that was broadly consistent with the children's accounts of carefulness as the first line of defence:

> With tiny children it [safety] has to be your first priority – you can't be too careful. (Health Visitor)

JG: So can you prevent accidents happening?
Accident Clerk: Yes, by being more careful...

Accidents could be prevented if enough care was taken to reduce risks. However, again, this advice was given in a general sense, and often individual accidents were seen as rather more complex in their causation – or at least the risk calculation involved in preventing them in practice was seen as being somewhat impractical.

Simon, for instance, points to the limitations of Sam's advice on accident prevention in the kitchen:

Simon (age 10):   When I was drying up ... [I was] trying to dry it too fast, and the plate slipped out of my hand, and I got grounded for a week. And I didn't think that was fair ...
Matthew (age 9):   Yeah, and like Sam said ... 'well you should have been holding it with two hands!'
Simon: Well, if I'd been holding it in two hands I wouldn't have been able to dry up, so Sam's a bit wrong!

The other practical limitation to the operation of safety advice was the empirical evidence that it could sometimes be ignored with impunity:

JG: So are there some people who have more accidents than others?
Leroy (age 10):   Like I've never had an accident before ...
Matthew (age 9):   But he was sitting on the chair right ... with two legs up like that – and he could have fallen back and broken his leg!

When pushed to describe how individual accidents could be avoided, children were quick to point to flaws in 'safety first' logic:

Jessica (age 6):   [You could prevent] falling off your bike, because someone could be there to catch you.
Amelia (age 8):   [laughs] I know, but someone might not be there! ... I was just riding along and I knew I was going too fast and I just pulled on my front brake and the back wheel went [makes noise] and I went flying over [demonstrates].
JG: So whose fault was that?
Amelia: I don't think it was anyone's fault, do you? The people who put the tarmac there! [laughs].

Safety advice, it appears, is not particularly useful for preventing specific accidental events. The children's recitation of 'look, listen, learn' suggests another role for safety advice, though. Precautions (be they wearing proper clothing for mountain walking or fixing cooker guards in the home) seem to have little causal relationship with specific accident events, either in research on accidents or in people's accounts of the causes of accidents. They do, however, demonstrate an adherence to the *concept* of prevention. The health visitor, for instance, describes how she burnt her leg on holiday:

> We're on this tiny little motorbike up a mountain – we had a helmet, would you believe – we were the only people in Kos to have a helmet! [laughs], so we took that precaution – but we were wearing only shorts ... I didn't think it would burn me. (Health Visitor)

When they are taken up, precautions are employed as *talismans* against misfortune, rather than as rational or instrumental attempts to reduce specific risk. Wearing a cycle safety helmet or providing a stair gate makes us feel safer not merely because it reduces in any causal way the likelihood of a head injury or a fall downstairs – but because it demonstrates that we did all we could, that we respected the calculability of risk.

Discussion

Both professional and lay people describe particular events as 'accidents' and utilise a working definition of 'ideal type' accidents which suggests that they are unpredictable and unwilled. Such definitions are tenuous, though; describing an event as an 'accident' is only a provisional explanation, pending more detailed investigation of the specific features of a case. This is clear in these everyday stories of accidents described above, in which events are analysed for precipitating factors and possible culpability. The tension between the accident as a random misfortune and the accident as a predictable outcome of known risks is not one between lay and professional accounts. Both lay and professional accounts are inherently paradoxical, in two senses. The first is that the ideal accident is constructed as a blameless event, yet in practice accidents are the subject of considerable debate about responsibility and culpability. There are few specific events that fulfil the criteria of ideal accidents.

Second, to define an event as an 'accident' relies on what are seen to be premodern beliefs (in fate, chance or *fortuna*), yet accidents can only exist within a modern, rationalist cosmology, in which there are known causes for most events and what is 'left over' gets defined as accidental. Accidents are the remnants of our classificatory system, defined not by their outcomes, but by what they are not. An event is accidental not because of any innate characteristics, but because it is *not* something else (a suicide, vandalism, child abuse). Inevitably, such definitions are provisional, since some other future verdict cannot be precluded and the designation is always, potentially if not overtly, in dispute. Even the coroner's officially 'final' verdict on a fatal accident, itself the result of a moral interrogation (Green, 1992), can be the subject of further public and private debate about whether 'accident' was indeed the appropriate classification. It seems that such a category of left-over events is a necessary one as there will always be (in our classification of misfortunes) some events that we cannot explain in terms of predictability or moral intent.

If this perhaps suggests that accidents will not stop happening because there is a need for such a category, it does not explain why specific interventions fail to prevent specific accidents. Castel (1991) has suggested that one feature of risk factors is that they are potentially limitless. In terms of accident prevention, we can certainly produce ever more sophisticated accounts of the risks for accidents: socio-demographic factors, psychological attributes, occupation, leisure pursuits, equipment design faults, etc. There is clearly a tension, though, between what we know to be risk factors at the population level and the logical impossibility of translating that population risk into an individual preventative action. This is not a problem of lay people failing to understand the patterned nature of accidents. Both professionals and lay people recognised this tension, and it seemed that engaging in accident prevention was an activity designed somehow to manage this. In short, preventative actions were taken not in an instrumental way to reduce personal accident risks, but as ritual actions to demonstrate an awareness of population risks.

There is perhaps a search for meaning for all misfortune at the individual level, where a statistical explanation of risk factors will not suffice. The accidental provides a provisional explanation for that which is at the limits of rational explanation. Public health departments have been charged with the thankless task of reducing accident rates through educational strategies. They may succeed in reducing injury and fatality rates for specific types of injuries, although Roberts and others (Roberts *et al.*, 1993) have pointed to some structural limitations to the likely success of this project. There will also presumably always be a category of events that lie outside current explanatory categories – the remnants of our classification systems that we provisionally call accidents. Events may be predictable on a statistical level; accidents are not. Accidents may prove rather difficult to prevent. [. . .]

References

Beck, U. (1992a) *Risk Society: Towards a New Modernity*, London: Sage.

Beck, U. (1992b) 'From Industrial Society to Risk Society: Questions of Survival, Social Structure and Ecological Enlightenment', in M. Featherstone (ed.), *Cultural Theory and Cultural Change*, London: Sage.

Carter, Y. H. and Jones, P. W. (1993) 'Accidents Among Children Under Five Years Old: A General Practice Based Study in North Staffordshire', *British Journal of General Practice*, 43, 159–63.

Castel, R. (1991) 'From Dangerousness to Risk', in G. Burchell, C. Gordon and P. Miller (eds), *The Foucault Effect: Studies in Governmentality*, London: Harvester Wheatsheaf.

Cliff, K. S. (1984) *Accidents: Causes, Prevention and Services*, London: Croom Helm.

Crawford, R. (1986) 'Individual Responsibility and Health Politics', in P. Conrad and R. Kern (eds), *The Sociology of Health and Illness: Critical Perspectives*, New York: St Martin's Press.

Croft, A. and Sibert, J. (1992) 'Accident Prevention – Environmental Change and Education', in J. Sibert (ed.), *Accidents and Emergencies in Childhood*, London: Royal College of Physicians.

Department of Transport (1985) *Compulsory Seat Belt Wearing*, London: HMSO.

Giddens, A. (1991) *Modernity and Self-Identity: Self and Society in the Late Modern Age*, Cambridge: Polity.

Green, J. (1992) 'The Medico-Legal Production of Fatal Accidents', *Sociology of Health and Illness*, 14, 373–90.

Henwood, M. (1992) *Accident Prevention and Public Health: A Study of the Annual Reports of Directors of Public Health Birmingham*, London: Royal Society for Prevention of Accidents.

Lake District Search and Mountain Rescue Association (LDSAMRA) (1992) *Mountain Accidents 1991*, Kendal: Lake District Mountain Rescue Association.

Roberts, H., Smith, S. and Bryce, C. (1993) 'Prevention is Better. . .', *Sociology of Health and Illness*, 15, 447–63.

Roberts, H., Smith, S. and Lloyd, M. (1992) 'Safety as Social Value: A Community Approach', in S. Scott, G. Williams, S. Platt and H. Thomas (eds), *Private Risks and Public Dangers*, Aldershot: Avebury.

Stone, D. (1991) 'Preventing Accidents – A High Priority Target', *Medical Monitor*, 24 May, 61–5.

Sutherland, R. (1992) 'Preventing Child Traffic Injuries', in J. Sibert (ed.), *Accidents and Emergencies in Childhood*, London: Royal College of Physicians.

12

Invisible Women? The Importance of Gender in Lay Beliefs about Heart Problems

Carol Emslie, Kate Hunt and Graham Watt

Introduction

[. . . Coronary heart disease] (CHD) is strongly patterned by gender and social class, as well as by place of residence. At all ages, men have higher rates of CHD than women (see Table 1). However, similar proportions of men and women eventually die of CHD as the disease occurs up to 10 years later in women (Sharp 1994b). The WHO MONICA project monitors trends in CHD amongst people aged 35 to 64 years in 21 countries; recent results show that women in Glasgow in the West of Scotland had a higher 10-year mean coronary event rate than women in any other geographical centre in the study (265 per 100,000 compared to a mean of 103), while men in Glasgow had the second highest rate (777 per 100,000 compared to a mean of 434) (Tunstall-Pedoe *et al.* 1999). Amongst both men and women, socio-economic disadvantage is associated with a higher risk of myocardial infarction (heart attack), and a lower chance of reaching hospital alive after a coronary event (Morrison *et al.* 1997). [. . .]

Some qualitative work has explored the experiences of people who have had a heart attack (Cowie 1976, Radley *et al.* 1998, Ruston *et al.* 1998, Wiles 1998), but little attention has been paid to more general perceptions of heart problems amongst women and men. The only detailed study of this kind explored the social and cultural context of CHD in South Wales in the late 1980s (Davison *et al.* 1991, Davison *et al.* 1989, Davison *et al.* 1992, Frankel *et al.* 1991). Davison and colleagues described the processes by which respondents assessed the possibility and probability of an individual becoming a 'victim' of heart disease. One cultural mechanism which they argued played a central role in lay theorising was the notion of the 'coronary candidate' or the 'kind of person who gets heart trouble' (Davison *et al.* 1991).

However, Davison and colleagues largely ignored gender when discussing 'coronary candidates'. In this paper, we argue that it is vital to pay close attention to gender when exploring lay beliefs about heart trouble, and we present data to support this from qualitative in-depth interviews with men and women in mid-life in the West of Scotland. We examine perceptions of the heart itself, and of heart problems, and explore how respondents talk about people who have had heart disease in their social networks and families. First, we summarise the findings in the South Wales study.

Table 1 Death rates from CHD per 100,000 population in 1997 by age, sex and country

Age	All	25–34	35–44	45–54	55–64	65–74	75–84	85+
Scotland								
Men	296	4	30	144	488	1180	2406	4688
Women	252	1	8	38	153	578	1540	3542
England & Wales								
Men	249	3	23	104	346	959	2179	3971
Women	203	1	5	20	105	417	1238	2773

(CHD is defined as ICD 9 codes 410–414. Source of figures: *Registrar General for Scotland Annual Report 1997*, Table 6.8, and *Mortality Statistics, Cause 1997, England and Wales*, Table 4.

Coronary candidacy in the South Wales study

Davison and colleagues collected their data from three communities in South Wales in 1988 and 1989. A high profile coronary prevention campaign had recently been carried out by 'Heartbeat Wales', which, like much coronary health promotion of the time, focused almost exclusively on individual behavioural change. Almost all of Davison's respondents were well aware of the behavioural risk factors associated with CHD, particularly smoking, eating a high fat diet and lack of exercise. However, this knowledge did not lead simply to behavioural change because respondents assessed this 'new' risk information in terms of their existing ideas about CHD. By noting regularities between individual CHD cases (through personal contact, reports from others' social networks or through the media) and the circumstances surrounding these events, respondents generated hypotheses (such as the notion of 'coronary candidacy') which could be proved or disproved through further observation. The authors judged this process to be closer to the 'questioning traditions of epidemiology than to the certainties of health education' (Frankel *et al.* 1991: 428) and so coined the term 'lay epidemiology' to describe it.

Davison and colleagues argued that the lay theory of coronary candidacy played a central role in helping respondents assess the personal risk to themselves and others, and in explaining why some people developed heart trouble while others did not. Respondents identified coronary candidates (or 'the kind of person likely to get heart trouble') in three main ways (Davison *et al.* 1991). First, respondents took note of physical appearance. People who were overweight, unfit and had a flushed or red complexion were thought to be more likely to be candidates for heart trouble. Secondly, respondents noted the relationship of the individual to the wider social world. This included their family background (people with a family history of heart trouble were more likely to be candidates), their position in the labour market (*e.g.* a stressful job, a sedentary job or hard manual labour) and their place of residence. Finally, respondents noted personal information. People who smoked heavily, ate a very fatty diet, drank large amounts of alcohol or were nervous or 'worriers' were more likely to be candidates. Some of these behaviours were similar to those highlighted by health promotion campaigns of the time. However, in contrast to these simple health promotion messages, respondents recognised that coronary candidacy merely increased risk, rather than inevitably leading to heart disease. Thus, some people who fitted the candidacy profile lived long and healthy lives while others who died from CHD did not have any of the acknowledged characteristics of a 'candidate'. Two categories of individuals illustrate this vividly: 'The fat "Uncle Norman" figure who ... survived into healthy old age, despite extremely heavy smoking and drinking' and '... the slim, clean-living "last person you'd expect to have a coronary" who is then unfortunate enough to succumb' (Davison *et al.* 1992: 682).

The coronary candidacy theory therefore suggests four outcomes (see Table 2). Two of these outcomes are explicable; a coronary candidate becomes a victim, someone who is not a coronary candidate survives. However, it also explicitly acknowledges that some outcomes are inexplicable; some candidates survive (the Uncle Norman figure) while some of those who do not appear to be coronary candidates will succumb to heart disease (the last person you'd expect to have a coronary). The authors summarise it in this way:

> On the one hand is a set of criteria which can be used in the post-hoc explanation of illness and death, the prediction of illness and death, and the assessment of risk. On the other hand, there exists the all-important knowledge that the system is fallible. It cannot account for all coronary disease and death, neither can it account for the apparently unwarranted longevity of some of those that the system itself labels as candidates. Thus the observation that 'it never seems to happen to the people you expect it to happen to' becomes integrated as a central part of the system itself. (Davison *et al.* 1991: 14–15)

Gender is largely ignored in this theorising. Davison *et al.* note only in passing that while 'in general, women are seen as being at less risk than men, it is clear that the candidacy system can be and is applied across gender boundaries' (Davison *et al.* 1991: 14). In contrast, we believe that gender is a key element of coronary candidacy.

Cultural representations of the heart and of heart problems

The human heart has particular symbolic resonance in many cultures. Its special psychological significance in Western culture, and its location in the body, is reflected in the expression the 'heart of things' which refers to the centre of activity in both the English and the French language (Jager 1996). Two seemingly contradictory representations predominate: the image of the heart as a machine, and the image of the heart as the centre of feelings and emotion. Following Ortner's (1974) argument that, to different degrees in different cultures, men are identified with 'culture' (human consciousness or the products of human consciousness, *e.g.* technology) while women are constructed as being closer to 'nature', we can think of these as masculine and feminine images, respectively.

Table 2 Our conceptualisation of Davison and colleagues' theory of coronary candidacy

	Explicable	*Inexplicable or anomalous*
'Candidate' for heart trouble	Victim	'Lucky' survivor ('Uncle Norman')
Not a 'candidate' for heart trouble	Survivor	'Unlucky' victim ('The last person you'd expect to have a coronary')

The feminine image of the heart as the centre of emotional life and of the self can be traced back to ancient Egypt (Walker 1983) and Greece (Erickson 1997). The heart is still associated with kindness and compassion (soft-hearted, warm-hearted), or lack of these virtues (hard-hearted, cold-hearted), courage (brave-hearted, stout-hearted) and, in particular, romantic love (Seddon 1993). The heart remains a symbol of both religious and romantic love despite the rise of anatomy and the development of more mechanistic models of the body (Hillman 1997). [. . .]

The masculine representation of the heart as a machine draws on images of clockwork mechanisms, combustion engines and plumbing systems within the body as a whole (Lupton 1994, Seddon 1993). In the 17th century, Descartes argued that the body followed the 'rules of mechanics'. This led to the body being compared to a machine, clock and engine and the heart being compared to a spring and piston (Synnott 1992). At the turn of the 19th century, Sir William Osler described the typical angina sufferer as a 'keen and ambitious man, the indicator of whose engine is always at "full speed ahead"!' (quoted in Friedman and Rosenman 1971: 303). In the early 1990s, the British government used a modern version of this mechanistic model to advertise a booklet promoting behavioural change based on *The Health of the Nation* (Department of Health 1992). The advertising campaign used illustrations of male and female bodies with cutaway sections showing the mechanics underneath. It suggested that 'with the right maintenance manual, the nation would be a lot healthier'.

[. . .]

The masculine construction of the heart as a machine has been particularly influential in shaping the 'metaphorical character' of heart disease (Price 1983). While emotions are sometimes seen as contributing to heart problems (Clarke 1992) and phrases such as 'heartsick', 'heartache' or 'dying of a broken heart' (Lupton 1994) reinforce this link, the masculine image of the heart as a machine is a much more common construction. Media representations (Clarke 1992) and lay perceptions (Weiss 1997) focus on heart attacks, rather than other manifestations of CHD. [. . .]

The mechanical image of heart problems facilitates its portrayal in morally neutral terms; a heart attack is seen as affecting a specific organ rather than transforming an entire person (Clarke 1992, Weiss 1997). Sontag (1991) suggests that, unlike the stigma associated with conditions like cancer and AIDS, there is nothing shameful about heart disease. 'Cardiac disease implies a weakness, trouble, failure that is mechanical; there is no disgrace . . . A heart attack is an event but it does not give someone a new identity, turning the patient into one of "them"' (Sontag 1991: 8–9, 124). However, this construction of heart disease as morally neutral can be contested. The strong emphasis on individual responsibility in coronary health promotion over the last 20 years has encouraged victim blaming (Davison and Davey Smith 1995).

[. . .]

Methods

Interview respondents for this qualitative research project were selected from a cross-sectional survey of cardiorespiratory disease (MIDSPAN) conducted in 1996 in the West of Scotland (Watt *et al.* 2000). [...]

We [...] wished to examine whether perceptions of heart problems varied by social class and gender, so we interviewed similar numbers of men and women, and similar numbers of contrasting socially non-mobile respondents [*both* respondents and their fathers were either in manual (*i.e.* working class) or non-manual (*i.e.* middle class) occupations]. We wanted to interview respondents at an age where heart disease would have some salience and so chose to interview people in their 40s (all respondents were aged between 41 and 51 years). [...] [O]ur sample comprised 15 working class men, 15 middle class men, 15 working class women and 16 middle class women, [all aged between 41 and 51. For further details, see Hunt *et al.* 2001.

[...]

Findings

The 'mechanical' heart and the 'emotional' heart

Respondents' conceptions of the heart emerged spontaneously from their discussions of heart *problems*, rather than being elicited by direct questioning. They frequently used mechanical metaphors to talk about the heart, comparing it to a car, a clock (or ticker), a pump and a hose. Weaknesses in the machine could exist from the start (such as in a 'defective heart') or could occur over time (for example, through 'leaky valves'). This discourse fitted well with ideas about stress, which was conceptualised as putting extra 'strain' or pressure on the heart or valves. The mechanical metaphor was used most often by middle class men. One middle class man compared a health check to a MOT. Two engineers used language which drew upon their professional background and echoed Birke's (1999) focus on the heart's electrical activity:

Greg: ... [heart problems] are a hidden failure unless you can pick up the signs ... from an engineer's point of view, I would term that as random failure mode. (R36, middle class)[1]
Simon: ... you have an electrical signal to your heart, it'll go to the left hand side and then the right hand side ... (later) A doctor is an engineer of the body. (R3, middle class)

Respondents suggested that it was important that this 'machine' was used appropriately, as both overuse and underuse could cause problems. The potential for repairing these 'faults' depended partly on age; if the machine was young enough, it could be repaired, but eventually wear and tear took its toll and the engine became clogged up or wore out. Kirsty conceptualised the heart as an organ like any other, which can be repaired or replaced (for a price):

Kirsty: ... [doctors] can patch you up, they can repair you, they can give you a new heart, they can give you a new liver and these are all parts of the body that we recognise can deteriorate quickly.... You're not going to change with somebody else's heart, you're not going to change with somebody else's liver, but they could change your character if they started mucking about with your genes. Your genes are you, they're born in you, the other parts, it's like a car, they're you, but they can be repaired or you can buy a new part. (R8, middle class)

Kirsty's account suggests that the location of the 'self' has moved from the heart to the genes. [...]

Other respondents, however, particularly women, still considered that the heart was an organ which held special significance. This significance was expressed in three ways. First, Morag commented that, like her mother, she would not want a heart transplant because 'I don't know if I would like somebody else's heart in my heart' (R13, working class). This contradicts Weiss's [1997] suggestion that hearts are regarded as standardised and so interchangeable. The worry that heart transplants might somehow 'change' people has also been reported amongst heart transplant patients (Boseley and Dyer 1999, Bunzel *et al.* 1992).

Secondly, the heart was seen as an importance source of strength in the body. This view was expressed mainly by working class women:

Josey: I think the heart's a lot stronger than what people realise, a lot stronger, it can take a lot. (R11, working class)
Morag: My gran lived till she was 86, she did bowling up till she was 79 or something... and yet she had a hard life, you know. So really, it must just be to do with your heart... if you've got a strong heart. (R13, working class)

[...] Thirdly, respondents referred to the link between the emotions and heart problems. 'Fiery' or 'nervous' people were seen as more likely to be at risk of heart disease than others, as were people who did not express their emotions (keeping things to themselves). Patricia and Jane explicitly linked romantic love and heart health:

CE: Do you feel prone to [heart problems] yourself?
Patricia: ...my heart has never let me down, it's been broken a couple of times but it's never let me down. (R21, middle class)
Jane: They say when somebody's in love, it's a very physical thing, that the heart slightly gets a wee bit bigger... if you've ever been in love... it's a nice feeling, you act daft, don't you?... so that's a happy acting when you're in love, so... if the good things are affecting the heart and you can feel it... but if feeling bad things, your heart's feeling it as well. I think the mental affects things, worry can affect the heart very much so. (R23, working class)

Gendering coronary candidacy

Respondents in the West of Scotland gave descriptions of 'the kind of people likely to have heart problems' which were very similar to those reported in the South Wales study. Coronary candidates were usually overweight, did not take sufficient physical exercise (and were often in sedentary jobs), smoked heavily and ate a fatty diet. As Davison and colleagues (1991) suggest, the notion of candidacy was used in three main ways. First, to predict coronary illness and death amongst other people:

Gary: You get lorry drivers and (they're) the type to go and sit on their bahookey and then going into cafes and big fry ups, well, what exercise are they getting? They're not burning all that excess fat so that's not obviously helping their cholesterol. (R41, working class)

Mary: (speaking about her male colleagues)...They're absolutely text-book. They're middle-aged, overweight, high blood pressure, very little exercise ehh, and what they say of their diet...chips and pies! (R45, middle class)

Secondly, coronary candidacy was used to explain in retrospect why other people have suffered or died from heart problems:

Shona: My friend's father had a heart attack...she said he was a prime candidate for a heart attack, he had a sedentary job, he smoked at his desk all day long...and he was getting fatter, and fatter and fatter, he was only about 44 when he died. (R14, middle class)

Paul: One of my friends was a taxi driver, a big chap, overweight, always perspiring and always eating fries and I thought to myself, he's heading for a, you know, heart attack and sad to say he did and has since died. (R25, working class)

Finally, and less commonly, coronary candidacy was used to assess one's personal risk of illness and death through heart problems:

Tom: Me probably!...I would be a prime example of a heart condition, 'cause I'm not fit. (R10, working class)

Our data, however, suggested some modifications to Davison and colleagues' work. First, even when asked about heart problems, our respondents almost always concentrated on heart attacks rather than other manifestations of heart disease. Thus, we would argue that coronary candidates are often 'the kind of people likely to have a heart *attack*' rather than 'the kind of people likely to have heart trouble' as Davison *et al.* suggest.

Secondly, Davison *et al.* (1991) note only in passing that, 'after the age of about 40, candidacy is seen to increase with age'. While we found that coronary candidates were typically around late middle age or retirement age, we would argue that age is more salient than Davison and colleagues suggested. A young person dying from, or having a heart attack is, by definition, unusual, so was often cited as an example of an 'anomalous death' (the last person you'd expect to have a heart attack). [...] In addition, the death of an elderly person was often put down to 'old age' rather than a heart attack; in such cases there was no need for respondents to draw on the mechanism of coronary candidacy to explain these deaths. [...]

Finally, and most importantly, accounts of coronary candidacy were structured by gender. Whenever respondents talked about specific coronary candidates, they were invariably talking about men. Only one respondent gave an example of coronary candidates who were women. He commented on 'these lassies that eat the chip butties day in and day out in our office...storing up problems for their heart' (R56, middle class). Given that respondents implicitly regarded coronary candidates as male, we were interested to examine their accounts of individuals who violated the candidacy system.

Inexplicable deaths and survivals

Like respondents in South Wales, our respondents were well aware that coronary candidacy was a fallible system. They also talked about the 'last person' (you'd expect to have heart problems) and the Uncle Norman figure (who does all the 'wrong' things but survives into old age):

Ruby: I mean you get some people who have a dreadful lifestyle but who are very healthy (laughs) and live for years... Others seem to be doing all the right things and still things go wrong, you know that (laughs). I don't suppose there's a hard and fast rule. (R54, middle class)

Both working class and middle class respondents acknowledged the role of luck and chance in this process. Shona's reference to Russian roulette and the use of phrases such as 'beating the odds' substantiate the assertion that coronary candidacy indicates an increased *probability* of heart problems, rather than certainty:

Shona: For every one fit... you think, there's another bloke going about smoking and beer belly out to here and living on for ever and ever and seeming to have no adverse effects anyone can see, what's going on? But that of course, is the kind of Russian Roulette aspect of life, I suppose [later]... There's always one that slips through the net that proves you to be wrong yet again, that proves everybody's theories out of the window. (R14, middle class)

Similarly, Jane's sophisticated analysis explicitly recognises that those who violate the rules of coronary candidacy *are* exceptions; for every 'Uncle Norman' (or 'Uncle Willie') who does all the wrong things and survives, there are 10 who do not survive:

Jane: You'll get somebody, who in spite of everything, can remain healthy, but maybe they're the lucky ones, it's like Uncle Willie smoked to a 100 and drank... but there are 10 Uncle Willies that never made it, so you know, there's a lot of different things going on there. (R23, working class)

In Davison and colleagues' original theory, Uncle Norman is implicitly an *old man*, by virtue of his name and the fact that he has survived to a ripe old age. When a specific Uncle Norman figure was identified by respondents, he was almost always a man. Interestingly, *Uncle* Norman frequently was a relative, often a grandfather. Stories about grandfathers who smoked 'Capstan full strength' but still survived into their 80s were often accompanied by indulgent chuckles.

More respondents gave examples of the 'last person' than of the Uncle Norman figure. Specific examples of 'the last person you'd expect to have heart trouble' concentrated on dramatic (often fatal) heart attacks, rather than other manifestations of CHD. Given that coronary candidates were almost invariably seen as male, we might expect the 'last person you'd expect to have heart trouble' to be female. However, where gender was made explicit, the 'last person'... was always male, making the 'last man' a more accurate description for this group. These examples fell into four categories. The most common group perceived as unlikely coronary candidates were young, active men. Male respondents were much more likely to talk about this group than female respondents. Young fit men in general were discussed, as well as specific examples of athletes and sportsmen. Working class men in particular gave examples of professional cyclists, runners and footballers who had unexpectedly had heart problems. For example, Phil talked about Graeme Souness, a professional footballer:

Phil: I know a few people that have had heart problems and they'd be the last people you'd think, you read in the paper about people that's out jogging and athletes that have heart problems...one of the fittest men you would look at on the television is Graeme Souness, he's had a triple by-pass operation, he'd be the last person on earth you'd think. (R35, working class)

Secondly, both men and women talked about friends or colleagues of around their own age who had died unexpectedly from a heart attack. They often gave quite long accounts of these sudden deaths, reflecting on their friend's health-related behaviours, temperament and job in order to attempt to make sense of why it had happened. In every case, these friends were male. [...]

Colin: A friend a year and a half ago keeled over and died (from a heart attack). 47. He kept himself relatively fit, he walked the dog, he played hockey and came off at half-time and died in the showers. It makes you think, but at the same time he wasn't someone you'd say did anything in excess.... But again there had been quite a lot of stress at work...it had been building up and building up and maybe that was enough to affect him. (R34, middle class)

The third, less commonly invoked, category of unlikely victims were children. More women than men gave examples of the untimely death of children from heart problems to illustrate the extreme difficulty in predicting who will get heart disease. Children were the most extreme example of 'innocent victims' which made the connection between poor health-related behaviours and heart problems doubtful.

Julie: A young kid that took a heart attack and died...I mean, was that a fault in that child's heart that went unnoticed? I say to myself, does it really matter what you do? (R6, working class)

Finally, respondents talked about unlikely coronary candidates within their family. Again, these accounts centred on men, usually fathers, and were characterised by sadness and bewilderment. Respondents in this situation also questioned health promotion messages which equated heart problems with smoking, drinking, lack of exercise and a fatty diet [...] [Iain's] account [is] striking. [He] cannot make sense of [...] [his] father's premature death, given that [he] did not fit the notion of a 'coronary candidate':

Iain: My father died, 52, of a heart attack. He'd never had a heart attack in his life, was fairly fit, never, didn't smoke or drink, he'd a heart attack and died within hours...you can be as careful as you like, because my father never had any heart condition, but two months before he took a heart attack he had a full-scale medical because he was getting a loan to buy a house and nothing was ever shown up in the medical...any time he put on say half a stone...he would just cut down on things, so he was ultra careful...His lifestyle was like that and it happened to him, so as I say, I don't think you can reduce the chance to nil. (R19, middle class)

[...] Thus, gender plays a key role in structuring lay perceptions about who is both likely *and* unlikely to have heart problems. Table 3 shows a summary of the coronary candidacy theory when it is extended to encompass gender. When respondents talked about specific coronary candidates, they were invariably talking about men. Similarly, accounts of the Uncle Norman figure (the coronary candidate who survives) tended to involve men, while accounts of the last person (you'd expect to have a coronary) typically referred to young, fit men. Therefore, three out of the four 'ideal types' (victim, lucky survivor, unlucky victim) in the table are made up of men. The only conceptual space for women in this schema is in the final, 'survivor' category which really exists as a reference point for the other categories.

Accounts of heart problems amongst family members

Given that women appear to be absent from these spontaneous references to 'likely' and 'unlikely' sufferers of heart problems, we turned to respondents' accounts of health amongst family members. [...] In this way, we could explore how respondents talked about female, as well as male, relatives with heart problems. Given the age of respondents, the high rates of CHD in the area in which they lived, and our sampling strategy (half the sample had indicated in an earlier survey that heart problems 'ran' in their family), it was not surprising that most respondents (55/61) reported that they had at least one relative who had suffered from heart problems. [...]

Male relatives – focus on sudden death

Like general descriptions about male 'victims', respondents' accounts of heart problems amongst male relatives usually focused on sudden, fatal heart attacks. Accounts were usually about fathers, but sometimes referred to grandfathers or uncles. The abruptness of these deaths was emphasised by the use of expressive language (*e.g.* 'dropped dead', 'literally dropped like a stone', 'wallop!'). Iain's use of the term 'massive' was typical in describing heart attacks among male relatives:

Iain: [Dad had a] massive heart attack, too much booze, he was out for the night, my mum phoned to say he had collapsed and we just thought he had too much to drink ... actually he had a massive heart attack. (R42, working class)

Respondents also used gestures to illustrate sudden deaths. For example, Gayle, like many others, snaps her fingers to illustrate the rapidity of her father's death:

Gayle: My dad went [clicks fingers] to his bed [clicks fingers] and got up and phoned us [clicks fingers] and [we] came right down, and by the time we got there, he was away. (R40, working class).

Table 3 Figure extending Davison and colleagues' theory of 'coronary candidacy' to include gender

	Explicable	Inexplicable or anomalous
'Candidate' for heart trouble	Victim (Typically a fat male smoker around retirement age who suffers a heart attack)	'Lucky' survivor ('Uncle Norman') (Typically an old man who smokes and drinks excessively)
Not a 'candidate'	Survivor (? woman)	'Unlucky' victim (the last person...) (Typically a young, fit man who suffers a heart attack, or a child)

[...]

Female relatives – focus on limiting illness

In contrast, accounts of female relatives with heart problems concentrated on morbidity, rather than mortality. Instead of sudden, fatal heart attacks, respondents often talked about the ill-health which limited the activities of women in their family, usually their mothers. Often this focused on difficulties with day-to-day activities such as getting out to the shops or dealing with stairs:

Gary: My mum's got angina . . . she's got to use a spray under her tongue especially when she's walking or trying to get up a flight of stairs, three flights of stairs where she stays, and sometimes she's got to use the spray before she goes up the stairs, sometimes she's got to use it when she gets to the top, or she's got to take a break halfway up the stairs. (R41, working class)

Sally: [My grandmother] . . . certainly died when my father was very young . . . someone had moved and stayed up the stairs, and she couldn't go up the stairs to them. Now that was when she had a reasonably young family so her . . . heart must have been pretty bad. (R49, middle class)

[...] When describing fatal heart disease in female relatives, respondents often used much softer, less dramatic imagery than was typically used for describing the cardiac deaths of male relatives:

Rose: It was quite strange when my mum died, she had been washing her hair and . . . she hadn't been feeling great for a couple of days but nothing that kept her in and em she had been washing her hair in the sink and she actually thought she had got cramp from bending over the bath and when the doctor came in that's what he thought it was as well. (R60, middle class)

[...] Alternatively, they stated in a matter of fact manner that their female relative had died from heart problems, rather than using any of the vivid imagery utilised when discussing male relatives:

Cath: Well my mum she had a heart condition for, I think it started in her sixties, but in saying that it was quite a bad thing, it was quite bad angina. I think she'd, it makes it three heart attacks and she eventually died you know of a heart attack. (R38, working class)

[...]

Conclusions

[...]

[...] [Until] recently, coronary health education has ignored women or else targeted them as a means of influencing their partner's risk of heart disease (Sharp 1994a). This may have had important consequences for lay perceptions of CHD. For example, there is evidence that women who experience chest pain are less likely than men to present these symptoms to their GP (Richards *et al.* 2000). [...]

In the last few years, some health promotion material has attempted to make women more visible as potential victims of heart disease. A leaflet produced in 1995 by the Greater Glasgow Health Board explicitly tried to challenge the perception of CHD as a man's health issue (Robertson and Scott 1995). It featured accounts from three women in their 40s who had had heart attacks. Similarly, a recent public awareness campaign by the American Heart Association aimed to publicise the fact that CHD is the major cause of death amongst women, both to the general public and to physicians. [...]

Given their relative invisibility in cultural and medical discourses, it is perhaps not surprising that women were absent from lay accounts of coronary candidates in our study in the West of Scotland. Our data thus suggest that the construction of a coronary candidate is not gender neutral. Asking respondents if there was a 'kind of person likely to have heart problems' was usually translated into 'the kind of person likely to have a sudden, dramatic fatal heart attack', an image associated with men rather than women. This is in stark contrast to the limiting effects of CHD morbidity described in respondents' accounts of the experiences of their female relatives. Interestingly, these accounts mirror the recently critiqued 'grand narrative' in gender and health research that 'women get sicker but men die quicker' (Popay and Groves 2000). In this paper, we have argued that women are 'invisible' in accounts of CHD mortality. However, it may also be that *men* are invisible in accounts of CHD *morbidity*. As Annandale and Clark (1996) have suggested, one danger of dividing men and women into two 'opposite' camps and concentrating on the *differences* between them is that '...women's health is constructed as "poor" against an implicit assumption that male health is "good"' (Annandale and Clark 1996: 32).

It could be argued that respondents' identification of coronary candidates (or the kind of people likely to have a sudden, fatal heart attack) as men is not surprising. Women are much less likely than men to die prematurely from CHD, and sudden death is a less frequent presentation of CHD in women than in men (Manolio and Harlan 1993). Coronary mortality rates in Scotland amongst people of a similar age to our respondents are nearly four times higher for men than for women, and are still three times higher for men than for women aged 55 to 64 (see Table 1). Thus, respondents' experience of coronary deaths amongst their own age-group may be limited to men. In addition, the general population perceive that heart disease is more prevalent in men. A cohort study in the West of Scotland found that 92 per cent of men and 79 per cent of women aged around 35 years thought that heart disease was more common in men than in women. Interestingly, however, similar proportions of men and women (33 per cent and 31 per cent respectively) thought that they themselves were likely to get heart disease (personal communication, Hunt). However, the absence of women from accounts of anomalous deaths from heart problems is more troubling. Given that men (with higher rates of CHD than women at all ages) are identified as coronary candidates, why are women so rarely identified as the 'last person' you'd expect to have a heart attack? If women rarely died from heart attacks, this might explain their invisibility in accounts of anomalous deaths. [...] [T]he prognosis for women after suffering acute myocardial infarction is worse than for men, even after controlling for age and treatment strategy (Chandra *et al.* 1998). Similarly, if very few women died from heart attacks, perhaps we might expect this exclusive focus on men. However, 55509 women (and 66923 men) died from CHD in England and Wales in 1997; amongst half (51 per cent and 52 per cent respectively), the underlying cause was considered to be acute myocardial infarction (ONS 1998).

There are many reasons for women's invisibility in lay accounts of heart problems as well as in cultural and medical discourses about CHD. Here, we suggest just two. First, the intersection of age and gender in the development of CHD may add to the problem. Our respondents tended to attribute deaths amongst older relatives with heart problems to old age rather than heart disease. This attribution particularly affected female relatives with CHD as they usually lived longer than male relatives. Thus, the death of a male relative in his 50s may require further explanations (perhaps in terms of coronary candidacy), but the death of a female relative in her 70s can more easily be put down to old age. Similarly, many past studies of CHD dismissed gender differences in mortality after MI [myocardial infarction] as 'normal ageing' because women were generally older than men (Wolinsky *et al.* 1999).

Our understandings of the impact of CHD, and other diseases, on the everyday lives of older women are incomplete because of the exclusion of both women and older people from research studies (Avorn 1997, Bowling 1999). Many older women face a form of 'double jeopardy' because of their relative lack of power and resources (Young and Kabana 1993). They have lower incomes and are more likely to have worked in lower status occupations than older men. As they are more likely to be widowed and live alone than men of a similar age, they are more likely to require formal or residential care if they are ill or become disabled (Arber and Cooper 1999, Arber and Ginn 1993). In addition, a combination of ageism and sexism means that older women are not particularly valued in our society. They are much more likely to be marginalised, stigmatised or written off as sexually 'past it' than men of a similar age (Foster 1995).

Secondly, Ortner's (1974) theory of how men and women are universally perceived may be pertinent. She suggested that, to different degrees in different cultures, men are identified with 'culture' (human consciousness or the products of human consciousness *e.g.* technology) while women are constructed as being closer to 'nature'. Ortner argues that this comes about because of women's procreative functions (in contrast with men's physiology, which frees them to take up 'the projects of culture'), their 'traditional' social roles (feeding and caring for children – also perceived as closer to nature than culture – in the private sphere) and socialisation. As cultures are engaged in changing and transcending nature in a generalised sense, women are associated with a lower order of being.

This association of men with culture and technology fits in with the notion of heart disease as the pathology of the (male) Fordist body, symbolised by mechanical metaphors. Sudden death, or the breakdown of this machinery, is abrupt and dramatic. In contrast, women's deaths from heart disease are constructed as much more organic, consistent with their association with nature. Accounts of their deaths are often undramatic, and may be perceived as due to old age rather than heart problems. This interpretation is strengthened by Prior's (1985) account of coroners' decisions about 'natural' and 'unnatural deaths'. He found that male deaths were more likely to be certified by a coroner than female deaths, even after excluding violent deaths. He suggests that either 'male deaths are more likely to be regarded as unnatural per se or... males are more likely to die "suddenly and unexpectedly" which is itself a socially structured judgement' (Prior 1985: 74).

Ortner concludes that cultural representations and social 'reality' feed off each other: 'various aspects of woman's situation...contribute to her being seen as closer to nature, while the view of her as closer to nature is in turn embodied in institutional forms that reproduce her situation...a different cultural view can only grow out of a different social actuality; a different social actual actuality can only grow out of a different cultural view' (Ortner 1974: 87).

Here we have argued that heart disease, like cancer, remains 'encumbered by the trappings of metaphor' (Sontag 1991: 5). Cultural representations, lay perceptions, medical research and provision, and health education policies that focus on heart disease primarily as a male disease are intertwined and need to be challenged.

Acknowledgements

We would like to thank the respondents who participated in this study as well as Mark Upton, Catherine Ferrell and Jane Goodfellow for work in establishing the study population of offspring, Carole Hart and Pauline McKinnon for follow-up of the parent generation and Alex McConnachie for help in establishing the sampling frame. Charlie Davison and Kathryn Backett-Milburn provided invaluable advice at different stages of the project. Finally, we are very grateful to Helen Richards, Mike Michael, Sally Macintyre, colleagues at Lancaster University, and the three anonymous referees for their helpful comments.

This qualitative project was funded by the UK Economic and Social Research Council Health Variations Programme, grant number L128251028.

Note

1   Each quote is followed by the interview number (*e.g.* R36) and social class. All names are pseudonyms.

References

Annandale, E. and Clark, J. (1996) What is gender? Feminist theory and the sociology of human reproduction, *Sociology of Health and Illness*, 18, 1, 17–44.

Arber, S. and Cooper, H. (1999) Gender differences in health in later life: the new paradox? *Social Science and Medicine*, 48, 1, 61–76.

Arber, S. and Ginn, J. (1993) Gender and inequalities in health in later life, *Social Science and Medicine*, 36, 1, 33–46.

Avorn, J. (1997) Including elderly people in clinical trials, *British Medical Journal*, 315, 1033–4.

Birke, L. (1999) The heart – a broken metaphor? In Birke, L. (ed.), *Feminism and the Biological Body*. Edinburgh: Edinburgh University Press.

Boseley, S. and Dyer, C. (1999) New heart for dying girl who refused consent, *The Guardian*, 16 July.

Bowling, A. (1999) Ageism in cardiology, *British Medical Journal*, 319, 1353–5.

Bunzel, B., Schmidl-Mohl, B., Crundbock, A. and Wollenek, G. (1992) Does changing the heart mean changing personality? A retrospective inquiry on 47 heart transplant patients, *Quality of Life Research*, 1, 251–6.

Chandra, N. C., Ziegelstein, R. C., Rogers, W. J., Tiefenbrunn, A. J., Gore, J. M., French, W. J. and Rubison, M. (1998) Observations of the treatment of women in the United States with myocardial infarction: a report from the national registry of myocardial infarction-I, *Archives of Internal Medicine*, 158, 9, 981–8.

Clarke, J. N. (1992) Cancer, heart disease and AIDS: what do the media tell us about these diseases? *Health Communication*, 4, 2, 105–20.

Cowie, B. (1976) The cardiac patient's perception of his heart attack, *Social Science and Medicine*, 10, 87–96.

Davison, C. and Davey Smith, G. (1995) The baby and the bath water. Examining socio-cultural and free-market critiques of health promotion. In Bunton, R., Nettleton, S. and Burrows, R. (eds), *The Sociology of Health Promotion*. London: Routledge.

Davison, C., Davey Smith, G. and Frankel, S. (1991) Lay epidemiology and the prevention paradox: the implications of coronary candidacy for health education, *Sociology of Health and Illness*, 13, 1, 1–19.

Davison, C., Frankel, S. and Davey Smith, G. (1989) Inheriting heart trouble: the relevance of common-sense ideas to preventive measures, *Health Education Research*, 4, 3, 329–40.

Davison, C., Frankel, S. and Davey Smith, G. (1992) The limits of lifestyle: reassessing 'fatalism' in the popular culture of illness prevention, *Social Science and Medicine*, 34, 6, 675–85.

Department of Health (1992) *The Health of the Nation. A Strategy for Health in England*. London: HMSO.

Erickson, R. A. (1997) *The Language of the Heart, 1600–1750*. Philadelphia: University of Pennsylvania Press.

Foster, P. (1995) *Women and the Health Care Industry*. Buckingham: Open University Press.

Frankel, S., Davison, C. and Davey Smith, G. (1991) Lay epidemiology and the rationality of responses to health education, *British Journal of General Practice*, 41, October, 428–30.

Friedman, M. and Rosenman, R. H. (1971) Type A behavior pattern: its association with coronary heart disease, *Annals of Clinical Research*, 3, 300–12.

Hillman, D. (1997) Visceral knowledge. In Hillman, D. and Mazzio, C. (eds), *The Body in Parts. Fantasies of Corporeality in Early Modern Europe*. New York and London: Routledge.

Hunt, K., Emslie, C., and Watt, G. [2001] Lay constructions of a 'family history' of heart disease: potential for misunderstandings in the clinical encounter? *Lancet*, 357 (14 April), 1168–71.

Jager, E. (1996) The book of the heart: reading and writing the medieval subject, *Speculum*, 71, 1–26.

Lupton, D. (1994) Representations in culture. In Lupton, D. (ed.), *Medicine as Culture. Illness, Disease and the Body in Western Societies*. London: Sage.

Manolio, T. A. and Harlan, W. R. (1993) Research on coronary disease on women: political or scientific imperative? *British Heart Journal*, 69, 1, 1–2.

Morrison, C., Woodward, M., Leslie, W. and Tunstall-Pedoe, H. (1997) Effect of socio-economic groups on incidence of, management of, and survival after myocardial infarction and coronary death: analysis of community coronary event register, *British Medical Journal*, 314, 541–6.

ONS (1998) *Mortality Statistics, Cause. England and Wales. Series DH2 No. 24*. London: HMSO.

Ortner, S. B. (1974) Is female to male as nature is to culture? In Rosaldo, M. Z. and Lamphere, L. (eds), *Women, Culture, and Society*. Stanford, California: Stanford University Press.

Popay, J. and Groves, K. (2000) 'Narrative' in research on gender inequalities in health. In Annandale, E. and Hunt, K. (eds), *Gender Inequalities in Health*. Buckingham: Open University Press.

Price, J. (1983) Epidemiology, medical sociology and coronary heart disease, *Radical Community Medicine*, 15, 10–15.

Prior, L. (1985) The good, the bad and the unnatural: some aspects of coroners' decisions in Northern Ireland, *Sociological Review*, 33, 1, 64–90.

Radley, A., Grove, A., Wright, S. and Thurston, H. (1998) Problems of women compared with those of men following myocardial infarction, *Coronary Health Care*, 2, 202–9.

Richards, H., McConnachie, A., Morrison, C., Murray, K. and Watt, G. (2000) Social and gender variation in the prevalence, presentation and general practitioner provisional diagnosis of chest pain, *Journal of Epidemiology and Community Health*, 54, 9, 714–18.

Robertson, M. and Scott, R. (1995) Women talking about heart attack, in *Women Talking: a Series of Mini-magazines on Women's Health in Glasgow*: Health Promotion Department of Greater Glasgow Health Board.

Ruston, A., Clayton, J. and Calnan, M. (1998) Patients' action during their cardiac event: qualitative study exploring differences and modifiable factors, *British Medical Journal*, 316, 1060–5.

Seddon, G. (1993) Imaging the mind, *Meanjin*, 52, 1, 183–94.

Sharp, I. (1994a) Attitudes to women and coronary heart disease. In Sharp, I. (ed.), *Coronary Heart Disease: Are Women Special?* London: National Forum for CHD Prevention.

Sharp, I. (1994b) Introduction. In Sharp, I. (ed.), *Coronary Heart Disease: Are Women Special?* London: National Forum for CHD Prevention.

Sontag, S. (1991) *Illness as Metaphor. Aids and its Metaphors*. London: Penguin.

Synnott, A. (1992) Tomb, temple, machine and self: the social construction of the body, *British Journal of Sociology*, 43, 1, 79–110.

Tunstall-Pedoe, H., Kuulasmaa, K., Mahonen, M., Tolonen, H., Ruokokoski, E. and Amjouyel, P. (1999) Contribution of trends in survival and coronary-event rates to changes in coronary heart disease mortality: 10-year results from 37 WHO MONICA Project populations, *The Lancet*, 353, 9164, 1547–57.

Walker, B. G. (1983) *The Women's Encyclopaedia of Myths and Secrets*. San Francisco: Harper and Row.

Watt, G., McConnachie, A., Upton, M., Emslie, C. and Hunt, K. (2000) How accurately do all adult sons and daughters report and perceive parental deaths from coronary disease? *Journal of Epidemiology and Community Health*, 54, 11, 859–63.

Weiss, M. (1997) Signifying the pandemics: metaphors of AIDS, cancer, and heart disease, *Medical Anthropology Quarterly*, 11, 4, 456–76.

Wiles, R. (1998) Patients' perceptions of their heart attack and recovery: the influence of epidemiological 'evidence' and personal experience, *Social Science and Medicine*, 46, 11, 1477–86.

Wolinsky, F. D., Wyrwich, K. W. and Gurney, J. G. (1999) Gender differences in the sequelae of hospitalization for acute myocardial infarction among older adults, *Journal of the American Geriatric Society*, 47, 2, 151–8.

Young, R. F. and Kabana, E. (1993) Gender, recovery from late life heart attack, and medical care, *Women and Health*, 20, 1, 11–31.

13

Beliefs and Accounts of Illness. Views from Two Cantonese-Speaking Communities in England

Lindsay Prior, Pang Lai Chun and See Beng Huat

On the status of lay belief

[...] Patients hold beliefs about illness, doctors know about them. During the 1990s, however, there appears to have been a major reassessment of the ways in which these various terms are ordinarily combined. Most notably, the words 'knowledge' and 'expertise' have come to be freely associated with the lay public as much as with professionals, whilst 'belief' has tended to be downgraded, and viewed as, somehow, a lesser form of knowledge (see, for example, Popay and Williams 1996). This switch of emphasis is appropriate, it is claimed, because lay knowledge is as important as scientific knowledge for an understanding of disease and illness, and consequently is deserving of parity of esteem [...] This contrasts somewhat with earlier standpoints in the sociology and anthropology of health and illness (such as that adopted by, say, Kleinman 1978, 1980, or Eisenberg 1977), which distinguished clearly between lay and professional viewpoints – a distinction that was, in large part, built around the twin concepts of 'disease' (seen as a biomedical reality) and 'illness' (viewed as a social interpretation). [...]

'Belief', in ordinary everyday usage, implies trust or faith or even certainty of some kind. In a late modern world where such notions tend to be regarded as heretical, or, at best, will-o'-the wisp, it is not surprising that the word should accumulate negative connotations (see Good 1994). Moreover, in line with a lack of concern with belief per se, authors such as Popay and Williams (1996: 766), Lambert and Rose (1996: 81) and Brown (1995) are also keen to question the notion that scientific medicine holds the primary vantage point from which health and disease can be understood, or that there are clear lines of division between scientific and lay knowledge (Williams *et al.* 1995: 118).

[...]

In this paper, we wish to outline an alternative approach to these issues. We do so in the context of a study concerning the health beliefs of Chinese people in England. In the first instance, we argue that what is wrong with a focus on belief is not so much that it denies parity of esteem with expert knowledge, nor that it is out of tune with the democratising tone of the postmodern ethic, but that it implies an inner state of believing. That is to say, a focus on 'belief' is suggestive of a psychological state that is somehow locked in individual minds. And although many social researchers refer to belief [...], we suspect that few would claim to have access to inner psychological states of believing or, indeed, of what is 'known'. What social researchers can legitimately lay claim to is 'accounts'. That is to say, they can rightly claim access to verbal accounts of what people believe. Such accounts are most frequently obtained from interview data (ours are obtained from focus group interchanges). Accounts are publicly available. They can be checked and re-checked without recourse to a secret inner mind in a way that beliefs cannot be so checked. And they contain claims and narratives, and identify problems, and their solutions are for one and all to see – so that conjecture about what people inwardly hold to be true or false is unnecessary. Radley and Billig (1996) consider the point crucial and have persuasively suggested that researchers 'shift their attention from "beliefs" to "accounts", in order to analyse what individuals say about health and illness' (1996: 221). [...]

[...] [W]hat ought to be researched in the realm of health beliefs/knowledge is not what is believed or 'known', but rather what it is that is enrolled into people's accounts of health and illness. Of equal interest is whether there are social variations in the enrolling and accounting processes, and what kinds of allies and strategies are drawn upon by different parties to advance their claims and counterclaims about the nature, sources and trajectories of specific forms of health and illness. [...]

In this paper we deal [...] with everyday accounts of health and illness in Cantonese-speaking communities in England. Our task is to map out the kinds of 'agents' that are drawn upon by Cantonese-speaking people to account for health and illness; the frames they use to define problems and to seek solutions to such problems; and how the processes of enrolment and recruitment of agents might vary according to the social location of the speaker. As we shall see, the range of agents available to Cantonese-speaking people is large and varied and the techniques of enrolment are complex. Running through all these processes is, of course, the agent commonly referred to as TCM [Traditional Chinese Medicine] – which is a complex object in itself. What we wish to indicate herein, then, is that what distinguishes the Cantonese-speaking community from others (both lay and professional) is not so much variations in the 'beliefs' that are displayed, but rather differences in the range and nature of objects that are recruited and assembled into accounts of health and illness.

[...]

Methods of data collection

[...]

Our focus groups were recruited in two urban areas: one area in the North of England and another in the South. We shall call them Northtown and Ferrytown.

At the outset we were interested in recruiting groups of males and females in three age bands. These were roughly of people aged 18–21 years, 25–45 years and 60 years or more. Recruitment was executed by a market research organisation. Respondents were recruited on the basis that they could speak Cantonese and that they were not engaged in health-related occupations (we deliberately wished to exclude 'experts'). [. . .] The main characteristics of the focus-group members are summarised in Table 1. The meetings were conducted in Cantonese and to our knowledge this is one of very few pieces of UK health research to be conducted in that language. (Members of the youngest age groups, however, tended to move into English more frequently than we would have wished.) Proceedings were audiotaped and later translated and transcribed (by the second author). [. . .]

Our opening gambit involved asking participants to react to brief and deliberately vague symptom patterns (cf. Koo 1984: 758) that we presented as individual 'cases' of illness. These are summarised in Table 2.

We would emphasise, however, that our brief descriptions were used only as stimulants to discussion, and that the focus-group leader posed direct and more telling questions about understandings of health and illness on the basis of the response to such examples. We used such cases because we felt that it would be particularly useful to ground any discussion about health in terms of specific examples, rather than abstract principles. To our minds, of course, the symptom patterns were suggestive of identifiable conditions, and abstract or generalised (epidemiological) knowledge could have been brought to bear on the analysis of each case had the respondents wanted. Thus the symptom pattern of the young woman was drawn up with an eye to developing discussions about clinical depression (yìyùzhèng) and 'nerves' (shénjingbìng) in the Chinese community.[1] Cases 5 and 6 are suggestive of a malignant growth (áiliú) and so on. Cases were both read out to the participants and presented on a card that was set amidst the tea table. Participants were then asked to discuss three issues. Did the details depicted in the case indicate the presence of a problem that required help in any way? If so, then what kind of help and attention might be appropriate? Where might they best get that help? After about 60 minutes, participants were asked to tell us about 'what makes for a healthy life?'

[. . .]

On the use of treatment systems

Under what kinds of conditions and, by whom, then, is TCM [traditional Chinese Medicine] commonly used? We need to note that three types of treatment system are routinely available to Cantonese-speaking people. First, there is what might be called popular medicine. That is, the medicine that is used and offered within the lay referral system. In our population it is a treatment system that circulates around the use of teas, soups, tablets, herbal preparations and tonics (bûyào). Second, there is Western professional medicine as offered by primary care practitioners or hospital doctors. Finally, there is TCM (zhòngyi), incorporating in itself a wide range of theories, therapies and practices – some medicinal, some physical and some supernatural.

Table 1 Some Characteristics of Focus Group Participants

	Northtown					Ferrytown		
	Group 1 Females	Group 2 Males	Group 3 Females	Group 4 Males	Group 5 Females	Group 6 Males	Group 7 Females	Group 8 Males
Mean Age	19.75	39.5	63.1	32.0	40.0	19.6	32.0	57.6
Age Range	18–21	35–50	62–65	25–39	33–50	19–23	25–36	52–63
Number not Married	8	0	1	1	4	0	4	1
Occupational Locus (Numbers in category)								
NEA+	Nil	Nil	8	Nil	4	2	6	7
Student	7	Nil	Nil	Nil	Nil	5	Nil	Nil
Restaurant	1	5	Nil	1	1	2	Nil	1
Other	Nil	1	Nil	4	6	1	2	Nil
Numbers	8	6	8	5	11	10	8	8

+ Not economically active

Table 2   The Vignettes

Case Number	Summary Description on Card
1	Woman aged 25. Waking unusually early in the morning. Crying without any apparent reason. Loss of appetite.
2	Three month old baby. Vomiting, diarrhoea, high temperature.
3	Woman aged 65. Runny nose, slight temperature.
4	Man aged 45. Dizziness. Headaches. Blurred vision.
5	Female 50. Lumps evident in breast. Otherwise well.
6	Male 50. Lumps evident in upper chest. Otherwise well.

Chinese people are adept at knowing when to use each of these three systems and they are also adept at judging the efficacy of the different systems (Gervais and Jovchelovitch (1998)) for specific problems. And in our work we found that there are markedly different approaches to the suitability of the different systems – approaches that tended to be related to social background (mainly, though not entirely, concerning the age and country of origin of respondents). There was certainly no single and coherent 'Chinese' position on the use of TCM. For example, in discussing the nature of the symptom pattern in our Case 3, the men in Group 4 saw a sequence of possibilities:

Ho: She may use her past experience to prescribe herself some medicine, either Western or Chinese.
Chun: Most people keep some Chinese tablets (zhòng yàopiàn). They may use these first for a few days, then they may see a Western doctor if the tablets don't work.

The discussants in Group 7 saw a similar development, thus:

> For old people, they should buy the Western tablets first, but some old people would take Chinese Herb tea which is more gentle, such as Gam Mo tea for the flu. Western tablets can get quick results … but Chinese herbs take time.

Members of all the groups made reference to the quick results available in Western medicine. Chinese medicine is thus regarded as 'slow', but, for those who approve of it, it is believed to deal with the root causes of disease (jībîng gēnyuán) at a more fundamental level than does Western medicine. Western medicine is quick and effective, but it only mops up the symptoms of disorder – only a Chinese doctor can, for example, truly rid a person of the unhealthy influences that cause disease (xié). Here are two Group 5 women discussing the runny nose symptoms of the 65-year-old:

Tan: … Western medicine (xiyào) has side effects.
Lau: Chinese medicine (zhòngyào) is better, because it is gentle. I think that this woman has wind and fire in the body. Chinese medicine can take the wind and fire out and I believe that only Chinese medicine can cure.
Sen: I agree that Chinese doctors (zhòngyi) are best.
Lai: Western medicines make you sleep.

Despite these references to the use of Chinese preparations and TCM, however, there were clear divisions in the community between those who approved of TCM as a mainstay of treatment and those who were reluctant to call upon it. In general, it was older people and people who had been born in China that sang the praises of TCM. Those born in Britain (who also tended to be younger) often had reservations about the use of Chinese medical preparations and TCM. The following respondent from Group 3 (talking about Case 2) laments her son's loss of faith in Chinese tablets. Referring to minor Chinese medical preparations (zhòngyào), she states:

> Look at our generation. We could manage that type of medicine. Even my son's generation took it. It can cure illnesses. It *really* works, but I never use this for my grandchild. My son does not allow me to give Chinese medicine to my grandchildren.

This reference to a generation effect in the use of Chinese preparations was reinforced in the comments of the younger participants. The latter being markedly more sceptical and wary about the use of Chinese medicine as compared to older people. The following extracts taken from Group 4 illustrate the doubts:

PLC: Would you take your child to see a Chinese doctor?
Mr YING: No. I wouldn't. This is my principle.

A negative position reinforced in the following comment from Mr Young (Group 4):

> I really don't trust Chinese doctors (zhòngyi) because they have no official scientific proof. It is very dangerous. Anyone can be a Chinese doctor. I am not against Chinese doctors, but I would never go to one.

Recruiting Chinese medicine to deal with illness is not, however, simply a matter of age. It also depends on the display of symptoms and other contingent factors. For example, not one of the respondents suggested that the baby exhibiting signs of tùxiè (Case 2) should be treated with anything other than Western medicine (xiyào) administered by Western-trained doctors. There were also numerous suggestions that for any form of acute illness, Western medicine would be superior. Chronic conditions, on the other hand, could well be susceptible to amelioration from a TCM practitioner – though it was often noted that such treatments could be very expensive, and, to that extent, economic factors also impinged on the decision whether to recruit TCM or not.

In sum, then, the responses of Chinese people to treatment systems were pragmatic and eclectic – a stance observed by Koo (1987) in her study of Hong Kong respondents. If a treatment (whether it be Western or Chinese) was thought suitable and effective, then it might be used; if not, then people would move on to another treatment system. Though, as we have noted, some respondents would simply 'never' use TCM. Others found it 'too expensive'. [...]

On lay aetiology

[...]

Contrasting schemes of aetiology were [...] evident. In particular, older people and people who had been born in China (these two groups, as we have been keen to indicate, overlapped considerably) were more likely to refer to what Young (1986) has identified as external factors in the causation of disease. The nature of the climate or the seasons, for example, would figure in their accounts. So too would references to spirits and demons. Among younger people, on the other hand, there tended to be fewer references to external factors and far more emphasis on an ethic of personal responsibility. The latter was in accord with the visions of health and healthiness that we shall refer to later. In any event, younger people tended to identify 'looking after oneself properly' (bàoyāng) as an important factor in health behaviour. Cutting across this age division, however, were references to nutrition and illness. In Young's schema, nutrition probably figures as internal/physiological type of factor. Nutrition can also be viewed as a cure for illness and so tends to have a dual role. Thus, in relation to an understanding of our Case 4 one of the older women in Group 3 stated:

> In the Chinese way of thinking there may be two parts of the [four] basic elements [earth, fire, water, air] missing. If there is a lack of fire and lack of earth, this person needs good nutrition Yes, somebody takes good wholesome food for a few months, he will improve.

Of the externalising factors, the 'environment' appeared in many forms. The quality of air was mentioned most frequently (there were, for example, diseases especially associated with dampness (such as, shibìng)). Clean versus dirty air, and damp air versus dry air were, consequently, some of the oppositions mentioned. The seasons also figured. Naturally, all such references might be read as pointing toward a nascent theoretical scheme that located disease as a product of inter-relationships between the human body and the wider environment – though any such scheme was clearly piecemeal and fragmented. For example, although relationships between humanity and the cosmos occasionally emerged from our discussions, they did not do so in any sophisticated manner. Here is Mr Tu (Group 2) speaking of his grand-daughter's uncle's mother, who, he says:

> ...loses her senses only with the incoming tides. When the tide is high, her madness (diānkuàng) is strongest. This is not very scientific (kēxué), but whenever the tides are high, she is mad.

The references to tides rather than the lunar cycle is distinctive, and the underlying reliance on astrological influences – apparent in everyday occidental, as well as oriental thought (Davison et al. 1992) – is clearly being used to distinguish between folk and expert scientific explanations for changes in affect and behaviour. This same division between what was scientific and what makes sense to 'us' was also evident in other discussions. For example, Mr Su (Group 8), thought that the woman referred to in Case 1 'might be carrying a spell' and continued to say that:

> In Western countries there are no such things. For Asian people maybe there are evil spirits (mózhàng) moving in to the body.

In a similar vein, one of the men in Group 2 stated:

In China, medicine is almost magical [...]. Chinese believe in magical things like spirits (shéndào). Hong Kong has plenty of spirits, they use spirits to cure illnesses. It is the truth.

And Mr Chang (Group 2) spoke of his son (dúshēngzi) when he was ill as a child. In fact, he provided an interesting narrative to account for the illness. Here, however, we concentrate solely on the reference to an evil eye:

The monk [daòshì] said that when my wife gave birth, my son saw something evil and got the illness.

Unlike these older men, younger people were more 'this worldly' in their accounts of illness, though their references tended to be every bit as fragmented and ad hoc as those of older people. Here is an extract from the women in Group 7. They are discussing the man in Case 4:

Lin: Not enough sleep can give you headaches, dizziness and blurred vision.
Kan: Smoking too many cigarettes, drinking a lot of wine and lack of nutrition, or gambling a lot, which leads to lack of sleep and no time to eat.
Ling: Some people go gambling for hours on end. They don't eat. They forget to take water. They sit on chairs until they get piles...

[...]

Framing symptoms

[...]

A world that is seen to hold at least two coherent medical frames (a Western one and a Chinese one) offers potentially fertile ground for the development of opposing views about the nature and sources of illness. Add to that variety of viewpoints a variety of languages and the ground is even richer for such developments. It is not surprising therefore that older Chinese people, in particular, often viewed themselves as being in conflict with the medical professionals that they encountered. [...] Here, for example, is an older male respondent. He points clearly enough to language differences as a source of difficulty, but hidden within the extract is a reference to something else. It is something to do with conceptualising illness as a state of being that involves more than diseases in autonomous organs:

Racism exists.... Western doctors are discriminating to us. Whenever they ask a question they know you can't answer it. For example, my doctor asks 'Are you a headache?' 'Are you a stomach ache?'. It is very quick, rapid, and then he stops. I can't express myself well. Our children are different....

This reported focus of the primary care practitioner on the anatomical site of an illness was regarded by a number of the older Chinese people as peculiar. When Chinese doctors came into contact with their patients, it was claimed, they took into account the whole person and their way of life. Western doctors simply asked where the pain was or 'where it hurt' and then provided a prescription. The criticism is, of course, familiar even in a Western frame. Rather than focus on different interpretations of 'illness', however, what we wish to do here is to draw attention to what Koo has referred to as the 'clinical horizon' (1984: 765). Koo used the term in relation to a discussion of the kinds of things that lay (Chinese) people included within the realm of medicine and illness and the kinds of things that they excluded. One of the most obvious and interesting candidates for testing the level of such a horizon is psychiatric illness and it was to such illness that we turned our attention.

Psychiatric problems are regarded as potentially stigmatising in most cultures. And Kleinman (1980) clearly indicates that a psychiatric interpretation of symptoms is generally shunned in Chinese culture. Serious mental illness (diānkuàng) is certainly stigmatised. Above and beyond that, however, it may be the case that what professionals recognise as symptoms of illness (depressed mood, sleeplessness, suicidal feelings and so on), are regarded by the lay public as non-medical problems – as problems in living perhaps. In that case a 'symptom' may well be recognised as a problem, but regarded as lying beyond the realm of medicine. In order to prompt discussion of psychiatric problems we used our Cases 1 and 4. They were intended to draw out any potential references to depression (yìyùzhèng) and 'nerves' (shénjingbìng). Case 1 involved reference to a female in her early 20s who was displaying symptoms of loss of appetite, sleep disturbance and frequent crying. A number of responses were made to the vignette.

First, we noted that [the] description failed to resonate in any of the male groups. It didn't 'make sense' they stated. They had never come across such things before. In so far as there might be a problem it was a family problem, or a problem in personal relationships and not a health problem. Perhaps the woman had lost 'face' (diū miànzi) and so on. In that respect the 'clinical horizon' of Chinese males certainly did not seem to stretch so far as to incorporate symptoms of the type outlined. Here is one (male) response from Group 4:

> I have never seen this situation before. I have no comment on this . . . but [.] if she cries in front of her husband then she is a whinger. I think that this is a family problem . . .

When the vignette was offered to the female groups, however, the circumstances seemed to resonate immediately. Here is a response from a woman in one of the Ferrytown groups:

> The first time I came to England I felt like I had gone to the moon. I knew nothing. I had rented a tiny room, and when I got up I just stared at the four walls . . . I didn't know why I would cry. I had no appetite and would feel tired. I didn't eat for days. This [pointing to the card that described Case 1] was my experience.

As in the male groups, however, the members of the all-female groups also tended to interpret the apparent symptoms as a product of social problems (especially family problems). It was certainly not regarded as a clear-cut and identifiable health problem. Indeed, even when the word depression was used, it was not at all evident that it was being used in a recognisable clinical sense. For example, one woman in Group 7 stated that the woman in Case 1 was unhappy and 'must be depressed', but she did not think that it was 'because of illness' (bìng zhèng). To that degree, the women in our groups seemed as reluctant as men to site such symptoms in a clinical frame. [...]

Overall, then, it was only in the female groups that the possibility of such things as psychiatric illness and, specifically, depression, were brought into the discussion at any level. So our results would suggest that an understanding of symptom patterns is clearly related to social position (a gender-structured position in this instance). The significance of a speaker's social location also emerged in other features of our discussions. For example, reactions to the 'lumps' in vignettes five and six showed a marked gender differentiation – women suggesting that some form of preventive action be taken and men being more likely to dismiss the notion that such signs ought to be taken seriously. [...]

On being healthy (jiàn kāng)

As was indicated above, questions about what make for a healthy life were left until the end of the focus group sessions. We had originally structured the focus-group membership so as to draw out what we assumed might be contrasting visions of health and illness in the Chinese community (say, between male and female, young and old, British born and Hong Kong born). As far as illness (bìng zhèng) was concerned we certainly saw some social variations. It was, however, something of a surprise to discover on analysis that, as far as images of health were concerned, there seemed to be a remarkable degree of agreement about how a healthy life was to be achieved. The similarity rested in the appeal to 'happiness' as a source of health. A simple content analysis of the translated transcripts, for example, revealed more references to 'happiness' (and unhappiness) in the context of talk about health, than any other factor. References to happiness were particularly marked among the female groups. Thus, the latter displayed an average of 14 citations to 'happiness' in the context of discussions on health, compared to an average of only five citations for the male groups – though none of the males in Group 2 made any reference to the term. Here is a selection of straightforward responses to our request for a discussion about the kinds of factors that might be associated with a healthy life:

Hong (Group 1):   You've got to be happy (kuàilè).

Yau (Group 3):   Having a peaceful feeling, happiness (xingfú), satisfaction, these can make you physically and mentally healthy.

Mr Chung (Group 4):   If your heart is happy then you are healthy.

Ling (Group 5):   If you are happy (kuàilè), have a happy family, have no heavy pressure, then you will be in good health.

Group 6. [With an instant response to the question.].

PLC: I want to know what you think makes people healthy?
KC: Being happy.

Kim (Group 7): The number one thing is being happy (kuàilè).

This focus on happiness and inner contentment implied that it did not really matter how you behaved in relation to what professionals might consider unhealthy activities. If smoking cigarettes made one happy then it was acceptable to smoke. If eating fatty foods led to contentment then that was acceptable also – all in the name of happiness. Some participants, of course, pointed toward other factors as being associated with health (exercise and fresh foods were also mentioned), but the overwhelming concern was with this state of inner contentment. [...] And in order to indicate the presence of some alternative ideas about health we offer an extract from an interchange between two men in Group 8:

[PLC]:   My final question. What do you think brings mental and physical health?
Mr Su: If you practise Tai Chi or Kung Fu every morning, because in the morning the air is fresh and.
Mr Mac interjects: /I don't think Kung Fu is very important. The main reason is if you have a happy family (kuàilè jiatíng).....
Mr Su: /If we want to keep young, physically and mentally we really need exercise and fresh air ... Of course, if your children do not rebel a lot and you can get a happy family...
To which Mr Mac responds: If you are happy, then you will be healthy. If you can laugh and are joyful and peaceful, you are especially healthy and fresh. If you are not happy, it does not matter how good you are in Tai Chi.

[...] [O]n re-reading the last dialogue, we can also catch a glimpse of a notion of 'health' that extends way beyond the physical body and into the social body. For our purposes, however, we merely note that of all the entities that could have been enrolled to account for health, it was an inner state of balance or contentment – a mental state – that proved to be the most popular candidate. In that sense, we can note that whilst there were a wide variety of agents (nutrition, the environment, demons and spirits) recruited so as to account for illness (bìng zhèng), the range of agents recruited to account for health (jiàn khāng) were much more limited. More interestingly, perhaps, we can also see how reference to 'belief' and other mental states such as feelings of being happy, are mobilised into the public process of accounting. In other words, rather than forming the basis for what is said (and possibly done), references to inner mental states (including beliefs) are used as building blocks for accounts. [...]

Conclusion

We opened this paper by making reference to a debate concerning the status of lay belief vis à vis professional knowledge. We noted and documented an emergent argument about the equivalence (or otherwise) of lay belief and professional knowledge. One of the claims incorporated into that argument is that reference to 'belief' downgrades the value of lay interpretation as against expert interpretation. Whether that is indeed so, it is not necessary for us to judge, for we have argued that there are other, and better, reasons for side-stepping a concern with belief (or, indeed, with what is 'known'). One such reason concerns the fact that a focus on belief is markedly psychologistic in emphasis. It concentrates attention on what is supposedly within the minds of individual subjects and thus rests on evidence that is unobtainable. What is obtainable is an account (Radley and Billig 1996). Accounts can be gathered from face-to-face interviews, from naturally occurring talk, or from focus-group interchanges. In each instance, of course, the accounts in question might differ one from the other according to the context in which they are offered – as is apparently the case with expert scientific discourse (Gilbert and Mulkay 1984). As far as focus-group accounts are concerned, it is clear that what people bring forward into the group arena are claims that they consider to be publicly acceptable. They reflect what people think the 'community line' is. As such the method offers another dimension of qualitative data for social scientific analysis. And, as we hope to have shown, they are certainly useful for demonstrating contrasts in the accounts of different social groups (male/female; young and old).

Our attention has, of course, been on what the accounts make reference to; on what is recruited and assembled within them; on what they connect and disconnect; and on how and, by whom, specific items and things are mobilised. As we have seen, many of our accounts recruited TCM and Western medicine as entities to be mobilised. Though detailed consideration as to exactly how TCM was assembled through text, talk and interaction was a problem that lay beyond the boundaries of this paper. Nevertheless, it was clear that the assembly process melded together various agents (materia medica, experts, concepts and theories) and that the mobilisation of TCM was triggered only under certain circumstances – for certain kinds of symptoms and people (vomiting, diarrhoeal babies, for example, were excluded) – and by particular segments of the community.

Yet, whether it be zhòngyàu or xiyào that is sought and used, the conditions that are excluded from the clinical frame of a community are no less interesting than those that are included. In most cultures, of course, wounds and body pains are recognised as things to be included. When it comes to psychological symptoms, on the other hand, opinions often alter. Thus, tears, sleeplessness, irritability and depressed mood and so forth, are often viewed as mere 'problems in living', or social problems that lay beyond medical help. That certainly seems to be the case in the Chinese community. Thus, few people seemed to think that the loss of appetite, crying and unusually early morning waking of the young woman was indicative of a medical problem. Even the somatic symptoms of Case 4 only just managed to find inclusion in a clinical frame (though not a psychiatric one). And it is, of course, in the interstices between alternative clinical frames that what are referred to as cultural syndromes often appear. So what is but an exaggerated social or personal problem for one group, is regarded as an illness (or even a disease) by another. Texts on Chinese culture highlight a number of such syndromes (such as koro and xié bíng), though we have not sought to list them, as they were not mentioned in our focus group discussions. (For further detail, see Prior et al. 1997.) Naturally, mapping the clinical boundaries of a population such as the one being discussed, could well throw considerable light on patterns and rates of primary care consultations in the community. Our major argument, however, is that what is contained within such boundaries is not to be found by examining people's beliefs – nor of what they inwardly 'know' – but is a matter of examining their accounts. Accounts link 'things', concepts and practices together in a seamless web. In that vein sociological health research becomes a matter not so much of dwelling on subjectivity and the inter-subjective, but of examining issues of enrolment, assembly, and mobilisation – in short, what Latour (1999) has referred to as patterns of 'interobjectivity'.

Note

1   Chinese words in brackets are pinyin equivalents of Cantonese terms used in the discussions. See, J. DeFrancis (ed.), *ABC Chinese-English Dictionary*, London: Curzon Press, 1996.

References

Brown, P. (1995) Popular epidemiology, toxic waste and social movements. In Gabe, J. (ed.), *Health, Medicine, and Risk. Sociological Approaches*. Oxford: Blackwell.

Davison, C., Smith, G. D. and Frankel, S. (1992) The limits of lifestyle: re-assessing 'fatalism' in the popular culture of illness prevention, *Social Science and Medicine*, 34, 6, 675–85.

Eisenberg, L. (1977) Disease and illness. Distinctions between professional and popular ideas of sickness, *Culture, Medicine and Psychiatry*, 1, 9–23.

Gervais, M-C. and Jovchelovitch, S. (1998) Health and identity: the case of the Chinese community in England, *Social Science Information*, 37, 4, 709–29.

Gilbert, G. N. and Mulkay, M. (1984) *Opening Pandora's Box. A Sociological Analysis of Scientists' Discourse*. Cambridge: Cambridge University Press.

Good, B. J. (1994) *Medicine, Rationality and Experience. An Anthropological Perspective*. Cambridge: Cambridge University Press.

Kleinman, A. (1978) Concepts and a model for the comparison of medical systems as cultural systems, *Social Science and Medicine*, 12, 85–93.

Kleinman, A. (1980) *Patients and Healers in the Context of Culture*. Los Angeles: University of California Press.

Koo, L. C. (1984) The use of food to treat and prevent disease in Chinese culture, *Social Science and Medicine*, 18, 9, 757–66.

Koo, L. C. (1987) Concepts of disease causation, treatment and prevention among Hong Kong Chinese, *Social Science and Medicine*, 25, 4, 405–17.

Lambert, H. and Rose, H. (1996) Disembodied knowledge? Making sense of medical science. In Irwin, A. and Wynne, B. (eds), *Misunderstanding Science? The Public Reconstruction of Science and Technology*. Cambridge: Cambridge University Press.

Latour, B. (1999) On recalling ANT. In Law, J. and Hassard, J. (eds), *Actor Network Theory and After*. Oxford: Blackwell.

Popay, J. and Williams, G. (1996) Public health research and lay knowledge, *Social Science and Medicine*, 42, 5, 759–68.

Prior, L., See, B. H., Pang, L. C. and Bloor, M. (1997) *The Health Needs and Health Promotion Issues Relevant to the Chinese Community in England*. Cardiff: SOCAS, Cardiff University.

Radley, A. and Billig, M. (1996) Accounts of health and illness, dilemmas and representations, *Sociology of Health and Illness*, 18, 2, 220–40.

Williams, G., Popay, J. and Bissell, P. (1995) Public health risks in the material world: barriers to social movements in health. In Gabe, J. (ed.), *Health, Medicine, and Risk. Sociological Approaches*. Oxford: Blackwell.

Young, A. (1986) Internalising and externalising medical belief systems: an Ethiopian example. In Currer, C. and Stacey, M. (eds), *Concepts of Health, Illness and Disease*. Leamington Spa: Berg.

Part III

Experiencing Illness

Introduction

The experience of illness is a fundamentally personal and private affair. Discomfort, pain and suffering reside within the anatomical frame of the body. And yet, sociological studies of illness have provided a rich vein of data which reveals that illness experience is profoundly social. How individuals identify, interpret, respond to, live with and manage their physical symptoms can vary according to their socio-economic context, their age, gender, sexuality, race and so on. Sociological studies of chronic illness have identified certain themes which appear to be relevant to a diverse range of conditions. These themes and concepts recur in the papers presented in this section. They include the management of illness, coping strategies, normalisation, stigma, the self and identity.

As we discussed in the Introduction to this Reader, there has been a change in the nature of the disease burden in the 'affluent' world. There has been a decline in acute and infectious diseases, and a corresponding increase in chronic conditions. A feature of many chronic conditions is that they are notoriously difficult to diagnose. After all, we all routinely experience symptoms of illness, such as stiffness, dizziness, aches and pains, but we tend to 'explain them away' until they become more enduring and less tolerable. Securing a medical diagnosis can also be a long process; this is especially so for an increasing array of illnesses which are referred to as 'syndromes' rather than diseases – so called because they have no identifiable organic pathology. From a biomedical perspective, diseases which can be 'explained' medically are essentially those which have an organic pathology, and form the basis of the biomedical model, which has its roots in the pathological anatomy developed within the context of the medical 'Clinic' at the turn of the eighteenth century (see the Introduction to Part I). There are, however, a number of conditions which cannot be defined in terms of organic pathology, and are in fact diagnosed on the bases of their symptoms. From a biomedical perspective, therefore, they remain 'unexplained', and are almost invariably contentious conditions. Myalgic encephalomyelitis (ME), which is discussed in our first paper by Cooper, is an example of such a syndrome. Cooper's analysis of the reported experiences of ME sufferers found that they had difficulty trying to secure a diagnosis, that they felt that their condition was not regarded as legitimate, and that their relationships with medical practitioners were particularly problematic.

The imperative to achieve a legitimate sick role status (see also chapter 2 above) is bound up with the moral dimension of illness, as illegitimate illness can be a threat to one's social identity. But so too can certain conditions which are potentially stigmatizing. For example, our identity may be 'spoiled' (Goffman, 1968) if we break social conventions, norms and rules. Nijhof, in his paper on Parkinson's Disease, reveals how the people in his study felt *shame* if they broke certain types of social rules – namely, those which are socially sensitive (e.g. rules associated with eating), those which are especially visible (e.g. involuntary body movements such as shaking and jerking), and those which would result in 'deviant' behaviour. A consequence of this shame was that the study participants reported how they tended to retreat to the security of their own homes and avoid public situations.

Carricaburu's and Pierret's investigation of men's experiences of being HIV-positive is an example of 'a situation at risk of illness'. Although the men in their study were not ill, unlike those in Nijhof's study, they altered their lives in the light of their at-risk status and had to cope with the emotional consequences of clinical risk and uncertainty. Carricaburu and Pierret develop Bury's notion of *biographical disruption* (the idea that the identification of a disease can force one to reflect and reassess one's life) to explore the impact of HIV on both gay men and men who are haemophiliac. From this exploration they further develop the notion of *biographical reinforcement*, which refers to the process of reinforcing components of identity that have been built around haemophilia or homosexuality. Such reinforcement also has a collective dimension. Biographical reinforcement involves not just the reassessment of the personal experiences of individuals, but is also shaped by the history of their reference group (be it AIDS activists or haemophiliacs).

A feature of the contemporary pre-occupation with risk is the emergence of a new health status. Any dichotomous notion of being either ill or healthy is undermined in a context of surveillance medicine where we are all potentially ill (see chapter 9 above). Certain types of risk status can propel people into what Gifford calls 'a grey zone that is between health and disease'. Taking the example of breast cancer, Gifford articulates three notions of risk: epidemiological risk (which is derived from population level data), lived risk (which is based on individuals' experiences of risk), and clinical risk (which involves the clinician mediating between the two). The clinician uses her or his knowledge of epidemiological risk to make decisions about an individual patient. In the case of benign cancer, clinical risk (in this case, benign lumps) can become a condition which has to be treated. Having a risk factor such as a benign lump can therefore be experienced as illness. As Gifford puts it, 'Women speak of risk in the same way they speak of experiencing other symptoms of illness.'

By definition, chronic conditions are incurable, so people have to learn to live with them and manage their illness. The management of illness involves a balancing between a medical logic (adhering to medical treatment and therapy) and a social logic (adapting to social life). The nature of the 'balancing' between such social and medical logics varies between social groups. For example, Atkin's and Ahmad's study of thalassaemia and chelation therapy shows that, for young people, non-compliance with the 'medical logic' can be understood in terms of their family relationships and, in particular, their struggle for autonomy and independence, especially during their early teenage years. It seems that the issue of compliance comes to the fore around the age of twelve, when young people are keen to forge their own identities and reject their parents', and health professionals', definitions of their interests. Over-protectiveness by parents was articulated as a concern for many of the study participants, and was a source of tension within the household. For the most part, the young people were keen to maintain their sense of normality, and were anxious that the illness itself did not form a defining feature of their identity.

Reference

Goffman, E. (1968) *Stigma: Notes on the Management of Spoiled Identity.* Harmondsworth: Penguin.

14

Myalgic Encephalomyelitis and the Medical Encounter

Lesley Cooper

Introduction

In the history of twentieth century western medicine several 'syndromes' have been denied the legitimate status of 'organic disease'. I shall entitle these syndromes 'non-diseases' or 'illegitimate illnesses', because they neither fit the category of organic disease, nor do they have the status of legitimate illnesses.[...] Sufferers often look perfectly well, and standard medical tests fail to find any clearly demarcated abnormalities. For instance, at present there is no accepted definitive test for ME [Myalgic Encephalomyelitis], even though a number of studies have shown that the condition can be diagnosed on the basis of specific highly complex pathologies using extremely sophisticated technologies [...] Given the context of scientific uncertainty, different specialties of medicine, both from within and outside of scientific medicine, construct opposing theories on aetiology which are usually centred on the question of whether the syndrome is primarily psychological or physical.

ME, or CFS [Chronic Fatigue Syndrome] as it is otherwise labelled, is perhaps unique amongst these syndromes in that estimates of prevalence have been much higher than estimates of other diseases – most literature quotes an estimate of 150,000 sufferers in Britain, and it has perhaps been the most vociferously contested of all such 'non-diseases'. In the last twenty years, the disease status of ME has been passionately debated in the scientific and medical community, whilst the controversy has had extensive coverage in the lay and medical press. Those committed to the validation of ME/CFS succeeded in getting the illness recognised by Parliament in 1987 (Private Member's Bill, Jack Ashley), and in initiating a Task Force, a body set up in conjunction with the government and the ME charity *Westcare*. The Task Force Report, published in 1994, validated the condition, whilst the government response to this report in the form of the Royal Colleges' Report on *Chronic Fatigue Syndrome*, published on 2 October [1996] also recognised that the condition existed as a valid illness. However, the latter report decreed that the term ME or Myalgic Encephalomyelitis should no longer be used, and still spoke of the condition as 'existing in the grey area between mind and body' with no single aetiology, and with an emphasis on psychological causes and management.

[...]

Given the background context of political and medical controversy, and the uncertainty of the label, I would argue that sufferers' own understandings and experiences are essential to an analysis of the political and social framework of ME. This paper is an attempt at an uncovering of these experiences. The respondents in the study reported here perceived major problems in their interactions with the medical profession. Their attempts at obtaining a diagnosis were constantly rejected, their symptoms were dismissed and disbelieved, and they were often labelled as bored housewives or depressed adolescents. Consequently, acting no longer as passive agents when their needs were not met, respondents actively pursued their own paths to knowledge and challenged the authority and status of their GPs and consultants. The supposition I wanted to investigate in this paper is that, if patients cannot find in the doctor someone who will diagnose, name, and accept their illness, they are more likely to challenge their doctors, and perhaps the legitimacy of medicine itself than patients with more easily diagnosed 'legitimate' illnesses.

[...]

Methodology

The analysis in this paper is based on the collection of data over a two-year period. This material was obtained through a postal survey of doctors' attitudes to ME, interviews with doctors, researchers and psychiatrists, attendance at international conferences and a review of papers in medical journals. More specifically, for the purposes of this paper, ten life history interviews were undertaken with sufferers of ME. Contacts were made through the local organiser of the self-help group, Irene, with whom a relationship had developed over time. Irene is a fifty-five-year-old, single woman, who has been chronically ill since 1971. She was severely ill and bedridden at the time of initial contact, living on a diet of potatoes and bottled water as she had experienced severe adverse reactions to all foods. Despite this, she was extremely active in running the local group providing advice and information, and organising occasional talks by experts.

[...]

The narratives

In the following discussion of my respondents' narratives it has to be noted that the three male patients had not shared many of the women patients' experiences. Two of the men had found that their GPs accepted their condition without really questioning it, even though they may have preferred not to have it labelled as ME, and one had the good fortune to find the only pro-active GP in the area very early on in his illness career. The numbers of respondents are so few in this study that it would be foolish to generalise on the implications of this observed gender difference.

Most, but not all, respondents related their stories within the broad framework of an 'illness career', and this framework provided a coherence and structure for their stories. An illness career can be defined as a progression of an individual through a series of positions in an institution or a social system, each having implications for the social status of the person concerned. Some respondents introduced other themes into their narratives; one woman, for instance, was concerned with her family's attitudes and reactions to her illness. Nonetheless, a major part of all the respondents' narratives was focused on framing an unknown set of physical and mental symptoms as a problem that could be defined, made meaningful and possibly solved by the institution of medicine, rather than by other means. The typical illness career began with sufferers starting to experience various inexplicable symptoms, severe enough to warrant giving up work or school. Often, because the symptoms were so mysterious, they were ignored or not 'given in to':

> Like most people I refused to give in at first. I didn't realise there was anything wrong. It was May the first symptoms started arriving...I had an ear infection, a terrible ear infection, I was in a lot of pain and I didn't stop working, I carried on...I was in dreadful pain and I think, gradually when you look back you can see all the things falling into place, I started to say things back to front, couldn't count with money, I was getting very tired when I woke up in the morning, it was as if I hadn't been to sleep, all those sorts of things – and it got to Christmas and I collapsed. (GB, 55-year-old, female, been ill 8 years, much better at time of interview)

Respondents often attempted to place their illness and its onset within the circumstances and emotions of their personal lives, so that causes of their illness were attributed to personal stress and traumatic events. One woman who had a Down's syndrome child at the age of 25, associated her illness throughout the whole of the interview, with the stress caused by looking after her daughter. Within the first few minutes of commencing her narrative, she had connected the stress of the birth of her daughter to contracting viral meningitis which developed into what was later diagnosed as ME, even though the latter event was many years after the first:

> She had always been poorly. She wasn't expected to live. I nursed her through so much which obviously really exhausted me. Yes I think it was the fact that I was stressed out and rundown when I got this virus, ... But there again I don't think I'd have had ME if I hadn't had Rachel. (AB, female, 52 years old, been ill 12 years, mobile but did not go very far outside own home)

[...] These attempts to make sense of illness in terms of biographical events are not specific to sufferers of 'illegitimate' illnesses (Williams and Popay 1994: 123), but in the face of uncertainty as to the scientific medical causes of their condition, and what [was] seen as a lack of understanding on behalf of their GPs, they were relied upon to give meaning and structure to an otherwise chaotic world.

Diagnosis

[...] Sufferers in this study found themselves seeing a number of doctors and consultants in an effort to find a diagnosis. The act of diagnosis was seen as a key even in the illness career, and a major part of the narratives was concerned with the difficulties in obtaining an acceptable diagnosis. Tests invariably gave negative results, visits to the psychiatrist proved unrewarding, as did visits to various consultants. Respondents often did not obtain a diagnosis for several years. Irene, the local contact, had become ill in 1971 and was not diagnosed with ME until 1987. A typical comment was:

> It was three years before we knew it was ME. At first we clutched onto everything that might be a diagnosis and no doctor could tell us what was wrong... (EB, 19 years old, female, been ill 6 years, mobile but unable to work or study)

This lack of a credible diagnosis led to problems with employers and family. By not being allowed full and decisive entry into the sick role, sufferers found that their social position was eroded, their social identity devalued and stigmatised, whilst they found it difficult to obtain legitimate absence from work or disability benefit. Interactions with doctors were thereafter conflictual and emotional. Respondents at this point perceived themselves as being at 'rock bottom', where the outlook was bleak and where positive support from physicians was nil. The turning point came when respondents discovered ME, often from newspaper or magazine articles, and diagnosed themselves, or were diagnosed by a 'pro-ME' professional who accepted the condition and recommended management and possible treatment routes. A teenager who had spent years trying to obtain a diagnosis finally read about it in a teenage magazine:

> We read this article in *Just 17* Magazine about a young girl who was ill at home and had got ME... As I read this article I thought this is what I've got and my friends started ringing me up to say it. (EB)

This diagnosis, especially when it was a self diagnosis, marked as it usually was by conflict and denial on the part of their own GP, could be seen as a symbolic turning point in respondents' change in attitudes towards their doctors.

[...]

When symptoms are eventually labelled as Myalgic Encephalomyelitis or Chronic Fatigue Syndrome this is often done in a manner that nonetheless denies the validity of the label. One woman whose daughter was ill, recounted that the paediatrician off-handedly mumbled a diagnosis of ME or glandular fever but said that he did not believe in it, and advised the mother not to get in touch with the ME Society. When another woman tentatively suggested [her] own diagnosis of ME, she was told: 'ME does not exist... it's all in your head!' [...]

Misunderstanding and disbelief

Respondents, with only the rare exception, reported that many people, and particularly doctors, misunderstood the nature of their illness. They complained to their doctors of multiple, vague symptoms, often with little physical sign of an organic disease. Various tests prove negative, and, according to both sufferers and doctors, they did not *always* look terribly ill. These individuals expressed the belief that they experientially 'knew' that something was wrong, and expected their doctors to take this knowledge and transfer it into their own understanding. However doctors and patients did not share the same understanding of simple descriptive terms. When patients talked of 'fatigue', they explained afterwards that they meant something different from what was commonly understood by the term. To sufferers, fatigue means being so tired they cannot brush their hair or even sit up in bed. To doctors 'fatigue' may simply mean a term to describe a common occurrence in the general population as a result of modern-day stress. Thus, what were to the sufferers severe symptoms of pain, depression and fatigue were trivialised by doctors, who saw them as common experiences not worthy of being brought to a doctor's attention. This breakdown of a shared meaning system, where the same term signifies different experiences, led to confusion and uncertainty. The common gap between medical and lay approaches in which neither party can find a common language was widened with respect to ME, where patients' experiences and doctors' understandings appeared to be so markedly incommensurate.

Female respondents gave accounts of invariably being dismissed and disbelieved by their doctors, despite in many cases experiencing quite severe symptoms. They recounted stories of doctors who labelled them as 'malingerers', 'school phobics', or 'bored housewives'. One informant who had worked as a health visitor for most of her life, had this to say:

> I had an hour with this chap and he just insulted me all the time ... He was a consultant physician ... it was obvious from the onset that he was trying to either break me down or I don't know what he was trying to do ... or make me come to my senses or something. But it was a bullying tirade ... that's all I can tell you. It started off with him bumping the table saying 'all right cards on the table now what's wrong with you? Something wrong with your marriage?' (HM, female, age 60 years, health visitor, ill 19 years, functioning and mobile but coughed constantly and still quite unwell)

Often, it was recounted that standard tests done did not reveal any abnormal pathology. Much of the misunderstanding, as far as the patients were concerned, stemmed from doctors' misunderstanding their symptoms as mere depression rather than as a severe physical illness in which depression played just one part. A female sufferer described the attitude of one particular doctor to both herself and her friend:

> I had got a list of symptoms – ... one written down was mild depression. Having to give up work and be ill at the same time was bound to cause a slight depression – I mean I wasn't gaga or on antidepressants or anything but I was fed up having to be at home and not feeling well. Of course having the depression written down on a piece of paper he said 'Oh you women, that's all you ever say ... you're depressed.' 'Bored Housewife Syndrome' that's what he called it. He told my friend she'd got too many children – she'd got four children. He said she got four children ... he told her 'Oh you housewives you've got too many children'. (GB)

[...] Even though relationships with their doctors deteriorated, patients kept on insisting they were ill, as sick role legitimacy and diagnostic certainty were still goals to be achieved and patients had to stay within the state medical system to achieve them. Attempts to attain legitimacy took on a moral face as patients took pains to show that they were really ill and 'good' or 'normal' patients: that they themselves were not deviant although they might have a 'deviant' illness, and that they were trying as best they could to get better:

> One thing also I've learnt is psychiatrists and doctors don't like you in a wheelchair. So my immediate thing I said to him was 'Do you mind if I sit in an ordinary chair?' and he looked at me and said 'Why?' I said 'I feel more normal there'. I didn't tell him, you know, something I had learnt, you know, what I say to them. (Irene W)

Part of playing the game of the good patient was to try and not incite the doctor by 'provoking' him with knowledge procured from other sources, particularly the self-help groups:

> When I last saw him I gave him some literature from ME and he got a bit up-tight. That was the only time I provoked him that far. (TT)

Public myth–private belief: the social stock of knowledge

Sufferers in this study came to their doctor with several expectations and needs. They needed to obtain relief of their symptoms, to have their pain and suffering named; in order to create some meaning out of a confusing plethora of symptoms, and to obtain validation of their illness to achieve entry into the sick role. As part of the social stock of knowledge (Berger and Luckman 1967), sufferers assume that the doctor *should* be able to help.

> I went back to the doctor and she said she couldn't help. I asked 'where do I go from here?' and she just shrugged her shoulders and said there was nothing she could do really. (EB)

Another way of viewing this social stock of knowledge is as myth. Thompson writes about the power of myth as a force that shapes and frames narratives in oral history, arguing for the universality of myth as a constituent of human experience. These interviews can be seen as both expressing and confronting an underlying myth, that of the doctor as a figure of both symbolic authority within society and as symbolic healer within our deeper consciousness. The implicit assumption that the doctor has the authority and knowledge to diagnose is challenged by these respondents in the stories of encounters with doctors as they fall foul of their assigned role. [...]

Fighting back

When doctors fell foul of their assigned role, contradicting the 'stock knowledge' of their patients, sufferers told of a specific turning point in their perception, of a moment of defiance when they challenged not only a particular individual, but their own internalised myth of the 'doctor'. The mother of a young girl who was seriously ill to the point where she could not eat recounted:

> ...that would be the eruption of the volcano if you like cos Dr X the paediatrician in C came to see her the next morning (our GP thought she needed a brain scan), and he came up to Kate and patted her on the head, she hated to be touched, and he patted her on the head and said 'Don't worry Kate we know where your brain is don't we', and walked off. And I was *so angry* I thought I don't care if the whole hospital hears me and I'm not one given to shouting and hollering, but I'd had enough, and he walked off... (AC, mother of KC, 14 years old, ill for two years, bedridden)

A young girl who had been sent to a psychiatric hospital had this to say:

> Yeah, I don't trust them at all, I don't trust doctors, because I knew I was ill and they were saying I weren't and I knew they were wrong...I'm not frightened anymore I used to be but I'm not frightened, I will say what I think, you know...I think actually after the day hospital, I couldn't put up with it anymore I spent at that point two and half years being pushed around by this specialist and that specialist, being pushed around from pillar to post, and I just said 'No More' and that was the turning point... (EB)

Some of my informants had collected their own information. For instance, the health visitor had undertaken her own research using facilities available to her because of her contact with medical institutions. She believed she had more medical knowledge of her condition than her own GP. When sufferers started to take a more active role in the diagnostic process sometimes diagnosing themselves, and pushing for other consultants or doctors who could give a more definitive diagnosis, they recounted that doctors could not accept this threat to their professional knowledge and power, and attempted to retain control not only over the patient but also over their claim to knowledge, often becoming angry and abusive. [...]

When the mother of a young patient asked for a second opinion, from someone who was known to be 'pro-ME', she experienced this kind of response:

> [...] I said 'Could I have this Dr Z?' and he went red in the face, I'll never forget, he was lost for words he didn't know what to say, and in the end I forget what he called him but it wasn't very complimentary – silly old crank or that old buffoon, or words to that effect...and he said 'Oh if you want to see him take her to see him a day out will do her good!' I stood there absolutely speechless, I felt awful, I said to him 'Can't he come and see her here?' 'Not in my hospital!' he said and walked off. He was absolutely furious and he realised that I must have gone behind his back if you like and gone to the ME society even though he'd asked me not to. (AC).

Conclusion

[...] Respondents found it difficult to obtain a satisfactory diagnosis, and because of a lack of diagnosis, they could not get easy entry into the sick role (Parsons 1951). Acceptance into the sick role legitimates an illness. It can also be seen as the ritual exculpation and legitimation of the patient (Young 1981). Naming an illness with an authenticated biomedical disease label is the ticket for entry into the sick role. Thus the *name* becomes the symbol for this legitimation and exculpation. Respondents failed to receive a bona-fide disease label, and thus a full passage into the sick role. Consequently the majority were not allowed passage into a state of legitimate patienthood free from responsibility and blame for their illness state. Also more concretely, their social position was to some extent eroded, their social identity devalued and stigmatised, and they found it difficult to obtain legitimate absence from work or disability benefit.

Furthermore, when confronted by patients who had obtained a diagnosis of ME from elsewhere, or gone to the self-help groups for advice, doctors sometimes became angry and abusive.

[...]

[...] Whilst sufferers may wish their understanding of their own symptoms and bodily experiences, their *illness*, to be prioritised over existing medical knowledge, they still argue for the acceptance of ME as an organic 'disease'. The legitimacy of doctors as holders of authoritative knowledge may be questioned in individual cases. Nonetheless, as a profession which holds the rights to possession of scientific medical knowledge, and as gatekeepers to social and community support, they are not seriously challenged.

References

Berger, P. and Luckman, T. (1967) *The Social Construction of Reality*. London, Allen Lane.

Chronic Fatigue Syndrome, Report of joint working group of the Royal Colleges of Physicians, Psychiatrists and General Practitioners, October (1996). Published by Royal College of Physicians, London.

Parsons, T. (1951) *The Social System*. London, Routledge.

Williams, G. and Popay, J. (1994) Lay knowledge and the privilege of experience. In J. Gabe, D. Kelleher and G. Williams (eds), *Challenging Medicine*, London, Routledge.

Young, A. (1981) The creation of medical knowledge: some problems in interpretation, *Social Science and Medicine*, 15B, 379–86.

15

Parkinson's Disease as a Problem of Shame in Public Appearance

Gerhard Nijhof

> Stories we tell ourselves about what is happening to us are dangerous because they are powerful. Stories come to us from many sources; some we seek, many happen without our notice, others impose themselves on our lives. We have to choose carefully which stories to live with, which to answer the question of what is happening to us.
>
> Arthur Frank, *At the Will of the Body*

[...]

Introduction

If someone shows signs of stiffness, trembling and shaking, these are likely to be taken as the symptoms of Parkinson's Disease. In this medical interpretation, these behaviours are taken to be a sign of a degeneration of parts of the brain resulting in a lack of dopamine. The interpretations of the diseased themselves are not necessarily restricted by medicine. For many chronic diseases, their interpretations appear to differ from those of doctors (for overviews, see Conrad 1987; Anderson and Bury 1988). Strauss and Corbin (1988: 34) speak of a 'mismatch' between the interpretations of medicine and those of the chronically ill. The medical care being offered to the chronically ill often appears not to be tuned to the problems they express.

[...]

The focus here will [...] be on the sequential patterning of the interpreting of Parkinson's Disease. The first question is whether a characteristic interpretation of the disease can be found. The second is whether this interpretation is part of a pattern, a set of related interpretations. If this appears to be the case, the third question will be whether in this pattern 'everyday explanations' (Antaki 1988) for the interpretation can be found. The last question is what consequences of the pattern are drawn from the interpretation.

Method and data

To find patterns in the individual interpretations, a method was chosen which allows informants to speak as freely as possible about their life with the disease. The interviews took place, therefore, in non-medical situations, mostly in the homes of the informants. For this reason we decided not to ask questions, but to invite the informants to tell a story. One of the techniques for gathering such stories is to solicit a 'life story'. In such a form of 'in depth interviewing', the interviewer is as unintrusive as possible to the informant's interpretation (Minichiello *et al.* 1990: 120). The narrative format of the life story allows the informant to speak with minimal interference. The life stories, thus, are not assembled for the reason of obtaining 'life stories', but to obtain free interpretations. The starting question was, therefore, a general one: 'Would you mind telling me about your life with Parkinson's Disease since it was diagnosed?' Only when hitches occurred did the interviewer interfere: as much as possible however, in words the informant had already been using. Questions were only asked for clarification, preferably at the end of the interview.

The influence of the researchers could not be eliminated completely, however. The interviewers introduced themselves as 'researchers from a university' and as 'interested in Parkinson's Disease'. The life stories are likely to be influenced by this knowledge. Our impression, however, was that the informants were speaking rather 'sincerely' (Scott 1990: 22) and felt free to choose their own words. In two cases, however, the partner participated in the story-telling. The life stories in these cases appeared to illustrate 'working together' (see for the collective character of the management of chronic diseases, Fagerhaugh and Strauss (1978); of Corbin and Strauss (1988): 127–66). Interference by onlookers in interviews is regarded as a disturbing factor which has to be avoided. In our research the partner took part in the interview several times, and it appeared difficult to stop this interference. The story of the informants in these cases appeared to be a collective undertaking. The focus on individual interviews in sociology seems in these cases to be artificial and a result of an atomised vision of society.

Life stories are not to be considered as descriptions of life, but as interpretations of it (Denzin 1989; Lejeune 1989). The story-teller is not only 'selecting' his or her own words (Searle 1983), he or she is also guided by the ways of speaking, the 'interpretative repertoires' (Potter and Wetherell 1987: 146–54) functioning in their social world. Life stories therefore are not just personal stories, they are socially constructed.

In these life stories we searched for the processes of social construction of Parkinson's Disease. This construction work was thought to be accomplished in the sequencing or patterning of interpretations. A pattern was conceived of as a set of connected interpretations.

The life stories were tape-recorded. In the text of each of the transcriptions, characterising interpretations of Parkinson's Disease were searched for. Only those interpretations found in a majority of the stories were analysed. In the context of these interpretations, explanations for the interpretation were sought and the consequences drawn from it.

The informants

From the files of a general practitioner, two neurologists and a physiotherapist, 24 men and women with Parkinson's Disease were selected; two were directly approached. The selection criterion required the subjects to be diagnosed as having Parkinson's Disease for at least three years, because it was assumed that their interpretations of the disease would be better developed. Three of those selected refused their cooperation.

The informants varied in age from 40 to 84 years, with a mean of 67.5. Ten were female, 13 male. The time since the diagnosis varied from three to 27 years, with an average of six. Four of the informants lived alone, 19 with a partner.

Shame

In the life stories several patterns of interpretation were found. One interpretation has 'shame' as its characteristic. Indications of this shame were: the direct use of the word itself; words considered as its equivalent, such as 'embarrassed', 'awkward' and 'disgrace'; words like 'terrible' and 'horribly' when used with a disqualifying connotation; indirect references such as speaking of efforts 'to hide' signs of the disease or of 'not daring something' because of the recognition that one will fail to act in accordance with accepted standards; expressions such as 'being noticed' or 'being looked at' when the behaviour referred to is seen as dishonourable; and downgrading descriptions like 'little old woman'.

In 12 of the 23 life stories signs of the disease appear to be related to such indications of shame. One of the informants, for instance, speaks of her shame for not being able to speak normally:

E: I feel ashamed about the way I'm sitting here talking, totally different. (...) Well, I don't talk any more when I'm in a large group, because of the fact that the words come out so awkwardly, don't you think?

Another points to shame because of her need for help when eating:

Y: Suddenly she [the informants' daughter] says, shall I cut the meat for you? I say, please. But then, I am embarrassed towards my environment. I think, won't all people stare at me? You've got that feeling and you get it more and more.

Several of the informants tell of the shame aroused by the physical dependence caused by the disease. For example:

F: I have to hold my wife's arm and lean onto her. It is annoying that suddenly you are a burden on someone, very annoying. Yes you do feel a bit embarrassed about it. That is a big part of it.

One informant points to his being in a poor condition as arousing feelings of shame:

E: I stopped walking in the streets during the day, I found it very awkward to be so visibly in a bad condition.

The shame appears in the life stories as part of a pattern of interpretation, consisting of several elements. In this pattern, explanations and consequences of the interpretation of shame can be distinguished.

Explanation: rule-breaking

Which 'explanations' for the interpretation of shame can be found in the life stories? What do the informants present as the grounds of their shame?

In the quotations expressing shame, the informants assumed that they were break-ing certain social rules. They spoke of their embarrassment for being in need of 'someone else to cut the meat for you', of having 'to lean on someone', of 'the words coming out so awkwardly'. Such utterances can be seen as indicating a breaking of the 'agreed upon rules of social behaviour' (Becker 1963: 9; Scheff 1966: 31).

Other informants speak of their shame for not following the rule of being able to rise up from a chair on your own:

A: It is also when I sit down. Then, I can hardly get up. That's terrible. When you are in a room full of visitors, for instance, and you have to stand up, it's embarrassing.

In all these cases, rules of 'competence' are at stake. Such competence is also spoken of when informants talk of breaking the rules of 'standing upright' and 'not trem-bling':

W: I mean, you can see that I walk strangely, that I can't stand upright anymore, that I tremble heavily. Terrible.

Another competence-rule referred to when interpreting the signs of the disease in terms of shame is 'to control your saliva':

B: Lastly, for already half a year, I have heavy secretion, spittle. It's a horror.
O: But as it changes to slavering and trembling in a corner, I will find that a horror.

Several informants refer to the rule of being able to eat independently, without help. For example:

B: I'm eating with difficulty. My wife has to put the pieces of bread into my mouth.

Eating according to the rules of good manners is also often mentioned:

J: You can take me to a restaurant. If not too difficult things are being served, then I can have dinner with you as usual, without people thinking: what is that old man sitting there, sopping and messing around.

Several times the rule of being able to speak normally is referred to:

E: But it's specially with speaking that I have difficulties. I keep my mouth shut. When there are visitors, then my wife speaks. Yes, because I can't speak so well. I have the feeling that people notice. Isn't it? Don't you notice it?

The rule of competence in social presentation, of a fit between one's situation and the facial expression, is also alluded to. Looking angry in situations not regarded as aggressive is mentioned as a violation of this rule:

M: Because of the stiffness of my face, people look at me. A boy, sitting opposite to me in a bus, asked his mother, why is it that this man looks so angry? I feel specially awkward in such a situation.

In many of such utterances, the informants relate their assumed rule-breaking to shame. A. speaks for instance of his 'embarrassment' when he indicates not being able to get up from a chair. M. expresses his 'awkwardness', when being stared at because of the stiffness of his face. Breaking rules appears to these informants as an explanation for their shame.

Conditions

However, there are also utterances of rule-breaking in which no explicit reference to shame is made. Obviously, the breaking of social rules is not always considered as causing shame. In the life stories three conditions are referred to when offering rule-breaking as an explanation for shame: the sensitivity of the rules; the public character of the behaviour; and the assumed labelling as a deviant.

1.   Valued rules of social competence

It appears to be the breaking of specific kinds of rules which is presented as a condition for shame. The rules the informants believe they are breaking have several characteristics in common.

Firstly, rules are seen as regulating everyday life. Everyday situations, such as speaking and eating, are mentioned. Secondly, the rules seem to be taken for granted. They are never mentioned explicitly, and never discussed, probably as a result of the internalisation of norms relating to physical, public behaviour and communicative competence. The interpretation of Parkinson's Disease as a problem of shame has its source not only in the breaking of rules belonging to prevalent social opinion, but to rules belonging to the selves which 'represent this social opinion' (Elias 1978: 292). Thirdly, most of the rules the informants mention refer to the need of behaving as an adult, for example, when they speak of their shame for needing help during meals. Most of the rules pointed out, appear to discriminate between the behaviour of children and adults. Fourthly, the rules mentioned are seen as representing sensitive social values, such as independence, competence and decency.

These informants seem to assume that the capacity to follow those everyday rules for adult behaviour, taken for granted but highly valued, is a condition for being a socially competent member of everyday society. Because they break these rules, they see themselves as socially incompetent. They appear to interpret the signs of the disease not primarily as a cause of physical, but of social, disability. The problem of Parkinson's Disease appears for them to be the defiance of valued rules of social competence.

2.   Public exposure

However, the breaking of the valued rules of social competence as such is not presented as a sufficient explanation of their shame. Almost all the rule-breakers locate their problems in the 'outside world':

G: In the beginning, when my Parkinson started, I had a lot of difficulties with the outside world. If you are in a hurry, your leg begins to swing, especially the left side. You can see that. If you are in the street it can happen quite involuntarily.

In the utterances of shame there is almost always a reference to a special kind of outside world: the 'public' domain. E. speaks of his words coming out so awkwardly when talking 'in a large group'; I. tells of her embarrassment when, being helped 'in a restaurant', she asks herself: 'Won't all the people stare at me?' Also, the rule-breaking mentioned by the informants is predominantly located in what can be described as the public world. The informants speak of 'the street', 'parties', 'visitors', and 'the bus', as places where the rule-breaking occurs.

Almost all the informants say that in the beginning they tried to hide, as much as possible, the public appearance of the signs of their disease:

G: You also hide yourself in the beginning. I always bought shirts and trousers with pockets.
T: [his wife] But in the beginning, he used to hide his hand. He hid it behind his back. Or he held one hand with the other.

Later, when hiding is regarded as no longer successful, Parkinson's Disease is described as a problem of public appearance. For example:

T: When we were having dinner with others, they sometimes used to stare at him. He was trying to eat. It doesn't work of course. He jerked a lot then. And they then began staring so much.

Utterances like this point to a domain where the breaking of rules is 'visible'. With this assumed visibility, it becomes a public affair: 'everybody sees it':

W: I was very good in disguising it. But one day, I went to the hair-dresser and he says, you must have a terrible back pain. I said, no, why? He said, you are walking very slowly. I said, I cannot walk fast at all. So then, yes, I was disguising it for myself. I found it terrible. Of course, you cannot hide anything. Whatever you wear, I mean, everybody sees it. You start to walk with difficulty, you start to act more crazily. I found that very hard. And, well, yes, the hanging over while walking, too. So it is definitely something you cannot disguise. Everybody sees it. You cannot say, as if it is a bad scar, I'm going to wear a dress. Everybody sees it.

It is due in part to the visibility of the rule-breaking behaviour, and thus the public disclosure of their social incompetence, that informants try to disguise their rule-breaking. It is this public disclosure which is seen as causing shame.

3. Labelled as deviant

It is not only the visibility of their rule-breaking which is said to be an explanation for shame; the assumed reactions of others are also brought into focus when informants speak of their shame. Those informants who mention the visibility of their behaviour often assume they are publicly labelled as 'a deviant'. *J.*, for example, is afraid of being viewed as 'an old man' when eating in a restaurant. Another informant feels embarrassed, when she assumes being seen as 'a thief':

W: Sometimes I have to sign my cheque. Then I think, these people must at least think I have stolen the cheque. . . . It's embarrassing.

G. talks of finding it terrible to be seen as a 'little old woman' because of the physical signs of her disease:

G: Yes, then I really got a fright [when the informant saw herself on a video]. I thought, is that me? Yes, that was terrible. I don't know that. No, that I was so . . . , a bit lopsided. Then I really thought, well, what does it mean, a little old woman? Yes, yes, terrible.

Thus, a third condition is added for the interpretation of rule-breaking as shameful: the assumed labelling as a deviant.

Consequences

In the pattern of interpretation involving shame, the informants not only explain the shame, they also allude to its consequences. Two are said to be attached to the shame Parkinson's Disease brings with it: a split of the life world into a 'public' and a 'private' domain; and a 'retreat' from the public domain.

1.   A split of the life world

The informants who speak of the disease in terms of shame appeared to attack this interpretation of their behaviour in the public world. This world is spoken of according to the double meaning Giddens (1991: 151–3) attaches to it. On the one hand there is a reference to people looking; what Giddens characterises as 'surveillance'. On the other hand the informants refer to a world where their behaviour is best concealed; 'not revealed' in Giddens' terms. It is in these public worlds that shame is said to arise.

In situations which are regarded as less public in character, the signs of the disease lose their shamefulness. In the private world described as 'at home', as being 'familiar' and 'safe', rule-breaking, deviancy and shame are never mentioned in the life stories. Through the ascription of shame to public life, Parkinson's Disease is constructed as a 'located illness'.

2.   Retreat

Almost all the informants who speak of shame in the public world also mention gradually giving up their participation in it:

Y: I used to like going out for dinner with the children, but I don't dare anymore. Then, I'm sitting there, fumbling, being all clumsy. You can do that at home, but not in a restaurant. No, I don't dare anymore. The children mind that I won't go anymore. But I already have towels which are used as a bib!

Others speak of their inclination to retreat from the public into the private world where the rules of competence seem to be regarded as less valid and their rule-breaking behaviour to be more easily tolerated. Shame discourages them from appearing in public any more:

N: I prefer to stay at home. I cannot bear the confrontation with others any more.

Some consider their withdrawal as ending in isolation:

Y: So you start to seclude yourself more and more, which isn't good. But what should I do? Gradually you start to feel a loner, I feel that myself as well.

The shame attributed to Parkinson's Disease is thus not only said to cause a split in the life world, but also a withdrawal from the public domain.

Conclusion and discussion

In the life stories of 23 men and women diagnosed as having Parkinson's Disease, half of them appear to interpret the signs of the disease in a pattern where shame is a characteristic element. This interpretation is partly explained by the references to behaviour where the informants assume they are breaking certain social rules. Not all rule-breaking behaviour, however, is said to be an explanation for shame. The following conditions for ascribing shame to rule-breaking behaviour are mentioned: the social sensitivity of the values to which the rules refer; the assumed visibility of the behaviour; and the labelling of it as deviance. It is under these three conditions, in particular, that the informants characterise the rule-breaking as causing shame.

As a consequence of this shame, the informants speak of a split of the life world, and their inclination towards retreat from the public into the private. Parkinson's Disease, in this pattern of interpretation, is the illness of a shameful withdrawal from public life.

The interpretation of shame has been found among other chronically ill groups, especially those running the risk of manifesting their symptoms in public because of their relative uncontrollability. Schneider and Conrad (1983) and Scambler and Hopkins (1986), for example, observed feelings of embarrassment among people with epilepsy. In accordance with the findings reported here, Schneider and Conrad ascribe shame to the perception that people with epilepsy have 'failed to meet others' expectations, and that these others have recognised this. Just how "embarrassing" seizures were, depends on how visible and public they were' (p. 110). They too declare the shame of manifesting seizures as dependent on the 'visible' and thus public 'violation of social expectations' (p. 110). Scambler and Hopkins (1986) suggest alternatively that the shame of people with epilepsy derives less from a sense of 'moral culpability' than from an unarticulated feeling that epilepsy is evidence of 'imperfection', of an 'ontological inferiority' (p. 33).

In this patterned shame-interpretation, Parkinson's Disease is seen as an example of a more common phenomenon: shame for public rule-breaking and deviance. Shame appears here to be a characteristic which relates Parkinson's Disease to societal processes. Some suggest that the interpretation of rule-breaking in Western societies is shifting from guilt to shame, self-identity becoming more 'internally referential' (Giddens 1991: 153), self-restraints 'becoming more comprehensive and differentiated' and therefore 'enhancing the feelings of shame' (Elias 1978: 293). Elaborating on these connections opens the possibility of the development of specific sociological theories of chronic diseases, for instance as phenomena of shame-conditioned social exclusion.

Acknowledgements

The research reported here is part of the programme 'Chronic Illness and Health Care' at the Department of Sociology of the University of Amsterdam. Participating researchers were: I. Bruins, R. Feis, P. Van der Ham, S. Helm, J. Van der Horst Bruijn and D. Lampe.

References

Anderson, R. and Bury, M. (eds) (1988) *Living with Chronic Illness: the Experience of Patients and their Families*. London: Unwin Hyman.

Antaki, C. (1988) *Analysing Everyday Explanation; a Casebook of Methods*. London: Sage.

Becker, H. S. (1963) *Outsiders; Studies in the Sociology of Deviance*. New York: The Free Press of Glencoe.

Conrad, P. (1987) The experience of illness: recent and new directions. In J. Roth and P. Conrad (eds), *Research in the Sociology of Health Care, Vol. 6, The Experience and Management of Chronic Illness*. Greenwich: JAI Press, 1–32.

Corbin, J. M. and Strauss, A. (1988) *Unending Work and Care: Managing Chronic Illness at Home*. San Francisco: Jossey-Bass.

Denzin, N. K. (1989) *Interpretive Biography*. Newbury Park: Sage.

Elias, N. (1978) *The Civilising Process*. Oxford: Blackwell.

Fagerhaugh, S. and Strauss, A. (1978) Negotiation and pain management of geriatric wards. In D. Maines and N. Denzin (eds), *Work in Problematic Situations*. New York: Crowell.

Giddens, A. (1991) *Modernity and Self-identity; Self and Society in the Late Modern Age*. Cambridge: Polity

Lejeune, P. (1989) *On Autobiography*. Minneapolis: University of Minnesota Press.

Minichiello, V. *et al.* (1990) *In-depth Interviewing*. Melbourne: Longman Cheshire.

Potter, J. and Wetherell, M. (1987) *Discourse and Social Psychology: Beyond Attitude and Behaviour*. London: Sage.

Schneider, J. W. and Conrad, P. (1983) *Having Epilepsy: The Experience and Control of Illness*. Philadelphia: Temple University Press.

Scheff, T. (1966) *Being Mentally Ill: A Sociological Theory*. Chicago: Aldine.

Scambler, G. and Hopkins, A. (1986) Being epileptic: coming to terms with stigma. *Sociology of Health & Illness*, 8, 26–43.

Scott, J. (1990) *A Matter of Record: Documentary Sources in Social Research*. Cambridge: Polity.

Searle, J. (1983) *Intentionality; An Essay on the Philosophy of Mind*. Cambridge: Cambridge University Press.

Strauss, A. and Corbin, J. M. (1988) *Shaping a New Health Care System; the Explosion of Chronic Illness as a Catalyst for Change*. San Francisco: Jossey-Bass.

16

From Biographical Disruption to Biographical Reinforcement: The Case of HIV-Positive Men

Danièle Carricaburu and Janine Pierret

Introduction

[...] With regard to the onset of a serious illness and its unsettling consequences, sociologists have studied the biographical accommodations made in everyday life as well as changes in self-conceptions and personal relationships. Concepts such as 'biographical disruption', 'biographical work' and 'identity reconstitution' have been used to shed light on how illness affects a person's identity or construction of a biography (see, in particular, Bury 1982, 1991; Corbin and Strauss 1987, 1988; Charmaz 1987). Herein, the concepts of biographical disruption and biographical work will be used to analyse the particular situation of asymptomatic carriers of the Human Immunodeficiency Virus (HIV).

Being HIV-positive is not a chronic illness of the sort sociology has investigated. Instead, it corresponds to what we have called 'a situation at the risk of illness' (Carricaburu and Pierret 1992). Being infected with HIV is not the same as having AIDS. What it does mean is that those infected will eventually come down with a fatal disease. No medical prognosis can predict when they will actually fall sick. As a consequence, asymptomatic HIV-positive persons must manage an apparently healthy life in conditions of uncertainty. For many of them, having a low CD_4 count or taking AZT for the first time is a signal that they are entering a new phase; but even then, they know neither when they will fall ill nor with what disease. At present, only one thing is sure: they have every chance of eventually dying from an AIDS-related disease. A further source of uncertainty has to do with medicine and science. Scientific knowledge and medical know-how about AIDS, much of it experimental, is still being developed. This has direct bearings on people's prospects and everyday lives. In this very special situation, even more than during chronic illness, medical and scientific uncertainty itself shatters certitude: any 'sure' knowledge may be invalidated.

[...]

Method

[...]

From January 1990 to June 1991, in-depth interviews, each lasting an average of two hours, were conducted with 44 HIV-positive men: 24 homosexual and 20 haemophilic men. None of them was a drug-user. All of them lived in the Paris Region; and all were under medical supervision. Most had known about their immune status for at least five years; and three of them, for as long as seven years.

Interviews, which were recorded and then transcribed in full, were conducted as follows. Focusing on their illness condition, we asked the haemophilic men:

> Could you tell me what everyday life is like for a haemophilic person? I'd like to understand what happens during the major phases of life (childhood, adolescence, adulthood...) and in various fields of life (at work, during leisure time, in the family, with doctors, and with friends).

With homosexual men, interviews were centred around HIV-infection:

> Could you tell me about being infected with the HIV? How did it happen to you? Tell me about everyday life, about what happens in various fields of life (at work, during leisure time, in relationships, in the family, with doctors, and with friends...).

[...]

Conceptual background

[...]

[...] Bury conceptualised chronic illness as a biographical disruption. He intended to show that it causes a break in people's lives, what Giddens (1979: 123) has called 'a critical situation':

> we can learn a good deal about day-to-day situations in routine settings from analyzing circumstances in which those settings are radically disturbed.

Bury (1982: 169), too, defended the idea that chronic illness

> is precisely that kind of experience where the structures of everyday life and the forms of knowledge which underpin them are disturbed.

It wreaks havoc in people's everyday lives and their 'forms of knowledge'. Bury (1982: 169–70) pointed out three aspects of this disruption:

> First, there is the disruption of taken-for-granted assumptions and behaviors; the breaching of commonsense boundaries (...) Second, there are more profound disrup-

tions in explanatory systems normally used by people, such that a fundamental rethinking of the person's biography and self-concept is involved. Third, there is the response to disruption involving the mobilization of resources in facing an altered situation.

[...] While reviewing 'research and prospects', Bury (1991: 453) tried to work out the concept of biographical disruption by taking into account the context [...]:

> The notion of biography suggests that meaning and context in chronic illness cannot easily be separated.

By placing chronic illness in its social context, attention can be turned to factors such as social policies, patients' associations, charitable organisations, consumerism and the mass media. In particular, two types of meaning can be distinguished (Bury 1991: 453):

> In the first place, the 'meaning' of illness lies in its consequences for the individual. The effects of the onset of disruptive symptoms on everyday life at home or at work, including, for example, giving time to managing symptoms or regimens (Locker 1983) may be uppermost (...) Second, the meaning of chronic illness may be seen in terms of its *significance*. By this, I mean that different conditions carry with them different connotations and imagery. These differences may have a profound influence on how individuals regard themselves, and how they think others see them.

[...] [W]e [...] [borrow] the phrase 'biographical work' from Corbin and Strauss (1987), which refers to what a person must do in order to face the new situation resulting from the onset of chronic illness. According to these two scholars, a person's biography has three 'major dimensions': 'biographical time', 'conception of self' and 'conception of body'. The combination of these three components shapes the individual's biography and gives it continuity in what Corbin and Strauss called the 'biographical body conception chain'. When chronic illness breaks this 'BBC chain' – what Bury has called a biographical disruption takes place – all three components are wrested. 'Putting the BBC chain back together' is what Corbin and Strauss meant by biographical work. [...]

The way people cope with a chronic condition and manage everyday life is intricately bound up with the interpretations they develop about the meaning of their illness condition. This holds even more in the case of the HIV-positive, whether they are asymptomatic carriers or have come down with AIDS. There is a collective dimension to HIV-infection that shapes the individual's experience. Interpretations of AIDS are rife. Everyone is familiar with public discourses about AIDS. The latter is usually presented as a 'disease others catch' – the others being persons with 'risky behaviors'. Coping with everyday, HIV-positive life means adopting a stance in relation to these discourses. For this reason, we have sought to understand:

—what people experience when infected by a disease that affects them as individuals and as members of a relatively stigmatised group.
—whether or not the HIV-positive, given that many of them have a past that has marked them as 'different', experience biographical disruption. If so, how do they

rework identities? Can the fact of being HIV-positive serve as the grounds for the emergence of new identities?

The consequences of HIV-infection for everyday life

All interviewees had been deeply disturbed by their HIV-infection and its menace to their health. But reactions to a positive immune status differed significantly. Some interviewees made thoroughgoing changes in their lives whereas others seemed to maintain the status quo. [...]

Managing the secret: to tell or not to tell

[...] Since all interviewees were asymptomatic, their immune status was not directly visible. For this reason, they could decide whether or not to reveal their immune status to others. In general, both the haemophilic and the homosexual men kept it secret, a secret shared with only a few people to whom they were, or came to be, close. The quandary about revealing one's immune status followed from public discourse about AIDS, wherein this 'shameful sickness' was presented as a stigma. To be infected by HIV, even though one is not yet sick, is both an 'enacted' and 'felt' stigma, to borrow two phrases Scambler and Hopkins (1988: 156–7) used when studying epilepsy:

> Enacted stigma refers to instances of discrimination against people with epilepsy based on the perception of them as somehow unacceptably different or inferior [...] Felt stigma refers principally to the fear of meeting with enacted stigma, although it also embraces a sense of shame that frequently attends 'being epileptic'.

All interviewees strongly experienced a 'felt stigma', because their bodies were both infected and, we might say, 'infectious'. The notion of an 'enacted stigma' refers to social discourse about AIDS.

But the decision to say nothing bore different meanings depending on the social situation wherein silence was kept. The fear of rejection or of dismissal from work motivated those interviewees who abstained from telling colleagues, as a 26 year-old haemophilic atomic engineer said, 'What's the use of looking for the switch to be spanked with?' Interviewees who did not inform family or friends mostly justified their silence by stating that they did not want to be pitied or did not want to hurt those they loved. A 36 year-old homosexual aeronautics engineer said,

> I don't want the others to look at me any differently. I don't want any condescension, and even less pity. I want to have the same relations with people, especially since, for now, there's no need to talk about it.

Keeping the secret entailed constant vigilance. It amounted to real 'work' in A. Strauss *et al.*'s (1982) sense. This work was all the harder whenever others knew the interviewee was haemophilic or gay, as a 43 year-old biologist pointed out:

Since they know I'm haemophilic, as soon as I catch one thing or another, I feel them looking at me, wondering. But I don't want to say anything, so I stick in my office.

As time went on, the least sign – whether a preventive treatment or the appearance of certain symptoms (shingles, herpes, etc.) – could make the potential stigma visible. This stressful situation forced interviewees to draw up strategies for dissimulating the sign's origins. A 35 year-old homosexual public relations employee preferred, since he often had to go to the hospital, saying he was diabetic. All interviewees knew they would have more and more trouble keeping the secret over time. In the words of a 46 year-old homosexual secondary school teacher:

If I fall sick, I'll probably change my mind. But for the time being, it's my secret, and I'm keeping it.

[...]

Constraints and self-restraints

[...]

Since childhood, all the *haemophilic men* had restricted their activities to varying degrees, depending on their age and medical treatment, itself related to the state of medical knowledge about haemophilia. This self-restraint affected their love life and, in particular, their plans for starting a family. Being HIV-positive reinforced the existing process of imposing self-restraints – and added further restraints. A jobless 27 year-old commented,

I've never had a sexual relationship, but I hope I'll not end up an old bachelor. A woman, she'd have to accept my being haemophilic and, in addition, my being HIV-positive. That's a lot! I don't think it's possible.

For interviewees who had been trying to lead a family and love life 'as normally as possible' (Strauss and Glaser 1975: 79), being HIV-positive made their efforts in vain. They now imposed restraints upon themselves of a sort from which they, as the carriers of a genetic disease, had, till then, escaped. In the words of the previously quoted 26 year-old engineer:

As for myself, I'd've liked to have had children. Now, with tests before birth, you can avoid transmitting the illness ... With being HIV-positive, no way!

[..] Haemophilic interviewees were used to living with uncertainty about, on the one hand, everyday life (given unpredictable, accidental haemorrhages) and, on the other, about their future (given their unforeseeable illness trajectory). But AIDS represented a different threat. Whereas haemophilia left room for the hope of avoiding any serious accident, AIDS was seen as an irreversible, deadly process from which there would be no escape. Even those interviewees who had always, despite haemophilia, tried to exercise maximum control over their own lives were conscious that 'the enemy's too strong', 'the fight'll soon be over' and 'it'll be necessary to give up'. The fear of dying – evacuated from consciousness since concentrated products for treating haemophilia had come on the market – revived in full force.

The sexual transmission of HIV produced major changes in *gay* interviewees' love and sex lives. Whereas homosexual men generally prize sexuality (Pollak 1988), our interviewees were changing sexual behaviours. Some of them had gone so far as to become sexually abstinent. A 34 year-old bookstore manager told us:

> For four years now, I've stopped having sex, having full sexual relations. I vaguely allow myself to masturbate now and then from a distance.

Gay interviewees insisted they were more tired and weak. They had gradually adopted restraints, as they carefully supervised their bodies and watched for signs of any coming illness. In this respect, they stood out from the haemophilic group. A 42 year-old secondary school teacher stated,

> Every morning when I get up, I look at myself to see if I'm ok, see whether I have anything looking like a Kaposi [He laughs]. I stick out my tongue to see if I have any fungus.

This self-supervision stemmed from the desire to keep their condition secret and from the need to struggle with time. Though constantly bringing to mind the idea of illness, this supervision, paradoxically, reassured these men by helping them believe that AIDS was still far off.

The uncertain prognosis led all the gay men to reconsider the plans they could pursue or allow themselves to pursue. They thus had to rethink both the present and future. They developed a paradoxical notion of time, often formulated as, 'You don't have time to lose, so you take it.' To quote the previously mentioned public relations employee,

> I might come down with AIDS in two years. I might no longer be here, so I may as well profit to the utmost from every minute. I'm a pretty optimistic person in life, but I don't like going to see the doctor and learning my T4 count has screwed up. With this illness, you're waiting. I'm waiting for a miracle cure. I'm waiting when I take a bath and I see a spot and hope it's not a Kaposi. There's something a little morbid about it, but I've gotten information about dying. I don't think about it all the time, but that cleared things up. Besides it's normal to think about it. Otherwise, I don't make any plans for the long run. I tend to live from day to day. Like I told you, it's a wait in all its glory.

Mobilising resources

[...]

When inquiring about the resources the *haemophilic men* had already tapped to deal with their haemophilic condition, we found that most of them developed diversified strategies and worked out concrete arrangements to cope with their illness condition in everyday life. They had spent considerable energy in order to be seen, especially at the workplace, as 'normal' instead of 'handicapped'. When faced with AIDS however, they no longer felt as combative. They did not seek out new resources, and they even tended to abandon those that had helped them organise their lives as persons with haemophilia. They withdrew into work, family and friends.

Furthermore, these haemophilic interviewees had misgivings about medicine, since they had been infected through medical products. A 38 year-old assistant accountant explained,

> Despite their good will, how can doctors possibly help me? I can't take my mind off it: they're responsible for what's happening to me.

AIDS upset their life plans and disrupted the biographies they had constructed. They were unable to cope with their immune status so as to allow room for hope. In the words of a 40 year-old man computer programmer,

> HIV-positive and AIDS, for me, they're the same thing. I've had too many encounters with sickness. I know how things are going to end.

For these interviewees, infection meant death. This pervasive idea kept them from planning for the future.

In contrast, most *gay* interviewees tried to maintain the status quo by using existing resources and/or finding new ones. First of all, jobs and relations with friends or family took on more importance, especially when infection was kept a secret. The already mentioned 46 year-old secondary school teacher commented,

> I've recentered my life around close relationships. I mean I devote more time to the people I like, whether exlovers who are now friends or straight friends. Simply put, we see each other more often. I'm more available. I'm more interested in them, in what they're doing, what they think. I have the impression my life has lost in diversity but gained in intensity.

These men looked for material, emotional and relational support from various sources so as to remain integrated in their affective environment and in society. A 39 year-old bank manager said,

> I'm more attentive and sensitive if something happens to my friends. I get more involved in their troubles than I could have before. I live more intensely whatever happens. I try to be closer to my family in the provinces, and I phone more often.

Secondly, gay interviewees developed a strong relationship with medicine. This provided them with a cognitive resource. These interviewees thought it important to follow up on appointments and treatments. Relations with medical care-givers became a source of emotional support, as for this 44 year-old antique-dealer:

Going to the hospital isn't a hassle. Besides, I'm telling you, it's friendly over there. The personnel's friendly too. And the room's been redone. I trust them a lot. I had no experience with hospitals before, didn't know anything about them. I realize it's great, from the nurse to the chief doctor. The dedication is extraordinary.

For these interviewees, such relationships were a source of emotional support that helped them exercise control over their bodies and cope with the current situation.

For a few of these gay interviewees, activism in associations provided emotional involvement and affective support. But all the gay men recognised that associations were an important source of knowledge and information.

A last point: gay interviewees believed in their ability to find resources so as to reinforce their psychological well-being and physical health and, thereby, delay the onset of illness. A 35 year-old journalist made this very point:

Now I have a test every three months, because my T4 count had dropped and I'd refused to take AZT. At that time, you had to take huge doses, but I waited for the next blood test and, thank God, it improved. It improved by itself. That's when I noticed something. It's a personal tip, but I don't know whether I should tell the doctor: when I stop taking vitamin C and magnesium, I feel a little weaker. Yeah, from the position where I am, I think vitamin C, magnesium, vitamins do work. They suit me to a T. They reassure me, make me feel safer. The test every three months is my race against the clock, a way of keeping an eye on myself. I think you take responsibility for your own body. It's a decision. The doctor can't do anything.

In effect, these interviewees adopted a wide variety of means to cope with HIV-infection: new eating habits, 'vitamin therapy', psychotherapy or even spirituality. Besides fighting against the passage of time, all this kept them from being passive and helped them take responsibility for themselves so as to go on living like everyone else for as long as possible.

Pursuing palliative strategies and constructing hope

Although HIV-infection means a limited future, some interviewees, regardless of how they had been infected, struggled against uncertainty by, paradoxically, taking risks. They were all the more capable of doing this insofar as they felt freed of certain social constraints and, therefore, free to do things they could not have before being infected. The risks thus taken figured in the 'palliative strategies' adopted to 'reopen the doors closed by AIDS'.

Citing a few examples of these strategies will show how diverse they were and how imaginative, and inventive, these men were. Several of the gay men had changed occupations or even their line of work, despite losing job security. In addition to his job, one gay interviewee, who lived with another man, started breeding pedigree cats despite the risk of toxoplasmosis. After counting how long he had left to live, one haemophilic man borrowed a large amount of money in order to travel as much as he wanted. Another asked his father to donate sperm so that if he and his wife were to want a child, the baby would be 'of the same blood' but without any risk of infection. These calculated risks can be interpreted as the will to keep some control over one's life. Indeed, being active, doing things, is a way to project one's life into the future and to refuse being taken prisoner by illness.

[...]

Understandably, most interviewees were deeply disturbed when they had to start taking AZT or DDI, even though doctors presented these drugs as means of helping the immune system defend itself. A 38 year-old musician told us,

> Thrice a day, I take two 100 mg. capsules. I don't often forget. That's pretty good. But it reminds me, necessarily in some way or another, that I'm HIV-positive. It brings my haemophilia back up. It's a kind of chain you can't break out of since it's all around.

Such a prescription amounted to a full-scale assault on the deep personal conviction that illness could be avoided. The previously quoted public relations employee emphasised,

> AZT has changed me a lot more psychologically than being HIV-positive. It upset me a lot because, without actually falling sick, it means I'm getting closer to it.

The work of constructing hope was jeopardised.

At this point, illness had to be accepted as part of the biography so that hope could be rebuilt on other grounds. This entailed a thorough reworking of one's identity. For this reason, as several interviewees pointed out, denying the difference between being HIV-positive and having AIDS impeded the work of constructing hope, which, however precariously built or however hard to build, was indispensable for the will to live.

Thinking over the past to reconstruct the present

[...]

Given this context – a pre-existing chronic illness and then HIV-infection via medical treatment – might haemophilic men consider their immune status to be a new illness, an addition to, or extension of, haemophilia? Can we analyse their reactions to being HIV-positive in terms of a biographical disruption, as happens at the onset of most chronic illnesses? Or do these reactions fit into the haemophilic situation without causing any disruption?

When analysing interviews, we observed two different reactions but with similar consequences. Whether or not HIV-infection caused a biographical disruption, it did reinforce, for all these interviewees, their identity as haemophilic persons. To state it in terms we prefer, it reinforced the components to their identity as haemophilic persons.

For some of these interviewees, HIV-infection was in continuity with haemophilia. They did not consider it to be a complication of their initial illness. Instead, it fit into the same illness logic. The previously mentioned 40 year-old computer programmer declared,

> Haemophilia is nature's mistake. Every so often something new crops up – AIDS proves that!

In this case, we cannot talk about a biographical disruption because, long before HIV-infection, these men had organised their biographies around their illness trajectories. They had not adopted (and some even forcefully rejected) the 'normalising' discourse of the Association Française des Hémophiles. In the words of a 24 year-old employee in a bookkeeping department,

> It's not true. You can't live normally with haemophilia. It's a ball and chain you drag with you through life.

Since it kept them from 'living like everybody else', these interviewees did not consider haemophilia to be something normal or ordinary. It had a central place in forming their identities and organising their lives. These men had already, long before HIV-infection, worked out a system of self-restraints. They had given up activities such as sports or travelling years ago. And their attitudes were directly affected by their awareness of themselves as carriers of a genetic illness; they refused to marry or to have children. On the whole, they had organised their biographies around their illness and its negative aspects. Being infected with HIV led them to reinforce measures of the sort already taken; there was no disruption. It proved 'the fatality of being haemophilic'. It was the sign of a deadly illness, and reinforced the individual and collective *fatum* (Herzlich and Pierret 1991). The process of context-ualising (Corbin and Strauss 1987) haemophilia continued relatively unchanged; or rather, it was reinforced. In this case, we can conclude that HIV-infection resulted in *biographical reinforcement*. The fact that there was no biographical disruption does not, of course, mean that these interviewees did not feel menaced by HIV-infection.

Among other haemophilic interviewees, we observed the second sort of reaction: HIV-infection caused a biographical disruption. This happened especially among those who had denied their haemophilia or had tried to consider it to be something ordinary. These interviewees had organised their lives to win the battle to 'lead a normal life'. Being HIV-positive disturbed this 'normalcy', which had been based on controlling haemophilia's effects if not haemophilia itself. Being HIV-positive disrupted this normalcy because haemophilia could no longer be kept at a distance. A 46 year-old personnel director admitted,

> I always pretended I was leading a normal life with haemophilia. It suited me to see things that way. Now, I realize I missed out on true life [...] If I hadn't been infected, I'd not have experienced this kind of questioning about my life. I'd've continued on the path I laid down for myself without changing one iota.

In this case, the person was forced to see himself both as the carrier of an incurable genetic defect (that he used to think he could control) and as the carrier of a deadly virus (that cannot, at least not yet, be controlled). Although these men had done everything to see themselves, and be seen, as 'normal', being HIV-positive forced them to face a hidden biological reality. It has jeopardised their identity as someone leading a normal life in spite of illness. Being infected with HIV threatened the future, disturbed everyday life and led to questioning the past and, thereby, the meaning of life as a haemophilic person. These men were caught up in barely manageable contradictions. Being HIV-positive upset the fragile balance they had reached. It forced them to think differently about their haemophilia and to direct attention to a body to which they had often paid little heed. The twofold experience of haemophilia and HIV-infection disrupted everyday lives and biographies. Given the serious implications of this infection, these interviewees could no longer keep up an identity that refused illness or tried to hold it off. This biographical disruption led them to think over the past. They thus came to see haemophilia as an essential component of their identities and biographies. During this process of contextualisation, HIV-infection resulted in a *biographical disruption that entailed a biographical reinforcement.*

Through this biographical reinforcement, identities were recomposed on the basis of not only individual components but also components closely related to the collective history of haemophilia. In France, about 1200 haemophilic men and boys have AIDS. Given the characteristics of HIV-infection – the cause of infection, its collective dimension and society's reaction – the AIDS social phenomenon has had a major impact on haemophilic men and their national association. HIV-infection is causing this group to lose much of what it had arduously won over the past 30 years.

Furthermore, HIV-infection has resuscitated the image of 'victim'. As Carricaburu's (1993) analysis of the positions adopted by the Association Française des Hémophiles has shown, haemophilic HIV-positive persons have to rework their identities around the twofold dimension of 'victim': victim of a life-threatening illness and victim as officially recognised by the December 1992 law about compensating persons infected through the medical use of blood products. Although this way of being infected is not stigmatised, the haemophilic interviewees were unable to recompose a sense of identity around positive components. In effect, the latter had been jeopardised by the individual and collective 'work of normalization' with and despite haemophilia.

Unlike haemophilic interviewees, all the *homosexual men* experienced a biographical disruption when they learned they were HIV-positive. This disruption set off a complex process wherein the components of their identity related to homosexuality assumed special importance.

Regardless of how these men had experienced their homosexuality in the past, all of them, when interviewed, spontaneously presented themselves in positive terms, as being gay. They placed their own biography within the history of the generation of men who fought for the recognition of homosexuality and the right to be different. This has coloured their way of thinking, as expressed by the 34 year-old bookstore manager already quoted:

> I don't want sidatoriums to be opened. . . . I don't want to have to wear a star of any color. . . I didn't approve of that for the Jews, Arabs or even homosexuals. I'm not going to approve of it for AIDS.

The onset of this epidemic has forced homosexual men as individuals and as a group to raise questions. In the meantime, AIDS activism has significantly modified society's perceptions of homosexuality and AIDS. A 35 year-old consulting engineer involved in an AIDS association revealed his motivations:

> I want to participate in a movement to acquire visibility in order to throw off this silence that, for so many and despite everything, is so shameful (. . .) I was never an activist, but I feel more and more like one – activist in the sense that I want to advance an idea. I believe there are ideas we have to get across to people, messages that are not always easy but that can make things change. I don't want to accept the idea that being sick means or amounts to something shameful. I think there's work to do, changes to be made in society so that this feeling of shame vanishes, lightens, so that, little by little, AIDS will be like any other illness in the collective subconscious.

Although being HIV-positive disrupted individuals' lives, this biographical disruption fits into the collective history of homosexuality. This twofold process – disruption of the individual's life but continuity in a collective history – led interviewees to reinforce the homosexual aspects of their biographies. But this process meant something different from the 'right to be different'. It also differed from our findings regarding haemophilic men.

Given this biographical reinforcement, how did these HIV-positive gay men actually rework their identities? The three 'steps' proposed by Corbin and Strauss (1987: 272) – defining and redefining the self, refocusing of direction, and integration – proved especially useful for analysing interviews. [. . .] All three steps might coexist in a single person; or one of them might prevail. In all cases though, this complex process of reworking identities led gay interviewees to establish priorities. They thus came to think of time differently and to attach a different value to it. In the words of a 35 year-old translator,

> I now know what does and doesn't work for me. I'm a lot more in the present than I used to be. I worry less about my future and am less stuck in the past. What works for me is to be in the middle run, to clear up my tax problems and get legal.

Interviewees defined new priorities for their personal lives and tended to give more importance to quality and intensity than to quantity in relationships, as a 33 year-old management consultant admitted:

> In the relations I have with others, I don't lose my time with people who bore me, because I no longer have time to lose.

They also took new interest in their jobs, which became a source of personal and social fulfilment. Moreover, it was important that others recognise these changes. While analysing these interviews, we realised that it was very important to these men that others should recognise the changes they were going through. This seemed paradoxical in light of what has already been pointed out about managing the secret.

These gay interviewees did not deem HIV-infection and the ensuing changes to be something 'ordinary'. Nor were these denied or idealised. To various degrees, these men had integrated this biological fact into their biographies by reinforcing whatever, in their pasts, had to do with homosexuality. They reworked their identities as though homosexuals were integrated in society. This was a far cry from the 1970s, when claims were made for the 'right to be different'. Gay interviewees were relatively willing to accept an integration based on recognising the normalcy of their situation. This need for social recognition was linked to the difference between being HIV-positive and having AIDS. As already pointed out, these interviewees emphasised that 'being HIV-positive is not the same as being sick'. AIDS was kept at a distance, it was a probability, something more or less accepted through the work of constructing hope. By relying on the new biological and (even more important) social category of 'HIV-positive', these gay men managed to work at recomposing a sense of identity.

Conclusion

For these asymptomatic haemophilic or homosexual men, the consequences for everyday life of being HIV-positive cannot be separated from how they interpreted their situation. This interpretation entailed reconstructing individual and collective pasts. The individual's life story could not be separated from his reference group's history. At this point, the characteristic of AIDS and of HIV-infection must be borne in mind: this illness, having reached epidemic proportions, is transmitted in specific, identifiable ways not just to isolated individuals but to individuals who are part of certain groups. By relating the reinterpretation and reconstruction of their individual and collective pasts to the current situation, interviewees recomposed a sense of identity and tried to give continuity to their biographies.

Whether or not biographical disruption occurred, all interviewees had to rework their sense of identity. This complex process entailed what we have called biographical reinforcement, *i.e.*, a reinforcement of the components of identity that, prior to HIV-infection, had already been built around haemophilia or homosexuality.

[...]

By drawing our attention to the interrelations between the individual's experience of infection, his life story and the history of his reference group, sociological research on AIDS sheds light on a little explored aspect of the illness experience: its shared, collective dimension. Being HIV-positive is not just a matter of being individually infected: it is also a question of being affected as part of a group that has its own history and has been decimated by AIDS. This experience bears little comparison with what happened during past epidemics, which felled victims more randomly (Herzlich and Pierret 1991). By observing *in situ* the evolution of the AIDS epidemic and its collective impact, we should advance our understanding, on the one hand, of the relations between micro- and macro-levels of social analysis and, on the other, of the feedback between individual experiences, cultural factors and macrosocial structures.

Acknowledgements

The French Agence Nationale de Recherche sur le Sida (ANRS) provided funds for this research. This article has been translated from French into English by Noal Mellott, CNRS, Paris.

References

Bury, M. (1982) Chronic illness as a biographical disruption, *Sociology of Health and Illness*, 4, 167–82.

Bury, M. (1991) The sociology of chronic illness: a review of research and prospects, *Sociology of Health and Illness*, 13, 451–68.

Carricaburu, D. (1993) L'Association Francaise des Hémophiles face au danger de contamination par le virus du sida: stratégie de normalisation de la maladie et définition collective du risque, *Sciences Sociales et Santé*, XI-3/4, 55–81.

Carricaburu, D. and Pierret, J. (1992) *Vie quotidienne et recompositions identitaires autour de la séropositivité*, a research report. Paris: CERMES-ANRS.

Charmaz, K. (1987) Struggling for a self: identity levels of the chronically ill, *Research in the Sociology of Health Care*, 6, 283–321.

Corbin, J. and Strauss, A. (1987) Accompaniments of chronic illness changes in body, self, biography and biographical time, *Research in the Sociology of Health Care*, 6, 249–81.

Corbin, J. and Strauss, A. (1988) *Unending Work and Care*. San Francisco: Jossey-Bass Publishers.

Giddens, A. (1979) *Central Problems in Social Theory*. London: Macmillan.

Herzlich, C. and Pierret, J. (1991) *Illness and Self in Society*, translation by E. Forster of the first edition (1984) of *Malades d'hier, malades d'aujourd'hui*. Baltimore: Johns Hopkins University Press, 1987.

Herzlich, C. and Pierret, J. (1991, 2nd ed.) *Malades d'hier, malades d'aujourd'hui*. Paris: Payot.

Locker, D. (1983) *Disability and Disadvantage. The Consequences of Chronic Illness*. London-New York: Tavistock Publications.

Pollak, M. (1988) *Les homosexuels et le sida: sociologie d'une épidémie*. Paris: A. M. Métailié.

Scambler, G. and Hopkins, A. (1988) Accommodating epilepsy in families. In Anderson, R. and Bury, M. (eds.), *Living with Chronic Illness*. London: Unwin Hyman.

Strauss, A. and Glaser, B. (1975) *Chronic Illness and the Quality of Life*. St. Louis-Toronto: Mosby.

Strauss, A., Fagerhaugh, S., Suczek, B. and Wiener, C. (1982) The work of hospitalized patients, *Social Science and Medicine*, 16, 977–86.

17

The Meaning of Lumps: A Case Study of the Ambiguities of Risk

Sandra M. Gifford

Molly is 27 years old and dying from breast cancer. She first noticed a lump in her breast when she was 21. Her girlfriend urged her to see a doctor and she did. Her doctor told her not to worry – that it was probably just a cyst. Five years later, in extreme pain and unable to walk, Molly was diagnosed as having breast cancer:

> I had this little knot and I thought, 'I'm sure it's nothing'. But she says (Molly's girlfriend) 'You should go get that examined . . . just because it's better to be safe than sorry'. So we ventured down to this little hospital and this doctor gave me an exam and said, 'Well, I feel something like the size of a pea and it seems like it's a cyst but I don't think it's anything you should be concerned about'. And I thought, 'Oh really? Well wonderful!' But he didn't explain to me the fact that sometimes you need to keep on these things, like cysts can grow into tumors. So I didn't even think about it at all. In my mind it was OK, it was a cyst. So the years after, every time I went for my physical, I would let the doctor know . . . I always made mention of the fact that I had this cyst and I always made mention of the fact that I had irregular menstrual cycles because I figured the more information they received, the better. But maybe because I didn't have a consistent doctor every year, they never thought much of it. . . . Then I was only 21 or 22 and they probably figured, 'Oh, no big deal!' Maybe I didn't take it as seriously . . . especially after I heard it was nothing to be concerned about. . . . But, I think they weren't conscientious enough and that really bugs me because that is what we pay them for. That's what they go to school for. And even if a patient doesn't come in and say, 'Well, give me a biopsy', they should say, 'Well, a cyst? And how long have you had this. Well, maybe we should take a biopsy just to see.' You know, I don't care how young you are or what. That really makes me angry because I think that maybe this could have been prevented.

Molly has none of the classic risk factors for breast cancer. She is young, black, and has no family history of the disease. Benign breast lumps are common in young women, breast cancer is not. Within the six months following her diagnosis, Molly underwent a mastectomy, an ovariectomy, radiotherapy and chemotherapy. She does not know how long she has to live.

Fiona is 44 years old and has been diagnosed as having mammary dysplasia – what some consider a serious benign breast condition. She has had several biopsies and is currently under close medical surveillance. Because of Fiona's benign condition, her doctor considers her to be at risk of developing breast cancer. Although Fiona knows her condition is serious, she is uncertain of the implications of her disease. Fiona explains:

> Dr. Smith said that there are things, mammary dysplasia for one, which could indicate the possibility of cancer in later years. He talked in Latin and much of what he said I did not understand.... I'm still not the hell sure what it is I got.... At any rate he has been seeing me now every three months. Now he inevitably finds something. He's found a couple of cysts in the left breast which he has aspirated. Now today I was up there and he found one in the right breast which he felt was a little bit more of a lump than it should have been... that more water should have come out of it than did. But he's going to send what little fluid that he did get to the pathologist again and I won't have their report till Wednesday. It has been an ongoing saga now for two years. As I say, he inevitably finds something. I have very lumpy breasts. I have mammary dysplasia. So it's one of those things. Nobody's sure if it's a disease or what the devil it is! But every time he finds something like he did today, he puts me on pins and needles again until he decides what else... I have told myself Sandy, I have told myself, I will not think about this anymore.... But it never goes away. It is always there.

Fiona has many risk factors for breast cancer. She is 44 years of age, white, never married, has no children, and has been given a diagnosis of benign breast disease. While Fiona does not have breast cancer, the uncertainty concerning her condition has resulted in the medicalization of her life.

Molly's and Fiona's experiences represent two extremes of the consequences of the ambiguities and uncertainties about risk, benign breast conditions and breast cancer. While Molly's experiences are the more tragic, one might pause to consider the physical and psychological consequences of Fiona's constant medical surveillance. Molly, Fiona and their doctors all are enmeshed in the dilemmas of medical uncertainty about what is known and what is unknown about the future of possible disease. This essay explores the ambiguities of risk which arise out of its translation from epidemiological findings to clinical knowledge and practice and thus to lay experiences of health and illness.

In both epidemiology and clinical medicine the concept of risk plays a central role in understandings about the etiology and prevention of chronic disease. For the epidemiologist, the concept of risk expresses a statistical measure of the degree of association between a characteristic and a disease within a defined population (Lilienfeld and Lilienfeld 1980). However, this epidemiologic concept becomes more broadly defined when translated into clinical practice and lay perceptions of health and illness. Within clinical and lay contexts, it is more appropriate to speak of the 'language of risk' in that the term is used to convey a constellation of meanings some of which are intended and some of which remain largely unconscious. The language of risk is about scientific uncertainty concerning causal relationships, and clinical and lay uncertainty concerning the prediction and control of unhealthy outcomes. The popularity of the concept is linked to the inability of epidemiologists and other medical scientists to produce models which adequately explain the etiology and population distribution of chronic diseases, and from the inability of clinical medicine to prevent and cure these diseases.

Currently there is much confusion and debate between epidemiologists and clinicians about how to translate concepts of epidemiologic risk into clinical risk. Part of this confusion arises because contextual differences in the meaning and use of the concept have not been fully recognized. To better understand these contextual differences, I present a model in which risk takes on two distinct dimensions; a technical, objective or *scientific* dimension and a socially experienced or *lived* dimension. The assessment and evaluation of risk with epidemiology is an objective, technical and scientific process but for the lay person it is a subjective, lived experience. Lay assessment and evaluation of risk is a social process, not a scientific, technical one. Clinical medicine bridges these two dimensions. Risk for the practitioner may sometimes be objective, sometimes lived, and sometimes both – as the practitioner is faced with the task of translating scientific risk into the treatment of individual patients.

The central argument of this paper is that although epidemiologists speak of risk as being a measured property of a group of people, clinicians speak of risk as a specific property of an individual. Risk becomes something that the patient suffers; a sign of a future disease that the clinician can diagnose, treat and manage. For the patient, risk becomes a lived or experienced state of ill-health and a symptom of future illness. To the patient, risk is rarely an objective concept. Rather, it is internalized and experienced as a state of being. These different dimensions of risk as understood and experienced by epidemiologists, clinicians and lay women – further blur the already ambiguous relationship between health and ill-health. This ambiguity results in the creation of a new state of being healthy and ill; a state that is somewhere between health and disease and that results in the medicalization of a woman's life. [...]

Epistemological assumptions informing epidemiological and clinical concepts of risk

[...]

The epidemiology of risk: benign breast disease and breast cancer

Although epidemiologic risk is a scientifically measured concept, there is much controversy concerning the precise nature and degree of risk associated with a given disease outcome. Thus, there is always an inherent degree of uncertainty concerning the understanding of specific risk factors. The risk factors for breast cancer provide a clear illustration of the complexities of accurately defining epidemiologic risk. [...]

Benign breast disease further illustrates the ambiguities of risk. Until recently it was thought that a diagnosis of benign breast disease, or what is also commonly referred to as fibrocystic breast disease, significantly increased a woman's risk for breast cancer. Most studies conducted indicated a two to four fold increase in risk (Kelsey 1979). However, there have been many problems in understanding the extent to which this benign condition actually contributes to the disease.

First, it has been difficult for epidemiologists to obtain accurate case definitions because the clinical and histopathological classification of benign conditions suffer from a lack of standardized criteria and terminology. [...]

A second problem with understanding the nature of risk that benign breast conditions represent concerns that of selection bias. Studies that show an increased rate of breast cancer among women with fibrocystic disease are based on a biopsy diagnosis. This means that risk has been based not on all women with lumpy breasts but rather only on those who have had a biopsy performed. This is a crucial point because not every woman with a lumpy breast is selected for a biopsy. Rather, other risk factors are taken into account, and women who have had breast biopsies tend to be in a higher risk group to begin with. [...]

These two problems have made it difficult for epidemiologists to estimate accurately the incidence and prevalence of benign breast disease within the population and to establish clear evidence for a causal relationship with breast cancer. Indeed, some studies have estimated that at least 50% of all women have palpably irregular breasts and as many as 90% of women may have some sort of histological changes! This has led some epidemiologists and medical practitioners to argue that many benign conditions simply represent a range of normal variation and that therefore, the condition should not be thought of as a disease entity (Ernster 1982; Love 1984).

Despite the problems inherent in the definition of risk, there does seem to be a general association between benign conditions and breast cancer. However, although epidemiologists have been careful to confine their understandings to populations, and to stick to the caveat that 'correlation is not causation', many doctors and women have tended to assume that in some as yet unknown way, benign conditions have the capacity to cause breast cancer. The crux of the problem thus lies in the translation of epidemiologic risk into clinical and individual risk.

[...] There is always an element of intrinsic uncertainty in the practice of clinical medicine because the practitioner is required to translate generalized knowledge to the treatment of a particular individual. And in these situations, there is always a certain amount of uncertainty which cannot be measured. Risk then, for the clinician, takes on the added dimension of unmeasured uncertainty.

There are thus, two kinds of risk: the first is 'measurable uncertainty' represented by the laws of probability; the second is unmeasured uncertainty, where numerical probabilities may not be entirely applicable. [...] The concept of measured and unmeasured risk can be applied to understanding the different dimensions of epidemiologic, clinical and lay knowledge of benign breast conditions and breast cancer. What distinguishes the two dimensions is the ambiguity of information. Scientific risk is quantitative, objective and relatively unambiguous. Lived risk is qualitative, subjective and highly ambiguous. Epidemiologists create scientific risk, lay people create and experience lived risk, clinicians mediate between and bridge these two dimensions of risk. It is to the clinical experience of risk that I now turn.

The clinical diagnosis and management of risk

Epidemiologists have identified certain groups of women who are unquestionably at higher risk for developing breast cancer.... For those of us who practice clinical medicine, it is essential to separate those factors that are significant enough to influence our own practice of medicine from those factors that are perhaps statistically important when dealing with large populations but which are not enough to make us alter the advice we give patients about the frequency of clinical examinations, intervals between mammograms, and so forth.... This then, becomes the crux of this discussion, namely, the clinical implications of these risk factors. Which if any, of the recognized epidemiologically significant risk factors should trigger special treatment or follow-up for women (or men) so affected? By identifying these groups of individuals can we detect breast cancer earlier and thereby alter the course and outcome of the disease? (Schwartz 1982: 26).

This passage from a recent article in the medical journal *Breast* clearly articulates the dilemmas facing the clinician in the management of women at risk for breast cancer. As the quotation suggests, the language of risk within clinical medicine is about uncertainty concerning the translation of scientific knowledge into clinical practice. A fundamental difference between clinical and epidemiological risk involves the application of risk knowledge. In contrast to epidemiology, which might be best understood as a science of populations, the practice of medicine can be understood as a science of individuals.

[...]

The assessment of risk factors plays an important role in helping the practitioner reach a clinical diagnosis. To make a risk assessment, the clinician must interpret epidemiologic risk to have clinical relevance, and this entails two shifts in meaning. First, the clinician must shift from thinking about risk as being a statement about disease rates in a population, to thinking of risk as applied to one patient. Second, risk is thus transformed from a statistical concept to a physical entity. The clinician comes to think about risk within existing modes of clinical thought and practice by transforming risk into a sign of a 'possible' current or future disease. Thus, objective clinical risk comes to be understood and talked about in the same sense as other objective clinical signs of disease.

[...]

Despite uncertainties about the clinical significance of benign conditions, clinicians do attempt to bring a sense of certainty to some risk factors. For example, practitioners often create risk profiles for individual patients based on statistical patterns. This is illustrated by the following surgeon's expressed concern over the chances that a benign condition might develop into breast cancer:

Those women who have multiple cysts, and I mean come in with four or five cysts in each breast over a period of a year, in this type of patient, 25% will develop cancer. I have one here who I am a little bit concerned about. She has been coming in since 1976 and each time she comes in she's got another cyst and she's been in seven times so far. I'm getting worried about her. There comes a time when you have to sit down and say, 'Well, look, statistically you've got about a 25% chance of developing breast cancer'. And you ask them to start thinking a little bit about having a subcutaneous mastectomy.

Considering this example, we might wonder about the clinical understanding of probability. Does this surgeon mean that this type of patient has a 25% chance of developing breast cancer over the next five years or over her lifetime? The concept of probability is poorly understood by clinicians and lay people alike. Faced with these uncertain understandings, this surgeon has translated a population risk into an individual risk and has suggested prophylactic mastectomy as a possible method of removing the risk.

When faced with management of a 'high risk' patient, surgeons have a tendency to treat risk as they would other undesirable physical conditions. Thus, we find that clinicians speak of risk as not only a sign of possible current or future disease, but also as something that resides in a particular part of the body and something from which a patient then suffers. Two surgeons explained:

> You really have to say to the woman, 'you have this much risk in each breast over the next 25 years'. Then they really have to decide how they feel about the risk.

> Consider you're at significant risk of developing breast cancer, but I can't tell you that you're going to develop cancer. All I know is that every woman suffers somewhere around a 1 in 11 chance of having breast cancer and your risk is greater than that and you're very young. That means for another 30 or 40 or 50 years, you suffer that risk.

This brings me to my final point about objective clinical risk. In the logic of medical thought and practice, if risk is understood as something from which the patient physically suffers, it then follows that risk is something that can be physically treated. In clinical language, risk is spoken of as if it were a sign of a possible future or current disease, a sign that resides in a particular part of the body and can be observed by the clinician. In the clinical management of risk for breast cancer, surgeons may remove the physical condition that they conceive of as being at risk: biopsies are performed to obtain a more definitive diagnosis and to remove the lump itself. Removal of the lump results in the removal of the risk of a possible pre-malignant condition. For example, a surgeon explains:

> I tend to be rather aggressive about doing biopsies and sometimes I get a little guilty about that. But you know, you have a situation that you will feel a little guilty about only to have it pop up to be pathologic! I mean we are legally at risk, emotionally at risk, and physically, the patient is at risk.

This comment is revealing as it introduces the second dimension of clinical risk, the *lived* dimension. Lived clinical risk refers to the clinician's own experience with the risk of being wrong. Lived clinical risk results from uncertainty concerning clinical knowledge and its application in practice. Such risk leads to changes in clinical perceptions of normality. As a result, patients diagnosed at risk fall into a grey zone that is between health and disease. This ambiguous state leads to clinical uncertainty concerning diagnosis, management and prognosis.

Clinical uncertainty has always been inherent to medical practice. The art of a diagnosis consists of bringing order and meaning to a complex series of signs and symptoms. The medical model within which most clinicians operate is based upon two basic assumptions. The first is that there exists an objective physical reality that medical and scientific knowledge can discover. Second, signs and symptoms refer to some underlying physiological or chemical change the meaning of which can be established and agreed upon (Feinstein 1973; McGehee et al. 1979). In theory, this process is straightforward. However, in reality, it is complicated by the fact that knowledge of states of ill-health is forever changing (Foucault 1973; King 1982). Clinicians are forced to make diagnoses based upon rapidly changing and often contradictory scientific knowledge. In the diagnosis of breast conditions the clinician must draw on the expertise of a number of different scientific and technological specialists which include pathologists, epidemiologists, radiologists, and geneticists. Much uncertainty exists in each of these areas concerning the etiology of both benign and malignant breast conditions. This makes the task of diagnosis particularly problematic as clinicians are faced with translating and integrating uncertain scientific knowledge in order to treat a particular patient.

[...]

Lay perceptions of risk and the state of 'non-health'

As discussed, a diagnosis of benign breast disease is thought to raise a woman's risk for developing breast cancer. Yet, there exists much uncertainty concerning the clinical and epidemiologic meaning of benign breast conditions, and thus the nature and degree of the risk involved is often unclear. For women, a diagnosis of benign breast disease often changes their perceptions of health and illness. For example, consider the following statements from women who have been diagnosed as having the risk factor of benign breast disease:

> I have very lumpy breasts. Nobody's sure if it's a disease or what the devil it is.

> I had some discomfort but I'd never had the thought that this was a disease!

> You know, one day you're walking down the street feeling wonderful and then all of a sudden somebody tells you that maybe you shouldn't feel so wonderful.

Risk for the lay woman is experienced as a symptom of a hidden or future illness, and thus serves to further blur the already ambiguous distinction between health and illness. Women speak of risk in the same way they speak of experiencing other symptoms of illness. Just as clinicians speak of risk as something that women suffer from, women speak of risk as a state of being. Being at risk is a state somewhere between health and illness. Inherent within lay perceptions of risk is a high degree of unmeasured uncertainty: risk for women is not objective or measured.

[...]

For women, information about their own individual risk will always be highly ambiguous because, (a) there exists much uncertainty within epidemiology concerning the significance of identified risk factors, (b) there exists much uncertainty within both epidemiology and other biomedical sciences concerning relationships between identified risk factors and the mechanisms of disease, (c) it is impossible to accurately translate population risk to individual risk and (d) it is impossible, accurately [to] know all the contextual factors and how they interact to determine risk for unique individuals. In sum, it is precisely because individuals are unique that we may be unable to know all of the information needed to accurately predict unique outcomes. Lay risk will always possess an inherent quality of unmeasured ambiguity and uncertainty as a central characteristic. It emerges from an individual's subjective feelings about the meaning of scientific and clinical risk mediated by their social and cultural background, context, and experiences. Lay risk is not objective, cannot be quantified or measured, and is not static. Rather, it must be understood as a dynamic experience of personal uncertainty about one's future. [...]

For women, risk represents potential changes in their experience of the relationship between their current and future state of health. In order for risk to have a personal reality, women must transform it from an objective entity to a subjective experience. Risk becomes internalized. One woman explained:

I knew *intellectually* that I was at high risk but I didn't feel it inside. And then my mother died of cancer of the pancreas and that's the same time I turned 30 and as a combination of my mother's death and my turning 30, I started to really be in touch with my own mortality...I started to really internalize it, that yes, this could happen to me and I started getting a little bit scared. (emphasis added)

[...]

The concept of subjective probability can be usefully applied to understanding women's experiences of lived risk of benign breast disease and breast cancer. First, women interviewed in this study were well aware of the uncertainty that exists in both epidemiology and clinical medicine concerning the meaning of identified risk factors, and were faced with having to make a subjective decision concerning the meaning of these risk factors within the context of their own lives. While women may discount their risk of getting breast cancer, a diagnosis of benign breast disease can act immediately to bring personal meaning to risk. In this sense, a diagnosis of benign breast disease can serve to make the possibility of future illness a physical reality. When a woman is diagnosed with benign breast disease she is thrown into a liminal state of being at risk, of being suddenly neither healthy nor ill. The discounting of risk until it becomes symbolically expressed in a physical condition is illustrated with the following quotes:

I read somewhere that women who don't have children before the age of 26 or don't breast feed are more likely to get it (breast cancer) but it doesn't seem like such a big thing.... But I think my risks are higher now that I have fibrocystic breast disease.

Now that I have fibrocystic breasts, I can't help but feel that I must have some sort of predisposition.

For women who have developed breast cancer, risk has resulted in certain unwanted and feared futures. What was once risk is now an experienced present. Here, risk loses much of its unmeasured uncertainty. Risk is certain and rather than experiencing 'being at risk', women experience 'risk' as becoming the illness they feared. In the same sense that women 'become ill', the onset of breast cancer can be understood as transforming a woman's experience of 'being at risk' to 'becoming risk'. One woman explained that not only was she at risk for a future cancer but that she had also become a risk statistic:

> After five years, if nothing has gone wrong, then you are free (of cancer). Then you don't have nothing to worry about. But I still have fear. The thing I do know is that I'm what you call a statistic and I am a cancer patient.

And another woman expressed similar feelings as she reflected why she had developed cancer:

> I had early menarche and late cessation of my menses so my risk is higher statistically. I've had no children and that's another risk factor. I mean we're all just bodies and I'm going to fall into some statistic eventually.

These last two women express what is perhaps most important about lay risk: the issue of control. Currently, there is little women can do to change their risk factors. Many of the women in this study expressed frustration concerning their lack of personal control over risk. For example, when I asked a 26 year old woman if the doctors had told her of anything she could do to prevent further breast problems, she said:

> Well, you know, no coffee, no tea, no caffeine, none of which I do anyway. Which was a great let down to the doctors, which was another thing that frustrated me because they said, 'Well, do you drink a lot of coffee?' I said no. I don't do any of that. And they would sigh, like, 'Um, what is going on?' You know, 'You really got a problem'. So part of my frustration was feeling like I already do everything that I'm suppose to be doing.

Ironically, the search for personal control over risk often leads to further medicalization. Because women often feel helpless to do anything to change their risk, they are left at the hands of medical experts. One woman expressed her own frustrations by explaining:

> I always feel that Dr. Smith is more in control than I am. Like I say, he's one of the few people who can intimidate me, and I don't think he does that, certainly not intentionally. But he does. I come out of there shaking all over. Now I have to wait until Wednesday to see if it's. . . . Then we have to wait till the next time to see if that's it. But as he said, 'What you have is serious and we have to watch it closely'. Now I could walk away from it, sure. I could say, 'It's been two years doctor, thank you very much for your help. I don't want to discuss it any more. I don't want to talk about it any more'. And maybe one day I will do that. But I am not ready to do that yet. I just simply am not ready to do that.

He keeps asking me if I keep getting my periods. I keep thinking that maybe it's true that once your periods stop some of these lumps go away with it. You know, I have no control over that. Who knows. So for the time being, we will play it his way and see what happens. But if he tells me something I don't want, I don't know what I'll do.

This woman raises several important issues concerning lay risk. While it is clear that she does not have cancer, her doctor has diagnosed her as having a serious benign condition and at risk for cancer. The doctor is not quite certain about the outcome of this condition and the woman is not quite certain if she should consider herself healthy or ill. The doctor deals with his own uncertainty by continuing his surveillance over her condition until it either goes away or becomes cancer. The woman is left thinking that her menopause might cause her lumps to disappear but she has no control over when this might occur and it is not at all certain whether this will clear up the problem. Therefore, the woman is left feeling that she has no alternatives but to continue with medical surveillance. Faced with the fear of breast cancer as a possible outcome, knowing that there is no way to prevent the disease and that early diagnosis is a woman's primary tactic for survival, this woman is caught in a bind of being both healthy and of needing medical surveillance until her condition either becomes cancer or goes away. In her current state, can this woman ever walk away from her doctor and declare herself well? In a very real sense, being diagnosed at risk is itself a risk factor. It represents the risk of medicalization and the risk of losing control over the definition of one's own health. [...]

What can women do to control their illness of risk? Some choose to create certainty by denying the existence of risk factors. However, this can sometimes lead to deadly consequences if the denial of risk results in the failure to take control over potential health problems. For example, Molly, quoted in the introduction, explained that she was consistently told that her lump represented no danger, yet five years later was diagnosed with a late stage breast cancer. Molly did not have the knowledge to take control over uncertainty. She did not have the power to judge whether or not her doctors were making responsible decisions about her risk of cancer. On the other hand, like clinicians, some women may choose to remove the risk through removal of the physical condition where the risk resides:

I don't know if I should tell this to you but I want to tell it to someone. I had a girlfriend die of breast cancer. It was terrible. Her death was worse than I imagined. The cancer went to her spine and liver. She was only 41 and had 3 little children. She had found the lump 2 years before and her doctor told her it was nothing to worry about and to come back and they would follow it. Well, she came back a year later and it was cancer. It had been cancer all along! With my lump, I was referred to Dr. Jones who I understand is a very good doctor. But he wanted to follow it. I wanted it out! Out of my body! There was no way I could live with that in me. I felt funny 'cause I had to insist on surgery. You normally don't do that. But I wanted it out! Out of there!

And in extreme situations, some women feel that they must control risk through prophylactic mastectomy. This extreme act is very much influenced by the practitioner's attempt to remove clinical risk. In other words, inherent to the construction of lay risk is the clinician's risk of being wrong, of failing to detect or predict a cancer. Lay risk incorporates a woman's experiences with her doctor's uncertainties. Rather than sharing responsibility for the diagnostic uncertainty with the doctor, some women choose to resolve this conflict by allowing the removal of that part of their body which makes the doctor and patient uncertain. But ironically, while the doctor is usually successful in removing his or her risk and regaining control over a physical condition, the woman suffers from the removal of her breast. Thus, while doctors treat risk through physical removal of part of the body, risk for women has been transformed into a new physical state of ill-health.

[...]

Discussion

I have argued that the concept of risk takes on fundamentally different meanings within epidemiology, clinical medicine and lay experiences of health and illness. For the epidemiologist, risk is an objective, scientific concept which describes relationships within large populations. However, for women, risk is an experienced condition of non-health. Women most often experience risk by transforming it into a symptom of a future or current illness. Once risk is experienced as an illness, a woman is at risk for further medicalization. For the medical practitioner, risk is understood as representing a sign of future disease from which a woman suffers, and as clinical uncertainty concerning diagnosis. Risk becomes a physical reality that can be manipulated and controlled by treating the affected individual or physical organ at risk for the disease. The desired clinical outcome is the removal of both clinical and lay risk. This process might be thought of as the medicalization of risk, and it results in greater clinical control over uncertainty by substituting an uncertain disease future with a certain state of ill-health. The medicalization of risk further removes the power to define states of health and illness from the individual. Instead, what is experienced are states of being ill, those individuals with less risk are simply less ill than those with more risk. Within current medical thought and practice one cannot be both healthy and at risk at the same time.

[...]

Acknowledgement

I would like to thank Anthony Colson, Kimberly Dovey and Ramona Koval for their critiques of earlier drafts of this essay.

References

Ernster, V. 1982 Personal communication.
Feinstein, A. 1973 An Analysis of Diagnostic Reasoning. Parts I and II. *Yale Journal of Biology and Medicine* 46: 212–32, 264–83.

Foucault, M. 1973 *The Birth of the Clinic: An Archaeology of Medical Perception*. New York: Vintage Books.

Kelsey, J. 1979 A Review of the Epidemiology of Human Breast Cancer. In *Epidemiologic Reviews*, vol. 1, The Johns Hopkins University of School of Hygiene and Public Health, pp. 74–109.

King, L. S. 1982 *Medical Thinking: A Historical Preface*. Princeton, NJ: Princeton University Press.

Lilienfeld, A. and D. E. Lilienfeld 1980 *Foundations of Epidemiology*. New York: Oxford University Press.

Love, S. M. 1984 Lumpy Breasts. *The Harvard Medical School Health Letter* X: 3–5.

McGehee, H., J. Bordley III, and J. A. Barondess 1979 *Differential Diagnosis: The Interpretation of Clinical Evidence*, 3rd ed. Philadelphia: W. B. Saunders Co.

Schwartz, G. F. 1982 Risk Factors in Breast Cancer: A Clinical Approach. *Breast* 8: 26–9.

18

Pumping Iron: Compliance with Chelation Therapy among Young People who have Thalassaemia Major

Karl Atkin and Waqar I. U. Ahmad

Introduction

[. . .] This paper explores how young people who have thalassaemia major view and respond to their treatment regimens. We examine the wider context within which chelation therapy – nightly infusion of an agent, through a slow operating pump, to break down excess iron – assumes meaning and significance. We begin with a brief description of thalassaemia.

Thalassaemia major is a recessive genetic condition in which individuals who inherit the thalassaemia gene from both parents (i.e. carriers) develop the disease. In the UK, the thalassaemia gene is more commonly found among Cypriot, South Asian and Chinese people, but also among African-Caribbean and indigenous 'white' British people. There are estimated to be around 600 people with thalassaemia major. A child born with thalassaemia major is unable to make sufficient haemoglobin and needs blood transfusions every four to six weeks, for life. Blood transfusions result in a potentially dangerous excess of iron in the bloodstream. Excretion of excess iron gained from transfusions requires injections of a drug such as desferrioxamine (desferal), using a battery operated infusion pump, eight to twelve hours a day, five to seven nights a week. Many of the complications associated with thalassaemia major result from non-compliance with these infusions (Modell and Anionwu 1996). Non-compliance causes 'iron overload' and can affect various organs. Specific complications include diabetes, delay or failure to enter puberty and heart problems. Non-use of the infusion pump is the most common cause of death among those with thalassaemia and many young people die in their 20s and 30s. The effects are cumulative and not immediately evident. The first signs of 'iron overload' are often apparent only after irreversible organ damage has occurred and this may be several years after non-compliance took place. Other problems associated with thalassaemia major include infections, such as hepatitis C, acquired through blood transfusions.

[. . .]

The study

The aim of the study was to provide a detailed understanding of young people's experience of living with a genetic condition, within the broader context of 'growing up'. We conducted in-depth interviews with 25 young people with thalassaemia [...] Each young person was interviewed twice over a six-month period. This enabled the young person's narrative to reflect the variability of the condition and its possible influence on their experience. The interviews illustrated the value of this approach as we were able to explore how young people's coping strategies changed over time as well as what might have been responsible for this change. This, as we shall see, proved especially valuable when making sense of a young person's response to chelation therapy.

[...] The eventual sample included 12 males and 13 females. Their average age was 13.9 years and the mode was 11 years. We interviewed two 10-year-old children; 12 young people were aged between 11 and 14 years; seven were aged between 16 and 17 years and four were aged between 18 and 19 years. In terms of ethnicity, 22 described themselves as Pakistani Muslim; one as Bangladeshi Muslim; one as Iranian Muslim and one Indian Hindu. Fifteen young people were still at school; seven were at college; two were seeking work and one was at university. In terms of family structure, 21 young people lived with their two 'natural' parents. Two lived with widowed mothers and one lived with his divorced mother, but still had regular contact with his father. Another young person lived with his brother and brother's wife, who were his legal guardians. The sample also included two young people who were married, but who were not living with their spouses. Three sample members lived in three-generation households and all but one lived with at least one sibling. The mean family size was 6.8 (including the person with thalassaemia).

[...]

The findings

Managing chelation therapy and its impact on the young person's life

Nearly all young people, irrespective of gender, cited the regular use of the infusion pump as the most difficult and disruptive aspect of thalassaemia major. All those over 13 years had failed to comply with chelation therapy at some stage and for those aged 13–16, non-compliance was more common than compliance. Seventeen-year-old Ashiq Javed remarked:

> I get stressed especially when I'm putting the pump on at night. I think, 'The hell, why?' I mean the pump is, I mean I don't like, I don't mind the transfusion at all, it's the pump, you know. I think every person with thalassaemia major will say, it's the pump. The pump's the problem.

Only those under 12 years of age were likely to play down the difficulties associated with chelation therapy. For them, chelation remained a parental responsibility and the young person did not yet dwell on the potential consequences of medical regimens for their sense of difference. Nonetheless, for older children, managing chelation therapy emerged as central to their illness narrative. They are physically and symbolically tied to the infusion pump and chelation therapy was seen to dominate their life. Not surprisingly, this caused resentment, with the use of the pump often becoming a focal point of the difficulties of living with thalassaemia major. Chelation therapy specifically evoked both practical and emotional difficulties and this explained why three-quarters of the sample specifically remarked that they *hated* using the pump. Nineteen-year-old Robina Begum described why she stopped using her pump:

> Because I started to hate it. I just didn't want it and, I don't know, things just got on top of me and I didn't want to wear my injections.

This sense of *hatred* is fundamental to understanding their relationship to chelation therapy and, as we shall see, will regularly recur throughout their narratives as we unpack these emotional and practical difficulties.

[...]

Coping with non-compliance

Despite their general ambivalence to chelation therapy, all – regardless of age – were clear about the importance of chelation therapy to their wellbeing. Balancing this tension is [...] a particular problem for young people when they reach their teenage years. Consequently, they were frustrated by the demands chelation therapy makes on them. Most were aware of the dilemma they faced in using the infusion pump to maintain their wellbeing while at the same time attempting to limit the impact of its use on their lives. Achieving this balance is part of a dynamic process and explains why their responses to chelation therapy were constantly shifting and at times appeared contradictory.

As part of this constant balancing process, the young person's response to thalassaemia is an important mediating factor in how they cope with chelation therapy. This is bound up with their general response to their illness and offers another reminder of the importance of discussing chelation therapy within the context of growing-up with a chronic illness. Young people's coping strategies are vulnerable and there are occasions when they are overwhelmed by the difficulties they face. These difficulties emerge from both the direct consequences of living with a chronic illness as well as the impact of the chronic illness in maintaining a sense of normalcy. The greater the sense of being overwhelmed the more likely they are to reject chelation therapy, as compliance becomes part of the symbolic struggle associated with living with thalassaemia.

For most of the time, the vast majority successfully adapted to their illness and coped with the difficulties they faced. The importance of this is increasingly being recognised in literature on childhood chronic illness (Beresford *et al*. 1996, Prout *et al*. 1999). None of the respondents was constantly overwhelmed by their illness and few perceived illness as a destroyer on a regular basis (see Herzlich 1973). Most, although occasionally engulfed by the illness, attempted to ensure that thalassaemia did not become the defining feature of their lives. Young people, for instance, try not to dwell on what might have been and several of the older respondents said it was important not to become angry and resentful. As part of this, they tried to maintain a sense of optimism and played down the negative aspects of the illness. This allowed them to maintain their sense of normality and similarity with peers.

Religion also emerged as an important coping resource, suggesting another possible ethnic difference in living with a chronic illness (see Currer 1986, Kelleher and Hillier 1996). Religion as a coping resource was more likely to be used by South Asian, irrespective of age and gender, than African-Caribbean respondents. The belief in Allah was seen as a source of strength, enabling them to come to terms with their illness. Chelation therapy was implicated in this. Several young people, for example, remarked that non-compliance was an insult to Allah. Eighteen-year-old Ashiq Javed explained:

> The fact is I have to do anything to stay alive. If I don't put the pump on, you know I'm committing suicide. Committing suicide is the highest sin. You have an obligation to keep yourself alive.

Several people were able to further sustain this sense of 'normality' by separating their condition or treatment from other 'normal' aspects of their life. Chelation therapy was often constructed as an activity with well-defined boundaries undertaken at specific times. Life was normal outside these boundaries; our previous work shows how parents often discounted the specific consequences of the condition in assessing the children's health and wellbeing (Atkin and Ahmad 2000).

However, this is part of a constant tension because [...] young people complain that chelation therapy often contributes to their sense of difference, reminding them that they have a disruptive and intrusive chronic illness and do not have the same opportunities as their peers. Attempts to construct normality and reduce the impact of thalassaemia on their life can therefore only ever be partially successful. The severity and technology-dependent nature of the condition provide too many reminders of the dangers and limitations they face. Young people are constantly juggling the difficulties associated with their condition and the possibility of relief from the consequences of their illness. Consequently, there are times when the young person's sense of sadness at having thalassaemia is greater than at other times. This is when they feel at the mercy of the illness, feeling that the world is against them. This is when their sense of difference, anxiety, frustration and powerlessness is especially strong. [...] [F]ive young people explicitly mentioned death in explaining their previous non-use of the pump. In three cases this reflected their belief that there was little point in complying with treatment because they were going to die young anyway. As 19-year-old Amir Jan said: 'I couldn't see the point, to be honest. I was going to die anyway so why bother'. Two young people saw the prospect of early death as offering release from the suffering and depression the illness caused them. This was not a deliberate attempt to end their life, but more an expression of the helplessness they felt. Nineteen-year-old Robina Begum explained:

I just felt a bit, you know, 'So what, big deal if I die', I die you know. That's what it was, that's why I stopped wearing my injections.

More generally, chelation therapy not only informs a young person's sense of estrangement, representing a symbolic reminder of the difficulties of living with a chronic illness and their sense of 'difference', these feelings of estrangement can also directly lead to non-compliance.

Negotiating responsibility: the relationship between the young person and their parents

As we have seen, young people, as they seek to develop their own identities and establish their 'normality', may reject their parents' or professionals' definitions of what is in their interests (see also Hill 1994, Mador and Smith 1989, Frydenberg 1997). Chelation therapy is often a focal point of these disagreements (Ratip *et al.* 1995) and can become a particular site of strategy and struggle as a child gets older (Ahmad and Atkin 1996). Parents, for example, often say that the most frequent cause of arguments with their teenage offspring concerned the use of the infusion pump (Atkin *et al.* 1998b). Respondents, in this study, would agree with this. Ashiq Javed, for example, described how his parents constantly reminded him about the importance of chelation therapy. This annoyed him:

> That really, really, really makes me angry and I can't stand it. I don't want to be treated differently. I mean, at the end of the day they should realise it's up to me what I choose to do.

The parent-child relationship becomes fundamental in negotiating responsibility for compliance with chelation therapy and gives specific expression to many of the issues discussed above. Exploring this relationship also helps to unpack further the young person's reasons for non-compliance.

As we have seen, those under 12 were largely dependent on parents for chelation therapy. As they got older, parents and professionals progressively encouraged them to take an active part in chelation therapy, such as mixing of the medication. Young people usually enjoyed this involvement as a sign of being 'grown up'. Most began to assume greater responsibility for their own care between the ages of 13 and 16 years. [...]

For many, however, the pump quickly became a chore as well as a symbol of their difference. This, as we have seen, led to a sense of estrangement and consequently, young people soon began not to use the pump as regularly as recommended. Ismat Javed, for instance, remarked how she used her newfound freedom to disregard the use of the pump. Young people hid non-compliance from their parents to avoid conflict (see also Drury 1991, Brannen *et al.* 1994). This was also apparent in the responses of African-Caribbean young people and suggests that ethnicity made little difference in hiding compliance from parents. South Asian young people concealed their non-compliance because they knew how angry their parents would be if they knew. Parents and children used various strategies in this regard. Ismat Javed, for example, said that her parents used to count her needles to ensure she was using the infusion pump. She systematically threw the needles away to create the impression that she was using the pump. Others described how they disconnected the needle at night, but still left the pump on. When their parents checked on them it appeared that the pump was connected. Gulab Maqbool explained:

> Sometimes [I] just, when my parents are asleep or something, take it out quickly, put it on the side and then in the morning attach it.

Such a strategy further illustrates the young person's complex relationship to chelation therapy. Disconnecting the pump seemed a futile form of resistance since the discomfort of connecting it had already been experienced, and reconnection would result in double the discomfort. However, as we have seen, the young person's response to chelation therapy is more than a reflection of the practical difficulties associated with using the infusion pump. It has an emotional dimension as well.

No respondent, however, was able to disguise this for long: non-compliance became evident during routine blood checks. [...] Seventeen-year-old Farzana Azam had also attempted to disguise non-compliance from her parents and described her mother's anger when she found out:

> My mum, she would say 'why you not having it, are you trying to die or what?' you know, 'what you trying to do to yourself? Have the injection, otherwise I'm not going to talk to you', and all that. I goes 'what's it got to do with you, why you asking me, I could take it if I wanted, don't have to take it if I don't want to'. So we did use to have arguments.

More generally, young people resented these arguments believing that parental objections undermined their ability to choose for themselves, although their non-compliance could be seen to provide parents with a legitimate reason for intervention. Many, however, did not necessarily recognise this contradiction. They were annoyed that parents compromised their sense of personal autonomy, found parental responses patronising and felt they were not treated as 'a grown up'. [...] This annoyance at their parents or guardians is perhaps another reflection of the young persons' complex relationship with chelation therapy. They want recognition of their growing independence by taking responsibility for chelation therapy, while at the same time using this sense of autonomy to make a choice not to use the pump.

Negotiating 'over-protectiveness'

Arguments about chelation therapy reflected another, more general concern of young people: 'over-protectiveness', a common theme in the literature on childhood disability (Eiser 1990, Davis and Wasserman 1992). For their part, many parents are aware of this problem but are not sure how to deal with it (Atkin *et al*. 1998b). Most young people, of all ages and both sexes, felt that their mothers and fathers were over-protective and prevented them pursuing activities they regarded as 'normal' among their peers. They provided many examples of the things they were prevented from doing. Several boys, for instance, said that their parents had stopped them playing sports because of their illness. Some mentioned not being able to stay overnight at a friend's house. Even when a young person was given permission to stay overnight, their parents still checked to ensure compliance. Sixteen-year-old Kaneez Mirza was glad her parents had eventually agreed to let her stay overnight with friends, but was embarrassed by their regular telephone calls to check that her infusion pump was working. [...]

In nearly all the families, parental 'over-protectiveness' had caused arguments. Young people felt that by over-emphasising chelation therapy, parents only saw the illness and not them. Consequently, many felt that the condition needlessly dominated their life. These concerns emphasised their difference, made it difficult to maintain a valued self-identity and sometimes resulted in conflict with parents. To some extent, this is an inevitable aspect of making sense of a chronic illness within the broader context of 'growing-up'. Respondents, as they attempted to develop and sustain a positive self-identity, described tensions in their relationships with their parents similar to those of young people in general. However, they seemed less desirous of living separately from parents. They also seemed less likely to challenge their parents' religious and cultural values than has been reported for white young people (Brannen *et al.* 1994). Discussion about independence and the more general process of 'growing-up' among different ethnic groups, therefore, is not entirely straightforward. Young Asian people are attempting to express the cultural assumptions in which they have become socialised, while at the same time needing to live within a more 'Western' frame of reference. Their peer networks reflect this; none of the respondents had friends confined only to their own ethnic group. Establishing autonomy and independence seems as important to Asian young people living in the UK as [to] their 'white' counterparts, albeit independence may have different connotations among Asian and white young people. The feeling that chelation therapy was imposed rather than negotiated made compliance more difficult to accept, although most attempted gradually to 'push back the boundaries' and demonstrate their sense of responsibility to their parents. Parental trust had to be earned. Despite their frustration about 'over-protection', they usually understood their parents' concerns and acknowledged that parents had a right to be concerned about non-compliance. This understanding, however, is caught up with the young person's constantly shifting response to their illness noted above.

Consequently, there are times when young people are more understanding than others. Our previous work also suggests there are times when parents are more conscious of non-compliance than at other times (Ahmad and Atkin 1996). Parental concerns become particularly heightened when they hear of a death of another child with thalassaemia major or when they are reminded of its importance by professionals or national organisations, such as the UK Thalassaemia Society. [...] Nineteen-year-old Ismat Javed, who went through periods of non-compliance which she now regretted, attempted to make sense of her parents' worries:

You expect families to be like that. I mean I always tell my mum, 'You're being too over-protective' but you know, what can you do? I'd probably do the same. I'm sure a lot of parents of children without thalassaemia are very over-protective of their children. But they [her parents] do worry too much. It's impossible. I mean obviously they don't worry as much now as they did before, I mean they still do in some ways but sometimes they just get a bit scared that something might happen.

Recognition of parental concerns did not, however, necessarily mean that it made their parents' approach any easier to deal with or that young people necessarily changed their behaviour. Acknowledgement of their parents' concerns and need to establish their own sense of autonomy added to confusion and made them feel guilty about arguing with their parents, even when they thought they had a just cause:

> Oh, when they're telling you to do things, you know, oh, you have to wear injections, that got to me sometimes, thinking, 'God man, this is me, I have to wear them, will you just leave me alone'. You know, 'let me do what I want to do'. But I know, I mean they do have your best interests at heart. (19-year-old Robina Begum)

Guilt, in fact, becomes an important feature of the young person's illness narrative, finding specific expression in the relationship with their parents. Their conscious non-compliance with chelation therapy and the distress this caused to their parents also fed this guilt. Older respondents mentioned this and emphasised how much their parents had had to come to terms with. Guilt could also be manifest in other ways. Unlike other reports (e.g. Nash 1990), respondents rarely blamed parents for having passed on the condition. On the other hand, parents of thalassaemic children fear being blamed by children because of professionals' assertions that their illness resulted from parental consanguinity (Atkin et al. 1998a, see Ahmad 1995 for a critique of the consanguinity debate). The few who did blame their parents were then in their early teens and struggling to make sense of the illness. Not surprisingly, the need for regular chelation therapy was often the reason for the young people having such feelings. Seventeen-year-old Farzana Azam remarked:

> And I used to think, why me? Because my brothers were all right. They did not need blood transfusions. They did not need to use the pump. They've got no problems. And why is it me that is going through medications and injections which I don't like at all. So I think I used to get cross and that I used to blame it on my mum.

More generally, however, most children admitted there were times when they took out the frustrations associated with chelation therapy on their parents (see Geiss et al. 1992). Respondents were, at times, 'awful' to their parents, being 'grumpy' and 'moody', and using parents as scapegoats for the problems associated with chelation therapy or the condition. As Jamil Rehman pointed out, 'who else is there' to be the target of these frustrations? Regrets over their behaviour did not stop them repeating it. Such frustrations caused guilt and sometimes undermined respondents' coping abilities and acceptance of treatment. [...]

Understanding the value of chelation therapy

The relationship between knowledge and non-compliance emerged as an interesting feature of the young person's behaviour. All, regardless of age, were clear about the importance of chelation therapy to their wellbeing. The value of the pump is strongly emphasised at patient group meetings, including the annual conference of the UK Thalassaemia Society, and by professionals. Deaths through non-compliance act as an unpleasant but strong reminder about the dangers of non-compliance. As noted, resistance to chelation therapy was related to practical, emotional and symbolic aspects of the therapy. Young people, however, still believed information was important in encouraging compliance and to some extent this reflects a belief in medical definitions of their problems.

Many of the older respondents, for example, felt they should have been told more about the consequences of non-compliance when they were younger. As we have seen, Ismat Javed, now 19, stopped using the pump during her early teens. This, she said, was partly explained by not understanding the value of the infusion pump:

> You see, I mean, I've only realised the importance of the pump recently. I didn't know how important desferal was and what it [does], you know. You think you're just going to grow like everyone else.

[...] Several young people were especially angry at health professionals for not telling them sooner about the problems of high feritin levels. Young people believe that service practitioners do not tailor information to their needs and fail to emphasise the value of compliance in a way the child would find useful. As we have seen, however, practical information is only one part of encouraging young people to use the pump. [...]

Those over 16, despite going through long periods of non-compliance when they were younger, were more likely to comply with chelation therapy than those aged 13–16 years. Moreover, those over 16 were not only more likely to comply but had also become passionate advocates of the infusion pump. Several reasons explain this return to compliance. Many, for instance, attributed it to a greater understanding of the problems of non-compliance, often gained from 'lived experience'. The consequences of non-compliance are not immediately evident and a child can go several years before being aware of the irreversible damage caused by iron overload. In many cases it was the emergence of problems that made them appreciate the value of chelation and using the infusion pump again. Sixteen-year-old Rashid Mustaq described how he began using his infusion pump again, after being told that he had an 'enlarged' heart. The fear of death encouraged Robina Begum to begin using her pump again, despite her initial non-compliance being associated with a wish to escape the suffering through death.

[...] In general, these young people hoped that others would not repeat their mistakes. Sixteen-year-old Gulab Maqbool's advice to others was: 'Don't be like me'. And Ismat Javed would advise them:

> ... if I met somebody who was 9, 10, 11, I'd say there is something you can do about it now, you know. Make sure, you know, look after yourself and do your treatment. It is impossible to turn the clocks back, isn't it?

Nonetheless, the response of these young people does not simply reflect their direct experience of the consequences of non-compliance. These older respondents also seemed better equipped to come to terms with living with a chronic illness. The sense of struggle associated with chelation therapy tended to reduce with age for both genders. They began to recognise the importance of working with the illness rather than against it. This is not to say that all older respondents had learnt to overcome the difficulties associated with thalassaemia. Sadness and frustration still occurred and became implicated in the compliance process throughout the person's life. Nonetheless, those over 16 seemed better adjusted to the difficulties associated with their illness; a range of coping strategies enabled them to cope with the illness. Compliance benefited from this and usually became more regular, although it rarely became absolute. [...]

Conclusion

[...] [Y]oung people's response to chelation therapy is both complex and dynamic. It represents a specific disruption to their biographies and is part of the wider process in which they make sense of the relationship between body, self and illness, and maintain relationships. Consequently the everyday experience of living with a chronic illness, the pleasures and tensions of growing-up, family relationships and social networks are all implicated in the compliance process. Thus the rejection of compliance therapy was rarely associated with practical difficulties alone. It more closely related to concerns around a valued self-identity, peer relations and being 'normal'.

[...]

Persuading users to follow treatment or advice remains an issue within health services. In relationship to thalassaemia, following treatment can make the difference between life and death. As this paper demonstrates, to understand young people's reasons for non-use of life-saving chelation therapy, one needs to move beyond a concern with practical difficulties. Instead the symbolic meaning of chelation therapy as a threat to their 'normalcy', and the importance of lived experience, are vital to recognise if more effective partnerships are to be built between young sufferers, their families and health professionals.

Acknowledgements

Our thanks to the National Lottery Charities Board for financial support; our Professional Advisory Committee and Young People's Advisory Group for valuable guidance; Kanwal Mand for assistance with interviews; and three anonymous referees for helpful comments on earlier drafts of this paper. This research is taken from a joint project with Al-Falah, a voluntary organisation based in Bradford offering welfare advice and support.

References

Ahmad, W. I. U. (1995) Reflection on consanguinity and birth outcome debate, *Journal of Public Health Medicine*, 16, 4, 423–8.
Ahmad, W. I. U. and Atkin, K. (1996) Ethnicity and caring for a disabled child: the case of children with sickle cell or thalassaemia, *British Journal of Social Work*, 26, 755–75.

Atkin, K., Ahmad, W. I. U. and Anionwu, E. (1998a) Screening and counselling for sickle cell disorders and thalassaemia: the experience of parents and health professionals, *Social Science and Medicine*, 47, 11, 1639–51.

Atkin, K., Ahmad, W. I. U. and Anionwu, E. (1998b) Service support to families caring for a child with a sickle cell disorder or thalassaemia, *Health*, 2, 3, 305–27.

Atkin, K. and Ahmad, W. I. U. (2000) Coping with childhood illness: experiences of parents whose children have thalassaemia major or sickle cell disorder, *Health and Social Care in the Community*, 8, 1, 57–69.

Beresford, B., Sloper, P., Baldwin, S. and Newman, T. (1996) *What works in services for families with a disabled child*. Essex. Barnardo's.

Brannen, J., Dodd, K., Oakley, A. and Storey, P. (1994) *Young People, Health and Family Life*. Buckingham: Open University Press.

Currer, C. (1986) Concepts of mental well- and ill-being: the case of Pathan mothers in Britain. In Currer, C. and Stacey, M. (eds), *Concepts of Health, Illness and Disease*. Leamington Spa: Berg.

Davis, J. K. and Wasserman, E. (1992) Behavioural aspects of asthma in children, *Clinical Paediatrics*, November, 678–81.

Drury, B. (1991) Sikh girls and the maintenance of an ethnic identity, *New Community*, 17, 3, 387–99.

Eiser, C. (1990) *Chronic Childhood Disease: an Introduction to Psychological Theory and Research*. Cambridge: Cambridge University Press.

Frydenberg, E. (1997) *Adolescent Coping: Theoretical and Research Perspectives*. London: Routledge.

Geiss, S. K., Hobbs, S. A., Hammersley-Maercklein, G., Kramer, J. C. and Henley, M. (1992) Psychosocial factors related to perceived compliance with cystic fibrosis treatment, *Journal of Clinical Psychology*, 48, 1, 99–103.

Herzlich, C. (1973) *Health and Illness: a Social Psychological Analysis*. London: Academic Press.

Hill, S. A. (1994) *Managing Sickle Cell Disease in Low-income Families*. Philadelphia: Temple University Press.

Kelleher, D. and Hillier, S. (1996) *Researching Cultural Differences in Health*. London: Routledge.

Mador, J. A. and Smith, D. H. (1989) The psychological adaptation of adolescents with cystic-fibrosis: the review of the literature, *Journal of Adolescent Health Care*, 10, 2, 136–42.

Modell, B. and Anionwu, E. (1996) Guidelines for screening for haemoglobin disorders: service specification for low- and high-prevalence district health authorities. In Ahmad, W. I. U., Sheldon, T. and Stuart, O. (eds), *Reviews of Ethnicity and Health*. York: NHS Centre for Reviews and Dissemination.

Nash, K. B. (1990) Growing up with thalassaemia: a chronic disorder, *Annals of the New York Academy of Sciences*, 612, 442–50.

Prout, A., Hayes, L. and Gelder, L. (1999) Medication and the maintenance of ordinariness in household management of childhood asthma, *Sociology of Health and Illness*, 21, 2, 137–62.

Ratip, S., Skuse, D., Porter, J., Wonke, B., Yardumian, A. and Modell, B. (1995) Psychosocial and clinical burden of thalassemia-intermedia and its implications for pre-natal diagnosis, *Archives of Diseases in Childhood*, 72, 5, 408–12.

Part IV

Social Patterning of Health and Illness

Introduction

Our chances of living a long and healthy life are strongly influenced by our social background. Illness and disease do not occur at random, but are socially patterned. This means that some social groups – mainly those who benefit from economic, social and psychological advantage – are less likely to suffer from illness than others. Social scientists have been aware of this for a long time, but there has been, and indeed remains, a considerable degree of controversy as to why this should be the case. The papers in this section document examples of the social patterning of health, raise some of the methodological issues associated with exploring the relationships between social attributes and health, and discuss some of the conceptual and theoretical developments in this area of study.

Graham draws upon empirical data which give insights into possible explanations for health inequalities. Her focus is on gendered differences in health across social classes. She establishes that since the 1970s there has been a widening in health inequalities between social classes for both men and women. Some of the reasons for this include changes in the labour market, such as the casualization of labour; changes to family structures, with an increase in female-headed lone-parent families; changes in the distribution of housing tenure with a loss of social housing; and a rise in poverty, particularly in childhood. She examines evidence based on material, psycho-social and behavioural factors, in order to elucidate reasons for such inequalities. These factors tend to cluster together, and it is therefore difficult to disentangle the contribution made by each of them. The data presented in the paper suggest that there is a complex interrelationship between structural, psycho-social and individual factors when attempting to understand the relationship between social groups and health.

It is now well documented that there are ethnic differences in health status, but there are competing explanations for this. Davey Smith and his colleagues provide 'descriptive epidemiological' data on this topic, and outline various explanations that have been offered to account for ethnic inequalities in health. The authors assess the contributions of various 'models of explanation', which they classify as 'artefact', 'migration', 'socio-economic factors', 'culture, beliefs, behaviour', 'racism', 'biology' and 'health service access and use'. The authors demonstrate how a great deal of care is needed when presenting and interpreting data on ethnicity and health. The data are of course contingent on the indicators used to measure differences. How ethnicity is categorized can be important. For example, if the measure used is country of birth, self-assigned ethnic group or a composite measure, different conclusions might be reached (Karlsen and Nazroo, 2000). Indicators of social class based on occupation can also make for inappropriate or misleading interpretations, as there may be considerable variations of income and experiences within social classes. The authors show, for example, how the mean household incomes of Pakistani and Bangladeshi households who are in social classes I and II are less than those of White households who are in social classes IV and V. The picture presented of the patterning of health by ethnicity is a highly complex one. The nature of the relationship between ethnicity and various conditions differs. For example, members of minority ethnic groups have an elevated risk of diabetes, which is maintained even after socio-economic differences are 'controlled for'. On the other hand, members of ethnic minority groups appear to be less likely to suffer from respiratory conditions, a relationship which again is maintained even after socio-economic differences are taken into account. The authors demonstrate that socio-economic factors do, however, play an important part in the ethnic patterning of health, and their contribution has been underestimated by those researchers who attempt to 'control out' socio-economic position to reveal the 'true' relationship between ethnicity and health. This is important because it

> gives the impression that different types of explanation operate for ethnic minority groups compared with the general population. While for the latter, factors relating to socioeconomic position are shown to be crucial, for the former they are not visible, so differences are assumed to be related to some aspect of ethnicity or 'race', even though socioeconomic factors are important determinants of health for all groups.

Levels of morbidity and mortality are linked to structural factors such as gender, class and race. Macintyre, MacIver and Sooman argue that research into these relationships almost invariably uses individuals as the unit of analysis, even when the focus of the study is on a geographical area. In their paper they make a case for carrying out research into 'places' as well as 'people'. They challenge the assumption that area variations in health are the result of 'variations in the composition of their population', suggesting that the quality of the social and physical environment has an important role to play in explaining health differences. As Macintyre has pointed out elsewhere:

> Although sociology is supposed to focus on social structures and social relationships, all too often in the field of social inequalities in health we have tended to focus on individuals and their behaviours rather than on the environments to which they are exposed (perhaps because health and illness is expressed in individuals). (2000: 18)

Macintyre, MacIver and Sooman support their argument by comparing data from two areas of Glasgow. They find that individuals who are similar in terms of income, housing tenure, etc., are likely to have better health if they live in the 'better off' area. This paper is an example of a growing body of literature which has emerged in recent decades on place and health, the policy implications of which can be seen in the development of urban regeneration programmes, health action zones and so on.

Health inequalities have long been debated by sociologists, and much of that debate centres on the reasons for the apparent differences in the health status of social groups, and what the mechanisms are that link class, gender, income, race or whatever to health status. Elstad summarizes the key developments in these debates which have occurred since the 1990s, and groups them under what he refers to as the 'psycho-social perspective on health inequalities'. This perspective, he notes, focuses less on material disadvantage and poor health behaviours, and turns our attention to 'psychological stress, relative deprivation, and the psycho-social injuries of inequality structures'. The perspective derives from both psychological and sociological literatures which draw upon issues of stress, emotions and social cohesion. One of the most influential writers in this field has been Richard Wilkinson, who in his book, *Unhealthy Societies*, (1996), brings together the work of psychologists, anthropologists, sociologists, economists, historians and demographers to make sense of health inequalities. Fundamentally, the psycho-social perspective represents a Durkheimian approach to the study of health and illness, in that it seeks to comprehend how social structures can alter the mental and physical states of individuals.

References

Karlsen, S. and Nazroo, J. Y. (2000) Identity and Structure: Rethinking Ethnic Inequalities in Health. In H. Graham (ed.), *Understanding Health Inequalities*, Buckingham: Open University Press, 38–57.

Macintyre, S. (2000) The Social Patterning of Health: Bringing the Social Context Back In, Plenary Address to the 1999 British Medical Sociology Annual Conference, *Medical Sociology News*, 26 (1), 14–19.

Wilkinson, R. G. (1996) *Unhealthy Societies: The Afflictions of Inequality*. London and New York: Routledge.

19

Socio-economic Change and Inequalities in Men and Women's Health in the UK

Hilary Graham

Introduction

Social class is 'written on the body': it is inscribed in our experiences of health and our chances of premature death. The invariable pattern, across time and between societies, is one in which men and women in higher socio-economic groups enjoy better health across longer lives than those in lower socio-economic groups. These inequalities in health are persisting – and in some cases are widening – in the context of rapid economic and social change. In the UK, for example, the rapid decline in manual occupations and the growth of more flexible employment contracts has brought with it greater job insecurity and unemployment. At the same time, men and women are reshaping their domestic lives, with more moving into and out of cohabitation and marriage. Changes in employment and household patterns are fuelling a wider process of socio-economic polarization. During the 1980s and 1990s greater prosperity for the majority has been at the cost of poverty for an increasing minority. [...]

In turning the spotlight on socio-economic stratification and socio-economic change, the chapter inevitably places other aspects of inequality in shadow. Age, ethnicity and sexuality, as well as gender, mediate the influence of socio-economic position on health. Socio-economic inequality, and its intersection with gender, therefore provides only a starting point for an analysis of how socio-economic change is structured into individual health. The focus on how health is framed by socio-economic circumstances also means that the chapter gives less attention to how individuals achieve agency 'in and against' these circumstances. However, the evidence it presents provides a corrective to perspectives on late modernity which suggest that the class based inequalities which have long characterized the UK are giving way to individually fashioned identities. Many men and women may, as sociological accounts have argued, be engaged in a reflexive and lifelong 'project of the self' (Giddens 1991). But increasing poverty and social polarization mean that the opportunity to participate in such projects is unequally distributed, with an increasing proportion of the population denied access to the lifestyles and life choices that the majority take for granted.

The chapter's focus on socio-economic inequalities is grounded in two fields of research: social policy and social epidemiology. Social policy research records what social change is doing to people's socio-economic circumstances, while social epidemiology is concerned with what their socio-economic circumstances are doing to their health. In their different ways, researchers in both disciplines map the pathways which run between the structure of society and the welfare of individuals. Researchers in social policy and social epidemiology share, too, a recognition of the difficulty of proving cause and effect, of demonstrating that structural factors have health outcomes. Demonstrating the health effects of changes in these structural influences is an even more complex methodological and theoretical task.

The task is complex partly because of the limitations of conventional measures of socio-economic position. In the UK, occupation and employment status have been and remain the primary measures of an individual's social class or socio-economic status (Rose and O'Reilly 1997). But, as in other countries, there are marked gender differences in employment status, with women more likely than men to be outside the labour market and in part-time employment. There is also a socio-economic gradient in full-time employment, with the proportion of men and women in full-time jobs rising with occupational social class (Office for National Statistics (ONS) 1998). Exposure to occupation related influences on health is therefore likely to be greater among men than women, and among those higher up rather than lower down the class ladder. As a result, analyses of socio-economic differences in health which are based on occupation are not, as Hunt and Macintyre (2000) put it, 'comparing like with like'. Demonstrating causal connections between socio-economic exposure and health effects is difficult, too, because an individual's health is shaped by long term processes which may be evident only when they materialize as symptoms: whether as self-defined ill health or as clinically validated indicators of disease. Further, there are likely to be time lags, of variable duration, between exposure to the cause and evidence of the effect, during which time other mediating factors may have altered the progress of the disease. [...]

Socio-economic inequalities in health

Patterns and trends

Socio-economic differentials in mortality have been recorded since the mid-eighteenth century (Woods and Williams 1995). By the mid-nineteenth century, these differentials were being systematically recorded in public surveys of Britain's new industrial cities (Whitehead 1997). In Liverpool in the 1840s, for example, the average age of death was 35 for the gentry and professional people, 22 for tradesmen and 15 for labourers (Whitehead 1997). This was the epidemiological period in which infectious diseases were the major causes of death. Today, the UK, like other western societies, has made the transition to a postindustrial society in which chronic diseases like coronary heart disease, stroke and cancer dominate the mortality statistics. These diseases have different specific causes, both from each other and from the killer diseases of the nineteenth century. But they share a common socio-economic profile. Consistent gradients are found for most major causes of death, including lung cancer, respiratory disease, heart disease and stroke (Smith and Harding 1997). Similar gradients are evident in self-reported health (Prescott-Clarke and Primatesta 1998; ONS 1998). [...]

Figures 1 and 2 describe the socio-economic gradient in men and women's health, as revealed in two measures of health status: self-assessed health and mortality. Figure 1 maps the proportion of men and women describing their health as 'very good' or 'good' in the Health Survey for England, which uses a measure of social class based on own occupation (Prescott-Clarke and Primatesta 1998). Figure 2 is based on the Office for National Statistics Longitudinal Study and classifies women's social class by the occupation of their (male) partners (Smith and Harding 1997). The gradients in mortality tend to be less steep for women but, as among men, higher socio-economic status protects women against the risk of ill health, while lower socio-economic status increases their chances of disease, disability and premature death. Compared to men and women in social class I, men and women in social class V have death rates which are respectively 1.7 and 1.5 times higher, while the proportion of men and women in good or very good health is around 30 per cent lower at the bottom of the class ladder than at the top.

The socio-economic differentials in health captured in Figures 1 and 2 are evident using different indicators of socio-economic position, including parental social class, education, income, housing tenure and car ownership (Filakti and Fox 1995; Smith and Harding 1997; Davey Smith *et al.* 1998). There are, of course, strong associations between these different measures of socio-economic status: staying on at school and gaining qualifications anticipates a career marked out by employment in secure and high paid non-manual occupations, which in turn provides the longer term income needed to buy a home and own a car. This suggests that the different measures are indices of an individual's socio-economic experience over the life-course, with parental social class indicating where a person comes from, education signalling where the person is going, and occupation and tenure marking the class of destination. [...]

How can the persistent and widening socio-economic differentials in health be explained? One possibility is that there is nothing to be explained: that the gradients are an artefact, produced through flaws in the measurement of socio-economic status and health and in the statistical analyses of their relationship. It is now generally

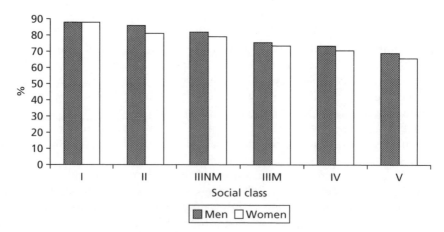

Figure 1 Adults' self-assessed health as 'good' or 'very good' (age standardized) by social class and sex, England 1996
Source: Prescott-Clarke and Primatesta 1998: Table 5.14

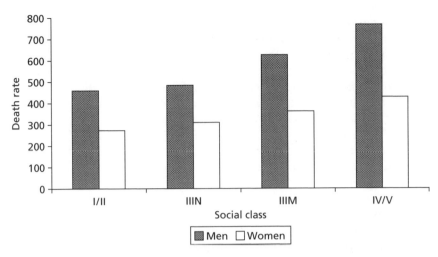

Figure 2 Age standardized death rates per 100,000 people by social class, men and women aged 35–64, England and Wales 1980–92

Note: Women are classified by partner's occupational details or, if absent, by their own.
Source: 1971 LS Cohort, England and Wales described in Smith and Harding 1997: Tables 11.4 and 11.7

accepted that statistical inaccuracies cannot explain the consistency and magnitude of the class gradient (Davey Smith *et al.* 1994). An alternative explanation suggests that the gradient is the outcome of health related mobility, in which healthier people climb up the class ladder, while those in poorer health slip down. However, while health status influences subsequent social mobility, the evidence suggests that its scale is insufficient to explain the overall socio-economic gradients in health (Power *et al.* 1996).

With neither statistical errors nor social mobility making a major contribution to health inequalities, the search for causes has focused on factors which run back to and from the broader structure of society. However, health outcomes are not easily tracked to their class origins. Both an individual's health and the class relationships in which they experience it are dynamic, with changes reflecting longer term processes which are hard to detect through the research designs currently available. Detection tends to be easier at the individual rather than structural level: at the point at which the underlying processes manifest themselves in people's home and work environments and in their daily habits and routines. As a result, studies have revealed considerably more about factors which are proximate (close) to the individual than about factors which are proximate to the social structure.

Constrained by these limitations, researchers have worked to identify the individual-level factors which link socio-economic status and health status. Attention has focused on three sets of factors: material, psychosocial and behavioural. Material factors include the physical environment of the home, neighbourhood and workplace, together with living standards secured through earnings, benefits and other income. Psychosocial factors include the life events and chronic difficulties which make demands that are hard to meet and the social networks and confiding relationships which can support people through them. Among the behavioural factors, diet, cigarette smoking and recreational exercise have been singled out for their contribution to the socio-economic gradient. The contribution of these factors to the socio-economic gradient in health obviously varies between different dimensions of health. Material factors figure more strongly than psychosocial factors in relation to causes of death like accidental injuries and respiratory disease, while both the material and psychosocial environments are implicated in the aetiology of many psychological illnesses.

Gender, as well as socio-economic position, mediates exposure to material, psychosocial and behavioural risks. For example, men have traditionally been more exposed to the industrial injuries associated with skilled manual work (in mining, engineering and construction, for example). Men also led the way into habits like cigarette smoking at a time when it symbolized affluence and high class living, and men still have higher rates of alcohol consumption: two behavioural factors seen as contributing to the male excess of mortality from lung cancer and coronary heart disease. Conversely, women are more likely to experience the disadvantages identified as contributing to affective disorders: a poor home environment, with heavy childcare responsibilities and low levels of social support (Brown and Harris 1978; Elliot and Huppert 1991; Macran et al. 1996). Reviewing the evidence on these divergent gender patterns, it has been suggested that women's disadvantaged position at home and in the labour market may hold the key to understanding both women's lower rates of mortality and their higher rates of morbidity from poor mental health and particularly from anxiety and depressive disorders (Johansson 1991; Popay et al. 1993; Macintyre and Hunt 1997).

Material, psychosocial and behavioural risk factors – among both men and women – tend to cluster together. Individuals exposed to material disadvantage are more likely to be disadvantaged with respect to their psychosocial environment and their health behaviour, while individuals protected from material hazards are more likely to have a protected and protective psychosocial environment and to engage in health promoting behaviours. Proximate influences not only cluster together, but also accumulate together. Children born into material disadvantage are exposed to more material, psychosocial and behavioural risk factors across their (shorter and less healthy) lives than children born into material advantage.

It is the clustered and cumulative nature of disadvantage – material, psychosocial and behavioural – which is seen to produce and perpetuate inequalities in men's and women's health. Research which addresses these key dimensions of class related exposure is discussed in more detail in the two subsections below.

The clustering of material, psychosocial and behavioural risks

Socio-economic gradients in exposure to material, psychosocial and behavioural risks have been consistently found in population surveys and in surveys of specific subgroups, like the Whitehall II Study of civil servants. Civil service grade provides a finely graduated measure of socio-economic status within a relatively privileged section of the working population. Clear socio-economic differentials in health are nonetheless produced among both men and women, as measured by height, body mass index, obesity, hypertension and self-reported health (Marmot and Davey Smith 1997; Marmot et al. 1997).

Socio-economic gradients in individual level influences are also strongly in evidence, with broadly similar gradients among both men and women. As Figure 3 describes, access to material resources, proxied by car ownership, and exposure to material problems, measured by neighbourhood environment, is related to civil service grade. Psychosocial risks and resources are similarly patterned by employment grade (Figure 4). Exposure to life events among men is inversely related to civil service grade, with rates of exposure in both sexes rising as employment grade falls. Poor working conditions, as measured by low control over the pace and content of work, are also related to low employment grade. Conversely, men and women in higher grades are significantly more likely to have access to a confiding relationship and to have high control at work. Health related behaviours display a similar socio-economic profile (Figure 5). Among both men and women, those in the lowest grade are most likely to smoke cigarettes and least likely either to be taking exercise or have diets high in recommended nutrients, like fresh fruit. Alcohol consumption, however, displays a different pattern, with higher mean consumption associated with higher employment grade for both women and men. The positive socio-economic gradient in alcohol consumption is also evident in national surveys (Colhoun and Prescott-Clarke 1996; ONS 1998). These surveys point to other socio-economic differences in alcohol consumption. While affluence is associated with higher consumption, the experience of being drunk and of problem drinking is more strongly associated with deprivation.

As Figures 3 to 5 suggest, individuals' access to health promoting environments and lifestyles is strongly patterned by their socio-economic position. However, the socio-economic patterning of health risks and resources is not identical for men and women. The most striking example is cigarette smoking, where the socio-economic gradient is reversed for women in the highest employment grade (Figure 5). Smoking prevalence in this group is 1.5 times higher than in the grade below. Women at the top of the civil service hierarchy also have the highest rates of alcohol consumption and, unlike their male counterparts, do not have the highest rates of leisure time exercise. These divergent lifestyles may reflect, as Marmot and Davey Smith (1997) suggest, the unique pressures on women working in high grades in the civil service. They may also reflect, and interact with, other differences between men and women in senior management.

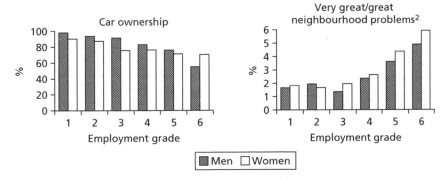

Figure 3 Material factors by employment grade, Whitehall II Study, men and women, age adjusted[1]

Notes

1 N = approx. 9000; tests for trend within sex by grade significant at p < 0.001 for men and women.

2 Neighbourhood problems as measured by answers to the question 'To what extent do you have problems with the neighbourhood you live in (e.g. noise, unsafe streets, few local facilities)?', using a five-point scale (very great, great, some, slight and little).

Source: Whitehall II, unpublished data

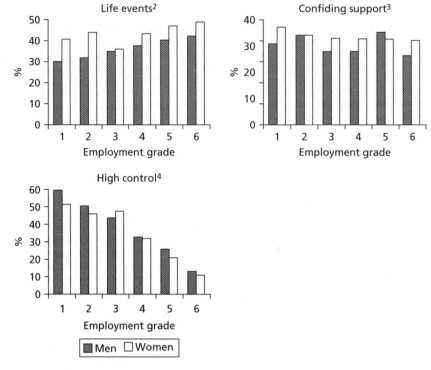

Figure 4 Psychosocial factors by employment grade, Whitehall II Study, men and women, age adjusted[1]

Notes

1 All analyses: N = approx. 9000; test for trend within sex by grade significant at p < 0.001 for men and women.
2 Life events = two or more major life events.
3 Confiding support = confiding support from closest person.
4 High control = high control of pace and content of paid work.
Source: Marmot and Davey Smith 1997: Table 3

[...]

With respect to the material environment, exposure to persistent poverty is more harmful than the experience of occasional poverty (Benzeval 1998). Studies have found large inequalities in physical and psychological health by income and by living standards, after controlling for other dimensions of socio-economic disadvantage, like education, occupation and marital status (Stronks *et al*. 1998; Weich and Lewis 1998).

With respect to the psychosocial environment, again there is evidence of its contribution to socio-economic inequalities in physical and psychological health. The Whitehall II Study has highlighted the importance of psychosocial work conditions, and low control in particular, to coronary heart disease risk. The experience of low control at work has been found to increase coronary heart disease risk independently of socio-economic status (as measured by employment grade) and other socio-economic related exposures, including social support (Marmot *et al*. 1997). In studies concerned with psychological health, however, social support has

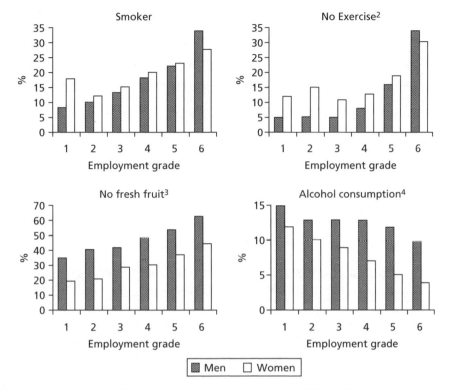

Figure 5 Behavioural factors by employment grade, Whitehall II Study, men and women, age adjusted[1]

Notes
1 All analyses: N = approx. 9000; test for trend within sex by grade significant at p < 0.001 for men and women.
2 No exercise = no moderate or vigorous exercise.
3 No fresh fruit = fresh fruit less than daily.
4 Alcohol consumption = mean units of alcohol in last seven days.
Source: Marmot and Davey Smith 1997: Table 2

been found to play a larger role in mediating the effects of material disadvantage. A study which tested the effects of material deprivation (enforced absence of one or more basic necessities) and lack of social support (emotional and practical) on psychological health found that material deprivation was the more important influence. However, access to social support moderated this influence. Low social support had a more negative effect on the psychological health of those living in poverty, and poverty had its most substantial effects on the psychological well-being of those who had limited access to social support (Whelan 1993).

With respect to behavioural factors, an early estimate of the behavioural contribution to health inequalities was provided by the Whitehall I Study. Socio-economic differences in behavioural risk factors were estimated to account for one third of the gradient in the relative risk of death from coronary heart disease (Marmot *et al*. 1984). More recent studies have estimated that between 10 and 30 per cent of the class differential in health may be explained by class differentials in health related behaviour (Lantz *et al*. 1998; Stronks 1997). However, because individual behaviour can be measured with greater precision than the material and social environment, estimates of its contribution to the socio-economic gradient may be inflated (Phillips and Davey Smith 1991).

[...] [W]omen are more likely than men both to be poor and to be responsible for maintaining the material and psychosocial environment of the home and the well-being of those who live there. Men are over-represented in higher income house-holds, while women (and children) are at greater risk of living in low income households, with limited access to material and psychosocial resources. They are also more likely to be restricted to, and to work within, these disadvantaged envir-onments. It is estimated that 40 per cent of women in Britain spend upwards of 50 hours a week caring for members of their household (Corti and Dex 1995). The patterns of work among fathers and mothers provide one illustration of the extent to which women (still) care for the family.

[...]

Cumulative exposure to material, psychosocial and behavioural risks

The way in which access to resources and exposure to risks combine can be captured in cross-sectional surveys, where measures are taken at one point in time. However, to track how these resources and risks accumulate over the lifecourse requires longitudinal studies, where measures are taken from the same population at differ-ent points in time. Birth cohort studies, which follow a cohort of babies into childhood and adulthood, are the research design of choice. They enable both the process of accumulation and its health effects to be monitored. The British birth cohort studies, and the 1958 National Child Development Study in particular, have recorded how exposure to disadvantage 'casts long shadows forward', both over a person's future socio-economic status and future health.

The long shadows of disadvantage mean that children born into poorer circum-stances accumulate more material, psychosocial and behavioural risks (Figure 6). In the 1958 cohort study, girls and boys born into social class IV and V (based on their father's occupation) were much more likely to grow up in overcrowded homes lacking household amenities than those in higher social classes. The psychosocial environment of childhood was similarly patterned by social class, with a socio-economic gradient in exposure to such life events as the divorce of one's parents. Parental health related behaviours, such as breast feeding, were also related to childhood social class.

The process of differential accumulation of risks continued into adulthood. By the time the 1958 birth cohort reached the age of 33 (in 1991), there were sharp socio-economic gradients by father's social class in the proportions of women and men living with material disadvantage (in rented housing, on means-tested benefits, having no savings and having debts). There were also socio-economic differences in the psychosocial environment (lacking emotional and practical support, doing work characterized by low control and monotony, perceiving one's job as insecure). Gender mediated these socio-economic differences in psychosocial factors (Figure 7). Women were less likely to experience poor social support than men at each level of

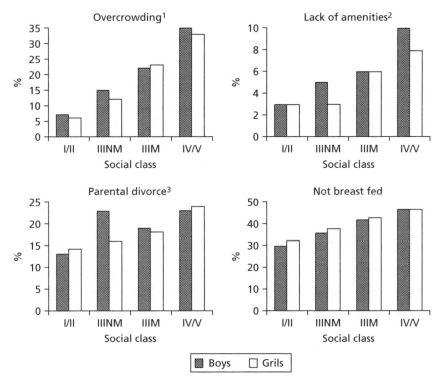

Figure 6 Exposure to material, psychosocial and behavioural risks in childhood by social class at birth, National Child Development Study

Notes
1 Overcrowding = more than one person per room.
2 Lack of amenities = lacking or sharing bathroom, toilet or hot water supply with another household.
3 Parental divorce = before child was 16 years old.
Source: Power and Matthews 1997: Tables 3 and 5

the class hierarchy. Conversely, women's main jobs (paid or unpaid) were characterized by more negative psychosocial characteristics.

[…]

While these findings point to the need to protect the living standards of (future) mothers and children, households with children have found themselves at the sharp end of rising poverty and increasing social polarization.

Widening socio-economic inequalities

Patterns and trends

[…] Britain's economic base has shifted away from the traditional manufacturing industries which provided full-time jobs to manual workers to service sector

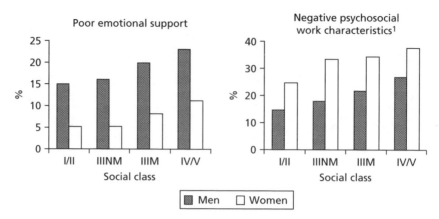

Figure 7 Exposure to a poor psychosocial environment at age 33 by social class at birth, National Child Development Study

Note
1 Negative psychosocial work characteristics => 2 of lack of learning opportunities, monotony, inability to vary work pace, inflexible break times in main paid or unpaid job, in or out of home.
Source: Power and Matthews 1997: Table 5

employment characterized by more flexible and less secure jobs. An increase in unemployment, and in male unemployment in particular, has been one outcome of this process. Male unemployment climbed from under 4 per cent in the early 1970s to 14 per cent in the mid-1990s. Changes in the structure of employment have coincided with changes in housing tenure and family structure. In 1950, 70 per cent of households rented their home; in the late 1990s nearly 80 per cent were owner-occupiers (ONS 1998). Household patterns have also changed radically across this period. In the 1950s and 1960s, men and women across the class spectrum followed a similar route through adult life. The vast majority married in their early 20s, had their first baby within three years of marriage and remained married until separated by death (Kiernan 1989). In the 1990s men and women are fashioning more diverse and dynamic household patterns as they move through adulthood and into old age. These new pathways are marked out by an increase in single adult households, in cohabitation, in births outside marriage and in separation, divorce and remarriage.

One result of these trends is a rapid growth in the number of one parent families, the vast majority of which are headed by women. In 1971, approximately one in thirteen (8 per cent) of all households with dependent children was headed by a lone mother. By the mid-1990s, it was one in five (20 per cent) (Haskey 1998). Since the late 1980s, it is the increase in single (never married) lone mothers which has fuelled the upward trend in the number of one parent families. Lone mothers in the UK are more disadvantaged than in other western countries, with a smaller proportion in employment and higher proportion in poverty (Bradshaw 1996). [...]

Trends in employment, housing tenure and household composition are combining in ways which are reshaping the social landscape of Britain. Among the features of the new landscape which are likely to affect the socio-economic patterning of men and women's health are the increase in poverty and childhood poverty and the wider process of socio-economic polarization of which the increase in poverty is part.

Increasing poverty and childhood poverty

Following the deep and widespread poverty of the 1930s, the UK experienced a long period of narrowing income differentials. Between 1939 and 1976, differences in the real incomes – and therefore the living standards – of rich and poor households narrowed. In other words, poorer households were able to afford more of the resources that better-off households took for granted. From the mid-1970s, the trend toward greater income inequality went into reverse (Goodman *et al.* 1997). Across the next two decades, inequalities in living standards in the UK increased at a pace and to a scale unmatched in Europe. [...]

The increased burden of poverty has not been equally shared by all age and household groups. At a time when the cohort studies have been highlighting the long term effects of childhood disadvantage on health and socio-economic status, there has been a shift in the risk of poverty down the lifecourse. Through the 1980s and early 1990s, the number of pensioners in the poorest groups fell, while the risks of poverty increased for children. In 1975, there were 1.4 million households with children under the age of 16 below the decency threshold, representing one in eight children. By the mid-1990s, the number had trebled to 4.2 million, representing one in three children (Goodman and Webb 1994). Underlying this trend is the increase in the poverty of lone parent households.

[...]

Socio-economic polarization

The 1980s and 1990s have been marked out by a polarization in the socio-economic circumstances of households. Underlying this process have been changes in the structure of the labour market and in the relationships of employment which tie individuals to it, changes which have had a more negative effect on the manual and unskilled workforce than on non-manual and professional groups. The 1970s and 1980s saw a major contraction of manual jobs in the UK, and unemployment rates for men in unskilled manual socio-economic groups rose from 15 per cent in the early 1970s to 30 per cent in the early 1990s. In contrast, the number of people in managerial and professional occupations increased sharply and recession and restructuring have had relatively little impact on employment rates of men in higher class groups. Men in social class I and II saw their rates of unemployment rise from 1 per cent to 5 per cent between the early 1970s and early 1990s (ONS 1998). Not only have opportunities for paid work become more unequal; so too have opportunities for high pay. Among adults in employment, the earnings of high paid workers have risen much faster than those in low paid jobs, widening earning differentials among both men and women (Hills 1998).

Changes in the structure of the labour market and in the dispersal of earnings have been associated with a more far-reaching change. They have fuelled a redistribution of employment between households. Across the 1980s and 1990s there has been a rapid shift away from households containing a mix of employed and non-employed adults and a corresponding increase in two-earner and no-earner households (Gregg and Wadsworth 1996). The proportion of no-earner households has doubled since the late

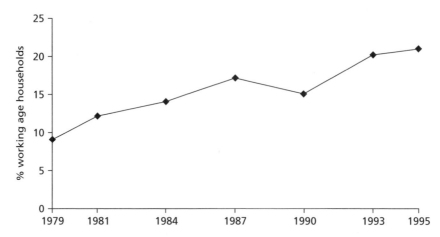

Figure 8 Households of working age with no member in paid work, UK 1979–97
Source: Hills 1998: Figure 15

1970s, from less than one in ten households in 1979 to more than one in five in 1995 (Figure 8).[...]

   The changing household distribution of work has fuelled a wider process of socio-economic polarization. During the 1980s, the clumping of households on middle incomes began to break up. In its place, a new income distribution has emerged, characterized by high and rising real incomes for working households and low and stagnant incomes for non-working households (Jenkins 1996; Cowell *et al.* 1997; Hills 1998). For no-earner households dependent on means-tested benefits, real incomes have not even been stagnant. [...] [T]hey have declined.

[...]

   The areas in which poor people live are also poor areas: they contain more health hazards and provide fewer health amenities than areas populated by better-off households. With respect to hazards, traffic volume tends to be higher in disadvantaged urban areas, with a resulting increase both in the rates of road traffic accidents and in car vehicle emissions (British Medical Association (BMA) 1997; Quality of Urban Air Review Group (QUARG) 1998). Motor vehicles are the major cause of accidental death among children over the age of 5 and an important contributor to the socio-economic gradient in childhood mortality (Quick 1991). Emissions from vehicles are the major cause of air pollution and a contributory cause of respiratory disease (Committee on the Medical Effects of Air Pollution (COMEAP) 1998). While exposure to hazards goes with living in poorer areas, access to amenities is a feature of more advantaged areas. A study in the Scottish city of Glasgow compared two contrasting areas displaying low and high levels of aggregate deprivation (as measured by male unemployment, overcrowding, households without a car and households in social class IV/V). Despite the fact that residents in better-off areas were much more likely to have a car to access health-promoting resources outside their local area, local levels of provision were consistently higher in better-off areas. This was true with respect to shops, recreational facilities, public transport and primary health care services (Macintyre 1997).

As the trends in employment, household income, housing tenure and area amenities indicate, dimensions of socio-economic disadvantage are both clustering and polarizing in the UK. Those most vulnerable to poor health and premature mortality find themselves on the wrong side of this process of polarization: living in households in which there is no one in employment, in social housing and in neighbourhoods high in health risks and low in health resources. These groups represent a mixture of the traditionally poor, like male unskilled manual workers and their families, whose lives have traditionally been punctured by unemployment and framed by low income. The process of polarization is linked, too, to newer social divisions, built around housing tenure, welfare dependency and lone motherhood. [...]

The polarizing of lifecourse patterns – and with them living standards and life chances – has profound implications for the socio-economic gradients in men's and women's health. At the least, it means that the class structure no longer consists of a hierarchy of unequal but relatively stable positions. Increasingly, it is a structure composed of unequal and divergent socio-economic trajectories.

[...]

Acknowledgements

I would like to thank Stephen Stansfeld for unpublished data from the Whitehall II Study and Tanya Richardson for moral support and help with typing the chapter.

References

Benzeval, M. (1998) Poverty and health, *Health Variations*, 1: 12–13.

Bradshaw, J. (1996) *The Employment of Lone Parents: A Comparison of Policy in 20 Countries*. London: Family Policy Studies Centre.

British Medical Association (BMA) (1997) *Road Transport and Health*. London: BMA.

Brown, G. and Harris, T. (1978) *The Social Origins of Depression*. London: Tavistock.

Colhoun, H. and Prescott-Clarke, P. (eds) (1996) *Health Survey for England 1994*. London: HMSO.

Committee on the Medical Effects of Air Pollution (COMEAP) (1998) *Quantification of the Effects of Air Pollution on Health in the United Kingdom*. London: Stationery Office.

Corti, L. and Dex, S. (1995) Informal carers and employment, *Employment Gazette*, 103: 101–7.

Cowell, F. A., Jenkins, S. P. and Litchfield, J. A. (1997) The changing shape of the UK income distribution: kernel density estimates, in J. Hills (ed.), *New Inequalities: The Changing Distribution of Income and Wealth in the United Kingdom*. Cambridge: Cambridge University Press.

Davey Smith, G., Blane, D. and Bartley, M. (1994) Explanations for socio-economic differentials in mortality, *European Journal of Public Health*, 4: 131–44.

Davey Smith, G., Hart, C., Hole, D. *et al.* (1998) Education and occupational social class: which is the more important indicator of mortality risk?, *Journal of Epidemiology and Community Health*, 52: 153–60.

Elliot, J. and Huppert, F. (1991) In sickness and in health: associations between physical and mental wellbeing, employment and parental status in a nationwide sample of married women, *Psychological Medicine*, 21: 515–24.

Filakti, H. and Fox, J. (1995) Differences in mortality by housing tenure and by car access from the OPCS Longitudinal Study, *Population Trends*, 81: 27–30.

Giddens, A. (1991) *Modernity and Self-Identity*. Cambridge: Polity.

Goodman, A. and Webb, S. (1994) *For Richer, For Poorer: The Changing Distribution of Income in the United Kingdom*. London: Institute of Fiscal Studies.

Goodman, A., Johnson, P. and Webb, S. (1997) *Inequality in the UK*. Oxford: Oxford University Press.

Gregg, P. and Wadsworth, J. (1996) More work in fewer households, in J. Hills (ed.), *New Inequalities: The Changing Distribution of Income and Wealth in the United Kingdom*. Cambridge: Cambridge University Press.

Haskey, J. (1998) One parent families and their dependent children in Great Britain, *Population Trends*, 91: 5–13.

Hills, J. (1998) *Income and Wealth: The Latest Evidence*. York: Joseph Rowntree Foundation.

Hunt, K. and Macintyre, S. (2000) Sexe et inégalités sociales en santé, in H. Grandjean (ed.), *Inégalités et disparités sociales en santé*. Paris: La Découverte.

Jenkins, S. (1996) Recent trends in the UK income distribution: what happened and why?, *Oxford Review of Economic Policy*, 12 (1): 29–45.

Johansson, S. R. (1991) Welfare, mortality and gender: continuity and change in explanations for male/female mortality differences over three generations, *Continuity and Change*, 6: 135–78.

Kiernan, K. (1989) The family: formation and fission, in H. Joshi (ed.), *The Changing Population of Britain*. Oxford: Blackwell.

Lantz, P. M., House, J. S., Lepkauski, J. M., Williams, D. R., Mero, R. P. and Chen, J. (1998) Socio-economic factors, health behaviours and mortality, *Journal of the American Medical Association*, 279 (21): 1703–8.

Macintyre, S. (1997) What are spatial effects and how can we measure them?, in A. Dale (ed.), *Exploiting National Survey and Census Data: The Role of Locality and Spatial Effects*, Catherine Marsh Centre for Census and Survey Research occasional paper 12. Manchester: University of Manchester.

Macintyre, S. and Hunt, K. (1997) Socio-economic position, gender and health: how do they interact?, *Journal of Health Psychology*, 2 (3): 315–34.

Macran, S., Clark, L. and Joshi, H. (1996) Women's health: dimensions and differentials, *Social Science and Medicine*, 42 (9): 1203–16.

Marmot, M. G. and Davey Smith, G. (1997) Socio-economic differentials in health, *Journal of Health Psychology*, 2 (3): 283–96.

Marmot, M. G., Shipley, M. J. and Rose, G. (1984) Inequalities in death: specific explanations of a general pattern, *Lancet*, 8384 (1): 1003–6.

Marmot, M. G., Bosma, H., Hemingway, H., Brunner, E. and Stansfeld, S. (1997) Contribution of job control and other risk factors to social variations in coronary heart disease incidence, *Lancet*, 350: 235–9.

Office for National Statistics (ONS) (1998) *Living in Britain: Results from the 1996 General Household Survey*. London: Stationery Office.

Phillips, A. N. and Davey Smith, G. (1991) How independent are 'independent' effects? Relative risk estimation when correlated exposures are measured imprecisely, *Journal of Clinical Epidemiology*, 44: 1223–31.

Popay, J., Bartley, M. and Owen, C. (1993) Gender inequalities in health: social position, affective disorders and minor physical morbidity, *Social Science and Medicine*, 36 (1): 21–32.

Power, C. and Matthews, S. (1997) Origins of health inequalities in a national population sample, *Lancet*, 350: 1584–5.

Power, C., Matthews, S. and Manor, O. (1996) Inequalities in self-rated health in the 1958 birth cohort: life time social circumstances or social mobility?, *British Medical Journal*, 313: 449–53.

Prescott-Clarke, P. and Primatesta, P. (eds) (1998) *Health Survey for England 1996*. London: Stationery Office.

Quality of Urban Air Review Group (QUARG) (1998) *Urban Air Quality in the United Kingdom*. London: Department of Environment, Transport and the Regions.

Quick, A. (1991) *Unequal Risks*. London: Socialist Health Association.

Rose, D. and O'Reilly, K. (1997) *Constructing Classes: Towards a New Classification for the UK*. Swindon: Office for National Statistics/Economic and Social Research Council.

Smith, J. and Harding, S. (1997) Mortality of women and men using alternative social classifications, in F. Drever and M. Whitehead (eds), *Health Inequalities*, series DS no. 15. London: Stationery Office.

Stronks, K. (1997) *Socio-economic Inequalities in Health: Individual Choice or Social Circumstances*. Rotterdam: Erasmus University.

Stronks, K., van de Mheen, H. and Mackenbach, J. P. (1998) A higher prevalence of health problems in low income groups: does it reflect relative deprivation?, *Journal of Epidemiology and Community Health*, 52: 548–57.

Weich, S. and Lewis, G. (1998) Material standard of living, social class and the prevalence of the common mental disorders, *Journal of Epidemiology and Community Health*, 52: 8–14.

Whelan, C. (1993) The role of social support in mediating the psychological consequences of economic stress, *Sociology of Health and Illness*, 15 (1): 86–101.

Whitehead, M. (1997) Life and death across the millennium, in F. Drever and M. Whitehead (eds), *Health Inequalities*, series DS no. 15. London: Stationery Office.

Woods, R. and Williams, N. (1995) Must the gap widen before it can be narrowed? Long term trends in social class mortality differentials, *Continuity and Change*, 10 (1): 105–37.

20

Ethnic Inequalities in Health: A Review of UK Epidemiological Evidence

George Davey Smith, Nish Chaturvedi, Seeromanie Harding, James Nazroo and Rory Williams

Introduction

[...] The approach we have taken is an epidemiological one. Descriptive epidemiology provides data on how disease, disability and death are distributed between and within populations. Analytical epidemiology aims at uncovering the causes of disease and thus the reasons for the distribution of disease that are seen. Epidemiological studies concerned with ethnicity have taken both descriptive and analytical approaches. [...] We will provide descriptive data on ethnic health differentials in the UK initially and then proceed to investigate the contribution of socio-economic factors to these differentials. We will conclude with a discussion of the different approaches that have been taken to understanding differentials in health status between ethnic groups. The main test of these approaches is their capacity to point to alterable causes of inequality, rather than to novel aetiological hypotheses (1)

Ethnicity and health: illustrative data

Adult mortality by country of birth

Mortality data according to ethnic group come from various sources, all of which have their limitations. Here we concentrate on data for England and Wales for the years around the 1991 census. Deaths around this census year have been classified according to country of birth, as given on the death certificate, and the population was classified according to country of birth in the 1991 census. This allows the calculation of mortality rates for country-of-birth groups. The country-of-birth groupings used in these analyses are those born in the Caribbean commonwealth, West and South Africa, the East African commonwealth, the Indian subcontinent (India, Pakistan, Bangladesh, Sri Lanka), Scotland and Ireland (both Northern Ireland and Republic of Ireland). The disaggregation of the African grouping is carried out because the majority of East Africans are of Indian origin while those from West/South Africa are of 'Black African' origin. Data are presented separately for those born in India, Pakistan and Bangladesh when numbers of deaths are high enough to allow disaggregation. Tables 1 and 2 present standardized mortality ratios (SMR) for deaths from all causes and from various specific causes, according to country-of-birth groups for men and women of working age. All-cause mortality is markedly higher for men and women born in West/South Africa, East Africa, Scotland and Ireland. Ischaemic heart disease and lung cancer are major causes of death, regardless of ethnic group. Ischaemic heart disease mortality is particularly high for men and women born in the Indian subcontinent, but low in people born in the Caribbean. Stroke mortality is elevated for all of the country-of-birth groups examined. Lung cancer mortality is lower for men and women born in all countries examined except Scotland and Ireland, who show high rates. Deaths from accidents and injuries are high for men and women born in Scotland and Ireland, as is suicide. Suicide is low among men and women born in the Caribbean (2). [...]

Table 1   Standardized mortality ratios (SMR) by country of birth, men aged 20–64 years, England and Wales 1991–93

	All causes	Ischaemic heart disease	Stroke	Lung cancer	Other cancer	Accidents and injuries	Suicide
Total	100	100	100	100	100	100	100
Caribbean	89*	60*	169*	59*	89	121	59*
West/South Africa	126*	83	315*	71	133*	75	59*
East Africa	123*	160*	113	37*	77	86	75*
Indian subcontinent	107*	150*	163*	48*	65*	80*	73*
India	106*	140*	140*	43*	64*	97	109
Pakistan	102	163*	148*	45*	62*	68*	34*
Bangladesh	133*	184*	324*	92	74*	40*	27*
Scotland	129*	117*	111	146*	114*	177*	149*
Ireland	135*	121*	130*	157*	120*	189*	135*

Note: *p < 0.05.

Table 2   Standardized mortality ratios (SMR) by country of birth, women aged 20–64 years, England and Wales 1991–93

	All causes	Ischaemic heart disease	Stroke	Lung cancer	Other cancer	Accidents and injuries	Suicide
Total	100	100	100	100	100	100	100
Caribbean	104	100	178*	32*	87	103	49*
West/South Africa	142*	69	215*	69	120	—	102
East Africa	127*	130	110	29*	98	—	129
Indian subcontinent	99	175*	132*	34*	68	93	115
Scotland	127*	127*	131*	164*	106	201*	153*
Ireland	115*	129*	118*	143*	98	160*	144*

Note: *p < 0.05; — = no data.

Morbidity in adulthood

Representative data on morbidity among minority ethnic groups have, until recently, been sparse. Data from the 1991 census show higher rates of long-standing illness reported to limit activities among all of the ethnic minority groups compared to whites, apart from the Chinese. While there have been several local studies and disease-specific investigations limited to particular ethnic groups the inclusion of a health component in the *Fourth National Survey of Ethnic Minorities* (3) has allowed a considerably more detailed analysis of morbidity differentials than has been carried out previously. We therefore concentrate on data from this source in the present paper, cross-referencing other studies where appropriate.

Table 3 presents age and gender standardized prevalence rates of various health problems according to ethnic group membership. Self-assessed general health is particularly poor amongst Pakistani/Bangladeshi and Caribbean people. The long-standing illness data in the *Fourth National Survey* show lower rates among Chinese people, in line with the census data, but also lower rates amongst South Asian groups, which are the reverse of the census. This may reflect the fact that the census question asked about limiting long-standing illness rather than long-standing illness alone. Data from other sources have suggested that there is a higher threshold for reporting ill health as constituting long-standing illness among ethnic minority groups. [...]

Taking the definitions of coronary heart disease used in the *Fourth National Survey*, Pakistani/Bangladeshi people had considerably higher rates than whites, although the prevalence rates for Indian and African-Asian people were very similar to those for the majority ethnic group (Table 3). This is not in line with the mortality data presented above, nor with the results of some other studies (4). This may reflect the self-reported nature of the data in the *Fourth National Survey*. The prevalence rates of hypertension also need to be treated with caution, since they are based on self-reports. The picture of a higher rate of hypertension amongst Caribbean people is consistent with the findings from surveys in which blood pressure is measured (see later). The higher prevalence rates of diabetes amongst all the ethnic minority groups for whom data could be analysed in the *Fourth National Survey* are also in keeping with several specific studies of this issue (5–7). All the ethnic minority groups studied except Caribbeans had considerably lower prevalences of respiratory symptoms than whites. A lower prevalence of respiratory symptoms amongst children of families originating from the Indian subcontinent has been found elsewhere(8), although not all studies agree on this (9). Similarly, some studies of respiratory symptoms in adults have found similar rates for South Asian groups and the majority ethnic population (10,11). The lower risk of having an accident resulting in hospital treatment for all the ethnic minority groups is consistent with the mortality data for the Indian subcontinent groups although not for Caribbeans. It may be that there are differences in the propensity to attend hospital following accidents between the groups.

Relative differences in cardiovascular disease and diabetes morbidity by ethnic group reflect the differences in mortality. Thus mean blood pressure is greater in South Asian (12) and African-Caribbean people than the general population [...] These differences are particularly striking for African-Caribbean women, where over a third of those in middle age are hypertensive. In contrast, blood pressure in Chinese people is similar to that of the general population (13). Assessing the burden of heart disease is difficult, as there may be ethnic differences in the proportion of people with heart disease being given this diagnosis by a doctor, and differences in interpretation of standard angina questionnaires. Changes consistent with ischaemic

Table 3 Age and gender standardized prevalence rates (per 100) of reported health problems according to ethnicity: Fourth National Survey of Ethnic Minorities (3)

	White	All ethnic minorities	Caribbean	All South Asians	Indian or African-Asian	Pakistani or Bangladeshi	Chinese
Fair or poor health	27	32	34	32	27	39	26
A long-standing illness	27	21	27	18	17	21	15
Long-standing illness limiting work	11	12	13	12	11	13	7
Diagnosed angina or heart attack	4.2	4.0	3.7	4.2	3.3	6.0	3.0
Hypertension	12	11	17	9	8	11	5
Diabetes	1.7	5.7	5.3	6.2	4.7	8.9	3.0
Accidents resulting in hospital treatment	13	6	9	4	4	5	8

heart disease on an electrocardiogram are less prone to an ethnic bias. Numbers of women with these changes are too small in existing studies, but in men it appears that whilst South Asian people have twice the prevalence of heart disease compared with the general population (5), African-Caribbean and Chinese people have rates which are about a quarter of that of the general population (6,13) [...]. The prevalence of adult diabetes is three and five times greater in African-Caribbean and South Asian people respectively compared with the general population [...] (6, 12). Current data suggest that diabetes prevalence is not different in Chinese people compared with the general population (7).

The contribution of socio-economic position to health differentials

In an analysis around the 1971 census, occupational social class was found to explain little or none of the mortality differentials between ethnic groups (14). We present more recent data from around the 1991 census in Table 4. Standardized mortality ratios adjusted for age are presented in the top line of each row in the table, with standardized mortality ratio following adjustment for social class as well as age being shown below these. Thus the standardized mortality ratio of 89 for all-cause mortality for Caribbean men is further reduced, to 82, after adjustment for social class. This is seen because Caribbean men are more likely to be in manual social class groups, which generally have higher mortality than non-manual social class groups. Thus the expectation would be that Caribbean men would have high, rather than low, mortality and taking social class into account in the statistical adjustments makes this discrepancy between what is seen and what would be expected more apparent. [...]

There is a clear social class gradient in perinatal, neonatal, post-neonatal and infant mortality for all countries of birth, with those born in the lowest social classes generally having the highest mortality rate (15). However, the lower occupational social class of many people from minority ethnic groups cannot account for the overall ethnic differences in mortality. Within each social class, for example, infant mortality rates were about twice as high in Pakistani children as in those born in England and Wales, except for those in social class I (possibly due to the small number of deaths observed in this group). Perinatal, post-neonatal and infant mortality is thus highest in children born to Pakistani parents, even when social class is taken into account. Conversely, when social class is taken into account, infants born to parents from Bangladesh, East and West Africa have lower post-neonatal mortality rates than those born to parents from the UK, and infant mortality rates are also lower in Bangladeshi children.

In the *Fourth National Survey* the role of socio-economic factors in accounting for the differences in morbidity and health-related behaviours according to ethnic group membership was studied in detail (3). As shown in Table 5, while the usual social class differences in morbidity are seen within each ethnic group, differences between ethnic groups are also seen within each social class stratum. A standard of living index was also constructed within this study, putting together various markers of socio-economic position. Information on overcrowding of accommodation, the presence of basic household amenities, the ownership of consumer durables and

Table 4 Standardized mortality ratios for men aged 20–64, before and after adjustment for social class*

	All causes	Ischaemic heart disease	Stroke	Lung cancer	Accidents and injuries	Suicide
Total	100	100	100	100	100	100
Caribbean						
Age	89*	60*	169*	59*	121	59*
Age/social class	82*	55*	146*	49*	109	57
West/South Africa						
Age	126*	83	315*	†	†	†
Age/social class	135*	79	372*			
East Africa						
Age	123*	160*	113	†	86	75*
Age/social class	137*	188*	128		104	75
Indian subcontinent						
Age	107*	150*	163*	48*	80*	73*
Age/social class	117*	165*	175*	52*	87	76*
Scotland						
Age	129*	117*	111	146*	117*	149*
Age/social class	132*	121*	112	151*	184*	160*
Ireland						
Age	135*	121*	130*	157*	189*	135*
Age/social class	129*	115*	124*	145*	169*	134*

Notes: *The standardized mortality ratios which are just age-adjusted are sometimes a little different from the equivalent age-adjusted standardized mortality ratios in Table 1. This is because the analyses only included the men on whom social class data were available on death certificates.
† numbers too small.
Source: Harding & Maxwell (1997) (2)

access to cars was used for this purpose. This, as is discussed later, was considered to be a more discriminatory marker of socio-economic position than social class. Differences in morbidity were then adjusted for social class, for housing tenure (a commonly used indicator of socio-economic position in UK studies) and the standard of living index. Table 6 presents data on reporting health as fair or poor according to ethnic group after adjustments for socio-economic measures. A relative risk of 1.25, for example, indicates a 25% higher chance of reporting fair or poor health among Caribbean people than among the majority ethnic community. When this is reduced to 1.15 on adjustment for social class (as well as age and gender) this indicates that after taking social class into account there is only a 15% higher risk of reporting fair or poor health among Caribbean people. For Pakistani and Bangladeshi people it can be seen that adjustment for the standard of living index produces considerably greater attenuation of the degree to which their reported health is worse than the majority ethnic community than does adjustment for social class or housing tenure. Tables 7, 8 and 9 report equivalent data for diabetes, respiratory symptoms and diagnosed heart disease. As can be seen, the elevated risk of diabetes among all the ethnic minority groups considered is largely independent of current socio-economic position. Similarly the reduced risk of respiratory symptoms is, as

George Davey Smith et al.

Table 5 Age and gender standardized prevalences per 100: Fourth National Survey of Ethnic Minorities (3)

	White	All ethnic minorities	Caribbean	Indian or African-Asian	Pakistani or Bangladeshi
Reported fair or poor health:					
Non-manual	21	24	25	20	30
Manual	23	30	29	27	35
No full-time worker in household	37	38	38	34	44
Respiratory symptoms (coughing up phlegm or a wheeze)					
Non-manual	23	14	16	13	13
Manual	23	17	28	13	12
No full-time worker in household	35	21	26	17	20
Diabetes:					
Non-manual	1.1	4.1	4.1	2.8	6.4
Manual	1.1	4.5	3.2	3.5	8.3
No full-time worker in household	2.1	6.3	4.5	7.1	7.6
Hypertension:					
Non-manual	8	8	15	5	6
Manual	12	11	15	9	10
No full-time worker in household	11	12	18	8	11
Angina or heart attack by tenure:					
Owner-occupier	3.0	3.2	2.7	2.5	5.2
Tenant	4.1	4.0	3.8	3.5	5.2
Regular current smoking:					
Non-manual	21	16	24	9	16
Manual	33	18	30	8	18
No full-time worker in household	46	25	39	19	18
Ever drinks alcohol:					
Non-manual	95	49	81	45	7
Manual	91	46	83	39	5
No full-time worker in household	84	46	84	41	2

would be expected, not a reflection of socio-economic differences, since in general socio-economic indicators are less favourable for the ethnic minority people and in all groups people in worse socio-economic circumstances report higher levels of respiratory symptoms. An elevated risk of diagnosed heart disease is only seen for Pakistani and Bangladeshi people after standardization for socio-economic factors, age and gender. The apparent reduced risk amongst Indian and African-Asian people for diagnosed heart disease after such standardization stands in contrast to other research on this issue (2, 4) and should be treated with caution.[...]

Table 6 Relative risk compared with the ethnic majority community of reported fair or poor health, standardized for socio-economic factors: Fourth National Survey of Ethnic Minorities (3)

	Caribbean	Indian and African-Asian	Pakistani and Bangladeshi	All ethnic minorities
Age and gender	1.25	0.99	1.45	1.17
	(1.1–1.4)	(0.9–1.1)	(1.3–1.6)	(1.1–1.3)
Class, age and gender	1.15	1.00	1.36	1.14
	(1.03–1.3)	(0.9–1.1)	(1.2–1.5)	(1.1–1.2)
Tenure, age and gender	1.17	1.04	1.45	1.18
	(1.04–1.3)	(0.9–1.2)	(1.3–1.6)	(1.1–1.3)
Standard of living, age and gender	1.15	0.94	1.24	1.08
	(1.03–1.3)	(0.9–1.04)	(1.1–1.4)	(0.99–1.2)

Note: 'All ethnic minorities' includes the displayed groups plus Chinese people.

Ethnicity and health: approaches to understanding the relationship

When considering differentials in health status between ethnic groups it is useful to categorize models of explanation. This is not intended to suggest that one explanatory category is adequate to account for the health differentials and it is likely that most, if not all, categories make some contribution to the pattern which is observed. Categories of explanation for sociodemographic differences in health have been developed and refined over many years (16) and have been modified and expanded for application specifically to health differentials between ethnic groups (17).

Artefact

Artefact explanations suggest that the relationships between ethnicity and health could be produced by the processes of data collection and analysis. For example, if country of birth is reported differently on death certificates than at the census, using these two sources to estimate mortality rates could be seriously misleading. The measurement of health status could also differ across groups. Self-reported health has been used in several studies discussed above and it could be that members of different ethnic groups have different propensities for reporting ill health at a given level of objective morbidity, although there is evidence against this (18). For other health outcomes ethnicity could also influence classification of illness status. For example it has been suggested that the apparently higher prevalence of schizophrenia amongst young African-Caribbean men than young men of the majority ethnic population is due to a greater propensity to diagnose schizophrenia amongst them, rather than any real difference in disease prevalence. While it is always important to consider the degree to which the processes of measurement and data analysis may generate apparent health differentials when no such differentials exist, it is likely that the overall contribution of artefact explanations to understanding the association between ethnic group and health is limited, although in particular circumstances it could be an important factor.

Table 7 Relative risk of diabetes compared with the ethnic majority community, standardized for socio-economic factors: Fourth National Survey of Ethnic Minorities (3)

	Caribbean	Indian and African-Asian	Pakistani and Bangladeshi	All ethnic minorities
Age and gender	2.6	2.6	4.9	3.0
	(1.6–4.0)	(1.7–3.9)	(3.3–7.2)	(2.1–4.3)
Class, age and gender	2.8	3.1	5.2	3.5
	(1.8–4.3)	(2.0–4.6)	(3.4–7.8)	(2.4–5.0)
Tenure, age and gender	2.3	2.7	4.8	3.1
	(1.4–3.6)	(1.8–4.1)	(3.3–6.9)	(2.2–4.4)
Standard of living, age and gender	2.2	2.4	4.1	2.8
	(1.4–3.4)	(1.6–3.6)	(2.9–6.0)	(2.0–3.9)

Table 8 Relative risk of respiratory symptoms compared with the ethnic majority community, standardized for socio-economic factors: Fourth National Survey of Ethnic Minorities (3)

	Caribbean	Indian and African-Asian	Pakistani and Bangladeshi	All ethnic minorities
Age and gender	0.89	0.53	0.65	0.66
	(0.7–1.05)	(0.4–0.6)	(0.6–0.8)	(0.6–0.7)
Class, age and gender	0.86	0.53	0.55	0.64
	(0.7–1.01)	(0.4–0.6)	(0.5–0.7)	(0.6–0.7)
Tenure, age and gender	0.85	0.58	0.65	0.68
	(0.7–1.01)	(0.5–0.7)	(0.6–0.8)	(0.6–0.8)
Standard of living, age and gender	0.83	0.50	0.50	0.61
	(0.7–0.98)	(0.4–0.6)	(0.4–0.6)	(0.5–0.7)

Table 9 Relative risk of diagnosed heart disease compared with the ethnic majority community, standardized for socio-economic factors: Fourth National Survey of Ethnic Minorities (3)

	Caribbean	Indian and African-Asian	Pakistani and Bangladeshi	All ethnic minorities
Age and gender	0.95	0.77	1.50	0.97
	(0.6–1.4)	(0.5–1.1)	(1.1–2.0)	(0.7–1.3)
Class, age and gender	1.05	0.92	1.49	1.10
	(0.7–1.6)	(0.6–1.3)	(1.1–2.1)	(0.8–1.5)
Tenure, age and gender	0.93	0.85	1.57	1.05
	(0.6–1.4)	(0.6–1.2)	(1.2–2.1)	(0.8–1.4)
Standard of living, age and gender	1.02	0.67	1.24	0.92
	(0.7–1.5)	(0.5–0.96)	(0.9–1.7)	(0.7–1.2)

Migration

A history of migration is often the root factor in the formation of self-conscious ethnic minorities and majorities, and is often a key issue in explaining patterns of health. The migration may have been of the current minority (e.g. South Asians or African-Caribbeans in Europe or Irish in Britain, America and Australasia) or of the current majority (e.g. the white populations amongst Maori or Aborigine or native American peoples in Australasia and North America). Among the migrants, this means that there is always biographical experience of at least two economic systems, one current and one in the past, and of at least two cultures. Among their descendants, likewise, there is a continuing consciousness of this dual experience. Hence all the factors enumerated below are complicated by this duality, e.g. material factors in both economic systems may have shaped migrants' health, and the culture of migrants is not straightforwardly that of the country of origin but will have been affected almost immediately by experiences in the receiving country.

Factors associated with the period immediately surrounding the migration also frequently present specific explanations for the health of ethnic minorities or, more often, alternative explanations which need to be ruled out in analysis or guarded against in the design of studies. Migrants tend to be selected by health characteristics from the population of origin – usually having better health if they are long-distance migrants (14). These health characteristics are present at the time of decision to migrate and will be reflected in the health of migrants in their place of destination. However, over time such differentials 'wear off' and the health of migrants will tend to revert to the mean standard of the population of origin, particularly when the next generation is considered. In the case of long-distance migrants, the 'wearing off' of the protection produced by the tendency of migrants to be a healthy subgroup of their source population may mean a relative decline in the health of migrants, compared to health in the country of destination, over time.

An alternative health-selection aspect of migration is the possibility that returning to one's birthplace when sick or through the desire to die in one's original home could lead to the selective return of those with high mortality risk. This phenomenon – which has been called 'salmon bias' (19) phenomenon – would therefore artificially reduce the mortality rate of migrant populations. This would occur whether or not there was complete recording of the return migrants leaving the UK. If recording is complete – and therefore denominators can be adjusted for those leaving the UK – then it is still the case that the remaining people born in a particular country and living within the UK would be a selected healthy group with low mortality. In addition, if there is incomplete recording of people who leave the country then they will erroneously remain part of the denominator for calculating mortality rates and artificially reduced rates of death will be generated. [...]

A second factor associated with the migration period is stress of various kinds (20). This would normally lead to worse health, but as it is a transitional phenomenon it should be followed by improvement over time, if other things are equal. The elevated risk seen long after migration and amongst second-generation migrants cannot be due to the acute stress of migration.

Socio-economic factors

Given that there is such a strong relationship between socio-economic factors and health, and there are important differences in the distribution of the socio-economic circumstances of different ethnic groups (summarized in Table 10) (3) it would seem to make sense to explore how far ethnic variations in health remain once socio-economic differences between ethnic groups have been controlled. This was the strategy adopted by Marmot *et al.* (14), but they found that once they had standard-ized for class differences in the immigrant mortality data they used, ethnic variations in health remained more or less unchanged. In addition, they found that class had a variable relationship with mortality rates for the different migrant groups. A more consistent picture, with social class differentials among minority ethnic groups being in the same direction as the general population, has emerged in the 1990s (2), but, as Table 4 shows, conventional adjustment for occupational social class still accounts for little if any of the differences in mortality risk between members of different ethnic groups.

However, there are two key reasons why class effects might be suppressed in immigrant mortality data. First, such data use occupation as recorded on death certificates to define social class. The inflating of occupational status on death certifi-cates (where, according to Townsend and Davidson (21), occupation is recorded as the 'skilled' job held for most of the individual's life rather than the 'unskilled' job held in the last few years of life) will be particularly significant for immigrant mortality data if migration to Britain was associated with downward social mobility for members of ethnic minority groups, a process that has been clearly documented (22, 23). So, the occupation recorded on the death certificates of migrants may well be an inaccurate reflection of their experience in Britain prior to death. In addition, given the socio-economic profile of ethnic minority groups in Britain, this inflation of occupational level would only need to happen in relatively few cases for the figures representing the small population in higher classes to be distorted upwards.

Second, there has been an increasing recognition of the limitations of traditio-nal class groupings, which are far from internally homogeneous. A number of studies have drawn attention to variations in income levels and death rates among occupations that comprise particular occupational classes (24). Within an occupa-tional group, it is certainly likely that, as a result of the racialization of disadvant-age, ethnic minorities will be more likely to be found in lower or less prestigious occupational grades, to have poorer job security, to endure more stressful working conditions and to be more likely to work unsocial hours (for example see the account of the situation in nursing (25)). Evidence from the *Fourth National Survey* illustrates this point clearly. Table 11 (3) shows that ethnic minority people had a lower income than white people in the same class, that unemployed ethnic minority people had been unemployed for longer than equivalent white people, and that some ethnic minority groups had poorer quality housing than whites regardless of tenure. Similar findings have been reported from elsewhere in the UK and in the USA (26–8). The conclusion to be drawn is that, while standard indicators of socio-economic position have some use for making comparisons *within* ethnic groups, they are of little use for 'controlling out' the impact of socio-economic differences when attempting to reveal a pure 'ethnicity' effect.

Another problem with using data that have been standardized for socio-economic position is worth highlighting. Such an approach to analysis and interpretation regards socio-economic position as a confounding factor that needs to be 'controlled

Table 10 Socio-economic position by ethnic group (percentages): Fourth National Survey of Ethnic Minorities (3)

	White	Caribbean	Indian	African-Asian	Pakistani	Bangladeshi	Chinese
Registrar General's Class:							
I/II	35	22	30	35	20	11	40
IIIn	15	18	19	23	15	18	26
IIIm	31	30	21	23	32	32	20
IV/V	20	30	30	19	33	40	13
Percent of economically active unemployed:	11	24	16	13	38	42	7
Percent lacking one or more basic housing amenities:*	16	17	19	10	39	32	19

Note: *i.e. exclusive use of: bath or shower; bathroom; inside toilet; kitchen; hot water from a tap; and central heating.

Table 11   Variations within socio-economic bands by ethnic group: Fourth National Survey of Ethnic Minorities (2)

	Whites	Caribbeans	Indians and African-Asians	Pakistanis and Bangladeshis
Mean income by Registrar General's class (pounds):[1]				
I/II	250	210	210	125
IIIn	185	145	135	95
IIIm	160	145	120	70
IV/V	130	120	110	65
Median duration of unemployment (months):				
	7	21	12	24
Percent lacking one or more basic housing amenities:[2]				
Owner-occupiers	11	12	14	38
Renters	27	23	28	37

Notes: [1]Based on bands of equivalized household income. The mean point of each band is used to make this calculation, which is rounded to the nearest £5.
[2]i.e. exclusive use of: bath or shower; bathroom; inside toilet; kitchen; hot water from a tap; and central heating.

out' to reveal the 'true' relationship between ethnicity and health (29). This results in the importance of socio-economic factors becoming obscured and their explanatory role lost. The presentation of 'standardized' data leaves both the author and reader to assume that all that is left is an 'ethnicity' effect, be that cultural or biological. This gives the impression that different types of explanation operate for ethnic minority groups compared with the general population. While for the latter, factors relating to socio-economic position are shown to be crucial, for the former they are not visible, so differences are assumed to be related to some aspect of ethnicity or 'race', even though socio-economic factors are important determinants of health for all groups. Theories based upon apparent 'pure' ethnic characteristics can in this way be used to explain the residual effects in models that claim to, but, as described above, cannot, take full account of socio-economic factors.

Culture, beliefs, behaviour

Culture is usually assumed to affect health through such factors as health-related behaviours and beliefs (e.g. smoking, drinking alcohol, diet, exercise, sexual behaviour, concepts of health, images of the body, lay theories of illness, etc.), or the organization of family and kinship (affecting child rearing, gender roles and patterns of social support), or language and communication (mainly affecting health service use).

Health-related behaviours are the best-documented of these factors. Smoking is generally at lower levels among Black and South Asian groups than in the general population, especially among women (30), although smoking levels of African-Caribbean and Pakistani men are approaching similar levels to the general population, and higher levels have been recorded for Bangladeshi men (31). Alcohol consumption, even more than smoking, is at low levels among Black and South Asian groups, again particularly among women (30). However, aggregated data may conceal high levels of alcohol consumption among Sikhs, and levels approaching those of the general population among Hindus (32). By contrast with this picture among Caribbean and South Asian groups, both smoking and drinking levels have been reported to be high among the Irish (33). Smoking and drinking patterns have been reported to persist into the second generation (34), but data on a longer-established Irish community in Britain suggest that differences are slight or non-existent, and rates of smoking and drinking in Ireland are generally similar to those in Britain (35).

Patterns of diet are more difficult to summarize, and have recently been reviewed (36). Concern has been expressed that dietary control may be needed to reduce coronary risk factors (especially abdominal obesity) among South Asian groups, and to reduce risk of hypertension and stroke (and excess weight for height) among African-Caribbeans. Among largely vegetarian groups such as Gujaratis saturated fat intakes are not an issue, but total fat intake may be. In addition, low vitamin D and iron intakes in vegetarian groups have been connected with TB and childhood growth problems. Among meat-eating groups such as Punjabis, intakes of saturated and total fat may be an issue. The other side of excess weight problems is exercise: low levels of exercise have been found among Black and South Asian groups, with the exception of young African-Caribbean men (31). Short stature among South Asian groups, and among people of Irish descent in Britain, suggests the possibility of a more general nutritional deficit, or a greater exposure to infections, in childhood. The stature of Irish people in Ireland is not shorter than that of the general population in Britain (37).

The organization of family and kinship is another complex subject. There are some recent statistical overviews (38), though the area has not been reviewed in relation to health. South Asian groups have larger average household sizes, both in number of adults and in number of children, and are more often looking after elderly relatives, than the general population. More Caribbean households are of children living only with a mother than in the general population. Irish households are similar to those of the general population on these crude measures: despite stereotypes of high Catholic fertility, the mean number of dependent children in households of the Irish-born, who include a high proportion of Catholics, is currently identical to that of the general population.

Religion may be an important influence on many of these patterns. There are religious limits placed on smoking among Sikhs, on drinking alcohol among Muslims, and on both among evangelical Protestants. There was also a temperance movement among Catholics in Ireland in the last century, which is still apparent in high levels of abstention there. The smoking levels of Pakistani and Bangladeshi men [...] which contrast with the low levels of smoking in South Asian groups otherwise, reflect the absence of a Muslim prohibition on smoking, although there is a general expectation of restraint for women. In the same way Sikh male levels of drinking reflect the absence of a specific Sikh prohibition on alcohol. Religion also influences diet, including the vegetarian patterns referred to earlier.

Language use has been considered an important influence on some health-related activities among South Asian groups (31). However the tendency to refer to this as a factor tends to mask more deep-seated difficulties of communication, some of which are related to racism.

There are special problems in using culture, behaviour or beliefs to explain health. The association of an ethnic group with a pattern of health does not indicate that the pattern of health is the result of a cultural difference. Crude assumptions of this sort, combined with the general tendency to focus on health problems more than health successes, have led to patterns of culture blaming which have received extensive criticism. A cultural explanation becomes an initial possibility only when particular beliefs or behaviours associated with the ethnic group concerned can be shown to account for the health pattern. [...]

Further exploration of these issues is needed. Many health-related behaviours have class or standard-of-living gradients, suggesting that they are also influenced by variations in income and wealth. Hence in relevant cases it may be necessary to test the possibility that any beliefs or behaviours concerned are influenced by class or standard of living. In a recent study, high levels of symptoms experienced by South Asian women were particularly elevated in Muslim groups and among those with poor English, suggesting cultural factors; however, when low standard of living, stress in work around the house and absence of kin and confidants were included in the analysis the cultural differences were no longer apparent (39).

Where beliefs or behaviours and material factors are jointly involved, care has to be taken in interpreting the direction of causation, which may be complex. For example bringing up children in deprived circumstances may lead to increased smoking as a way of reducing tension; however, the proportion of a group in deprived circumstances is increased by barriers to jobs and income, and access to jobs and income may be restricted by racism. In this review racism is treated separately in a later section, but it provides an important illustration of ways in which cultural and material factors can interact.

[...]It is important that cultural factors are described in the terms used by cultural insiders, even if these descriptions are set beside other descriptions. Early research on reporting of symptoms assumed that South Asian languages lacked terms for identifying depressive states; but this assumption has been challenged by qualitative interviews with South Asian women (40). Again, even when the behaviours or beliefs associated with an ethnic group can be shown to account for a particular health pattern, the fluidity of these factors and the way in which they are constantly refashioned within a culture need to be recognized, especially after migration when people have access to the resources of two different cultures. [...] Nor does the association of beliefs or behaviours with the health of an ethnic group in Britain guarantee that they are associated in the country of origin. Victorian explanations of Irish ill health in Britain blamed Irish culture, yet levels of mortality in Ireland were much lower than in the receiving towns in Britain (41). The situation in the new country, especially if hostile, may itself alter the beliefs and behaviour of incomers, or change their implications.

Racism

Racism and discrimination could possibly have an effect on health in three ways. First, there could be an indirect effect on health as a result of consequent socioeconomic disadvantage. Second, ethnic minority people will have a clear recognition of the relative disadvantage they face as a result of the obvious inequalities, discrimination and racism that they experience in virtually all spheres of their lives (42).

This sense of relative disadvantage, as Wilkinson has argued (43), may have a significant impact on health.

Third, the experience of racial discrimination and harassment may have a direct detrimental effect on health. There has been recent evidence of both the nature and extent of the harassment members of ethnic minorities experience (42, 44, 45) and the multiple victimization that some are subjected to could lead to mental distress and poor health. For example, it has been demonstrated that experiencing racial harassment is associated with reported acute illness (after controlling for other relevant variables) and that experiencing any form of discrimination at work is associated with both acute and long-standing illness (46).

However, evidence is not consistent. For example, the *Fourth National Survey* showed that variations across ethnic minority groups in the reported experiences of racial harassment did not match those for health (42). Bangladeshis, who had the poorest health, were less likely than both African-Asians and Chinese, who had the best health, to report that they had been racially harassed. Part of the reason for this inconsistency in evidence is undoubtedly the difficulty of assessing the extent of racial harassment individuals experience. For example, studies in the USA have shown that Black Americans who report and challenge racial harassment and discrimination have *lower* blood pressure than those who say they would tolerate harassment and discrimination and do not report experiencing it (47,48). The authors suggest that, in the case of hypertension at least, the negative health effect is a consequence of internalized anger, which would be more likely among those who experience, but do not report, racial harassment.

Biology

The use of studies of ethnic differences in health to point to presumed underlying biological – usually genetic – factors has been much discussed and criticized (49). There is, however, generally more genetic variation within ethnic groups than between ethnic groups. This does not mean that differences in some health problems – for example haemoglobinopathies and melanoma – are not strongly influenced by genetic factors which alter propensity to disease. However, as contributors to overall health differentials between ethnic groups, these play a relatively minor role. Several research groups are investigating whether differences in common chronic diseases, such as diabetes, coronary heart disease and hypertension, may be influenced by genetic factors which are differentially distributed between ethnic groups. Opinion on this differs with, for example, some researchers considering epidemiological evidence to demonstrate that the higher prevalence of hypertension amongst African-Caribbeans and people of African origin in the UK or USA is strongly influenced by genetic factors (50), while focused studies of this issue find little support for this hypothesis, instead identifying environmental factors as of primary importance (51). The 'racialization' of research and health policy which focus on genetic differences is, and should be, resisted for many obvious reasons. Similarly the failure of many approaches based on genetic factors to acknowledge the often necessary role of environmental factors in the expression of any genetic differences is particularly unhelpful.

The understandable reluctance – on both empirical and ideological grounds – to accept a major role for genetic differences in explaining health differentials between ethnic groups has sometimes led to a reluctance to consider biological factors as having any role in generating health differentials. However, many important determinants of health are physiological characteristics which are strongly influenced by socio-economic and other environmental factors, and in turn have a long-lasting influence on health. Thus low birthweight, which is strongly influenced by adverse material circumstances acting over the lifetime of the mother, is associated with high rates of diabetes, coronary heart disease, respiratory disease and hypertension in adult life. Similarly, short stature, influenced by nutrition in early life, is related to an increased risk of respiratory and cardiovascular mortality. Several aspects of bodily habitus, such as birthweight, growth in childhood, achieved height and lung function, are factors which are at the same time socially produced and biological. Similar considerations apply to the role of such factors in explaining socio-economic differentials in health status within ethnic groups. An understandable tendency to reject any form of explanation presented in biological terms fails to recognize the extent to which socio-economic and environmental forces become embodied and, through this embodiment, influence the health of people throughout their lives, and may even influence the health of subsequent generations.

Health service access and use

The role of health services in determining health status has often been underestimated in comparison to environmental and genetic factors. But surgery for heart disease or arthritis, medical treatment for diabetes, and immunization can have a major impact. There are several reasons why people from minority ethnic groups have inequitable access to care. Studies from the USA show large inequities in health care access, especially when comparing African-Americans to US whites, largely due to the relationship between wealth and ability to obtain health care.

But equity in access to health care, particularly by ethnicity, has been poorly researched in the UK, as it is assumed that there should be no inequity in a service which is free at the point of delivery. Such a simplistic argument ignores the complexity of the route to obtaining appropriate care, so that barriers can occur at any stage of the care-seeking process. At the patient level, individuals differ in their perceptions of the severity of their symptoms, and the urgency with which they seek care. Once the decision has been made, physical barriers to the GP, such as lack of access to a car, and unavailability of an appointment at a convenient time, may also cause delay. The outcome of the consultation depends largely on the GP being able to arrive at a correct diagnosis, which is influenced by patient demographic characteristics, including social class, and the quality of the GP. These factors may also influence the receipt of hospital care, once a referral has been made.

Earlier studies have simply examined utilization of primary or hospital services, and suffer from several methodological limitations, which results in confused interpretations. GP consultations were found to be higher in Pakistani, Indian and Caribbean adults compared with the general population (31, 52), but no account was taken of differences in morbidity or need. Consultations for specific conditions show that whilst Caribbean people attend more for diseases of the circulatory system, Asian attendance rates are similar to that of the general population (53, 54). The latter finding is not reassuring given the substantially higher rate of heart disease observed in South Asians.

Use of screening services, such as breast and cervical cancer screening, has often been reported to be low in people from minority ethnic groups, especially South Asian women (31). The explanation provided for this is that there is a poor understanding of the value of preventative care, and a general lack of knowledge about such services. However, these explanations are contradicted by the finding that immunization rates are generally higher in people from minority ethnic groups (55).

These studies tell us very little about whether, or where, inequalities in access to care occur. More recent studies, generally focusing on a specific condition, have provided better information. In the management of chronic heart disease, South Asian people have to wait twice as long for specialist intervention as Europeans (56). But again this study could not show where the barrier to care occurred. An examination of proposed action in the event of chest pain indicated that South Asian people were more likely to be concerned about such symptoms, and more likely to seek immediate care than the general population (57). This finding is confirmed by a study of mothers, which showed that Bengali mothers were more likely to seek immediate care for an unwell child than their counterparts from other ethnic groups (9). Thus it would appear that barriers are unlikely to occur before the health care service is approached. There is some evidence that physical access to the GP is more difficult, and obtaining an appointment is harder in South Asian people, particularly Bangladeshi people, compared with the general population (31). But at the consultation, South Asian people are more likely to report that they have satisfactorily communicated their needs (58). This is confounded by studies of the outcome of consultations. South Asian people are less likely to leave the surgery with a follow-up appointment (53), and less likely to be offered services such as a district nurse, despite being keen to use this service once offered to them (59). Difficulties in communication between the doctor and patient have often been ascribed to language (60), but this is less of a problem than it at first appears. Facility with English is now high in the younger South Asian groups (58), and around 80% of South Asian people are registered with a South Asian GP (31). But there are indications that cultural perceptions about symptoms may differ, and may make it hard for people from minority ethnic groups to articulate their needs within the framework used by the UK general population. In those who had a confirmed heart attack, South Asians are less likely to present with classical symptoms, and the diagnosis is therefore often missed (61). Others have shown that referral rates from general practice for a barium meal examination are higher in South Asians than Europeans, but that abnormalities are reported much less often (62). As a result of this, GPs may find it harder to arrive at an appropriate diagnosis.

It appears that people from minority ethnic groups may have poorer access to health care in the UK compared with the general population, but the reasons for this, its extent and the degree to which it influences health outcomes are unknown.

Conclusions

[...] Influences considered under each of the explanatory categories we have discussed above will all make some contribution to the production of ethnic differentials in health. Different influences will act during different periods of peoples' lives and the accumulation of such factors over the entire lifecourse – and even the lifecourses of previous generations – must be considered if an adequate framework for understanding ethnic differentials in health is to be developed.

A key issue relates to the ways in which measurement and conceptual issues regarding socio-economic position can influence studies of the contribution of socio-economic differences to ethnic group differentials in health status, as has been discussed by several authors (e.g. 63–5). A failure to appreciate these problems when studying the contribution of socio-economic position to health differences between ethnic groups produces a form of reasoning by elimination, which leads to explanations concentrating on assumed genetic or cultural differences. For example, a [...] study of ethnic group differences in stroke in London (66) compared stroke rates among two groups they defined as black (Afro-Caribbean, 'black African' and 'black other' according to the 1991 British census categories) and white (a group they do not define). The stroke rates among blacks were around twice as high as among whites, and statistical adjustment for occupational social class only partly accounted for this elevated stroke rate. On the basis of this the authors suggest that 'Ethnic differences in genetic, physiological and behavioural risk factors for stroke require further elucidation'. As discussed earlier, adjustment for occupational social class will capture only some of the aspects of socio-economic environment that influence stroke risk and may not provide an index of social circumstances in the same way among the group Stewart *et al.* refer to as blacks and whites. This then produces data which apparently – but spuriously – demonstrate that health differences are due to genetic or cultural/behavioural factors.

As some minority ethnic groups are among the most disadvantaged sections of British society, measures which misrepresent the standard of living of minority ethnic groups risk not only perpetrating but exacerbating disadvantage through inadequate investment of public resources. Equally, an improved understanding of the processes which underlie ethnic differences in socio-economic position and health has the potential to lead to more appropriately targeted interventions. There is therefore a pressing need to develop more sensitive indicators of socio-economic position, particularly for use in research into the causes of ethnic inequalities in health.

Acknowledgements

The authors would like to thank Anne Rennie and Claire Snadden for help in preparation of the manuscript and Roy Maxwell for help with providing data. George Davey Smith and James Nazroo have received support from the ESRC Health Variations Program. The Afiya Trust, Kings Fund and Health Education Authority supported this review. A full version of this paper is represented in George Davey Smith, *A Lifecourse Approach to Health Inequalities* (Bristol: Policy Press, 2002).

Note

Since the completion of this review the provisional results of the 1999 Health Survey for England 'Health of Minority Ethnic Groups Supplement' have appeared on the World Wide Web (http://doh.gov.uk/public/hs99ethnictables.html), although only simple tabulations of the data have so far been presented and the preliminary findings cannot be regarded as being reliable. The publication of a formal report of this survey will constitute an important addition to the literature on ethnic group differentials in health in England.

References

1 Bhopal R. Is research into ethnicity and health racist, unsound, or important science? *BMJ* 1997; 314: 1751–6.

2 Harding S, Maxwell R. Differences in mortality of migrants. In: Drever F, Whitehead M, editors, *Health Inequalities*. London: The Stationery Office; 1997.

3 Nazroo JY. *The Health of Britain's Ethnic Minorities: Findings from a National Survey*. London: PSI; 1997.

4 McKeigue P. Coronary heart disease in Indians, Pakistanis and Bangladeshis: aetiology and possibilities for prevention. *Br Heart J* 1992; 67: 341–2.

5 McKeigue PM, Ferrie JE, Pierpoint T, Marmot MG. Association of early-onset coronary heart disease in South Asian men with glucose intolerance and hyperinsulinemia. *Circulation* 1993; 87: 152–61.

6 Chaturvedi N, McKeigue PM, Marmot MG. Resting and ambulatory blood pressure differences in Afro-Caribbeans and Europeans. *Hypertension* 1993; 22: 90–6.

7 Unwin N, Harland J, White M, Bhopal R, Winocour P, Stephenson P, Watson W, Turner C, Alberti KG. Body mass index, waist circumference, waist–hip ratio, and glucose tolerance in Chinese and Europid adults in Newcastle. *J Epidemiol Community Health* 1997; 51: 160–6.

8 Duran-Tauleria E, Rona RJ, Chinn S, Burney P. Influence of ethnic group on asthma treatment in children in 1990–1: national cross sectional study. *BMJ* 1996; 313: 148–52.

9 Watson E. Health of infants and use of health services by mothers of different ethnic groups in East London. *Community Med* 1984; 6: 127–35.

10 Jackson SHD, Bannan LT, Beevers DG. Ethnic differences in respiratory disease. *Postgrad Med J* 1981; 57: 777–8.

11 Williams R, Bhopal R, Hunt K. The health of a Punjabi ethnic minority in Glasgow: the comparison with the general population. *J Epidemiol Community Health* 1993; 47: 96–102.

12 McKeigue PM, Shah B, Marmot MG. Relation of central obesity and insulin resistance with high diabetes prevalence and cardiovascular risk in South Asians. *Lancet* 1991; 337: 382–6.

13 Harland JO, Unwin N, Bhopal RS, White M, Watson B, Later M, Alberti KGMM. Low levels of cardiovascular risk factors and coronary heart disease in a UK Chinese population. *J Epidemiol Community Health* 1997; 51: 636–42.

14 Marmot MG, Adelstein AM, Bulusu L. Immigrant mortality in England and Wales 1970–78. In: *Immigrant Mortality in England and Wales 1970–78*, OPCS Studies of Medical and Population Subjects No 47. London: HMSO; 1984.

15 Raleigh VS, Balarajan R. The health of infants and children among ethnic minorities. *The Health of our Children*, Decennial Suppl. London: The Stationery Office; 1995: 82–94.

16 Davey Smith G, Bartley M, Blane D. Explanations for socioeconomic differentials in mortality: evidence from Britain and elsewhere. *Eur J Public Health* 1994; 4: 131–44.

17 Andrews A, Jewson N. Ethnicity and infant deaths: the implications of recent statistical evidence for materialist explanations. *Sociology of Health and Illness* 1993; 15: 137–56.

18 Chandola T, Jenkinson C. Validating self-rated health in different ethnic groups. *Ethnicity and Health* 2000; 5: 151–9.

19 Abraido-Lanza AF, Dohrenwend BP, Ng-Mak DS, Turner JB. The Latino mortality paradox: a test of the 'salmon bias' and healthy migrant hypotheses. *Am J Public Health* 1999; 89: 10: 1543–8.

20 Hull D. Migration, adaptation and illness. *Soc Sci Med* 1979; 13A: 25–36.

21 Townsend P, Davison N. *Inequalities in Health: The Black Report*. Harmondsworth: Penguin; 1982.

22 Smith D. *Racial Disadvantage in Britain*. Harmondsworth: Penguin; 1977.

23 Heath A, Ridge J. Social mobility of ethnic minorities. *J Biosoc Sci* (Suppl.) 1983; 8: 169–84.

24 Davey Smith G, Shipley MJ, Rose G. The magnitude and causes of socio-economic differentials in mortality: further evidence from the Whitehall Study. *J Epidemiol Community Health* 1990; 44: 265–70.

25 Beishon S, Virdee S, Hagell A. *Nursing in a Multi-Ethnic NHS*. London: Policy Studies Institute; 1995.

26 Lillie-Blanton M, Laveist T. Race/ethnicity, the social environment, and health. *Soc Sci Med* 1996; 43: 83–91.

27 Williams DR, Lavizzo-Mourey R, Warren RC. The concept of race and health status in America. *Public Health Reports* 1994; 109: 26–41.

28 Williams R, Wright W, Hunt K. Social class and health: the puzzling counter-example of British South Asians. *Soc Sci Med* 1998; 47: 1277–88.

29 McKenzie K, Crowcroft NS. Describing race, ethnicity, and culture in medical research. *BMJ* 1996; 312: 1054.

30 Office for National Statistics. *Social Focus on Ethnic Minorities*. London: HMSO; 1996.

31 Rudat K. *Black and Ethnic Minority Groups in England: Health and Lifestyles*. London: Health Education Authority; 1994.

32 Cochrane R, Bal S. The drinking habits of Sikh, Hindu and white men in the West Midlands: a community survey. *Br J Addict* 1990; 85: 759–69.

33 Balarajan R, Yuen P. British smoking and drinking habits: variation by country of birth. *Community Med* 1986; 8: 237–9.

34 Pearson M, Madden M, Greenslade L. *Generations of an Invisible Minority*. Liverpool: University of Liverpool, Institute of Irish Studies; 1991.

35 Mullen K, Williams R, Hunt K. Irish descent, religion and alcohol and tobacco use. *Addiction* 1996; 91: 243–54.

36 Bush H, Williams R, Sharma S, Cruickshank K. *Opportunities for and Barriers to Good Nutritional Health among Ethnic Minorities*. London: Department of Health and Health Education Authority; 1999.

37 Abbotts J, Williams R, Ford G, Hunt K, West P. Morbidity and Irish Catholic descent in Britain: an ethnic and religious minority 150 years on. *Soc Sci Med* 1998; 45: 3–14.

38 Owen D. *Black People in Great Britain*, census statistical paper no. 6. Warwick: University of Warwick, Centre for Research in Ethnic Relations; 1994. Owen D. *South Asian People in Great Britain*, census statistical paper no. 7. Warwick: University of Warwick, Centre for Research in Ethnic Relations; 1994. Owen D. *Irish-Born People in Great Britain*, census statistical paper no. 7. Warwick: University of Warwick, Centre for Research in Ethnic Relations; 1995.

39 Williams R, Hunt K. Psychological distress among British South Asians: the contribution of stressful situations and subcultural differences in the West of Scotland Twenty-07 Study. *Psychol Med* 1997; 27: 1173–81.

40 Fenton S, Sadiq-Sangster A. Culture, relativism and the expression of mental distress: South Asian women in Britain. *Sociology of Health and Illness* 1996; 18: 66–85.

41 Williams R. Britain's regional mortality: a legacy from disaster in the celtic periphery? *Soc Sci Med* 1994; 39: 189–99.

42 Modood T, Berthoud R, Lakey J, Nazroo J, Smith P, Virdee S, Beishon S. *Ethnic Minorities in Britain: Diversity and Disadvantage*. London: Policy Studies Institute; 1997.

43 Wilkinson RG. *Unhealthy Societies: The Afflictions of Inequality*. London: Routledge; 1996.

44   Virdee S. *Racial Violence and Harassment*. London: Policy Studies Institute; 1995.

45   Hickman M, Walter B, editors. *Discrimination and the Irish Community in Britain*. London: Commission for Racial Equality; 1997.

46   Benzeval M, Judge K, Solomon M. *The Health Status of Londoners*. London: King's Fund Institute; 1992.

47   Krieger N. Racial and gender discrimination: risk factors for high blood pressure? *Soc Sci Med* 1990; 30: 1273–81.

48   Krieger N, Sidney S. Racial discrimination and blood pressure: the CARDIA study of young black and white adults. *Am J Public Health* 1996; 86 (10): 1370–8.

49   Herman AA. Toward conceptualisation of race in epidemiology research. *Ethnicity and Disease* 1996; 6: 7–20.

50   Wild S, McKeigue P. Cross sectional analysis of mortality by country of birth in England and Wales, 1970–92. *BMJ* 1997; 314: 705–10.

51   Cooper R, Rotimi C, Ataman S, McGee D, Osotimehin B, Kadiri S, Muna W, Kingue S, Fraser H, Forrester T, Bennett F, Wilks R. The prevalence of hypertension in seven populations of West African origin. *Am J Public Health* 1997; 87: 160–8.

52   Balarajan R, Yuen P, Raleigh VS. Ethnic differences in general practitioner consultations. *BMJ* 1989; 299: 958–60.

53   Gillam SJ, Jarman B, White P, Law R. Ethnic differences in consultation rates in urban general practice. *BMJ* 1989; 299: 953–7.

54   McCormick A, Fleming D, Charlton J. *Morbidity Statistics from General Practice. Fourth national study 1991–1992*. London: HMSO; 1995.

55   Baker MR, Bandaranayake R, Schweiger MS. Differences in rate of uptake of immunisation among ethnic groups. *BMJ* 1984; 288: 1075–9.

56   Shaukat N, de Bono DP, Cruickshank JK. Clinical features, risk factors, and referral delay in British patients of Indian and European origin with angina matched for age and extent of coronary atheroma. *BMJ* 1993; 307: 717–18.

57   Chaturvedi N, Rai H, Ben-Shlomo Y. Lay diagnosis and health care seeking behaviour for chest pain in South Asians and Europeans. *Lancet* 1997; 350: 1578–83.

58   Rashid A, Jagger C. Attitudes to and perceived use of health care services among Asian and non-Asian patients in Leicester. *Br J Gen Pract* 1992; 42: 197–201.

59   Badger F, Atkin K, Griffiths R. Why don't general practitioners refer their disabled Asian patients to district nurses? *Health Trends* 1989; 21: 31–2.

60   Ritch AES, Ehtisham M, Guthrie S, Talbot JM, Luck M, Tinsley RN. Ethnic influence on health and dependency of elderly inner city residents. *J R Coll Physicians Lond*. 1996; 30: 215–20.

61   Lear JT, Lawrence IG, Pohl JE, Burden AC. Myocardial infarction and thrombolysis: a comparison of the Indian and European populations on a coronary care unit. *J R Coll Physicians Lond* 1994; 28: 143–7.

62   Malcolm PN, Chan TYK, Li P-L, Richards J, Hately W. Management of dyspepsia among Asians by general practitioners in East London. *BMJ* 1995; 10: 910–11.

63   Kaufman JS, Cooper RS, McGee DL. Socio-economic status and health in blacks and whites: the problem of residual confounding and the resiliency of race. *Epidemiology* 1997; 8: 6: 621–8.

64   Davey Smith G. Learning to live with complexity: Ethnicity, socio-economic position, and health in Britain and the United States. *Am J Publ Health* 2000; 90: 1694–8.

65   Nazroo JY. Genetic, cultural or socio-economic vulnerability? Explaining ethnic inequalities in health. *Sociology of Health and Illness* 1998; 20: 714–34.

66   Stewart JA, Dundas R, Howard RA, Rudd AG, Woolfe CDA. Ethnic differences in incidence of stroke: prospective study with stroke register. *BMJ* 1999; 318: 967–71.

21

Area, Class and Health: Should we be Focusing on Places or People?

Sally Macintyre, Sheila MacIver and Anne Sooman

Research on areas and health

There is a long tradition of research in Britain into the effects on various aspects of health of living in certain types of area. John Graunt noted area variations in mortality over 300 years ago (Graunt, 1662). Mortality statistics by local area have been presented in annual reports of the Registrar General since 1938 [...].

Despite this long history of interest in area variations in morbidity and mortality in Britain, there has been relatively little investigation of the socio-economic or cultural features of areas which might influence health and the likelihood of death. Most of the recent British studies in this field can be divided into two categories according to the focus and explanatory variables of interest.

First, there are a number of studies whose aim is to provide clues to the etiology of disease, and which focus on specific properties of the physical environment. The explanatory variables used include air pollution, water hardness, nitrates in the drinking water, distance from the coast, latitude, altitude, mean temperature, rainfall, and toxins or other threats from industrial processes (for example, West and Lowe, 1976; Roberts and Lloyd, 1972; West, Lloyd and Roberts, 1973; Pocock *et al.*, 1980; Shaper *et al.*, 1981; Chinn *et al.*, 1981; Williams, Lloyd and Lloyd, 1988; Gardner, 1989; Britton *et al.*, 1990). As Gardner has pointed out, much of this work examines the relationship between a particular cause of death and a particular feature of the environment (for example, respiratory death rates and rates of population density); this specificity may be appropriate for infectious diseases but be less appropriate for chronic diseases of multifactorial origin, or for risk factors which may contribute to a range of conditions (1973, p. 422). [...]

Second, there are studies of the relationship between deprivation and either morbidity or mortality which use area level analysis. The work in Scotland of Crombie *et al.* (1989) and Carstairs and Morris (1989; 1991), and in England of Townsend and his associates (Townsend, Simpson and Tibbs, 1984; Townsend, Phillimore and Beattie, 1988) exemplifies this approach. In this tradition small areas (local government districts, post code sectors, or wards) are classified according to characteristics of their populations as ascertained at the latest decennial census (1981 in the case of the above studies). Either individual census indicators, such as percentage of men unemployed or percentage of individuals in social classes

III and IV, are correlated with mortality (Crombie *et al.*, 1989) or a number of census indicators are combined to form indices of deprivation which are then examined in relationship to mortality. (Carstairs and Morris, 1989, for example, use a deprivation measure consisting of an unweighted combination of four standardised census variables: male unemployment, no car, overcrowded housing and low social class; Townsend *et al.*, 1988, use a measure comprising percentages with no car, in overcrowded dwellings, living in non-owner occupied housing, and unemployed). This type of research explicitly uses aggregate measures of deprivation, and of morbidity or mortality, as surrogates for individual measures of deprivation and health or death. It does not use area or ecological variables other than those created by aggregating the characteristics of the people living in them. The main interest in areas is to see whether deprivation (measured at the 'area' level) can explain observed differences between areas in mortality or morbidity.

[. . .] [A]lthough ostensibly about area variations in health or life expectancy, many of these studies are not, *per se*, about the role of areas in influencing health; rather they use areas as vehicles for exploring hypotheses about the role of physical exposure or material deprivation in the etiology of ill health.

Research on social class, area and health

Social class is often brought into such analyses as a control factor. [. . .]

In general much of this work has been undertaken to explore whether apparent differences between areas can be 'explained away' (Gardner, 1973; Crombie [*et al.*], 1989). In relation to theories of the role of social deprivation or social class, area level indicators were initially used as surrogate measures for individual level deprivation but the interest has now moved on to explore the issue of the different predictive value (and, by implication, causal role) of individual level of deprivation as compared with living in a deprived area.

An important analysis from the Alameda County Study in California showed that residents in 'poverty areas' experienced higher age, race and sex adjusted mortality over a follow up period compared with residents of non-poverty areas. This increased risk of death persisted when there was multivariate adjustment for baseline health status, race, income, employment status, education, access to medical care, health insurance coverage, and a whole range of behavioural factors often assumed to be the link between socio-economic status and poor health. The authors conclude that 'these results support the hypothesis that properties of the socio-physical environment may be important contributors to the association between low socio-economic status and excess mortality, and that this contribution is independent of individual behaviours' (Haan, Kaplan and Camacho, 1987, p. 989). In other words this suggests that over and above individual level attributes of deprivation, people of low socio-economic status may have poorer health because they tend to live in areas which in some ways are health damaging.

Another recent analysis, this time from Britain and using health-based rather than death-based measures, supports this conclusion. Blaxter examined various aspects of health ('illness', 'psycho-social health', 'fitness', and 'disease/disability') among men and women in non-manual and manual class groups living in different types of area. She found that 'while the health of manual men and women was almost always poorer than that of non-manual, it is clear that types of living area do make a difference' (1990, p. 82). She suggests, however, that the relationship between social class and area of residence is more complex than is sometimes assumed. For example, there are larger social class differences in health in 'good' residential areas and in industrial areas than there are in rural or resort type areas. Living in rural or resort neighbourhoods seems equally beneficial for non-manual and manual families. Cities seem to have a particularly adverse effect on 'psycho-social health' and 'illness' among non-manual men and women. Industrial areas by contrast seem to have a particularly bad effect – in terms of 'illness', 'fitness' and 'psycho-social health' – among manual families. [. . .]

These findings suggest that we should be looking at features of local areas which might be health damaging or health promoting. Perhaps surprisingly, little work of this sort has been conducted. Although, as described above, there has been research into features of the physical environment such as water hardness and climate, there has apparently been very little corresponding curiosity about what aspects of the social, cultural or economic environment might contribute to area variations in health. Although there are many studies of differences between areas in terms of the composition of their populations, based on census returns, there are few which directly examine features of the places themselves. Most studies on area variations in health actually examine who lives in certain places rather than what certain places are like, or used to be like, to live in (exceptions include Barker and Osmond's analysis of Burnley, Colne and Nelson in Lancashire, (Barker and Osmond, 1987), and Peter Phillimore's study of working class communities in Middlesborough and Sunderland (Phillimore, 1991).

This lack of interest we attribute to three main reasons. First, we suspect that some investigators tend to think of census-type classifications of areas (Craig Webber, ACORN, Townsend, Scotdep) as if they actually describe properties of the areas rather than the characteristics of their residents.

Second and relatedly, we suspect that many researchers and policy-makers tend to think of the mechanism for any area effects on health as being compositional, that is, as being due to the characteristics of the residents. Differences between neighbourhoods' health outcomes (such as the twofold differences in mortality between different areas in Glasgow (GGHB, 1984, 1989) are often treated as being explicable in terms of the social class or deprivation level of their inhabitants, and therefore as being of no further analytical or policy interest. The finding, for example, that high status leafy suburbs have good health indices is assumed to be because the people who live there are rich, upper class and well educated. This assumption that area variations in health are a product of variations in the composition of their populations may have inadvertently been encouraged by the way in which area level analysis has been used in order to make the case that social class or material deprivation is related to health. It may also stem from the epidemiological tradition of research, which tends to focus on individuals rather than on supra-individual variables, and to be concerned with ruling out problems arising from the ecological fallacy.

Third, lack of curiosity about the features of place which might influence health may relate to the commonsense assumption that 'we all know' what different areas are like to live in. Just as 'social class' is often treated as though it explains things, rather than providing a starting point for more detailed examination of the processes producing health and illness, 'area' may be also treated as though its relationship with health is obvious (for a discussion of the role of 'space' in British health policy see Moon, 1990).

Analysing 'class' controlling for 'area' may lead us to ignore the role that the social and physical environment might play in influencing people's life chances and ability to lead healthy lives; analysing 'area' controlling for 'class' may lead us to ignore the role of political and economic factors in determining what areas are like to live in and how society's resources are distributed to different places. We therefore want to argue that the important research which partials out the relative effects of individual social class from the effects of area of residence should be complemented and extended by research which directly examines features of local environments which might influence health, and which might be amenable to social reform.

Rather than treating the characteristics of areas as the sum of the individual characteristics of their residents, and instead of taking for granted 'what we all know' about different sorts of places, this approach would seek to examine, systematically, those characteristics of areas which might influence the physical or mental health of their residents. Such a systematic approach would allow for the generation of hypotheses about people's experiences of social class and of living in different types of areas, and contribute towards the testing of hypotheses about the influence of these features on the health of the population.

The local environment and health

What aspects of the physical, social and cultural environment might promote or damage health? Much of the existing literature on socio-environmental influences on health tends to focus on specific domains, such as work, housing, or health services. Looking in a holistic way at the cumulative or interactive impact of an individual's local environment is a novel approach for which previous research does not provide clear guidelines. Nevertheless we suggest that it might be profitable to conceptualise socio-environmental influences on health as falling into five broad types:

1 *Physical features of the environment shared by all residents in a locality*   These include the quality of air and water, latitude, climate, etc. and are likely to be shared by neighbourhoods across a wide area. (For example, all the drinking water in Glasgow City comes from one source, Loch Katrine, therefore variations in water hardness cannot explain twofold differences in mortality between neighbourhoods in Glasgow (GGHB, 1984).)

2 *The availability of healthy/unhealthy environments at home, at work, and at play*   Areas vary in their provision of decent housing, secure and non-hazardous employment, affordable and nutritious food, and safe and healthy recreation. These environments may not affect everyone living in an area in the same way as do air or water quality; they are opportunities which may or may not be taken up, with various degrees of choice and/or constraint.

3 *Services provided, privately or publicly, to support people in their daily lives*   These include education, transport, street cleaning and lighting, policing, churches and other community organisations, and health and welfare services.

4 *Socio-cultural features of a neighbourhood*   These include the political, economic, ethnic, and religious history and current characteristics of the community;

norms and values, the degree of community integration, levels of crime and of other perceived threats to personal safety, and networks of community support.

5 *The reputation of a neighbourhood* How areas are perceived, by their residents, outsiders, and service or amenity planners and providers, may influence the self-esteem and morale of the residents, and also who moves in or out of the area.

There are some obvious possible interactions between these categories. For example, houses with lead piping (category 2) may pose more of a risk to health than those with other types of pipe, given the same quality of mains water (category 1). Certain types of design of house (category 2) may be more susceptible than others to damp, mould and condensation, given the same climatic conditions (category 1). Some types of industry, for example, nuclear plants or chemical works (category 2), may pose risks not just to those employed in them but also to those living nearby. Individuals or families with better personal resources may be better placed than their poorer neighbours to avail themselves of certain opportunities (category 2): for example, by driving to out-of-town supermarkets to buy their food, using recreational facilities outside the area, or sending their children to 'better' schools outside the area. They can also avoid living in areas with 'a bad name' (category 5). Areas with poor reputations (category 5) may find it extremely difficult to attract decent private or publicly funded services (category 3), or to generate the sort of community spirit needed to fight for improved local environments (category 2). Local norms and values (category 4) may prescribe what is regarded as appropriate employment or recreation (category 2) for certain social categories such as men, women, or people of different religious or ethnic minorities. The extent of community integration and political activism in a neighbourhood (category 4) may influence actions taken to improve local services (category 3).

Aspects of the physical and social environment may influence both mental and physical health, and may do so directly or in interaction with individual attributes. Health services, for example, may not be a major determinant of variations in mortality between areas. However, inaccessible or poorly resourced local health services may be an additional stressor for people already stressed by other personal and local circumstances – for example, poor, disabled, or unemployed people, or those caring for children or disabled relatives. The provision of facilities for outdoor recreation – tennis courts, football fields, bowling greens – may not only enhance opportunities to develop or maintain cardiovascular fitness, but may also promote mental health via self-esteem, social contacts, and social participation. A generalised sense of a threatening environment – one with high noise levels and traffic density, dirty and poorly lit streets, high rates of crime, vandalism, litter and graffiti, and an ugly and uncared for built environment – may demoralise people and affect their mental health, as well as directly threatening their physical health.

Is it possible to study these features of the social and physical environment directly, that is, separately from the characteristics of the inhabitants of areas? We suggest that it is possible to examine some elements of the five types of influence outlined above, though there are a number of difficulties in so doing. We illustrate these points in the following section, which uses two urban localities in Glasgow as examples.

Comparisons between areas

We selected two areas in Glasgow known to differ in their socio-residential characteristics and in their mortality experience, and attempted to gather data about aspects of their social and physical environments which might help to explain these different health profiles. We used a socio-residential classification of enumeration districts, based on 1981 census data, devised by the Information Services Division of the Greater Glasgow Health Board (GGHB). It contains eight socio-residential types, which had standardised mortality ratios (SMRs; standardised to 100 for the GGHB area) ranging from 78 in the 'best' area type to 124 in the 'worst' area type. We selected areas which were towards the better or worse poles of this continuum, but not at the extremes. Criteria for selection are given in MacIver and Macintyre (1987).

The 'better' area is in the North West of Glasgow City. It includes the neighbourhoods of Anniesland, Dowanhill, Hyndland, Knightswood, Blairdardie, and Jordanhill. In 1981 its population was 51,000, 43.9 per cent of whom lived in households headed by someone in social classes I or II, and 12.4 per cent in households headed by someone in social classes IV or V. Its SMR for 0–64 year olds was 83 in 1980–2 (standardised to the GGHB area). The 'worse' area is in the South West of Glasgow City and contains the neighbourhoods of Craigton, Mosspark, Pollok, Levern, Darnley, South Nitshill, Carnwadric and Arden. In 1981 its population was 60,000, 5.9 per cent of whom lived in households headed by someone in social classes I or II and 36.4 per cent in households headed by someone in social classes IV or V. Its SMR for 0–64 year olds was 114 in 1980–82. Further details of these areas can be found in MacIver (1988).

Some data are available from statistics routinely collected by various agencies for their own purposes, although there is often a difficulty of non-comparable boundaries. We have thus been able to collect information on our two study areas from the Planning, Environmental Health, Parks and Recreation, and Cleansing Departments of Glasgow City District Council (GDC); the Social Work and Education Departments, and the Police and the Passenger Transport Executive, of Strathclyde Regional Council (SRC); and the Greater Glasgow Health Board (GGHB).

Other data have to be collected by specially designed surveys or observations. We have conducted a survey of the structure of primary medical care in our two localities; this involved approaching all the general practices in the areas and interviewing a representative from each practice (Wyke, Campbell and MacIver, 1992). We also undertook a survey of social work provision, although this proved extremely difficult and the results were hard to interpret (Erskine, 1991). Two surveys were conducted into the price and availability of food; in both cases this involved researchers going into a stratified sample of food shops in both areas and checking on the availability of a standard basket of food stuffs (MacIver and Bowie, 1989; Sooman and Taggart, 1992). In the second food survey comparisons were made between 'healthy' and 'less healthy' versions of the same foods (for example, wholemeal as compared with white bread).

This directly collected information tends to suggest that whatever one's personal characteristics, the opportunity structures in the poorer area are less conducive to health or health promoting activities than in the better off area. These local disadvantages are magnified when combined with the less adequate personal resources of those living in the poorer areas. Some illustrations are given below, divided into the five categories outlined earlier.

1 *Physical features of the environment shared by all residents in a locality*   The two localities are only a couple of miles apart, and share the same climate and water supply, therefore macro-environmental influences cannot explain the differences between them in health.

2 *The availability of healthy/unhealthy environments at home, at work, and at play*   Despite such macro-environmental similarities, it appears that there may be more of a problem of high lead content in the drinking water in the South West. In 1989, of the 79 houses in the North West whose drinking water was sampled, 5 per cent exceeded the EC guidelines for lead; of the 65 houses sampled in the South West, 11 per cent did so. The overall rate for Glasgow is 7 per cent above EC guidelines (data from Environment Health Department, GDC).

In 1989 the North West had 11 shops per 1,000 population compared with four in the South West. The North West had six strategic shopping centres and nine major local centres compared with three and five respectively in the South West. There was the same number of minor local centres in both localities, and the South West had more single outlets (13 compared with 10 in the NW) (MacIver and Bowie, 1989). In 1992 both a 'less healthy' basket of foodstuffs (white bread, whole milk, sausages, etc.) and a 'healthy' basket (wholemeal bread, semi-skimmed milk, low fat sausages) cost more in the SW than in the NW; £9.03 in the SW compared with £8.98 in the NW for the 'less healthy' basket, and £10.48 in the SW compared with £9.94 for the 'healthy' basket. The difference in price between the 'healthy' and 'less healthy' versions was proportionately greater in the SW than the NW (£1.45 (16 per cent) more expensive in the SW, compared with £0.96 (10.7 per cent) more expensive in the NW) (Sooman and Taggart, 1992).

Table 1   Recreation facilities, NW and SW localities 1990

Number of	NW	SW
Athletic tracks	2	1
Boating ponds	3	0
Bowling greens	12	8
Cycle tracks	1	0
Golf courses	1	2
Indoor bowling rink	1	0
Pitch and putt	0	1
Playing fields	15	1
Putting greens	2	0
Recreation centres	0	3
Sports centres	0	1
Sports hall	3	3
Swimming pools	4	4
Tennis courts	17	4
Total	61	28

Source: Parks and Recreation Department, Glasgow City Council

Table 2 Selected transport statistics, NW and SW localities 1988

	NW	SW
Population (1981)	51,000	60,000
% Households with no car (1981)	52.6	74.5
Bus services: number of routes		
ordinary (public and private)	3	3
works' service	4	3
night service	4	5
shoppers' bus service	3	0
hospital bus service	2	0
Taxi stances (official)	8	5
Railway stations	8	4
Peak trains per hour	65	8
Off peak trains per hour	44	5
Sunday trains per hour	20	< 1

Source: MacIver and Bowie, 1989

There is also less local access in the SW to healthy recreation. The data given in Table 1 show a strikingly higher availability of both publicly and privately provided sporting recreation facilities in the NW compared with the SW; in total people in the NW have access to 61 facilities within their local area, while those in the SW have access to only 28 (data from Parks and Recreation Department, GDC).

3 *Services provided, privately or publicly, to support people in their daily lives*
Transport services show a marked contrast between the two areas to the disadvantage of the SW. In 1981, 75 per cent of households in the SW had no car, compared with 53 per cent in the NW. Yet as Table 2 shows, there is no compensatory better provision of public transport services in the SW. In 1988 the SW was worse off in terms of special bus services and taxi stances and markedly worse off in terms of train services. This quantitative analysis does not take into account additional, more qualitative, contrasts such as the inconvenient siting of stations in the SW, or their less attractive physical appearance (MacIver and Bowie, 1989).

The quantity of primary health care services is also less in the SW than in the NW. Table 3 shows that there are nearly twice as many community clinics, three times as many GP practices, over twice as many GPs, three times as many dentists, nearly four times as many opticians, and one and a half times as many pharmacies in the NW than in the SW (MacIver and Finlay, 1990).

A more detailed survey of primary medical care in the two localities revealed that the SW is not at quite such a disadvantage as these summary figures might suggest. A larger proportion of practices in the SW practised from purpose-built accommodation, more of the GPs there had qualified more recently, and more of its practices had attached community nurses and provided special clinics. However, the SW had fewer doctors, proportionally to population, than the NW; GPs in the SW allocate less time on average per consultation; practices in the SW are less likely to own certain items of equipment (for example, ECG machines, microscopes, blood glucose testing equipment); and the average list size per whole time GP is slightly greater in the SW (though not by as much as the numbers of GPs, given above, would suggest; many people

Table 3 Selected primary care statistics, NW and SW localities 1989

Number of*	NW	SW
Health centres	1	2
Clinics	4	2
GP practices	36	12
GPs	92	37
Dental practices	24	10
Dentists	38	13
Community dental clinics	4	2
Opticians	18	5
Pharmacies	29	17

*Including those on the locality peripheries.
Source: Primary and Community Care Unit, Greater Glasgow Health Board

Table 4 Monthly average of reported crime rates NW and SW localities 1990

	NW (Partick)	SW (Pollok)
Serious assault	4	16
Assault and robbery	12	16
Vandalism	70	96
Breaking into houses	120	138
Breaking into other premises	100	28
Theft of car	100	57
Theft from car	100	61
Attempted theft of/from cars	100	9
Breach of peace	110	61

Source: Strathclyde Police

resident in the SW are registered with practices outwith the locality) (Wyke, Campbell and MacIver, 1992). The relative similarity in the structure of primary medical care in the two localities also has to be seen against the backdrop of higher all-cause SMRs, and higher SMRs for all major causes of death, in the SW compared to the NW; the lower car ownership in the SW; and the higher mean number of GP consultations in the SW compared to the NW (3.5 for 35 year olds and 3.9 for 55 year olds in the SW in the previous year, compared with 2.2 and 2.8 in the NW (Wyke, Campbell and MacIver, 1992)). In relation to these admittedly crude indicators of 'need', even identical primary care provision in the two areas could be interpreted as relatively diadvantageous to the SW.

Data on 'manual sweeping and delittering' of streets in sub-areas of the two localities were obtained from the GDC cleansing department. The mean number of weekly delitterings was higher in Pollok, in the SW (1.98 per week), than in two areas of the NW, Knightswood (1.51 per week) and Partick (1.26 per week). This would seem to indicate that the worse off area is allocated more cleaning resources. What is not clear is to what extent this means the streets in the SW are actually cleaner as a result. Certainly the perceptions of the residents are that litter is more of a problem in the SW (see Figure 1) and this is borne out by the impressions of

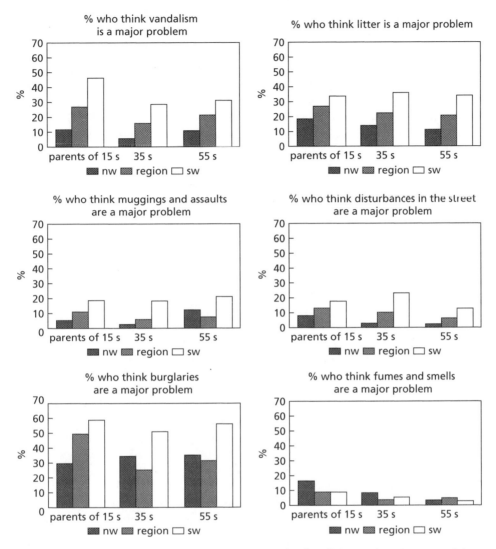

Figure 1 Percentage of various age groups in the localities and region perceiving selected socio-environmental threats as a major problem in their area.

researchers. Researchers have also noted that the litter in the SW locality is more likely to contain items potentially injurious to health, such as broken glass, dog faeces, beer cans and used syringes; in the NW locality litter is more likely to be composed of paper and leaves (Forsyth, *pers comm*).

4 *Socio-cultural features of a neighbourhood*   Data were obtained from Strathclyde Police on reported crime rates in the sub-divisions or divisions covering our two study areas, and are presented in Table 4. This shows a greater incidence of crimes against the person, and against personal space, in the SW; and a greater incidence of crimes against commercial premises and cars in the NW, where there are more cars to steal or steal from, and more shops and other premises from whom theft might be profitable. (The police stress that the figure for serious assault in Pollok, in the SW, is a conservative one

since many assaults go unreported. They also point out that the figure for breach of the peace in the SW is an underestimate since there is a policy in this area not to arrest for this offence. In the Partick sub-division, in the NW, there is a high density of pubs and most of the breach of the peace offences occur at closing time.)

What do the residents say about these areas? As part of the *West of Scotland Twenty-07 Study, Health in the Community* (described more fully in Macintyre *et al.*, 1989), 15 year olds, their parents, and 35 and 55 year olds in these two localities, and samples of these age groups throughout the Central Clydeside Conurbation (called the 'regional samples'), were asked a number of questions about how they felt about their local area, including whether they thought items on a standard list were a major problem, minor problem, or not a problem at all, in their local area. Figure 1 shows the proportions of parents of 15 year olds and of 35 and 55 year olds reporting vandalism, litter, muggings and assaults, disturbances in the street, burglaries, and fumes and smells as being a major problem in their area. All these features of their local environment, with the exception of fumes and smells, were consistently seen as more of a problem by residents of the SW than by the regional sample, who in turn saw them as more of a problem than those in the NW. Whether or not these perceptions are 'objectively' true, this suggests a degree of pessimism about the local area which is more marked in the poorer area and which may contribute to low morale and poor mental health and community self-esteem.

5 *Reputation*   There are sub-areas within the SW which have an extremely bad reputation, as evidenced, for example, by descriptions in local papers (for example, 'in the last 10 years Dormandside Road has established a notorious reputation as the place no one wanted to live in', *Evening Times*, 4 August 1988: 'The Darnley area which has been named "Tem City" because of the extent of dealing and injecting of the painkiller, temgesic', *Evening Times*, 20 September 1990). Another measure is the rate of requests for transfers out of Council Housing Areas; in an earlier period, 1977, the percentage of requests for out transfers, as a proportion of total households, was 30.54 per cent in Pollok, in the SW locality, compared to 4.84 per cent in Anniesland, in the NW (Pacione, 1979). We are currently investigating the extent to which certain street addresses or postcodes may, because of their poor reputation, render people at a disadvantage in terms of access to services such as GP registration, credit, taxis, etc.

Research and policy implications

The examples just given of differences between these two study areas tend to suggest that the broad hypothesis with which we started – that the physical and social environments in our more middle class area might be systematically better than those in the more working class area, in ways which might promote the physical and mental health of residents of the former – would be generally confirmed. Even for individuals who are similarly situated in terms of their personal circumstances (for example, with the same income, family size, and tenure of house), it seems likely that living in the NW would be more conducive to good health than living in the SW; healthy foodstuffs are more available, and cheaper, locally, there are more sporting recreation facilities within easy reach, better public transport, more extensive primary health services, and a less threatening local environment.

This conclusion may appear so predictable as to be trite. We all know that areas inhabited by less affluent people are less pleasant than areas inhabited by more affluent people, and that is why the more affluent people live where they do. However, many health promotion or public health policies focus on individuals and their behaviours (DH, 1992; SOHHD, 1991; Reid, 1992). A large proportion seem to be based on the principle that if working class *people* could become more like middle class *people*, then their rates of illness and premature death would become more like those of middle class people. An alternative approach would be to try to make working class *areas* more like middle class *areas* by improving the social and physical environment. Rather than encouraging individuals to eat more healthily or take more exercise, perhaps it would be more useful to try to improve the availability, quality and prices of healthy foodstuffs in poor localities, or to improve the availability of sports grounds and green spaces there.

Our research to date suggests that, for a number of reasons, it is important to make *systematic* comparisons between areas rather than relying on 'what everyone knows'. First, this is because this may reveal fewer differences than expected or differences in the opposite direction to that anticipated. For example, residents in the NW reported more fumes and smells in their local area than those in the SW, contrary to expectations. (This unexpected finding was confirmed on further research and found to be attributable to two sources, a rape-seed processing factory on King George V dock and the Shieldhall sewage plant; both are on the South bank of the Clyde, near the SW locality, but the prevailing winds blow the fumes into the NW locality.) The fact that the generally poorer rating of problems in their area in the SW was reversed for fumes and smells also suggests that these ratings are not simply attributable to a generalised pessimistic response-set among people in less advantaged areas. This example also points to the importance for policy-makers of looking at extremely local, as well as general, environmental features.

Second, systematic and quantified information is more useful for policy-makers than general impressions. A general perception that public transport is poorer in some areas can be dismissed as impressionistic; a list of bus and train routes and of numbers of services per hour or per day is a much more effective tool for advocates or policy-makers. Complaints from people in poor areas about the difficulty of complying with healthy diet guidelines may be dismissed as laziness or special pleading; data collected by independent researchers assessing the availability and price of healthy foodstuffs is more difficult to rebut. Although data on social deprivation in different areas is usually based on census information, there is a wealth of other quantifiable information available in a variety of public and private agencies (for example, on land values, house prices, the buying rates of council houses, road accidents in relation to car ownership, insect/rodent infestation, fires, vacant properties, etc.), which is rarely presented systematically by area or related to health outcomes.

A disadvantage, however, of such quantifiable information is that it may fail to capture more subtle and intangible features of local environments which may nevertheless influence people's lives and health. One of the problems for this type of research is the difficulty of capturing in words, let alone in figures, a sense of what these places look like and feel like. We have collected some photographs of the two localities which convey their atmosphere more immediately than words can do, but these are difficult to analyse, or to present in academic papers. An additional problem is that of analysing or describing the cumulative impact of these environmental features, as opposed to presenting them one by one as we have done above.

A further problem is that the data we want may not be the data available, and *vice versa*. Although there is a wealth of information available about local areas, particularly in local government departments, the boundaries in which these data are organised may not be co-terminus with those in which the researcher is interested, the data may not be available in quite the form one wants, or the theoretically really interesting data may not be available at all. [...]

[...] Research into the magnitude of the influence of social class or area of residence on health may become sterile unless we can go beyond treating 'social class' and 'area of residence' as though they were, in themselves, explanatory factors. What we need for policy formation is more information on the *mechanisms* by which social class or area of residence might influence health in positive or negative ways. One of the correlates of individual social class position is the type of area one is likely to live in. It may not be possible to make everyone middle class, but it might be possible to try to upgrade the social and physical environments of poorer areas in ways that might be health promoting. This would cut through the defeatism sometimes underlying the assumption that area differences in health are entirely attributable to the social class composition of its residents and to personal correlates of their social class position, and that there is thus nothing that can be done about these health differences. We therefore advocate research which focuses directly on the health promoting or health threatening features of local social and physical environments, and local and national health promotion policies which take into account features of places as well as features of people. [...]

Acknowledgements

The work on which this paper is based is supported by the Medical Research Council of Great Britain. We are grateful to Patrick West, Kate Hunt and Graeme Ford for access to data on 15, 35 and 55 year olds as part of the *West of Scotland Twenty-07 Study; Health in the Community*; to the Greater Glasgow Health Board, Glasgow District Council and Strathclyde Regional Council for making data available to us; and to Jean Money and Jean Leiper for typing various drafts. We are grateful to Annie Anderson, David Blane, Russell Ecob, Graeme Ford, Alasdair Forsyth, Gill Green, Mike Kelly, Ken Mullen, Peter Phillimore, Danny Wight and Sally Wyke for comments on an earlier draft. The authors are solely responsible for the opinions expressed in this paper, an earlier version of which was presented at the Society for Social Medicine Conference in September 1990.

References

D. J. P. Barker and C. Osmond (1987), 'Inequalities in health in Britain: specific explanations in three Lancashire towns', *British Medical Journal*, 294, 749–52.

M. Blaxter (1990), *Health and Lifestyles*, Routledge, London.

M. Britton, A. J. Fox, P. Goldblatt, D. R. Jones, and M. Rosato (1990), 'The influence of socio-economic and environmental factors on geographic variations in mortality in OPCS', *Mortality and Geography*, HMSO, London.

V. Carstairs and R. Morris (1989), 'Deprivation: explaining differences in mortality between Scotland and England and Wales', *British Medical Journal*, 299, 886–9.

V. Carstairs and R. Morris (1991), *Deprivation and Health in Scotland*, Aberdeen University Press, Aberdeen.

S. Chinn, C. du V. Florey, I. G. Baldwin and M. Gorgol (1981), 'The relation of mortality in England and Wales 1969–73 to measurements of air-pollution', *Journal of Epidemiology and Community Health*, 35, 174–9.

I. K. Crombie, M. B. Kenicer, W. C. S. Smith, and H. D. Tunstall-Pedoe (1989), 'Unemployment, socio-environmental factors and coronary heart disease', *British Heart Journal*, 61, 172–7.

Department of Health (1992), *The Health of the Nation: A Strategy Document of Health in England*, Cmnd. 1986, HMSO, London.

S. Erskine (1991), *Social Work Services and Resources in Two Contrasting Localities in Glasgow City*, MRC Medical Sociology Working Paper No. 24, Glasgow.

M. J. Gardner (1973), 'Using the environment to explain and predict mortality', *Journal of Royal Statistical Society*, 136:3, 421–40.

M. J. Gardner (1989), 'Review of reported increases of childhood cancer rates in the vicinity of nuclear installations in the UK', *Journal of Royal Statistical Society (A)*, 152, 307–25.

J. Graunt (1662), *Natural and Political Observations made upon the Bills of Mortality*, London.

Greater Glasgow Health Board (1984), *Ten Year Report 1974–1983*, Information Services Division, GGHB, Glasgow.

Greater Glasgow Health Board (1989), *The Annual Report of the Director of Public Health*, Glasgow.

M. Haan, G. A. Kaplan and T. Camacho (1987), 'Poverty and health: prospective evidence from the Alameda County Study', *American Journal of Epidemiology*, 125:6, 989–98.

S. Macintyre, E. Annandale, R. Ecob, G. Ford, K. Hunt, B. Jamieson, S. MacIver, P. West, and S. Wyke (1989), 'The West of Scotland Twenty-07 Study: health in the community', in C. Martin and D. MacQueen (eds), *Readings for a New Public Health*, Edinburgh University Press, Edinburgh.

S. MacIver (1988), *West of Scotland Twenty-07 Study: Socio-demographic and Mortality Profiles of the Study Areas*, MRC Medical Sociology Unit Working Paper No. 10, Glasgow.

S. MacIver and F. Bowie (1989), *A Survey of Retail Provision: Price and Availability of Selected Food Items in Two Localities in Glasgow City*, MRC Medical Sociology Unit Working Paper No. 15, Glasgow.

S. MacIver and A. Finlay (1990), *Health Service Provision in the Twenty-07 Study Localities*, MRC Medical Sociology Unit Working Paper No. 19, Glasgow.

S. MacIver and S. Macintyre (1987), *West of Scotland Twenty-07 Study: Selection of the Study Localities and Region*, MRC Medical Sociology Unit Working Paper No. 4, Glasgow.

G. Moon (1990), 'Conceptions of space and community in British health policy', *Social Science Medicine*, 30, 165–71.

M. Pacione (1979), 'Housing policies in Glasgow since 1988', *The Geographical Review*, 69, 395–412.

P. Phillimore (April 1991), *How do Places Shape Health? Rethinking Locality and Lifestyle in N-E England*, paper presented at British Sociological Association Annual Meeting, Manchester.

S. J. Pocock, A. G. Shaper, D. G. Cook, R. F. Packham, R. F. Lacey, P. Powell and P. F. Russell (1980), 'British regional heart study: geographic variations in cardiovascular mortality, and the role of water quality', *British Medical Journal*, 280, 1243–9.

M. Reid (1992), *Long Live Glasgow!*, Greater Glasgow Health Board and *Evening Times*, Glasgow.

C. J. Roberts and S. Lloyd (1972), 'Association between mortality from ischaemic heart disease and rainfall in South Wales and in the County Boroughs of England and Wales', *Lancet*, i, 1091–3.

Scottish Office Home and Health Department (1991), *Scotland's Health: A Challenge to Us All*, HMSO, Edinburgh.

A. G. Shaper, S. J. Pocock, M. Walker, N. M. Cohen, C. J. Wale, and A. G. Thomson (1981), 'British regional heart study: cardiovascular risk factors in middle aged men in 24 towns, *British Medical Journal*, 283, 179–86.

A. Sooman and J. Taggart (1992), *Price and Availability of a Selection of Basic Food Items in Two Localities in Glasgow City*, MRC Medical Sociology Working Paper No. 33, Glasgow.

P. Townsend, P. Phillimore and A. Beattie (1988), *Health and Deprivation: Inequality and the North*, Croom Helm, London.

P. Townsend, D. Simpson and N. Tibbs (1984), *Inequalities of Health in the City of Bristol*, Department of Social Administration, University of Bristol, Bristol.

R. R. West and C. R. Lowe (1976), 'Mortality from ischaemic heart disease – inter-town variation and its association with climate in England and Wales', *International Journal of Epidemiology*, 5, 195–201.

R. R. West, S. Lloyd and C. J. Roberts (1973), 'Mortality from ischaemic heart disease – association with wealth', *British Journal of Preventative and Social Medicine*, 27, 36–40.

F. L. R. Williams, O. L. Lloyd and M. M. Lloyd (1988), *Animal and Human Disease around a Site with Two Incinerators: A Review*, Asia-Pacific Symposium on Environmental and Occupational Toxicology, 8, 475–83.

S. Wyke, G. Campbell, and S. MacIver (1992), 'Comparison of the provision of, and patient satisfaction with, primary care services in a relatively affluent and a relatively deprived area of Glasgow', *British Journal of General Practice*, 42, 271–5.

22

The Psycho-social Perspective on Social Inequalities in Health

Jon Ivar Elstad

[...]

The psycho-social perspective: towards a paradigm shift?

[...] One emerging perspective has been proclaimed a 'paradigm shift' (Evans *et al.* 1994a: ix) that will become 'enormously important' and 'destined to transform social and economic policy' (Wilkinson 1996b: 5, ix). It employs the familiar social causation type of explanation, assuming that the roots of social inequalities in health are found in the varying environment of social positions. But instead of material shortages and negligent behaviour, focus is now on psychological stress, relative deprivation, and the psycho-social injuries of inequality structures.

To give an overview of this *psycho-social perspective* is the purpose of this paper. The term 'perspective' is chosen because I consider it a set of related approaches rather than a unified theory. It can, however, be identified by three core assumptions: (1) the distribution of psychological stress is an important determinant of health inequalities in present-day affluent societies, (2) psychological stress is strongly influenced by the quality of social and interpersonal relations, and (3) the latter are determined to a large extent by the magnitude of society's inequalities. First, I will make some remarks on the aetiological basis. Then follows a presentation of what I consider the four main sources of the perspective: the *social stress* approach, the related *self-efficacy* approach, the newer *sociology of emotion*, and the *social cohesion* approach. [...]

Aetiology

[...] That grief, loneliness, and similar distressed feelings can impair health, have been part of lay notions of illness for centuries. Since the 1960s a growing number of academic studies have also addressed this topic. Accumulating doubts about the material deprivation explanation for health inequalities has further stimulated interest in the psycho-social environment. The aetiological basis for the psycho-social perspective is the health-damaging potential of psychological stress. Two somewhat different pathways from stress to poor health are proposed: a *direct* effect on disease development, and an *indirect* route, when stress is expressed by health-damaging behaviour.

The indirect pathway implies that people react to adverse circumstances by excessive alcohol use, smoking, accident-prone behaviour, etc., sometimes as conscious or subconscious self-destructive acts, sometimes more 'innocently' in order to alleviate stress. That health can suffer from such behaviour is well documented – and sometimes self-evident, as in the case of violence and homicide.

More controversial is the direct pathway – not as regards mental illness, but as regards somatic disease: can it occur because of psychological stress? Generally, this implies that experiences transmitted by the central nervous system provoke changes in other human organs in a way that threatens health (Kelly *et al.* 1997). Many recent reviews are in favour of this view (see for instance Maes *et al.* 1987, Thoits 1995, Uchino *et al.* 1996, Cohen and Herbert 1996). Evans *et al.* state that 'There is now no longer room for doubt as to the existence of a complex web of linkages, having important implications for health, between the nervous system and other body systems' (1994b: 182). Others are not so sure (see, for instance, Davey Smith and Egger 1996). Despite a rapidly increasing number of studies, reflecting the expansion of fields such as psychoneuroimmunology and psychoneuroendrocrinology, uncertainty remains.

[...]

How to conceptualise the role of psychological stress in aetiological processes is [...] a disputed topic. That social inequalities are found for a wide range of diseases has been interpreted to indicate that stress has a general negative effect on health (Syme and Berkman 1976, Wilkinson 1996b: 71). If so, the mechanisms can be understood in different ways. Stress can be seen as a specific causal factor in the various chains of events which lead to particular diseases (see Uchino *et al.* 1996). Alternatively, stress could influence the body's general capacity for homeostasis, by conditioning 'biological responses...in ways that lead to systematic differences in resilience and vulnerability to disease' (Kelly *et al.* 1997: 438). [...] Notions of stress-related *general susceptibility* is often part of the aetiological understanding of the psycho-social perspective. [...]

In summary, the aetiological basis for the psycho-social perspective is complex. That psychological stress may contribute to mental illness and health-damaging behaviour is usually agreed; the direct link to specific somatic diseases, or to somatic disease in general, is more contested. One objection to the psycho-social view is that disease aetiology, even in the most affluent societies, cannot be constructed solely in terms of psychological stress. Both the psycho-social *and* the physical environment, and their interaction and interpenetration over time, are perhaps imperative elements of any convincing aetiology, and correspondingly the key to understand health inequalities. [...]

The social stress approach

The social stress approach developed especially from Hans Selye's investigations, during the 1940s and 1950s, of physiological responses to external exigencies (see Pollock 1988: 384). In this tradition, stress was defined as 'a state of arousal resulting either from the presence of socioenvironmental demands that tax the ordinary adaptive capacity...or from the absence of the means to attain sought-after ends'

(Aneshensel 1992:16). Thus, socioenvironmental demands – stressors – engender psychological stress, *i.e.* a troubled state of the mind which can surface in many ways, as anxiety, fear, hopelessness, or anger.

Stress research is extremely multifaceted (see, for instance, Thoits 1995). Two main tendencies, one more medically, the other more sociologically, oriented, can be distinguished (Aneshensel 1992, Aneshensel *et al.* 1991, Pearlin 1989). While the former is primarily concerned with consequences of stress in terms of ill health, the latter focuses on the social origins of stress, and includes social inequalities and the stratification system in its models. The two tendencies utilise social variables differently: medically oriented researchers employ information on social back-ground as controls in order to accentuate the links from stressors to stress reactivity, while sociologically oriented researchers focus on how the distribution of stressors depends on people's location within social structures.

The sociologically oriented tendency within stress research can be regarded as the original source of the psycho-social perspective. To explain social inequalities in health has always been part of its agenda. Since the 1960s, various developments have further underlined how people's location in the social structure could result in health differences. What I have in mind are four reorientations: from *any* type of stressors to *negative* stressors; from the 'objective' features of a situation to the 'subjective' impact; the substitution of chronic strain for life events; and the focus on buffers which could reduce the health-damaging potential of stressors.

Stress research started out with the assumption that any kind of event was a potential threat to health (Pearlin *et al.* 1981: 339). This was in line with Selye's preoccupation with reactions to change itself (see Oatley and Jenkins 1992: 72). Thus, not only divorces and deaths, but also marriages and births, could constitute health-damaging experiences, given that the event required overburdening adaption. Poor empirical evidence for this 'neutral' attitude to stressors led to a focus on negative stressors: stressors characterised as unfortunate and unwelcome. As there was little doubt that less privileged social strata tend to face negative circumstances more frequently than those more favourably located in society, the connection between stress processes and the social gradients in health was underscored.

Second, when negative events were highlighted, the subjective impact of events came into focus, because the definition of 'negative' could hardly exclude subjective evaluations. Attention was directed away from the 'objective' characteristics of stressors, towards the way they were appraised by those afflicted (see, for instance, Lazarus 1993). This development put the social environment on the agenda. Ap-praisals could hardly be seen as isolated individual judgements, but rather as constructed judgements within a social setting. Prevailing norms, types of classifica-tions, and systems of labelling would influence the subjective impact. If events led to social isolation, loss of respect, or other distressing interpersonal relations, the subjective impact would make matters worse. Less exclusionary attitudes towards 'deviants' and more supporting practices towards those who were hit by misfortunes would alleviate the subjective impact. This directed attention to the quality of society's social relations and networks, the cultural representations it favoured, and furthermore towards how such attributes were related to the material differ-ences in society.

Third, findings indicated that the 'deleterious health effects of life changes are of consistently modest magnitude' (Aneshensel 1992: 17). Thus, the one-sided focus upon short-term, abrupt events, as compared with more longstanding stressors – 'enduring problems, conflicts and threats that many people face in their daily lives' (Pearlin 1989: 245) – was criticised. Chronic strain was given a more prominent place in stress research (see, for instance, Turner *et al*. 1995). When stressors were conceptualised as enduring life problems, the association between stress experiences and location in the social structure became more marked, as longstanding economic problems, difficulties related to subordinate positions in the workplace, and the burden of poor neighbourhoods were typical examples.

A fourth reorientation was to focus on vulnerability, *i.e.* why the impact of similar adverse circumstances differed between individuals. One answer was the existence of buffers. Coping resources of diverse types could help people master and overcome adverse circumstances without suffering health setbacks (Maes *et al*. 1987). Social support is the main example, but almost any type of resource connected to personality, social background, education, and financial resources, has been proposed as a moderator of the harmful effects of stressors. Access to buffering factors is related both to the supportiveness of the social environment, and to a person's location in the social structure. Thus, the connection between social position and the circumstances that influence psychological stress was underlined even more.

In this way, the social stress approach explains how social inequalities in health arise. Stressors, particularly long term, chronic stressors, are unevenly distributed in society, basically in line with its structural inequalities. The impact of stressors depends on their subjective appraisal, which follows not only from stressors' factual character, but also from the distribution of buffering resources. Accordingly, psychological stress could be expected to vary with social position and to result in social variations in health. The other approaches outlined below build in many ways on this social stress model, but they also develop particular points and introduce new aspects, thereby contributing to a more comprehensive understanding.

Developing the social stress model: the self-efficacy approach

Social stress research has brought forward a multitude of concepts and hypotheses, addressing topics such as the types of external circumstances that provoke psychological stress, the types of mechanisms that connect circumstances to stress, and the contextual and buffering factors that will influence this process (see, for instance, Maes *et al*. 1987, Pollock 1988, Thoits 1995, Pearlin 1989). In spite of this diversity, it can be argued that stress research has been biased in two respects. It had tended to view people as *passive recipients* of external circumstances, and it has tended to focus solely on *health deterioration*. Moreover, although the emphasis on chronic strain introduces a more longitudinal view, it could be argued that the social stress approach has often avoided a lifecourse perspective on health.

The *self-efficacy approach* (see Aneshensel 1992: 27–30) can be considered a development of the social stress model which counters all these drawbacks. It addresses the first of these tendencies by pointing to capabilities and power as crucial stress-protecting factors. Humans are conceptualised as acting subjects and not only as being governed by external and structural forces. By emphasising human agency, connections to fundamental theoretical debates in sociology are made. In addition, the self-efficacy approach also opens up for a life-time perspective and for notions about growth in health.

Self-efficacy can be defined as a 'cognitive orientation attributing outcomes such as success and failure to personal attributes, such as ability and effort' (Aneshensel 1992: 27). Mirowsky and Ross (1984) observe that its meaning is virtually synonymous with other frequently employed terms within stress research, such as mastery, internal locus of control, personal control, perceived control of the environment, and instrumentalism. Opposite concepts are fatalism, external locus of control, powerlessness, and learned helplessness. Whatever the term used, the kernel is 'the extent to which people see themselves as being in control of the forces that importantly affect their lives' (Pearlin et al. 1981: 339). Self-efficacy is linked to various other phenomena often studied by stress researchers, such as self-esteem, self-concept, social support, and coping style. To emphasise self-efficacy, instead of other related concepts, is therefore somewhat arbitrary. These phenomena are all correlated, and the division of them into separate units, each with a special term, may be artificial, as the sense of support, mastery, self-esteem, and similar traits within an individual is often a tightly connected bundle.

The feeling of mastery, self-efficacy, and being in control, can be assumed a health-promoting factor by itself, as it goes together with a balanced, non-stressed, state of mind. However, it is more common to regard it as a buffer which protects against the damaging effects of adverse external circumstances. Self-efficacy maintains the belief that one can influence one's lot, and this constitutes a defence against feelings of frustration and hopelessness. Thus, self-efficacy makes people less vulnerable to external stressors, and it can be equated with a kind of mental strength which maintains self-esteem and protects against distress.

What generates self-efficacy? The characteristics of the social environment, and social location, seem to be two important factors. Satisfying interpersonal relations will support and enhance self-efficacy. But this is probably also associated with placement in the social structure. Gecas and Schwalbe suggest that the formation of self-esteem is heavily influenced by 'the possibilities that social structures afford for individuals to engage in efficacious action' (1983: 82). Thoits summarises that '[p]erceived control over life circumstances is inversely distributed by social status' (1995: 60). Thus, the formation of self-efficacy is rooted in the structural features of society, including its system of material inequalities, but also in the supportiveness of the social environment.

The contribution of the self-efficacy approach to the psycho-social perspective is particularly, therefore, that it specifies *mechanisms* involved in the stress process, and that it takes into account the active, participating actor. It is moreover closely linked to studies which examine the relationship between work organisations and health. Karasek's hypothesis, made credible by many empirical studies, that work-related stress is not dependent on job demands in themselves, but on the combination of a low level of decision latitude with large job demands (see Peterson 1994), points to the significance of having the capability to influence circumstances. Thus, self-efficacy could be importantly involved in the processes whereby health inequalities are formed by hierarchical work organisations.

Furthermore, the notion that health develops over the lifecourse can be viewed as part of the self-efficacy approach. Thus, it parallels the expanding lifecourse perspective on health inequalities (see, for instance, Carroll et al. 1996, Davey Smith et *al*. 1997, Wunsch *et al*. 1996). Self-efficacy is commonly seen as a result of a lifetime development. The importance of early life is not only emphasised by biomedically oriented researchers, but also by researchers who focus on psycho-social circumstances. Attachment theory, for instance, argues that inner feelings of security, with important consequences for stress resistance, result from the characteristics of social relations in infancy and childhood (Fonagy 1996). The notion of a life-span development of one's health potential is a prominent part of Antonovsky's concept 'sense of coherence' (1987: 89–127). The principal components of this concept are that the external world is experienced as comprehensible, manageable, and meaningful (1987: 16–19). Given a strong sense of coherence, resistance against deleterious effects of stress, as well as against physical risk factors, is enhanced. Social variations in health are related to the way the sense of coherence is formed. It is no short-time personal characteristic, but develops through life, influenced by placement in the social structure and the availability of resources. [...]

The sociology of emotions: filling black boxes

[...] The structural resemblance between the social stress model and the standard approach of sociologists of emotions is easily recognised. The former addresses the link between social position, stressors, psychological stress, and health outcomes; the latter examines how the social world is experienced in emotionally loaded categories which have bodily correlates: blushing cheeks when feeling shame, muscular tension when angry, throwing up when feeling disgust, etc. Thus, the link between a person's social, subjective, and corporal existence is emphasised by the sociology of emotions. Accordingly, dichotomies such as mind/body, culture/nature, and society/biology are challenged, because such mutually excluding concepts block the understanding of their inner connections (Williams and Bendelow 1996: 28).

In the context of this paper, I will argue that the study of emotions contributes to the psycho-social perspective by addressing certain unclear aspects of the social stress model. Put simply, an awkward problem for the social stress approach is why experiences, which could be regarded as nothing but perceptions of the external world, could possibly be fateful to health. Why aren't they simply mental reflections arousing no more excitement than a dull TV commercial? The general reason is that significant experiences are emotionally loaded. Lots of experiences are irrelevant. Those which have an important meaning also engender emotional responses. Oatley and Jenkins maintain that 'emotions are usually elicited by evaluating events that concern a person's important needs or goals' (1992: 60). As Lazarus puts it: 'there is a world of difference between a non-emotional and an emotional event' (1993: 11). In general, we would expect that emotional experiences have an impact both on mental and physiological processes, while perceptions without this quality would hardly effectuate significant alterations, neither in behaviour nor in physiological functioning. [...]

[...] In order to be relevant for the psycho-social perspective, not only a focus on the micro-world of social relations is required, but also a connection to inequality structures at the macro level. The 'positivist' Kemper is more explicit in this respect: he argues that emotions like security, guilt and fear-anxiety arise from social relations formed by dimensions of power and status (Kemper 1979, see also Thoits 1989: 325, Hochschild 1981). Highly relevant, furthermore, is the existential-phenomenological approach of Freund (1988, 1990), who argues that people exhibit 'emotional modes of being' strongly influenced by their positions in social hierarchies, and that these modes become embodied and expressed through various bodily states, including illness.

In order to support the psycho-social perspective, empirical studies should indicate increasing experiences of negative emotions the further 'down' the social ladder people are located. That the frequency of social disadvantages increases in lower social positions is hardly contested, but are they correspondingly associated with emotional responses of a negative character?[. . .]

To clarify such topics is a challenge for the sociology of emotions, but also of considerable interest for the further development of the psycho-social perspective on health inequalities. It can be added that investigations of the social distribution of negative emotions present many methodological difficulties. Not only are emotions subjective, but they are often partly subconscious and even prelinguistic. Standard research techniques based on verbal responses may therefore miss the target, and this difficulty is an obstacle to empirical studies of how negative emotions are involved in the generation of health inequalities.

The social cohesion approach

The current interest in psycho-social explanations of social inequalities in health has been spurred on not least by the research of Richard G. Wilkinson (1986, 1990, 1992, 1993, 1994, 1996a, 1996b, 1997). Paradoxically, his interest in psycho-social explanations followed from empirical studies using an indicator of material circumstances, income, as the principal independent variable. His findings, now widely diffused, indicate that in present-day affluent societies, the absolute level of income is no straightforward determinant of health. As absolute deprivation is reduced, health variations become more linked to relative deprivation (or relative income or relative poverty), and life expectancy is influenced by the magnitude of society's income inequalities.

[. . .]

With Wilkinson's more recent writings (see especially 1996b), a more general framework which addresses the transforming of social inequalities into health inequalities has been suggested. The kernel is that social inequalities, *i.e.* not only income inequalities, but also power inequalities (for instance, authoritarian hierarchies and non-democratic social organisations) and status inequalities (for instance, as between the two genders, or between ethnic groups), have a fundamental influence on the content of social relations and interactions. The greater the social inequalities (longer distances from top to bottom of the income scale, more authoritarian patterns in families, schools, etc.), the more will the quality of social relations suffer. Inequalities will tend to produce anger, frustration, hostility, fear, insecurity, and other negative emotions. Material inequalities will often go together with fear of, or the actual distressing experience of, failures to secure a socially acceptable

material standard of living. Authoritarian power patterns engender feelings of
hostility and anger. Differences in status produce contempt from those above and
fright and insecurity among those below. Thus, an overall association is assumed to
exist between the amount of inequalities in society and the amount of negative
feelings and emotions signifying psychological stress. From this, health problems
would follow, along both the direct and indirect pathway as described above in the
section on aetiology. Smaller social inequalities are, on the other hand, associated
with better social relations, *i.e.* more trust, more security, more social support, more
self-esteem and self-respect, and more sense of belonging; and also with less financial
insecurity and fewer feelings of being materially disadvantaged. Democratic, partici-
patory styles in social organisations, from the family to the political system, ensure
self-respect and feelings of being appreciated by one's surroundings, and have
therefore additional health-enhancing effects.

Wilkinson substantiates his view both by studies of stress and by accounts of
actual societies (1996b: 113–36). He points out, for example, that the low death rate
of Roseto (a small US town), which has astonished researchers, could be related to
its egalitarian ethos; that variations in infant mortality between Italian regions
depend on the degree of 'civic community' which in its turn is associated with the
magnitude of social inequalities; and that the remarkable increase in longevity in
Japan should be explained not only by economic progress but also by the increased
sense of community and the reduced rigidity of the stratificational order developing
since 1945.

Social cohesion is accordingly a key concept. It implies a *Durkheimian* view
(Durkheim 1964) that 'social facts', *i.e.* societal and collective traits, are more
than the sum of individual attributes, and that individuals cannot be understood
without grasping the collectivities they are part of. This contrasts with the approaches discussed above, which are mainly individualistic in focus. Wilkinson not
only asks questions relating to individual variations in health, but also addresses
macro health profiles such as population health and average life expectancy. Instead
of analysing individual health as functions of individual variations in income and
health behaviour, Wilkinson advances the importance of global characteristics of
social life, for instance in terms of the amount of social capital. This has been defined
as 'networks, norms and trust...that enable participants to act together more
effectively to pursue shared objectives' (Wilkinson 1996b: 221, quoting Putnam
1995: 664–5). The underlying hypothesis is that the degree of social inequalities is
highly influential on the formation or deformation of social capital, which is, in its
turn, significant for people's health. This theme has also been dealt with by several
newer studies, for instance a study of 39 American states (Kawachi *et al.* 1997)
which found associations between average mortality, levels of trust, density of group
memberships, and income inequality.

Critical views have been raised. There are methodological objections to the studies
finding associations between income inequality and population mortality (Judge
1995, but see also Kawachi and Kennedy 1997); and West has maintained that the
evidence has 'striking gaps' (1997). The association between population mortality
and social inequality is suggestive; nevertheless, this does not release one from examining why the level of individual (or household) income is still closely related to
mortality risk within most present-day affluent societies (see, for instance, Davey
Smith *et al.* 1996). The hypothesis that material circumstances are without significant

influence after certain threshold levels are surpassed, is not necessarily true, and increasing material wealth could have a positive health effect also on higher levels than has often been assumed. Or could it be that the focus on current income is irrelevant, compared with accumulated material disadvantages over the lifecourse (Davey Smith 1996, Bartley *et al.* 1997)? Moreover, Wilkinson's underlying social theory is not always convincing. At the base of the social cohesion approach is the idea that the larger the material inequalities, the more will social environments that lack social support prevail. Thus, it is assumed that social life is more or less directly determined by material structures, which arguably is a much too uncomplicated answer to the perennial question about the relationship between society's material, social, and cultural structures.

In my view, the main contribution of the social cohesion approach to the psycho-social perspective is that it takes components of individual-centred approaches and develops them at the macro level. Wilkinson shows that individual attributes are closely related to collective characteristics. Individual experiences of hostility and social support parallel, on the level of society, the overall occurrence of altruism, trust, and generosity. Individual traits correspond to collective phenomena, and individual processes are insufficiently understood when it is overlooked that individuals are to a large degree formed by the social facts of society, its inequality structures, and its social capital.

[...]

References

Aneshensel, C. S. (1992) Social stress: theory and research, *Annual Review of Sociology*, 18, 15–38.

Aneshensel, C. S., Rutter, C. M. and Lachenbruch, P. A. (1991) Social structure, stress, and mental health: competing conceptual and analytic models, *American Sociological Review*, 56, 166–78.

Antonovsky, A. (1987) *Unraveling the Mystery of Health. How People Manage Stress and Stay Well.* San Francisco: Jossey-Bass Publishers.

Bartley, M., Blane, D. and Montgomery, S. (1997) Socioeconomic determinants of health. Health and the life course: why safety nets matter, *British Medical Journal*, 314, 1194–6.

Carroll, D., Davey Smith, G. and Bennett, P. (1996) Some observations on health and socio-economic status, *Journal of Health Psychology*, 1, 1, 23–39.

Cohen, S. and Herbert, T. B. (1996) Health psychology – psychological factors and physical disease from the perspective of human psychoneuroimmunology, *Annual Review of Psychology*, 47, 113–42.

Davey Smith, G. (1996) Income inequality and mortality: why are they related? *British Medical Journal*, 312, 987–8.

Davey Smith, G., Neaton, J. D., Wentworth, D., Stamler, R. and Stamler, J. (1996) Socio-economic differentials in mortality risk among men screened for the Multiple Risk Factor Intervention Trial: I. white men, *American Journal of Public Health*, 86, 4, 486–96.

Davey Smith, G. and Egger, M. (1996) Commentary: understanding it all – health, meta-theories, and mortality trends, *British Medical Journal*, 313, 1584–5.

Davey Smith, G., Hart, C., Blane, D., Gillis, C. and Hawthorne, V. (1997) Lifetime socio-economic position and mortality – prospective observational study, *British Medical Journal*, 314, 547–52.

Durkheim, E. (1964 [1895]) *The Rules of Sociological Method*. New York: Free Press.

Evans, R. G., Barer, M. L. and Marmor, T. R. (1994a) Preface. In Evans, R. G., Barer, M. L. and Marmor, T. R. (eds), *Why are Some People Healthy and Others not? The Determinants of Health of Populations?* Berlin/New York: de Gruyter, ix–xix.

Evans, R. G., Hodge, M. and Pless, I. B. (1994b) If not genetics, then what? Biological pathways and population health. In Evans, R. G., Barer, M. L. and Marmor, T. R. (eds), *Why are Some People Healthy and Others not? The Determinants of Health of Populations?* Berlin/New York: de Gruyter, 161–88.

Fonagy, P. (1996) Patterns of attachment, interpersonal relationships and health. In Blane, D., Brunner, E. and Wilkinson, R. G. (eds), *Health and Social Organization. Towards a Health Policy for the 21st Century*. London and New York: Routledge.

Freund, P. E. S. (1988) Bringing society into the body: understanding socialized human nature, *Theory and Society*, 17, 839–64.

Freund, P. E. S. (1990) The expressive body: a common ground for the sociology of emotions and health and illness, *Sociology of Health and Illness*, 12, 4, 452–77.

Gecas, V. and Schwalbe, M. L. (1983) Beyond the looking-glass self: social structure and efficacy-base self-esteem, *Social Psychology Quarterly*, 46, 77–88.

Hochschild, A. R. (1981) Power, status and emotion, *Contemporary Sociology*, 10, 1, 73–7.

Judge, K. (1995) Income distribution and life expectancy. A critical appraisal, *British Medical Journal*, 311, 1282–5.

Kawachi, I. and Kennedy, B. P. (1997) The relationship of income inequality to mortality: does the choice of indicator matter? *Social Science and Medicine*, 45, 7, 1121–7.

Kawachi, I., Kennedy, B. P. and Lochner, K. (1997) Social capital, income inequality, and mortality, *American Journal of Public Health*, 87, 9, 1491–8.

Kelly, S., Hertzman, C. and Daniels, M. (1997) Searching for the biological pathways between stress and health, *Annual Review of Public Health*, 18, 437–62.

Kemper, T. D. (1979) *A Social Interactional Theory of Emotions*. New York: Wiley.

Lazarus, R. S. (1993) From psychological stress to the emotions: a history of changing outlooks, *Annual Review of Psychology*, 44, 1–21.

Maes, S., Vingerhoets, A. and Vanheck, G. (1987) The study of stress and disease – some developments and requirements, *Social Science and Medicine*, 25, 6, 567–78.

Mirowsky, J. and Ross, C. E. (1984) Mexican culture and its emotional contradictions, *Journal of Health and Social Behavior*, 25, 1, 2–13.

Oatley, K. and Jenkins, J. M. (1992) Human emotions: function and dysfunction, *Annual Review of Psychology*, 43, 55–85.

Pearlin, L. I. (1989) The sociological study of stress, *Journal of Health and Social Behavior*, 30, 3, 241–56.

Pearlin, L. I., Menaghan, E. G., Lieberman, M. A. and Mullan, J. T. (1981) The stress process, *Journal of Health and Social Behavior*, 22, 337–56.

Peterson, C. L. (1994) Work factors and stress – a critical review, *International Journal of Health Services*, 24, 3, 495–519.

Pollock, K. (1988) On the nature of social stress – production of a modern mythology, *Social Science and Medicine*, 26, 3, 381–92.

Putnam, R. D. (1995) Tuning in, tuning out: the strange disappearance of social capital in America, *Political Science and Politics*, December, 664–83.

Syme, S. L. and Berkman, L. F. (1976) Social class, susceptibility and sickness, *American Journal of Epidemiology*, 104, 1, 1–8.

Thoits, P. A. (1989) The sociology of emotions, *Annual Review of Sociology*, 15, 317–42.

Thoits, P. A. (1995) Stress, coping, and social support processes – where are we – what next, *Journal of Health and Social Behavior*, Extra Issue, 53–79.

Townsend, P. (1979) *Poverty in the United Kingdom*. Harmondsworth: Penguin.

Turner, R. J., Wheaton, B. and Lloyd, D. A. (1995) The epidemiology of social stress, *American Sociological Review*, 60, 104–25.

Uchino, B. N., Cacioppo, J. T. and Kiecolt-Glaser, J. K. (1996) The relationship between social support and physiological processes: a review with emphasis on underlying mechanisms and implications for health, *Psychological Bulletin*, 119, 3, 488–531.

West, P. (1997) (Book Review) Wilkinson, R. G., Unhealthy societies: the afflictions of inequality, *Sociology of Health and Illness*, 19, 5, 668–70.

Wilkinson, R. G. (1986) Income and mortality. In Wilkinson, R. G. (ed.), *Class and Health. Research and Longitudinal Data*. London and New York: Tavistock Publications.

Wilkinson, R. G. (1990) Income distribution and mortality: a natural experiment, *Sociology of Health and Illness*, 12, 4, 391–412.

Wilkinson, R. G. (1992) Income distribution and life expectancy, *British Medical Journal*, 308, 1113–14.

Wilkinson, R. G. (1993) The impact of income inequality on life expectancy. In Platt, S., Thomas, H., Scott, S. and Williams, G. (eds), *Locating Health. Sociological and Historical Explorations*. Aldershot: Avebury.

Wilkinson, R. G. (1994) The epidemiological transition: from material scarcity to social disadvantage, *Dædalus*, 123, 4, 61–77.

Wilkinson, R. G. (1996a) How can secular improvements in life expectancy be explained? In Blane, D., Brunner, E. and Wilkinson, R. (eds), *Health and Social Organization. Towards a Health Policy for the 21st Century*. London and New York: Routledge.

Wilkinson, R. G. (1996b) *Unhealthy Societies. The Afflictions of Inequality*. London and New York: Routledge.

Wilkinson, R. G. (1997) Health inequalities: relative or absolute material standards? *British Medical Journal*, 314, 22, 591–8.

Williams, S. J. and Bendelow, G. (1996) Emotions, health and illness: the 'missing link' in medical sociology? In James, V. and Gabe, J. (eds), *Health and Sociology of Emotions*. Oxford: Blackwell Publishers, Sociology of Health and Illness Monograph Series.

Wunsch, G., Duchêne, J., Thiltgès, E. and Salhi, M. (1996) Socio-economic differences in mortality. A life course approach, *European Journal of Population*, 12, 167–85.

Part V
Health Care Work

Introduction

We noted in the Introduction to this Reader how late modernity is a period that is characterized by rapid social and technological change. Social structures and social relations are in a relative state of flux; traditional social hierarchies are being altered; and confidence in scientific and technological progress is being undermined. These broader social transformations impact upon the social organization of formal health care (Hertzman, 2000). For example, relationships between health professionals and the public are changing, the dominance of biomedical science is being challenged, and in general the content of health care is coming under greater scrutiny.

It has been argued that the medical profession dominates Western health care systems. The source of the medical profession's power and authority has formed an important strand of medical sociology since the 1960s. Particularly influential here is the work of Freidson (1970), who developed the twin concepts of medical autonomy and medical dominance. The former refers to the profession's ability to regulate itself and its immunity from evaluation by others. The latter concept refers to an occupation's right to control the work of other, related occupational groups. The paper by Harrison and Ahmad documents in some detail the bureaucratic procedures and ideological shifts that have led to a decline in both the medical profession's autonomy and its dominance. They conclude that the medical profession's autonomy has been curbed at both the micro (individual) and meso (institutional) levels, but not so at the macro (ideological) level. They suggest that although there have been policy initiatives to address the social aspects of health and illness, these organizational developments have not 'made inroads into the biomedical model'. Thus, according to their analysis, the dominant medical paradigm of biomedicine remains intact.

Professional dominance refers then to the control of related occupational groups. Griffiths's paper examines how such 'control' is challenged or negotiated in practice within the context of the community mental health team. Such psychiatric teams, comprising a psychiatrist, community psychiatric nurses and social workers, manage the care of people with mental health problems in the community. Griffiths's paper illustrates how the rank-and-file members of the team use humour as a strategy to resist instructions coming from the dominant professionals – in this case the psychiatrists. Team members are also able to counter the psychiatrist's medicalized version of a 'case' by normalizing the actions and behaviours of their clients and so implicitly constructing the clients in non-medical terms. They are construed as sufferers living with 'normal' social problems. We see here how relationships between occupational groups are 'accomplished' and how relationships are sustained at the level of day-to-day interactions.

Biomedicine may indeed be the dominant paradigm in Western medicine, but there is also evidence that 'patients' (or health care users) are discerning in the sense that they are shopping around for the most appropriate 'treatments' for their medical problems. People are increasingly making use of alternative or complementary therapies, particularly for those conditions – often chronic illnesses – where biomedicine has little to offer. Cant and Sharma take the example of the registration of chiropractors in the UK to examine the changing relationship between the state, biomedicine and complementary medicines. The issue of consumerism is evident here, in that the medical profession has had to respond to the fact that complementary medicines are becoming increasingly popular. What is more, there is growing evidence that chiropractors effectively deal with symptoms such as back pain, whereas conventional medicine has little to offer for these conditions. Cant and Sharma trace how the chiropractors from different 'schools' united and worked together to win the favour of the dominant profession of medicine. They adopted strategies such as limiting their sphere of work to parts of the body and ensuring that practitioners would have sufficient biomedical training to know when to refer patients back to conventional practitioners. As Cant and Sharma put it, they 'linked themselves to the established medical paradigm', and this enabled them to achieve state sponsorship. Thus they conclude that the government has responded to consumer demand for alternatives to conventional medicine by permitting the support of complementary practices and so paving the way for greater medical pluralism.

The next paper, by Annandale, examines how organizational changes and the emergence of consumerism affect the work of nurses in hospital settings. Making use of Giddens's reflections on risk (see Introduction to this Reader), Annandale illustrates how the dual impact of growing patient expectations and organizational accountability has contributed to a 'risk culture' within the health service. Drawing upon both survey and observational data, she reveals how nurses develop 'self-protective strategies' as a means of managing the risks. Examples of 'risks' in this context include errors in decision making, providing inappropriate care, or indeed any action which might have negative repercussions in the future. In some instances such strategies may enhance the quality of care, by making nurses more aware of the consequences of their actions, but very often the reverse is the case. Self-protective strategies can result in defensive practices which do not serve the interests of either staff or patients.

Notions of consumerism, which presume that people act as rational actors, work on similar assumptions to ideas about late modernity which speak about the 'reflexive self'. The 'reflexive self', like the 'consumer', implies that individuals act in calculated ways to further their own interests. Although sociologists are in general agreement that we live in a consumer society, the extent to which individuals invariably behave in rational and entrepreneurial ways is an empirical question. Lupton examines this question empirically through the analysis of sixty interviews which were carried out in Australia to ascertain people's views on health care. While she finds some evidence to suggest that people are discerning and questioning of medical practice, she also finds that in general people still retain a considerable degree of faith in, and respect for, medical practitioners. This, she suggests, may be to do with the nature of the doctor–patient relationship itself, where on occasion patients may have a 'felt desire' to take on a 'passive patient' role and appreciate the opportunity to be dependent on others, especially those whom they can trust.

References

Freidson, E. (1970) *The Profession of Medicine: A Study of the Sociology of Applied Knowledge*. New York: Harper & Row.

Hertzman, C. (2000) Social Change, Market Forces and Health: *Social Science and Medicine*, 51, 1007–8.

23

Medical Autonomy and the UK State 1975 to 2025

Stephen Harrison and Waqar I. U. Ahmad

This paper is concerned with the decline of medical professional dominance and autonomy. That such a decline has occurred in both the United States (Freidson 1988; Mechanic 1991) and Britain (Allsop and Mulcahy 1996; Harrison 1999) is hardly contentious, though detailed accounts are rare and there are differences of interpretation of its form and extent. [...]

The dimensions of medical dominance

There are differences amongst analysts about the nature of dominance. For Freidson (1988: 369), it refers to the position of an occupation in the division of labour, sustained by a combination of autonomy (immunity from regulation or evaluation by others) and dominance (control over other occupations). For Coburn (1992), these form a 'continuum of control' along with subordination to other occupations. Alford (1975: 14–15) adopted a broader approach, defining 'structural interests' in terms of the extent to which their 'interests [are] served or not served by the way in which they "fit" into the basic logic and principles by which the institutions of society operate'. In Alford's study of New York, medicine was the *dominant* structural interest, 'served by the [current] structure of social, economic and political institutions'. *Challenging* interests included hospital administrators and government health planners 'created by changing technology and division of labour in health care production and distribution', sharing an interest in 'breaking the monopoly of physicians over the production and distribution of health care'.

[...] This paper examines the decline in the autonomy and dominance of the British medical profession over the last twenty-five years, noting both changes in the institutions of medicine and the National Health Service (NHS), and evidence from empirical studies. The account focuses on medicine's relationship with the state and NHS management: how autonomous is medicine from management and how far does medicine dominate management? The institutions which have underpinned medical autonomy/dominance in the past can be discerned at various levels.

At the *micro level* is clinical autonomy, which can be seen to include several elements (Schulz and Harrison 1986: 340–1). *Control over diagnosis and treatment* covers decisions about what tests and examinations to order, what drugs and procedures to prescribe, to whom to refer. Restrictions to such autonomy might in principle relate to individual patients but are in practice more likely to circumscribe aggregates (for instance, through pre-set budgets), identify 'outliers' with untypical treatment patterns, or channel certain treatments through a 'gatekeeper'. 'Clinical guidelines' are another important vehicle for circumscribing practice. These are documents which guide the clinician to courses of (diagnostic or therapeutic) action, dependent upon stated prior conditions, though guidelines do not claim to determine clinical action completely. *Control over evaluation of care* concerns judgements about the appropriateness of the care for particular patients; peer review or clinical audit are common vehicles for such evaluation, whilst clinical 'performance indicators' (such as surgical mortality rates) are becoming pervasive. *Control over the nature and volume of medical tasks* represents the ability of doctors not to be managed in the industrial sense: the extent to which they are left to determine their own movements, priorities, times and workloads. Finally, *contractual independence* refers to the characteristics of doctors' contracts of employment: the extent to which they contain unilateral rights such as to engage in private medical practice or to criticise employers.

At the *meso level* are the institutionalised relationships between the medical profession and the state. The legal basis of state licensure and self-regulation is part of this, but so are the various corporatist arrangements (Schmitter 1974) through which medical interests are mediated, including numerous joint government/professional standing committees and official recognition of the British Medical Association (BMA) as the profession's 'peak association'. These arrangements also impact on the local NHS through, for instance, the constitution of governing bodies. At the *macro level* is the phenomenon of the 'biomedical model' (Mishler 1989), the pervasive assumption that ill-health equals individual pathology, and that health care therefore consists of individual medical interventions. This ideology did not simply arise autonomously in the NHS; rather, the possibility of a broader public health approach was rejected in the early 1940s by medical interests in alliance with civil servants (Colwill 1998).

Evidence from the micro level: clinical autonomy

Formal commitment to clinical autonomy for doctors figured prominently in the official pronouncements of governments from the gestation of the NHS until the 1980s. The wartime coalition government's 1944 White Paper stated that 'whatever the organisation, the doctors taking part must remain free to direct their clinical knowledge and personal skill for the benefit of their patients in the way which they feel to be best' (Ministry of Health 1944). Similar statements followed at regular intervals (for details, see Harrison 1999) and as late as 1979 it was stated by the then newly-elected Conservative Government (whose successors went on to make some of the radical changes described below) that 'It is doctors... who provide the care and cure of patients and promote the health of the people. It is the purpose of management to support them' (DHSS and Welsh Office 1979: 1–2).

The arrangements for employing doctors reinforced this freedom from subordination to managers. Consultants' contracts of employment were carefully insulated from managerial discretion by being held at the regional, rather than operational level. There were unilateral rights to engage in private practice and to appeal to the Secretary of State against dismissal. General practitioners (GPs) were self-employed contractors to the NHS, remunerated through capitation fees, fees for service and various allowances, and were somewhat insulated from the remainder of the NHS. Their contracts were held by separate public bodies and specified their duties in only the vaguest terms: 'A doctor shall render to his (*sic*) patients all necessary and appropriate personal medical services of the kind usually provided by general medical practitioners' (Ellis and Chisholm 1993: 12). GPs were able to refer their patients freely to any specialist in any hospital anywhere in the United Kingdom, the financial consequences of such decisions falling upon the hospitals. Subject to administrative intervention in only the most extreme cases, they could prescribe from the wide-ranging NHS pharmacopoeia in whatever quantities they chose. Haywood and Alaszewski (1980) were thus able to show that the pattern of health care delivered by the NHS was simply the aggregate of individual clinical decisions rather than the outcome of planners' or managers' decisions.

The reality of medical dominance was also reflected in formal management structures. Until 1974 the local statutory bodies which ran the NHS had large numbers of doctors in membership (Ham 1981) and were afterwards dominated by multidisciplinary consensus management teams, half the places on which were occupied by doctors, each with a power of veto (Harrison 1982). The practice of NHS management until the mid-1980s has been likened to the practice of diplomacy. Rather than conforming to the stereotype of an authoritative individual, pursuing organisational objectives by means of proactively generated change, the manager possessed little influence relative to doctors, was very much focused on responding to the demands of internal organisational actors, and procured only incremental change. A summary of the evidence from some twenty-five empirical studies conducted up to 1983 (Harrison 1988: 51) concluded that: 'Managers neither were, nor were supposed to be, influential with respect to doctors...Managers in general worked to solve problems and to maintain their organisations rather than to secure major change'.

The recommendation of the 1983 Griffiths Inquiry that individual general managers (later 'chief executives') should replace consensus teams therefore represented a major defeat for the medical profession, despite a good deal of resistance over a prolonged period. The BMA wrote to the Secretary of State in the following terms:

> It could be interpreted from the report that a somewhat autocratic 'executive' manager would be appointed with significant delegated powers, who would – in the interests of 'good management' – be able to make major decisions against the advice of the profession... it should be clearly understood that the profession would neither accept nor cooperate with any such arrangement – particularly where the interests of patients are concerned.

This virtual declaration of independence (quoted in *British Medical Journal* 288, 14 January 1984: 165) was accompanied by demands for modifications to Griffiths' scheme and a trial period. Despite all this and some diffidence by the Secretary of State, the new arrangements were accepted by the Government in 1984 when it became clear that they had the Prime Minister's support (Harrison 1994: 90–1). Alongside the new general managers, various systems of budgets, performance indicators and internal organisational structures related to clinical workloads were introduced (Packwood *et al*. 1991, 1992). A number of management posts came to be occupied by doctors, albeit on a part-time basis.

A review of empirical research carried out between 1984 and 1990 concluded that, despite the defeat over the *form* of the Griffiths innovations, the medical profession had experienced little resulting loss of autonomy (Harrison *et al*. 1992). [...] However, three changes did result which, with hindsight, can be seen as necessary conditions for subsequent developments. First, managers became much more externally focused; they were increasingly compelled to respond to governmental agendas and were consequently less able to respond to internal professional agendas (Flynn 1988). Secondly, the new arrangements meant that hospital doctors increasingly 'rubbed shoulders' with managers, and the appointment of doctors to management posts had considerable symbolic importance. Thirdly, by 1985 there was no longer any desire, in medicine or elsewhere, for a return to consensus team management. General managers had thus achieved legitimacy if not substantial influence and since this time NHS management has become an increasingly attractive career option for people whose original training was in the nursing or therapy professions.

The NHS quasi-market introduced in 1991 represented a major departure from this by providing a radically different institutional structure. [...]

As with the earlier reforms, the government faced a good deal of opposition from the BMA (1989: 2):

> [The BMA Council] is convinced that many of the proposals would cause serious damage to NHS patient care, lead to a fragmented service and destroy the comprehensive nature of the existing service. The Government's main proposals would appear to be to contain and reduce the level of public expenditure devoted to health care. The proposals would undoubtedly increase substantially the administrative and accountancy costs of the service, and they ignore the rising costs of providing services for the elderly and of medical advances. In the absence of any additional funding the proposals would inevitably reduce the standards of NHS patient care.

By mid-1989 there was a widespread perception that the government was losing political ground on the issue, evidence for which continued to be apparent in opinion polls throughout 1990 and 1991. However, the government persisted with the necessary legislation, and in June 1992 the BMA formally ended its campaign against the changes, more than a year after they had been implemented.

[...]

After its massive election victory of May 1997, so-called New Labour's initial NHS reform proposals retained Trusts but abolished GPFH [GP Fundholding]. The latter is replaced initially by Primary Care Groups (PCGs) which compulsorily federate groups of general practices with a cash-limited unified budget for providing primary health care and purchasing most hospital and community services. Although the self-employed status of GPs will not change, PCGs will have governing boards accountable to HAs [Health Authorities] and be required to enter into annual 'accountability agreements' with them as well as to produce a public annual accountability report. Initial GP enthusiasm for PCGs was far from general

(*British Medical Journal*, 28 March 1998: 1025) and the government found it necessary to make a number of concessions, including allowing GPs to occupy a majority of seats on PCG boards and hence to chair them. Although there remain strong concerns that the new arrangements will offer much less autonomy than did GP fundholding (McIntosh 1998), GPs have accepted that participation is unavoidable. From 2000, PCGs will be able to transmute into Primary Care Trusts (PCTs), independent of HAs; crucially, the process of transmutation can be triggered by local actors other than GPs, and there is no formal GP veto on it. Moreover, PCTs will not have GP majorities on their governing bodies. Although there has been an initially high level of PCG interest in attaining PCT status, the emergence of the planned governance arrangements for the latter has led to some medical discontent (*Health Service Journal*, 25 February 1999: 3).

Labour has also introduced the policy of 'clinical governance', officially defined as 'a framework through which NHS organisations are accountable for continuously improving the quality of their services and safeguarding high standards of care by creating an environment in which excellence in clinical care will flourish' (NHS Executive 1998: 33). Though it builds on the development of an NHS Research and Development strategy (Baker and Kirk 1996) which took place under the previous government, this anodyne formulation masks a significant challenge to clinical autonomy as previously practised. The new institutions of clinical governance are as follows.

The National Institute for Clinical Excellence (NICE) was established in 1999 with three broad functions (NHS Executive 1998: 13ff). First, it will make recommendations to the government as to whether specific treatments are sufficiently cost-effective and affordable to be provided by the NHS. Secondly, it will give its *imprimatur* to thirty to fifty per annum 'evidence-based' (for a discussion, see Harrison 1998) clinical guidelines for the management of medical conditions. Thirdly, it will be responsible for approving models of clinical audit for compulsory use by hospital doctors (*British Medical Journal* 316, 20 June 1998). In addition to this central specification of *clinical* models, there is to be central specification of *service* models, beginning with coronary heart disease and mental health. Thus 'National Service Frameworks' (NSFs) will be developed as a means of defining the pathway through primary, secondary and tertiary care which a particular type of patient will be expected to pass. The Commission for Health Improvement (CHI) will be established as a statutory body and will 'conduct a rolling programme of reviews, visiting every... Trust over a period of around 3–4 years' (NHS Executive 1998: 51–3). Such reviews will include local compliance with clinical guidelines issued by NICE, and with NSFs. In addition to routine reviews, the NHS management hierarchy will be able to initiate inquiries where local problems are suspected. [...]

These proposals have not been strongly resisted by the medical profession. The manner of their reception has been influenced by the media and public response to the discovery in 1998 that paediatric cardiac surgeons in a Bristol hospital had a poor survival record for particular surgical procedures and that attempts by colleagues to draw attention to this had been obstructed (Klein 1998). Three doctors, including the hospital's medically qualified chief executive, were dismissed, of whom two were disqualified by the General Medical Council from the practice of medicine (Dyer 1998). [...]

Evidence: the meso and macro levels

There have always been conflicts within British medicine or between the state and medicine, not least at the creation of the NHS in the 1940s (Webster 1998). At times since then, there has been considerable tension between specialists and doctors in training (Harrison *et al.* 1992: chap. 4) and between specialists and GPs, whilst doctor's pay has been a source of recurring friction with governments (Seifert 1992). Such conflicts, however, occurred beneath the close meso-corporatist relationship between the profession as embodied in the BMA and medical Royal Colleges, and the government Health Departments (Cawson 1982). At national level, this resulted in workforce planning practices very much in the profession's interests (Harrison 1981), as well as parallel medical and administrative hierarchies within these departments. Moreover, some hospital specialists were able to receive substantial 'distinction awards' in addition to their salary; these permanent awards were unilaterally and secretly determined within the profession.

The Conservative Governments of the 1980s (and especially Mrs Thatcher's) notoriously regarded the professions as indistinguishable from trade unions and this led to a downgrading (though by no means the abandonment) of the corporatist relationship with the medical profession (Lee-Potter 1997). [. . .]

The piecemeal dismantling of some of the unilateral rights conferred on medicine as part of its corporatist relationship with the state has been continued by New Labour. The committee which allocates distinction awards to senior doctors has lost its medical majority and gained patient representatives in addition to senior NHS managers (Crail 1998), and individuals' awards may now be discontinued (*Health Service Journal*, 25 March 1999: 4–5). The Parliamentary Health Service Commissioner may now investigate complaints against GPs, which had previously been excluded from the ambit of the office (Warden 1999). New legislation will allow the government more easily to change the self-regulating status of the health professions (Smith 1998), though it appears that the recent decision by the General Medical Council to work towards a system of compulsory competence reaccreditation may have pre-empted any immediate government attempt to modify the system of medical registration (Healy 1999).

Despite the above changes at the micro and meso levels, the dominance of the 'biomedical model' at the macro level remains largely intact. The NHS reorganisation of 1974 ostensibly recognised the social and environmental aspects of ill-health and placed great emphasis on institutional integration between the NHS and other agencies such as local government authorities. These arrangements were substantially downgraded by the Conservatives, but the philosophy of integration has re-emerged in current New Labour reforms. These include Health Improvement Programmes, a statutory requirement for all HAs to work with local government authorities, NHS Trusts and PCGs to address local health needs through economic, social and environmental policies in addition to health care services (Secretary of State 1997: 26–7). Another such initiative, Health Action Zones, allowed NHS institutions to bid for centrally-allocated funds to develop multi-agency programmes to improve the health status of their local populations. However, there is little to suggest that the model of ill-health implied by these organisational developments has made inroads into the biomedical model, and indeed it might be argued that the constitution of PCGs around doctors reinforces the latter, at least until the advent of PCTs. However, as we note below, there is a sense in which recent managerial changes have turned the biomedical model back on doctors, suggesting that it is not *necessarily* a source of autonomy.

Theorising the decline

It is clear that a not insignificant decline in the autonomy and dominance of British medicine has occurred over the last twenty-five years, though this has not been linear and developments in primary care have occasionally run against this trend. The decline is clearest at the micro level of clinical autonomy and at the meso level of corporatist relations with government. [...] [I]t may become plausible to conclude that (in Alford's terms) medicine is no longer the dominant structural interest in the NHS. This is despite the fact that no significant weakening of the macro-level biomedical model has yet occurred. Paradoxically, this has underpinned management as much as medicine, and many of the manifestations of managerialism outlined above depend upon it; observation of medical practice variation, clinical performance indicators, the quasi-market and clinical guidelines are examples.

[...] An alternative perspective represents the change mainly as (re-)stratification *within* medicine rather than overall decline (Freidson 1988; Reed 1994) and sees little evidence that the overall social or intellectual place of medicine has been eroded (Mechanic 1991: 495). There have always been differences of status within medicine, especially between its various specialties. But whichever perspective is adopted, the conclusion remains that, for the ordinary medical clinician, autonomy has been eroded, partly by the imposition of new frames of reference (Lukes 1974), and that this is as much the case for high-status specialties such as surgery as for the less prestigious ones such as general practice. Thus it has increasingly become the case that doctors must adopt a managerial perspective in order to progress within the profession, and that clinical decisions must be justified by reference to external research findings. Though it does not capture the totality of the changes to medical autonomy and dominance outlined above, one way of labelling the medical labour process as it is now emerging is as 'scientific-bureaucratic medicine'. It is 'scientific' in the sense that its prescriptions for treatment are drawn from an externally-generated body of research knowledge (for a discussion, see Harrison 1998), and 'bureaucratic' in the sense that it is implemented through bureaucratic rules (albeit of a very specialised kind), namely, clinical guidelines.

The dissonance of this development with post-Fordist analyses is striking. Such theories suggest that continued economic growth in capitalist states depends on a direct relationship between the new patterns of consumption (which may be labelled 'consumerism') and new modes of production. Crudely, a shift takes place from standardised mass production accompanied by highly specified and routinised work, to flexible production in which workers develop close relationships with customers and are given the autonomy to produce outputs which satisfy the latter's individual demands. Yet medical work seems to be moving in precisely the opposite direction. The principle of clinical autonomy was based precisely on the assumption that each physician would thus be able to respond to the individual needs of each patient. It is doubtful whether this ideal was met. Studies of variations in the rates at which medical procedures are performed have found no straightforward relationship to the severity of illness or other plausible proxies for patient need (Andersen and Mooney 1990) and there is ample evidence that access is influenced by patients' gender (Graham 1984), ethnicity (Ahmad 1993) and social class (Acheson 1998). Nevertheless, it is clear that the NHS medical labour process as it stood at the beginning of the period covered by this paper is better described as flexible production than as mass production. [...] [T]he rhetoric of consumerism associated with the NHS quasi-market of 1991 to 1997 was not accompanied by any mechanisms of consumer choice. Rather, 'purchasing' decisions were to be made by managers or GPs [...] rather than patients. It was thus not uncommon for the needs of marginalised groups to be absent from purchasing agendas on grounds such as 'low numbers', lack of resources or (for minority ethnic groups) 'they look after their own' (Walker and Ahmad 1994). And the notion of 'clinical governance' implies much more than 'the progressive decentralisation of production under conditions of rising flexibility and centralised strategic control' (Hoggett 1990: 5); the controls inherent in scientific-bureaucratic medicine largely introduce to medicine the central Fordist notion of 'one best way'. As it is now developing, the medical labour process is better described as mass production than flexible production.

A plausible explanation for this direction centres on the observation that a key element in the post-Fordist schema does not apply to the NHS. As noted above, a good deal of explanatory weight for the breakdown of Fordism is carried by the growth of more individualistic patterns of consumption. In this formulation the concept of 'consumer' is of a person willing and able to pay for a good or service and hence endowed with some degree of choice. But the NHS consumer only consumes; whatever choice is available must be negotiated with NHS providers rather than exercised through the medium of cash. [...] The NHS, which accounts for some 85 per cent of UK health care expenditure (Office of Health Economics 1997), is both a near-monopoly provider of medical care and a near-monopoly purchaser (strictly, monopsonist) of medical labour; most doctors who undertake private work do so in addition to their NHS contracts. [...]

Of course, [...] underlying legitimation requirements are not unaffected by contemporary cultural change. The attempt to reduce professional autonomy by bureaucratic devices can also be seen as a governmental response to greater public awareness of risk (Alaszewski *et al.* 1998: 91), as exemplified in the Bristol case cited above. From this perspective, it represents a strategy to maintain the legitimacy of the state in the face of an increasingly decentred political culture (Beck 1992: 198), that is to assert modernity in the face of postmodernity (Harrison 1998).

The next twenty-five years: some implications for sociology

[...] [S]tudies of medical autonomy/dominance can illuminate much larger sociological questions.

One area of enquiry concerns the *managerial capacity of the state*. At first examination, the twenty-five year history outlined in earlier sections suggests that the ostensible corporatist bargain between medicine and the state is rather one-sided, in favour of the latter. Specifically, it seems that the relationship can be downgraded when no longer deemed convenient. Such observations fail, however, to consider whether the new arrangements are capable of delivering the state's agenda. The New Labour arrangements for governing medicine are not classically bureaucratic, but nevertheless represent a form of neo-bureaucracy which has rules (such as NSFs and clinical guidelines) but enforces these as much through regulatory agencies as through a conventional hierarchy. This Fordist programme of clinical governance clearly runs counter to two (related) contemporary trends. First, government has increasingly become transmuted into 'governance', that is public sector hierarchies have been replaced by self-organising networks (Rhodes 1996); it is particularly ironic that, in the NHS context, the term 'governance' has been appropriated to signify virtually the opposite. Secondly, other organisations have generally adopted post-Fordist labour processes, namely those based on 'the progressive decentralisation of production under conditions of rising flexibility and centralised strategic control' (Hoggett 1990: 5; Hirst and Zeitlin 1992). Such processes often also involve 'core–periphery' distinctions and attempts to manipulate 'organisational culture' (Peters and Waterman 1982). [...]

The other area of enquiry concerns the *legitimacy of the state* as an agent of health care rationing (Harrison and Moran 1999). This may be subdivided into two sets of considerations, of which the first relates to social exclusion both inside and outside the NHS. Existing patterns of stratification within medicine work against women and ethnic minorities and it seems probable that the new forms of stratification implied by the above analysis will also follow the lines of 'race', gender (Annandale 1998: 212ff) and class. Bluntly, the medical academic researchers whose output contributes to the production of guidelines, and the doctors who occupy managerial positions, may turn out to be white males from middle-class backgrounds. Outside NHS organisation, much of the rhetorical force of clinical governance derives from its potential to level out variations in medical practice in the interests of fairness (Secretary of State 1997: 15). But these problematic variations are largely seen in spatial terms, especially as 'postcode prescribing', and the advice of NICE to government will substitute rationing of treatments, a criterion which relates no more closely to the needs of obviously socially excluded groups than its predecessor. [...] And, as examination of just one social cleavage, ethnicity, shows, institutionally discriminatory practices and attitudes remain in the form of racism within medical ideology and the systematic deprivileging of minority ethnic health concerns and racist definitions of their needs (Ahmad 1993). Substantive citizenship rights are likely to be a crucial determinant of how legitimate the UK state is seen [by] its minorities.

Second, there are more general questions about state legitimacy in the context of postmodern consumerist culture (Smart 1996), the social construction of risk (Douglas 1992), the knowledgeable consumer (Haug 1988), and the internet-informed public (Coiera 1996). Whilst it may be argued that a rational consumer would seek only that medical care known to have a 'reasonable' probability of effectiveness (Evans 1990), there are numerous reasons why this may not be so. There is evidence that actors may espouse quite different criteria for the allocation of medical care, and may have widely varying thresholds of what is reasonable (Harrison 1998). [...] From this perspective, therefore, the explicit attempt of clinical governance to privilege science and destabilise professionalism risks repoliticising the previously depoliticised (Reed 1994). Part of the durability of clinical autonomy lay in the advantages it offered to profession, government and patient (Harrison 1999); the impact of deprofessionalisation on the legitimacy of the welfare state, and ultimately the state itself, is an open question.

References

Acheson, D. 1998. *Independent Inquiry into Inequalities in Health: Report*. London: Stationery Office.

Ahmad, W. I. U. (ed.) 1993. *'Race' and Health in Contemporary Britain*. Buckingham: Open University Press.

Alaszewski, A., Alaszewski, H. and Harrison, L. 1998. 'Professionals, Accountability and Risk'. In A. Alaszewski, L. Harrison and J. Manthorpe (eds.), *Health, Risk and Welfare*. Buckingham: Open University Press.

Alford, R. R. 1975. *Health Care Politics*. Chicago: University of Chicago Press.

Allsop, J. and Mulcahy, L. 1996. *Regulating Medical Work: Formal and Informal Controls*. Buckingham: Open University Press.

Andersen, T. F. and Mooney, G. (eds.) 1990. *The Challenges of Medical Practice Variations*. London: Macmillan.

Annandale, E. 1998. *The Sociology of Health and Medicine: A Critical Introduction*. Cambridge: Polity.

Baker, M. R. and Kirk, S. (eds.) 1996. *Research and Development for the NHS: Evidence, Evaluation and Effectiveness*. Oxford: Radcliffe Medical Press.

Beck, U. 1992. *The Risk Society: Towards a New Modernity*. London: Sage.

British Medical Association. 1989. *Special Report of the Council of the British Medical Association on the Government's White Paper 'Working for Patients'*. London.

Cawson, A. 1982. *Corporatism and Welfare: Social Policy and State Intervention in Britain*. London: Heinemann.

Coburn, D., 1992. 'Freidson Then and Now: An "Internalist" Critique of Freidson's Past and Present Views of the Medical Profession'. *International Journal of Health Services* 22: 497–512.

Coiera, E. 1996. 'The Internet's Challenge to Health Care Provision'. *British Medical Journal* 312: 3–4.

Colwill, J. 1998. 'Professionalism and Control in Health Services Provision: Some Lessons from the Health Service in Britain'. *Journal of Contemporary Health* 7: 71–6.

Crail, M. 1998. 'Distinct Improvement'. *Health Service Journal* 12 (November): 12.

Department of Health and Social Security and Welsh Office. 1979. *Patients First: Consultative Paper on the Structure and Management of the National Health Service in England and Wales*. London: HMSO.

Douglas, M. 1992. *Risk and Blame: Essays in Cultural Theory*. London: Routledge.

Dyer, C. 1998. 'Bristol Doctors Found Guilty of Serious Professional Misconduct'. *British Medical Journal* 316: 1924.

Ellis, N. D. and Chisholm, J. 1993 (2nd edn). *Making Sense of the Red Book*. London: Routledge.

Evans, R. G. 1990. 'The Dog in the Night-time: Medical Practice Variations and Health Policy'. In T. F. Andersen and G. Mooney (eds.), *The Challenges of Medical Practice Variations*. London: Macmillan.

Flynn, R. 1988. *Cutback Management in Health Services*. Salford: University of Salford.

Freidson, E. 1988 (2nd edn). *Profession of Medicine: A Study of the Sociology of Applied Knowledge*. Chicago: University of Chicago Press.

Graham, H. 1984. *Women, Health and the Family*. Hemel Hempstead: Harvester Wheatsheaf.

Ham, C. J. 1981. *Policy Making in the National Health Service*. London: Macmillan.

Harrison, S. 1981. 'The Politics of Health Manpower'. In A. F. Long and G. Mercer (eds.), *Manpower Planning in the National Health Service*. Farnborough: Gower Press.

Harrison, S. 1982. 'Consensus Decision Making in the National Health Service: A Review'. *Journal of Management Studies* 19: 377–94.

Harrison, S. 1988. *Managing the National Health Service: Shifting the Frontier?* London: Chapman and Hall.

Harrison, S. 1994. *Managing the National Health Service in the 1980s: Policymaking on the Hoof?* Aldershot: Avebury.

Harrison, S. 1998. 'The Politics of Evidence-Based Medicine in the UK'. *Policy and Politics* 26: 15–32.

Harrison, S. 1999. 'Clinical Autonomy and Health Policy: Past and Futures'. In M. Exworthy and S. Halford (eds.), *Professionals and the New Managerialism in the Public Sector*. Buckingham: Open University Press.

Harrison, S., Hunter, D. J., Marnoch, G. and Pollitt, C. J. 1992. *Just Managing: Power and Culture in the National Health Service*. London: Macmillan.

Harrison, S. and Moran, M. 1999. 'Resources and Rationing: Managing Supply and Demand in Health Care'. In G. Albrecht, R. Fitzpatrick and S. Scrimshaw (eds.), *The Handbook of Social Studies in Health and Medicine*. New York: Sage.

Haywood, S. C. and Alaszewski, A. 1980. *Crisis in the NHS: The Politics of Management*. London: Croom Helm.

Haug, M. 1988. 'A Re-examination of the Hypothesis of Deprofessionalisation'. *Milbank Quarterly* Supp 2: 58–6.

Healy, P. 1999. 'Regulation Issue'. *Health Service Journal* 18 Febuary: 10.

Hirst, P. and Zeitlin, J. 1992. 'Flexible Specialisation Versus Post-Fordism: Theory, Evidence and Policy Implications'. In M. Storper and A. J. Scott (eds.), *Pathways to Industrialisation and Regional Development*. London: Routledge.

Hoggett, P. 1990. *Modernisation, Political Strategy, and the Welfare State: An Organisational Perspective*. Bristol: SAUS Publications.

Klein, R. E. 1998. 'Competence, Professional Self-Regulation and the Public Interest'. *British Medical Journal* 316: 1740–2.

Lee-Potter, J. 1997. *A Damn Bad Business: The NHS Deformed*. London: Gollancz.

Lukes, S. 1974. *Power: A Radical View*. London: Macmillan.

McIntosh, K. 1998. 'What the Doctors Ordered'. *Health Service Journal* 12 November: 10–11.

Mechanic, D. 1991. 'Sources of Countervailing Power in Medicine'. *Journal of Health Politics, Policy and Law* 16: 485–98.

Ministry of Health and Department of Health for Scotland. 1944. *A National Health Service*. Cmnd 6502. London: HMSO.

Mishler, E. G. 1989. 'Critical Perspectives on the Biomedical Model'. In P. Brown (ed.), *Perspectives in Medical Sociology*. Belmont, Calif.: Wadsworth.

Moran, M. and Wood, B. 1993. *States, Regulation and the Medical Profession*. Buckingham: Open University Press.

NHS Executive. 1998. *A First Class Service: Quality in the New NHS*. London: Department of Health.

Office of Health Economics. 1997. *Compendium of Statistics*, 10th edn. London.

Packwood, T., Keen, J. and Buxton, M. 1991. *Hospitals in Transition: The Resource Management Experiment*. Buckingham: Open University Press.

Packwood, T., Keen, J. and Buxton, M. 1992. 'Process and Structure: Resource Management and the Development of Sub-Unit Organisational Structure'. *Health Services Management Research* 5: 66–76.

Peters, T. L. and Waterman, R. H. 1982. *In Search of Excellence: Lessons from America's Best-Run Companies*. New York: Harper and Row.

Reed, M. 1994. 'Expert Power and Organisation in High Modernity: An Empirical Review and Theoretical Synthesis'. Paper presented at ESRC seminar, Cardiff.

Rhodes, R. A. W. 1996. 'The New Governance: Governing without Government'. *Political Studies* 44: 652–67.

Schmitter, P. C. 1974. 'Still the Century of Corporatism'. *Review of Politics* 36: 85–131.

Schulz, R. I. and Harrison, S. 1986. 'Physician Autonomy in the Federal Republic of Germany, Great Britain, and the United States'. *International Journal of Health Planning and Management* 1: 335–55.

Secretary of State for Health. 1997. *The New NHS: Modern, Dependable*. London: Stationery Office.

Seifert, R. 1992. *Industrial Relations in the NHS*. London: Chapman and Hall.

Smart, B. 1996. 'Postmodern Social Theory'. In B. S. Turner (ed.), *The Blackwell Companion to Social Theory*. Oxford: Blackwell.

Smith, R. 1998. 'Repositioning Self-Regulation: The Influence of the GMC May Be Leaking Away'. *British Medical Journal* 317: 964.

Walker, R. and Ahmad, W. I. U. 1994. 'Windows of Opportunity in Rotting Frames? Care Providers' Perspectives on Community Care and Black Communities'. *Critical Social Policy* 40: 46–68.

Warden, J. 1999. 'Role of Chief Medical Officer has been Eroded'. *British Medical Journal* 317: 1340.

Webster, C. 1998. *The National Health Service: A Political History*. Oxford: Oxford University Press.

24

Humour as Resistance to Professional Dominance in Community Mental Health Teams

Lesley Griffiths

Introduction

This paper contributes to the sociological study of humour in health care settings by analysing its use by social workers and nurses in community mental health teams (CMHTs) dealing with referrals made by consultant psychiatrists. It is about humour and hierarchy, and specifically about humour as a strategy used by rank-and-file team members to resist or attenuate instructions coming from powerful professionals.

[...]

Humour emerged as a pervasive feature of CMHT work, featuring in almost all the tape-recorded meetings. It was central to CMHT members' skilful negotiation of potential points of conflict between immediate work pressures and wider organisational requirements, such as the tension between individual workloads and the duty to deal with the large numbers of patients requiring care in the community. In the empirical sections of the paper I describe how humorous challenges to the psychiatrist's medicalised version of a case often provided a way for CMHT members to resist excessive workloads. By implicitly constructing patients in non-medical terms – as the sufferers of normal problems of living or as 'malingerers' – team members harnessed trans-situational understandings about the boundaries of the target population to control the entry of patients to their caseloads.

The study and the setting

The two CMHTs studied were set up in 1991 in response to the *All Wales Strategy for Mental Health*. Each CMHT comprised community psychiatric nurses (CPNs) and social workers specialising in mental health and a team psychiatrist. Both operated in urban areas, serving predominantly working class populations.

One team had accommodation both at the psychiatric hospital and in the social services area offices; the second team was split between a local health centre and the area offices. The two CMHTs studied were selected on pragmatic grounds and there is no suggestion that they represent opposite poles on a theoretical continuum. They were simply the first teams operating in an area where several other CMHTs were planned.

[...]

Contrasting versions of teamwork

The psychiatrists had been the most powerful actors in shaping local arrangements, and each had opted for a different role and a different way of constituting weekly team meetings. The *Team A* psychiatrist favoured a division of labour in which a semi-independent team drew upon his clinical expertise, but exercised its autonomy in managing work activity rather than through involvement in diagnosis or clinical review. He did not generally attend meetings, and the function of meetings was characterised as 'allocation'. The *Team B* psychiatrist similarly emphasised his expert clinician role, but was prepared to involve the team more directly in some areas of clinical decision-making. The weekly gatherings were presented as 'clinical review meetings', which the psychiatrist or his senior house officer always attended. Although referrals and the basis of referral decisions were not usually discussed in *Team B*, nurses and social workers would frequently feed back their assessments of patient progress to the psychiatrist, so that cases were subject to an ongoing review in which all team members played a part. In this team the allocation function was also present, but was carried out as a brief preliminary to the weekly meeting or – with the occasional urgent case – outside the meeting. Referrals to *Team A* came from GPs directly or from the psychiatrist; in *Team B* all referrals came through the psychiatrist.

CMHT work may be seen as people-processing work, not dissimilar to the work of other 'street-level bureaucrats' (Lipsky 1980) who exercise discretion in categorising a clientele and providing a service. CMHT members develop routine ways of managing the work of allocating cases, classifying patients, and monitoring progress through the talk of the meeting – what we might call 'talking the work'. However, there are striking differences in the way definitions of patients and CMHT work are constructed in the two teams, which seem to be directly attributable to the participation or non-participation of the psychiatrist and the framing of the meeting as 'allocation' or 'review'.

On the surface one psychiatrist has embraced the team concept and participated fully, while the other has taken a more qualified position, with a more distant relationship with the rest of the team. However, in practice, both approaches had the consequence of keeping substantial decision-making authority with the psychiatrist, albeit with different costs and risks. The *Team A* psychiatrist gains the time and professional detachment from the team which non-attendance at team meetings allows, but through his absence creates the space for other team members to resist his definitions and instructions. The *Team B* psychiatrist structures meetings to encourage full staff participation in discussions and an appearance of joint decision-making but – because of his control over referrals, hospital admissions, prescribing, and wider professional contacts – continues to be the most powerful team actor.

Humour as resistance

Humour is an important feature of meetings in both teams. In part this reflects a shared concern with the volume of work coming through from the psychiatrists, and a perception that many referrals involve patients who are not seriously mentally ill. From time to time, team members challenge the patient history put forward by the referring psychiatrist, and seek to re-formulate the information to suggest an alternative explanation for the patient's behaviour. Often these challenges are packaged as humorous comment.

In *Team A* these comments are addressed, not to the absent psychiatrist, but to the team leader who makes the referral request on the psychiatrist's behalf and must report back to him. Typically the team leader introduces the referral in the format of the case report, cast in the standard language of case presentation, and making heavy use of direct quotations from the referral letter and attached papers. Team members respond by questioning the team leader about the case, and sometimes suggesting re-formulations of the history. Without an author to provide clarification, the referral letter must stand on its own: it is scrutinised for sense and consistency, and for evidence that the referral is appropriate. *Extract 1* illustrates the delicate interplay between team leader (TL) and team, as the team's scepticism about the referral becomes clear. 'Rory' is the psychiatrist.

Extract 1

```
 1   TL:     Right. Ray Daniels, 8, W__ Rd__, C__,
 2            referred by Rory, seen at South health centre on the
 3            30th of April, he's going through a divorce from his
 4            wife, and he believes she has been unfair to him, she
 5            has stolen his car and sold it =
 6   N1:      = Paah! Good for her          Stolen his car =
 7   N2:                      [Heh heh] heh heh [heh heh]
 8   N1:      = That's my girl =
 9   N2:      = Hmmmmmm Eeeeh//heh
10   SW1:     I think that's unspeakably low, that's possibly
11            the worst thing a woman could do
12   N1:                     [I think that's absolutely] brilliant
13   N2:      Heh heh   heh heh heh
14   SW1:              [heh he   heh heeh
15   TL:                        [It's not very nice and not only his
16            car but his jacket as well
17   SW1:     Ooo/aoh
18   N1:        [[Nooooh, □□ not his jacket □□ haah ha haaah
19   N2:        [ Noooooh
20   SW2:     Oooahhhh =
21   TL:      = And has taken his furniture and has gone to live with
22            her mother
23   N1:      Ooh//no
24   N3:      What ahh   How about the microwave?
25   TL:      She has apparently also taken the microwave
```

26	N1:	[ha ha ha huuh heh]

27 TL: = and television
28 N1:   [Hah ha ha   heeh heeh heeh
29 N2:   [uh huh huh huh huh huh =
30 TL: = I feel sorry for this //chap
31 SW2:   Heh   heh heehh
32 N2:   [Heeh hah ha =
33 N1:   What diagnostic category is that then?
34 N3:   Desmond's got empathy here =
35 TL: [[Well, he   = He tends to cry a lot
36 N1:   = Why? =
37 TL: = He has three children, two by his wife's first
38   marriage and one by theirs. His appetite//
39   is poor
40 N1:   ((inaudible overlap))
41 TL: He has attempted suicide New Year's Eve when he had
42   been drinking. Is he known to anybody?
43 N2:   No =
44 N1:   = A lot of people do that New Year's Eve though,
45   don't th//ey?
46 N2:   eh heh eh heeeh =
47 SW2:   = Can't face the new//year
48 N2:   Heh eh heeeh
49 TL: He is reluctant to go back to his home situation and
50   is and is due in court on the 12th of May and =
51 N2:   [There's nothing there]
52 TL: = also the 4th of May for assault
53 SW1:   Ooo//oh
54 SW2:   [[Oooh
55 N1:   ((inaudible overlap))
56 TL: He is being prosecuted for assault
57 N1:   Oh =
58 TL: = Oh, she is prosecuting =
59 SW2:   = He gave her a pasting
60 TL: He admits to drinking five pints a//night
61 SW2:   Sue was there. Sue would know
62 N1:   Heh heh he doesn't heeh heh
63 SW2:   [[heeh, heh heeh
64 TL: Past medical history nil, except the patient had been
65   in before. He also tried to ahh kill himself on New
66   Year's Eve. Well there we are
67 N1:   Oh all right
68 N2:   What's he referred him for?
69 TL: Hey?
70 N2:   What's he referred//him
71 N1:   Poverty
72 TL: I've got (all the details) on his marital problems.
73   Summary: a 37-year-old married man who is

74		undergoing divorce for the second time. He drinks
75		approximately five pints a night =
76	N1:	= And the re//st
77	TL:	And is depressed due to the impending divorce
78		from his second wife. He's put him on Prozac, he
79		says refer to social services for urgent
80		attent//ion
81	N1:	Nooo not =
82	TL:	= due to his chronic housing problem
83	SW3:	What is he looking at? What is his housing
84		problem? He's got a house
85	N2:	With nothing in it = heh hehh heh
86	N1:	= Nothing [in it heh ha heh]
87	SW3:	= The best thing to do now … (inaudible). Well he should
88		see a solicitor shouldn't he?
89	N1:	Yes, if he … What about STEPS, Desmond, for him?
90	TL:	Well you see, the tone of this suggests to me that his
91		alcohol abuse isn't the thing that's concerning him at
92		this point =
93	N1:	= No but that's what they all think at STEPS as well =
94	TL:	= Yeah that's right and he's presumably depressed
95		about his wife leaving him and seeking a divorce.
96	N1:	So what will we do, send Jane up for therapy
97		three times a week?
98	N3:	Yeah, Jane, get him another house
99	N1:	Get him a woman
100	N2:	Huh heeh/heh
101	N3:	By next week
102	N2:	Huummh heh
103	SW1:	Give him one
104	SW2:	Hehh heh heh heh Oh Jane =
105	N1:	⌈Huuh huuuh hu]uuh = No, you want to cure
106		him not kill him
107	TL:	You see, I mean, social services, for urgent
108		attention due to his chronic housing problem. Well have
109		we got any houses//then?
110	SW2:	Is it a chronic//prob
111	SW3:	Well, he's … He's got a house, a council house.
112		They won't give him another house =
113	N1:	No
114	TL:	[[There's … There's insufficient information here

Mulkay (1988) has suggested that humour depends on a juxtaposition of disparate elements in such a way that familiar patterns are challenged by other less obvious ones, so that an interpretive shift occurs. There is 'a sudden movement between, or unexpected combination of, distinct interpretive frames' (1988: 26). Sacks (1992) has described the way in which second speakers in arguments hold the stronger position as they are able to draw attention to weaknesses in the case being made by the first speaker. He pays special attention to the role of clarificatory questions, which, while hearable as a simple request for information, can also allow for the introduction of a new interpretation. Taken together these two ideas offer us a way of developing an explanation for the way humour is used in this team.

The inter-disciplinary nature of CMHTs means that members have available to them two discourses and thus two sense-making frameworks within which they can categorise patients. Social workers draw on a set of ideas which tend to 'normalise' or 'socialise' symptoms which might be presented within a medical model as evidence of mental illness. The nurses in the team move between this social discourse on symptoms and the medical discourse of the psychiatrists. The kind of interpretive shift between frames that Mulkay refers to often occurs as team members challenge the medical framing of the case by offering an alternative social framing packaged as humorous content. Typically, such interventions will suggest an interpretation of supporting case-report information which casts doubt on the appropriateness of the referral by poking fun at it. While the referral report de-personalises the 'case', the team's challenge reverses that process and reconstructs the case as a person with human motivations.

Coming from the second speaker's position, such challenges have the strength that they can be constructed elliptically as comments or questions requiring further clarification, rather than as a direct contradiction of the preceding formulation, and the risk to the speaker is further reduced by their overtly humorous nature. Unlike a serious evaluation which must be heard seriously and responded to, humorous challenges leave open the possibility that the next speaker will ignore the attempted frame shift and reassert the serious agenda of the meeting. Yet if sufficient support for the challenge can be mustered, a change of agenda may be forced. In *Extract I* the shift of frame comes as a nurse (N1) offers an evaluative comment, 'Good for her. Stolen his car. That's my girl!' (lines 6–8), after the first segment of the case presentation. Although this is ostensibly an evaluation of the action of the client's wife who has stolen his car, it also serves as a channel to mount a challenge to the referral as a serious matter.

Glenn (1995) draws a useful distinction between 'laughing at' and 'laughing with', which helps to shed light on the affiliative and disaffiliative functions of laughter in CMHTs. Glenn notes that conversational laughter contributes to displays of both alignment and distancing, but that 'which (if either) laughter helps accomplish at any particular moment may be displayed and redefined over several turns' at talk (1995: 43). In negotiating laughter's affiliative status, participants attend to: the nature of the utterance to which laughter refers ('the laughable'); the first laugh; any (possible) second laugh by another participant; and subsequent activities. In a typical 'laughing at' situation: the 'laughable' identifies some co-present member as the butt of a joke; the first laugh will be from the perpetrator or another participant (as opposed to the putative butt); there is shared laughter from others present (but not the butt); and subsequent talk continues on the topic taken up in the 'laughable', with possible attempts at repair.

The sequence that includes the 'Good for her' comment displays many of these features. Although the butt at first appears to be the referred patient (whose status as the kind of patient presented in the referral is cast in doubt), it becomes apparent that the absent psychiatrist ('What's he referred him for?'), and his proxy, the team leader ('Desmond's got empathy'), are also implicated. The first laugh (at line 7) comes not from the staff member who produces the humorous challenge (N1) but from a second community psychiatric nurse (N2). One may hypothesise that, in the hierarchical CMHT context, there are advantages for the perpetrator of a 'laughable', in terms of minimising the risk of offending superiors, if the first laugh comes from another team member. When a social worker (SW1) uses irony to extend the joke at lines 10–11 ('that's possibly the worst thing a woman could do') and joins in with the second laugh at line 14, it is clear that at least three participants support the challenge. The team leader takes up the joking tone with his comment at lines 15–16 that it is not only the car but 'his jacket as well'. In the subsequent talk the joking tone is amplified and another nurse (N3) becomes involved (line 24). A shared team alignment begins to emerge, which is at odds with the account of the case contained in the referral letter. Team members construct an alternative version which highlights the tragi-comic elements of the wife's appropriation of domestic property, the assault of the wife by the husband, and the current situation of a man living in an empty house and affected by heavy drinking and depression.

A significant shift in the direction of the interaction comes at line 30. In continuing the joke ('I feel sorry for this chap'), and laughing with the team, which serves affiliative functions for him as he selects the role of team member, the team leader opens the way for other members to raise the issue of the point of the referral. N1's sarcastic question about the nature of the diagnosis (line 33), and N2's mocking answer that the team leader has 'got empathy there' (line 34), threatens to turn the joke on him. The team leader risks being 'laughed at' and distanced from the rest of the team, while at the same time having lost the authority he might have retained by resisting the earlier frame shift to the humorous mode. He tries to steer talk back to the serious business of the referral by quoting from the psychiatrist's letter, but other team members respond by asserting the basic normality of the case (and by implication the absence of underlying mental illness) culminating in the suggestion that the problem is 'poverty' (lines 44–5, 47, 61, 71). This takes place in a stretch of talk where the team leader's paraphrasings of the psychiatrists' points are challenged, and in which team members eventually move to offer alternative suggestions for action (seeing a solicitor and referral to a voluntary agency – STEPS). These suggestions support the construction that the case is not suitable for treatment by the team. At lines 107–9 the team leader changes tack by acknowledging the inappropriateness of the CMHT referral for what is presented as a 'housing problem'. He finally suggests that there is 'insufficient information' to proceed (line 114). Later the discussion moves on to the type of advice or help that this client could get, and the need for a policy to cover referrals of this kind. The social work team leader is obliged to take the case back to the psychiatrist, but has managed to re-formulate the problem as one of lack of information – something that can be communicated to the psychiatrist with less risk of offence than straightforward refusal to accept the case.

The dynamic of meetings in *Team A* is substantially shaped by the communication of information between absent psychiatrist, mediating team leader and team. Rank-and-file team members use humorous comments to signal their unease about certain referrals to the team leader, who must then choose whether to respond to this by delaying acceptance of the referral. The team leader's position as the link between team and psychiatrist gives rise to a difficult dilemma: an over-close identification with the psychiatrist risks negative reaction from the team, but open opposition is even more damaging because it challenges the operative system of referral and allocation. To maintain credibility with team members the team leader needs to be seen to have a degree of detachment from the psychiatrist, but – at the same time – must chair meetings in a way that ensures that the process of referral and allocation continues to be taken seriously. In *Extract 1*, the team leader is able to distance himself from the referral by locating the psychiatrist as its author, and even commenting negatively on the reasonableness of its content: 'Well have we got any houses then?' (lines 108–9). This technique is used on several occasions by this team leader, who has a social work institutional affiliation which is problematised at times by his 'managerial' role in this team.

Negotiating laughter's affiliative status

In *Team B*, humour is again a resource that less powerful team members can put to work to question the psychiatrist's definitions and preferred course of action. *Extract 2* involves a male client who is significantly underweight and complains of a variety of illness conditions, for which no physical basis has been established. The case is little different from cases referred back in *Team A* as inappropriate or requiring more information, and team members use similar strategies to communicate scepticism. However, in *Team B* the psychiatrist (P) is present to respond to team members' humorous jibes and resist their attempts to reframe the situation.

Extract 2

1	P:	I mean I think a lot of it is driven by him
2		consciously, and it's malingering and it's manipulating
3		things. But I'm sure there's an unconscious element
4		here, gaining a lot. I mean I was asking him how it's
5		affected his life, this not being able to hold solids
6		down and the story was like that he spends his time on the
7		sofa, watching TV and sipping this high calorie stuff
8	N1:	Yeah, I asked him if he went out and he said, no, he
9		said, I can't, I'm not strong enough to walk
10	P:	Good, good, so I mean I thought that was it, if there
11		was anything we could do it's to look at that, at the
12		secondary gain that he's getting, that you know, he
13		has … he's ill and therefore he doesn't have to do
14		anything in the house or anywhere else, he just sits
15		there ((multi-turn segment omitted))
16		Okay. I mean I wonder just, er if we've any input it's
17		to look at the secondary gain for him and … and try and
18		push him out of the house. I mean I'm aware that it's
19		probably … I mean it's attention he wants. I think it's
20		some form of attention … some form of intervention
21	SW1:	Where does he live, John?
22	N1:	Hmmmmmp?
23	SW1:	Where does he live?
24	N1:	Redbridge

25	SW1:	Redbridge. Oooh get him to the club man. Cos he could
26		come to the club if we get him off the sofa
27	N1:	Yeah get him on the bus, it's right on the main//road
28		((inaudible overlap)) Yeah =
29	N1:	= nearly opposite Val
30	SW1:	Is it? Right. We ought to get her to go there,
31	N1:	He heh heh heh
32	P:	heh heh heh
33	SW1:	She'd sort him out. heh heh heh heh
34	P:	⌈heh heh heh
35	N1:	⌈heh hheh
36	N2:	⌈heh heh//hehh
37	SW1:	And have some cash heh heeh
38	N1:	⌈Yeh ha heh heh heh =
39	P:	= But I think if there's one thing we could do, it's
40		that: look at the secondary gain and try and shift
41		that. Like get him involved with things
42	SW1:	Yes =
43	P:	= Because I can imagine he just drifts from place to
44		place with his symptoms and he sits in a certain area
45		for a certain space of time and goes into the hospital
46		and he gets attention and then whenever he gets known =
47	SW1:	= Hmmm =
48	P:	= and he gets a bit of negative feedback he moves on
49		somewhere. But I mean that's like a typical
50		Munchausen's. All that energy and drive to get
51		attention, if you could divert it somewhere else, he'd
52		be Prime Minister.
53	SW1:	hm//hhhmmmm
54	N2:	heh heh
55	P:	But I wonder if that's . . . if that's probably all. I mean
56		I said to the GP that that's all we're going to be able
57		to do. And I said to him like you know anything else
58		is going to be counter-productive. If it gets to the
59		point where he does collapse and it's a real collapse,
60		then he's need to go to a medical ward to be re-fed ahm
61		but not here.
62	SW1:	Would he come to the club Phil?
63	N1:	Well I didn't ask him really, I asked him about his
64		social life and he said he didn't have much social life
65	SW1:	Well tell him then, tell him that we . . . we've got the
66		ambulance calling up the valley to pick him up. heh
67		heh heh heh
68	N1:	⌈Heh heh heh
69	N2:	⌈yeah heh heh
70	P:	That's . . . that's in a sense, I mean . . . The thing about
71		this chap, that that's a more socially acceptable =
72	N2:	= Yes =

```
 73  P:       = place and it's more acceptable for him. It's
 74            intervention, it's help and it's him being special,
 75            which is all these sort of issues that go round chaps
 76            like this. I mean maybe =
 77  N2:      = Tell him they'll drip feed him down there. heh heh
 78            heh
 79  N1:      ⌈Heh
 80  SW1:     ⌊Heh heh heh
 81  P:       Tell him it's a special club for you know whatever
 82  N2:                    ⌊shove him on the bus⌋
 83  N1:      For malingerers
 84  N2:      Heh heh heh heh heh heh heh
 85  SW1:        ⌊heh hchh hch heh heh
 86  P:              ⌊heh heh
 87  N1:             ⌊heh heh hehh heh heh
 88  P:       I think that =
 89  SW1:     = Would be great for the patient heh//heh
 90  N1:      heh heh heh.
 91  N2:         ⌊huuh heh heh
 92  P:       I mean he's malingering, but there's always an
 93            unconscious element to these people
 94  SW1:                    ⌈Yes⌉
 95  N2:        Hmmm
 96  N1:      ⌈⌈Yes
 97  P:       I mean you can get like ((pause)) I'm sure there is a
 98            hysterical conversion bit to this chap
 99  N1:      Hmmm
100  P:       You know he shifts all over the place ... the way he
101            shifts his symptoms is so typical of that
102  N1:      That's right
103  P:       I think if he was a straightforward malingerer, I mean
104            maybe I'll get to the point of saying that, I don't
105            know. But I have a feeling he's typical Munchausen's
106  N2:      Hmmmmmmm =
107  P:       = That what you need to do is just say, yeah, you've got
108            a problem, we'll help you with it, and if the help is
109            just getting him to the club or whatever, getting him
110            involved somewhere, just getting him out of the house,
111            I think maybe is all we can do, yeah?
112  N1:      Mmmmmm
113  P:       But I'll send you the ... I've got a file here
114            which I haven't written up, I'll do it
```

Here the interplay between the medical and social definitions of psychiatrist and team members overlaps with attempts by the psychiatrist to preserve the medical frame as serious, and by social worker and nurse to juxtapose elements of a humorous frame that pokes fun at the patient and challenges the medical interpretation of the case. As in *Extract 1*, some team members appear doubtful about the presence of psychiatric pathology. Scepticism is introduced by the social worker's query at lines 25–6 about the difficulty of getting the patient 'off the sofa', and the joking observation that a second patient (Val) living nearby would 'sort him out' (with its obvious sexual innuendo). The remarks elicit laughter from several team members. The psychiatrist attempts to re-assert the primacy of the medical framework by talking of the need to 'look at the secondary gain' (line 40) and formulating the patient's behaviour as 'his symptoms' (44). 'Secondary gain' here is used as a technical term which is represented as a symptom of mental illness rather than being used as a moral evaluation. He suggests that the patient is 'typical Munchausen's' (lines 49–50), and talks of the possibility of a 'real collapse' (line 59). However, the psychiatrist's attempted return to the medical frame is resisted as the social worker produces another joke (lines 65–7). Once again he gets others to join in the laughter, and once again the psychiatrist tries to re-assert the serious medical agenda (line 70). But a CPN (N2) again brings talk back within the humorous frame in line 77 ('they'll drip feed him down there'). [. . .]

In line 92 the psychiatrist moves forcefully to regain the floor. He acknowledges that the team's version has some validity ('I mean he's malingering'), but sets this within the context of 'hysterical conversion' and the typical symptomatology of an established disease syndrome (Munchausen's). In this he receives support from N2 and N1, who produce appreciations to signal agreement with his account (lines 95, 96, 99, 102, 106, 112). While it is not clear that the dissenting members are wholly convinced, the psychiatric definition is publicly sustained, and the psychiatrist's suggestions for action are enforced. [. . .]

The above exchange highlights the continuing reality of professional dominance in the apparently democratic context of the *Team B* setting. While the psychiatrist stops short of any bald assertion of decision-making authority in the face of the humorous challenge, he carries the argument by emphasising his specialist expertise in psychiatric diagnosis (notably through his references to the typicality of symptoms). This is an effective tactic, though one that may have negative consequences for team unity if repeated too often. Challenges to definitions which are framed humorously are permissible since they allow for the withdrawal of the challenge without loss of face on the part of the challenger. However, a challenge made outside this frame and based on claims to superior expertise, for example, would pose a serious threat, both to the psychiatrist's expert status and to the cooperative ethos of teamwork. The psychiatrist's problem is that excessive emphasis on specialist medical knowledge will also have negative consequences by devaluing the contribution of the other disciplines to the team enterprise.

[. . .]

Conclusion

[. . .] CMHTs are clearly organisations which manifest a high degree of paradox and strain. They are intended to exemplify team working, but must also accommodate existing occupational hierarchies and the professional power of the psychiatrists. The need to work closely together is contradicted, not just by status differences, but also by different disciplinary perspectives that favour different explanations of mental illness. Team members are bound together by the need to conform with the current orthodoxy in mental health policy, but – because the teams are so new – have not fully worked out their respective roles and decision-making powers. Humour reflects these paradoxes and strains. It helps rank-and-file team members to support each other in dissent, and communicates their dissatisfaction to organisational superiors. Superordinates, too, join in the banter to avoid being marginalised and to try to deal with implicit challenges packaged as jokes. [...]

Acknowledgement

I am grateful to David Silverman, David Hughes and the anonymous referees of the Journal for comments on an earlier version of the paper.

References

Glenn, P. (1995) Laughing at and laughing with: negotiations of participant alignments through conversational laughter. In ten Have, P. and Psathas, G. (eds), *Situated Order: Studies in the Social Organisation of Talk and Embodied Activities, Studies in Ethnomethodology and Conversational Analysis No. 3*. Lanham, Maryland: International Institute for Ethnomethodology and Conversation Analysis and University Press of America.

Lipsky, M. (1980) *Street-Level Bureaucracy. Dilemmas of the Individual in Public Services*. New York: Russell Sage Foundation.

Mulkay, M. J. (1988) *On Humour: Its Nature and Its Place in Modern Society*. Cambridge: Polity.

Sacks, H. (1992) *Lectures on Conversation*, 2 volumes (edited by Jefferson, G.). Oxford: Blackwell.

25

The State and Complementary Medicine: A Changing Relationship?

Sarah Cant and Ursula Sharma

[If] the relationship between the orthodox medical profession and the state has been exclusive, where does this leave complementary medicine? We could conceive of complementary medical practice as entirely marginal to the interests of the state and history would suggest we should draw the same conclusion. The exclusion of complementary medicines from the NHS in 1948 was disastrous for their practice, and it is at this time that we see the decline in number of practitioners.[1] There are also instances of damaging legislation such as that which banned the use of the comfrey herb (Whitelegg 1996). Notwithstanding such evidence, it is possible to locate occasions when the government has acted in a more favourable way – although these are few and far between – for example, the BMA was not able to prevent the entry of spiritual healers to the NHS in the 1950s and 1960s (Inglis 1980). The last decade has seen increasing instances of supportive action by the state, partly generated no doubt by the increased interest in complementary medicine by consumers, so that it is possible to ask whether the orthodox medical profession–state relationship has run its course, to be replaced by a more pluralistic phase.

Larkin (1983) suggests that practitioner groups have historically attempted to break the state–physician alliance by relying on three strategies: first, through public support, secondly, by securing a Royal Charter and inclusion under the Companies Act, or thirdly, by state registration.[2] Within complementary medicine it is the first strategy that has been used most widely until recent times. Indeed, the twentieth century has largely been characterized by the thwarted attempts of complementary medical groups to gain recognition from the state. At a time when the registration of midwives (1902), nurses (1919), dentists (1921) were successful, albeit placing them in subordinate positions in the medical division of labour, the complementary therapists met with no success. The osteopaths and herbalists made several submissions during the 1920s and 1930s (Larkin 1996), but were dismissed with incredulity. Larkin shows that this dismissal was the product of the state's use of the medical profession as advisors. The herbalists, for example,

> discovered that what they regarded as their correspondence with the Minister of Health in fact was being passed onto the General Medical Council (GMC) to advise the Ministry of Health, and in turn being relayed to the pharmacy profession to stimulate its opposition in addition to that of the medical profession. (Larkin 1996:49)

[...] The 1980s and 1990s have been witness to a changing relationship between the state and complementary medicine in Britain. In 1989 the All Party Group for Complementary and Alternative Medicine was set up with the remit to prevent damaging legislation and to promote the use of complementary medicine within the NHS (PGACM 1993). A research study conducted for the Research Council of Complementary Medicine assessed the general degree of support for complementary medicine by Members of Parliament (RCCM 1992) and revealed high degrees of support for therapies to be included in the NHS, especially osteopathy (74 per cent), acupuncture (62 per cent), chiropractic (50 per cent) and homoeopathy (53 per cent). Levels of support did, however, vary when controlled for party affiliation, Labour MPs being more supportive.

When we turn our attention to specific responses that have emanated from government we see there have been three policy initiatives that have had knock on effects for complementary medicine. In the first place, following the NHS reforms (1990) the then Junior Minister for Health, Steven Dorrell, was asked to clarify the position for complementary medicine. His statement confirmed that GP fundholders could use their budgets to purchase complementary medical services. [...]

Secondly, a number of statements have been issued regarding the criteria under which the government might contemplate the statutory registration of complementary medicine. The expected criteria were that the therapy should be based on a systematic body of knowledge, there should be voluntary registration in place that embraced an appropriate and enforceable code of conduct, the profession should exhibit unity and finally should have the support of the medical profession (HMSO 1987). Since that time we have seen the successful passing of the Osteopaths and Chiropractors Acts. The acupuncturists and homoeopaths were also, at the time of writing, in the process of preliminary discussions.

Thirdly, the NHS reforms have given the opportunity to reorientate health care services, in particular, a large number of Family Health Service Authorities (FHSAs) are using the 'health promotion clinic' budget to support complementary therapists. A study undertaken by NAHAT in 1992 estimated that £1m of the NHS budget, a small sum in the light of the overall expenditure on health, had been spent on complementary medical services (NAHAT 1993).

Generally then, the Conservative Government made some positive overtures to the complementary therapists. The Labour Government, elected in 1997, had published a discussion document about complementary medical services prior to election which suggested stronger commitment, with calls for strategic policy to integrate osteopathy, chiropractic and acupuncture into the NHS (Primarolo 1992) and the establishment of an Office for Complementary Medicine through the Department of Health.

This shift in attitude towards complementary medicine is not peculiar to Britain alone and in many instances the UK has in fact lagged behind other countries. In the United States, some individual states have allowed certain groups (e.g. trained acupuncturists) to practice independently of the medical profession (Saks 1995). Chiropractic has achieved state regulation in all American states since 1974 although the realities of this regulation vary, in some states for instance, the medical profession retains control and has dictated the content of chiropractic education. Chiropractic has also attracted state regulation in Australia (Willis 1989), Canada (Coburn & Biggs 1986) and New Zealand. [...]

How might we explain this intensified interest? One explanation must hinge on economic factors. There has been increasing global concern about the escalating costs of medical care, not only the rise of health budgets (at a time when the range and application of health care becomes increasingly wide) but also the time and money lost on intractable conditions, those not amenable to cure by the medical profession. It was in the light of such concerns that the Back Pain Group was inaugurated in 1976 in the UK (Baer 1984b) with the remit to assess other services that might be more cost effective. [...] Secondly, it is possible that the development of other therapies fill a gap in supply of medical personnel and certainly this is the explanation given by Baer (1984a) for the inclusion of chiropractic in the United States. This interpretation would appear to lack the same explanatory power in the United Kingdom. Thirdly, it could be that the government is responding to popular opinion (the therapists and their patients have been involved in very well orchestrated lobbying, e.g. letter writing campaign by chiropractic patients). It is no surprise that the softening of the government's approach coincided with the publication of numerous polls that showed the public support for and use of other services. Other strategic elites may also have been influential, the Royal Family being the most public supporter of complementary medicine[3] in the UK, and certainly the medical profession has become more open to the development of complementary medicine. We explore the explanatory power of these factors and the extent to which the support of a plural health market can be witnessed in a detailed case study of chiropractic in the UK. We detail the steps that were required by the group themselves, the response of the medical profession and the actual rewards of state support.

The chiropractors: a case study

After over 60 years of campaigning, 1993 saw the passing of the Osteopaths Act and 1994 saw the chiropractors receive similar state regulation. Yet, it was only in 1991 that Baer concluded his study of these two therapeutic modalities with, 'in the foreseeable future the Conservative government is unlikely to grant statutory recognition ... particularly as independent practitioners' (Baer 1991:45). What produced this apparent sea change in the government's approach to complementary medicine?

Origins and history of chiropractic

Chiropractic is the third largest primary health care profession in the world after medicine and dentistry (Wardwell 1992). In the UK, despite the small number of members (900 in March 1994), it is the most widely used complementary approach after osteopathy and it has been estimated that chiropractors see 75,000 patients a week (HMSO 1994a). Chiropractic was actually 'discovered' in 1895 by Daniel David Palmer who had experimented with the manipulation of vertebrae, and the technique was imported to the UK in the early 1920s.

There has also been an on-going division within chiropractic relating to scope of practice. A consensus exists that chiropractic has the ability to resolve musculoskeletal conditions – 'type M' problems. However, it was also believed, by the early chiropractors and a body of the profession today, that energy from the brain is transmitted by the spinal cord and then to every organ in the body. Any abnormal function in organs has also been associated with subluxations at specific levels of the spine and so can be alleviated by manipulation. Thus, chiropractic has been said to alleviate 'type O' (organic) problems.

Competition from the osteopaths, who put a bill before parliament in 1925, prompted the then 19 British chiropractors to form the British Chiropractic Association (BCA). The coming of the NHS proved problematic for chiropractic because they were no longer covered by insurance and consequently the profession went into decline. As a result of this descent in popularity the BCA decided to shift to a broader range of technical chiropractic methods, rejecting their previous adherence to the 'straight' technique (Copeland Griffiths 1991). In 1965, the Anglo-European College of Chiropractic (AECC) opened its doors prepared to teach these various methods of chiropractic and significantly, in May 1988, the Council for National and Academic Awards (CNAA) accredited the course, making the AECC the first college of complementary or alternative medicine in Europe to offer a validated degree.

The operation of common law in the UK has meant that the BCA could not prevent other schools and practitioners setting up practice. There are currently two other forms of chiropractic in the UK (McTimoneys and McTimoney Corleys) which both conform to a 'straight' form of practice with concentration on a single technique of manipulation.

This description is by way of background to the latest successful claim made by chiropractic to gain state regulation. A review of the BCA newsletters reveals that it was during 1988 that debates about regulation were renewed (an earlier submission had been made to the Professions Supplementary to Medicine in 1975 but had been rejected) because the BCA committee were anxious to police the profession:

> We need a protected title, every Tom, Dick and Harry can come under our banner, I mean ten years ago there wasn't any McTimoney, if we had had regulation then... well we didn't, and it's not going to be as easy now, because we have to unify with them... we want to come in line with other recognized bodies so that we can police the profession and get basic standards. (Cant & Sharma 1994)

Making ready for registration

Following the regulation criteria set down by the government in 1987, it was recognized that to even begin a regulation campaign the three groups of chiropractors needed to come together and agree about standards. This was not going to be an easy task; for years the BCA membership had berated the McTimoneys and indeed wanted state regulation simply to get rid of this competition. Despite their differences the groups came together, convened a steering group (later a limited company) and worked very well together constituting, in effect, an umbrella body to represent the profession.

Unification was only part of the project to make themselves acceptable to the state. The preparations also included being able to prove they had a legitimate and scientific approach. This requirement has not been peculiar to Britain, indeed there have been international attempts to de-emphasize the more controversial elements of their treatment and secure a scientific paradigm to underpin their techniques (Coburn 1991). In other words, chiropractic has developed into a musculo-skeletal speciality. This is the way that the BCA portray themselves in their public relations literature:

> The zealous and unsupportable assertion of many chiropractors was that vertebral subluxation influencing the nervous system was the source of all or most of disease. This is as historical as the then current medical technique, bloodletting with the leech. This skeleton in the cupboard, rattled by a fringe movement of extremists as exist in any profession, has sometimes been the barrier to understanding and co-operation between the chiropractor and medical profession... no responsible chiropractor today claims to cure organic disease through adjustment of the spine. (BCA 1993)

Moreover, the BCA has also consciously aligned chiropractic to established scientific theory. As one member of the BCA stated:

> The biggest obstacle to increasing the therapy's potential is having an adequate knowledge base to fit to your hypotheses. I mean with the greatest respect to the homoeopaths their model is flawed, our model is based on standard orthopaedic principles and biomedical principles, so it is not our model – it's somebody else's that has been validated.
>
> (Interviewer) So you borrowed a model?
>
> Stolen basically... we know we are empirically correct and now we have the science to prove it, the reason other therapies hate science is that they know they are correct but can't prove it. We are lucky that our empirical results are being supported by theory.

In other words, the chiropractors have linked themselves to the established medical paradigm. As in other countries, the development of chiropractic has been characterized by a *public* narrowing of practice and philosophy and the adoption of the scientific paradigm.

The medical profession – a steel fist in a velvet glove?

Until recently [...] the attitude of the medical profession towards complementary medicine in general has been unfavourable. This has taken the form of attempts to discredit the therapies as quackery. For example, [...] in the 1986 BMA report, chiropractic was described as follows:

> chiropractic... stem(s) from particular beliefs about the nature and causation of disease... These systems are incompatible with the corpus of scientific knowledge, and must be rejected by anyone who accepts the validity of the latter. (BMA 1986:35)

An uproar followed the publication of the BMA report and this may have served to temper the reactions of the medical profession as the discreditation model had been shown to lack strength. The latest BMA report (1993) is certainly more favourable. In response to 'discrete clinical disciplines' (such as homoeopathy and chiropractic) the report does not cast judgement about their efficacy but suggests that they should be subject to statutory regulation so as to ensure high standards and training and that medical science should be included in a core curriculum. There is a recognition that orthodox practitioners' training may be insufficient in these areas and that general practitioners and complementary therapists should work together.

While we have shown that the attitude of the medical profession has been changing, the BCA representative suggested that the medical profession had to be wooed by the chiropractors.

> We deliberately did not go straight and officially to the medical profession, because I think had we done that we would have run into opposition because if it had gone to a committee there would have bound to have been someone or several on the committee who would have been opposed and would have stopped it moving forward...it was important not to get a 'no' answer, you have to be non-confrontational. I have acted like this for our profession.

It was thus decided that the best thing was to win the medical profession round in more relaxed and informal circumstances...those of a dinner party:

> I had this idea, because the Prince of Wales had got people together from the medical profession before in a dinner party situation, that this was the way we could do it. Fortunately I knew X who had arranged previous dinner parties and he agreed to help, so we invited key people and the Kings Fund, and they all came. This was after the M R C trial and it was pretty clear that they supported us...After this the Department of Health decided that we appeared to have the support of the medical profession.

To summarize then, the attitude of the medical profession has undergone significant change and it appears that their support has been secured. This was not an easy or straightforward task but required extensive networking and was dependent to some degree upon the energy and persistence of the chair of the steering group and positive scientific results. Acceptance by the medical profession has meant compromise. Chiropractic has portrayed itself as a specialist and fitted into a gap in the medical market (back pain), an area in which the medical profession has had little success.

State registration and its provisions

The Chiropractors Bill was passed easily in 1994 and makes the provision for regulation, high standards of education and protection of the title of chiropractor, in the name of safeguarding the patient.[...]

In essence, this regulation provides for a *state supported profession in the private sector*. Moreover, a monopoly was not granted, rather it was clearly stated that other groups could practice chiropractic:

> The Bill protect(s) the title chiropractor...and makes it a criminal offence for other than a registered practitioner to call himself by that name. I know that provision interests many related professions. I confirm that it is not intended to prevent other professions...from using chiropractic techniques in the course of their treatment and from telling their patients that they are using such techniques. (HMSO 1994b:1169)

[A]nd certainly there is nothing in the law to stop practitioners calling themselves a 'bonesetter', for example, and practising chiropractic techniques.

What explanations can be provided for this statutory support? First, the issue of cost was certainly raised in the parliamentary debate:

> 310,000 people in the United Kingdom are off work each day with back pain. That costs the country more than £3 billion a year in lost production. Disability from lower back pain is increasing faster than any other form of disability. (HMSO 1994b:1184)

[A]nd references were made to the Medical Research Council (MRC) report which compared the outcomes of chiropractic treatment with outpatient hospital treatment and concluded:

> For patients with low back pain in whom manipulation is not contraindicated chiropractic almost certainly confers worthwhile, long-term benefit in comparison with hospital outpatient management. (Meade et al. 1990)

The government sponsorship was limited only to registration and was not concerned to extend any financial commitments and there were certainly no plans to provide blanket funding for chiropractic:

> The overwhelming majority of chiropractors practise in the private sector and that position is unlikely to alter even if the Bill succeeds. (HMSO 1994b:1176)

Nor was there provision for educational grants. So, while it was hoped the Bill would increase collaboration with orthodoxy there was no discussion of bringing chiropractic into the NHS. Rather, there was a direct linkage of chiropractic practice to the private sector:

> I hope the Bill will encourage more private insurers to cover chiropractic treatment, because they will judge it more cost effective than orthodox medical treatment. (HMSO 1994b:1181)

However, at a practical level, there are only a small number of chiropractors (900 at our last count) who are not dispersed evenly throughout the country. Thus, state regulation has not made the service more available to the public despite the arguments about the clinical and cost effectiveness of the approach.

Secondly, the incorporation of chiropractic has not challenged the current direction of health care. Chiropractic, as in other parts of the world, has taken on board a narrower definition of practice. Whereas state regulation may encourage a more favourable attitude on the part of purchasing GPs, the funding and health care system have not altered. Thus, chiropractors who want to take state patients will be dependent upon the GP as a gatekeeper. As such they will, in the final analysis, be subject to the attitudes of individual GPs and will be employed in a delegated role, with patients and problems defined by the GP. Stacey (1994) has warned that the advantages and disadvantages of state registration balance out differently for each therapy but that on the whole the price of state registration has been subordination to biomedicine. The disadvantages will, in the long run, depend on the extent to which each therapy sees its position in relation to biomedicine. Those that see themselves as truly complementary will have fewer problems. For others, registration may restrict the way they practice and only afford them a small space in the market and provide little more than boundary definition. Thus, by specializing, the chiropractors, like the dentists, have been bestowed a 'part' of the body but, in the final analysis, may not have autonomy and control over this area. We see then that the state has been involved in the refiguring of expertise but without a radical change in the complexion of the health services.

Finally, the impact of public opinion and the more favourable attitude of the BMA were important contextual changes that must account partly for the more favourable attitude of the government. The chiropractors engaged their supporters in a massive letter writing campaign to MPs that heightened the awareness of the therapy. This, of course, occurred under a Conservative Government, who, as we have seen, were less influenced by professional advice and more by the mandate from the public and at a time of broader crisis for universalistic welfare provision.

Conclusions

The preceding discussion points to a number of shifts in governmental responses to complementary medicine, particularly changes to the content of medical care and context in which policy decisions are made. Historically, health care provision could be depicted as plural, simply by virtue of the inattention of the government. This shifted in the nineteenth century with a state–physician alliance, to monopolistic control by orthodox medicine, and more recently we have seen a refiguring of expertise. These changes are not peculiar to Britain and seem to have occurred even in countries with very different systems of government, partly, of course, because they have been consumer led. How pervasive are these changes and what are the implications for complementary medicine, the medical profession, and the intervention of the state in health matters?

Paradoxically, an ideology that supports the rolling back of the state coexists with a situation where governments are passing legislation to regulate therapies. This regulation has often tended to curtail practice and bring it in line with more medical definitions of the therapy. At the same time the increased state jurisdiction has not been activated by the orthodox medical profession alone, rather the state has taken account of public demand (it has had to pursue policies that society demands) and broader economic decisions relating to cost curtailment. However, the influence of an ideological commitment to neoclassical economics does not suffice in our explanation of these changes. [. . .] [S]tate intervention is also propelled by the need to constrain and regulate the population. Therefore, the changes in the government's response should be seen as the product of the need to balance public demand with economic constraint and the prerequisite that there be social stability. Drawing on the contradictions of capitalism (specifically the need to curtail costs) and upon Foucault's concept of governmentality, we suggest that we are witnessing the restructuring of expertise. [. . .] [I]n Foucault's conception, the state and the medical profession are not separate entities but rather are intimately entwined, thus the professionalization of medicine cannot simply be explained by the success of its occupational strategies but rather as the institutionalization of expertise that is crucial to governmentality – the regulation and surveillance and normalization of populations. [. . .]

The shift in the government's response can be understood as the refiguring of this governmentality. At the same time it is no coincidence that the organizational framework for this refiguring has been established in the private sector.

Practically, we have seen the refiguring of expertise as the government has intervened to ratify who is a legitimate provider. This is a significant change. Previously patients of chiropractors would choose their practitioner by word of mouth and recommendation. In other words, the charisma of the therapist (Cant 1996) and perceived success of the treatments provided by the practitioners would have been influential. Now we have a situation of the state identifying which practitioners may be viewed as 'expert', based on training, credentials and internal organization. Thus, new criteria underpin the legitimacy of provider groups, and the clinical legitimacy as simply experienced by patient is less important. The state has stepped in to legislate where consumers did so before.

There has been a refiguring of exactly what types of expertise will attract state support. Orthodox medicine is no longer the only medical provider to receive sponsorship, indeed there has been some depreciation of the claims to expertise on behalf of the orthodox medical profession. Markets have not been freed, as neoclassical economists would have us believe, but restructured. The state has reduced direct provision but allowed the restructuring (albeit limited) of expertise in new ways, which has had some knock on effects for the jurisdiction of orthodox medicine and the relations between orthodox and complementary medicine. More broadly [...], with the intervention of the European Union, there has been an 'internationalization' of expertise in the context of a single market.

So, to reiterate, why has there been a need to refigure the expertise? Certainly there has been a loss of faith in orthodox medicine, and governments have needed to confront the problems of financial crisis and chronic illness. There has been a balancing of a number of contradictory demands, between those financial constraints of capitalism, the need to order and survey the population and yet also the need to respond to civil demands. As Johnson (1993) points out, the perception of the consumer has been incredibly important:

> Government initiated reform has, in these recent reforms, been securely linked with the political commitment to the 'sovereign consumer'. In the case of reform in the NHS, this translates into a shift of behaviour from the primary obligation of the sick to seek medical advice, as a means of social control, to a new set of obligations including the stress on prevention, the obligation to care for the self by adopting a healthy lifestyle...The changes initiated in state-expert government structures are, then, the product of new policy goals which include as part of the process, changing the way the citizen-subject normally relates to health care provision. (Johnson 1993: 149)

The passing of the osteopaths and chiropractors acts served to 'normalize' their practice and legitimate their extended use. What we have seen, then, are changes to the boundaries of what is acceptable medical practice, a settlement that has tried to limit the demands upon the public purse and has rearticulated the state–profession relationship to create a new set of techniques and roles for the purposes of governmentality.

Why have only certain therapies, particularly, osteopathy and chiropractic, been endorsed in this way? In the first place, they do not significantly challenge orthodox medicine, indeed their acceptance has hinged on the therapies taking on board orthodox science and training [. . .] However, it is possible to envisage a scenario in the future where other therapies may become more legitimate (certainly, the government in Britain and elsewhere has accepted the practice of other therapies and encouraged their use so long as practitioners are self regulated), especially those that emphasize healthy living and preventative medicine. [. . .]

Overall, we have seen changes to the practices of government. The government has responded to consumer demand, the need to cut costs, the failures of orthodox medicine and in addition, has extended its regulative agenda. Consequently, the developments have often been contradictory, on the one hand we see the support of groups but on the other they are insufficiently financed. The consequence has been a refiguring of expertise rather than a radical alteration to the system of health care delivery.

Notes

1 The number of chiropractors dwindled at this time; see Gaucher-Peslherbe (1986).
2 Groups can of course be self-regulated, have state-sanctioned self-regulation or be directly administered by the state. Our discussion related to state-sanctioned self-regulation.
3 The Royal Family has always supported homoeopathy. Prince Charles has been involved in private talks with representatives of the main complementary therapies and Lady Diana (as she was then) gave her support to the Chiropractors' campaign for state support.

References

Baer, H. 1984a. A comparative view of a heterodox health system: chiropractic in America and Britain. *Medical Anthropology* 8, 151–68.
Baer, H. 1984b. The drive for professionalisation in British osteopathy. *Social Science and Medicine* 19 (7), 717–25.
Baer, H. 1991. The socio-political development of British chiropractic. *Journal of Manipulative and Physiological Therapeutics* 14 (1), 38–45.
British Chiropractic Association 1993. *Chiropractic Report Special Issue* BCA No. 7, 3.
British Medical Association 1986. *Alternative Therapy Report of the Board of Science and Education*. London: BMA.
British Medical Association 1993. *Complementary Medicine. New Approaches to Good Practice*. Oxford: Oxford University Press/BMA.
Budd, S. & U. Sharma (eds) 1994. *The Healing Bond*. London: Routledge.
Cant, S. 1996. From charismatic teaching to professional training. See Cant & Sharma (1996), 44–66.
Cant, S. & U. Sharma 1994. *The Professionalisation of Complementary Medicine*. Project report to ESRC.
Cant, S. & U. Sharma (eds) 1996. *Complementary and Alternative Medicines. Knowledge in Practice*. London: Free Association Books.
Coburn, D. 1991. Legitimacy at the expense of narrowing of scope of practice: chiropractic in Canada. *Journal of Manipulative and Physiological Therapeutics* 14 (1), 14–21.
Coburn, D. & L. Biggs 1986. Limits to medical dominance: the case of chiropractic. *Social Science and Medicine* 22, 1035–46.
Copeland Griffiths, M. 1991. *Dynamic Chiropractic Today*. New York: Thorsons.

Gaucher-Peslherbe, P. 1986. Chiropractic as a profession in Europe. *Journal of Manipulative and Physiological Therapeutics* 15 (2), 323–30.

HMSO 1987. *Hansard* 489, cols 1379–1416.

HMSO 1994a. *Chiropractors Act*. London: HMSO.

HMSO 1994b. *Hansard* Feb., [cols] 1168–1222.

Inglis, B. 1980. *Natural Medicine*. Glasgow: Fontana.

Johnson, T. 1993. Expertise and the State. In *Foucault's New Domain*, Gane, M. & T. Johnson (eds), pp. 139–53. London: Routledge.

Larkin, G. 1983. *Occupational Monopoly and Modern Medicine*. London: Tavistock.

Larkin. G. 1996. State control and the health profession in the United Kingdom: historical perspectives. See Johnson, Larkin, Saks (1996), 45–55.

Meade, T., S. Dyer, W. Browne, J. Townsend, A. Frank 1990. Low back pain of mechanical origin: randomised comparison of chiropractic and hospital outpatient treatment. *British Medical Journal* 300 (6737), 1431–7.

National Association of Health Authorities and Trusts 1993. *Complementary Therapies in the NHS*. Birmingham: NAHAT.

Party Parliamentary Group for Alternative and Complementary Medicine 1993. PGACM Newsletter vol. 1.

Primarolo, D. 1992. *Complementary Therapies with the NHS*. London: Labour Party.

Research Council for Complementary Medicine 1992. *Complementary Therapies. A Survey of MPS*. London: Research Council for Complementary Medicine.

Saks, M. 1995. *Professions and the Public Interest. Medical Power, Altruism and Alternative Medicine*. London: Routledge.

Stacey, M. 1994. Collective therapeutic responsibility. Lessons from the GMC. See Budd & Sharma (1994), 107–34.

Wardwell, W. 1992. *History and Evolution of a New Profession*. St Louis: Moseby Year Book.

Whitelegg, M. 1996. The Comfrey controversy. See Cant & Sharma (1996), 66–87.

Willis, E. 1989. *Medical Dominance*. Sydney: Allen & Unwin.

26

Working on the Front-Line: Risk Culture and Nursing in the New NHS

Ellen Annandale

Introduction

Nurses and midwives increasingly talk of working in a climate of fear and uncertainty. The risks that they confront emanate not only from the long-standing concern with clinical uncertainty that has traditionally marked practice, but also from the great emphasis that health care organisations now place on nurses' and midwives' individual accountability. [...] This concern for individual accountability is heightened by the broader self-reflexive culture of late modern society. The shifting parameters of risk and uncertainty that thread through everyday life call for individuals to be constantly questioning, not only the conditions of their own lives, but also the authority of others (Lash, 1994). Thus, when expert individuals or expert-systems fall short of consumer expectations, they are increasingly called to account. The patient has been reborn as 'consumer' who, in theory, is newly empowered to make health care choices and to hold providers to account through new citizens' rights embodied in the Patient's Charter (Walsh, 1994). These changes force risks to the surface that were previously veiled (such as errors of practice) evoking a new vigilance and heightened concern.

Devolved responsibility and accountability to patients and colleagues need not in principle pose a problem for health care providers, but in a risk culture they can fuse to provoke stress and fear. The purpose of this paper is to explore the consequences that this has for practitioners as they engage in the everyday work of caring for patients. It will be argued that the increased surveillance of individual practice by self and others can have a backlash effect. Colleagues and patients are increasingly perceived as 'risk generators' who need to be watched at all times. While the self-protective strategies that emerge to cope with this pressure can enhance quality of patient care, they can also be counter-productive, generating defensive practices which are neither in the interest of health care providers nor patients. Moreover, it will be suggested that attempts to 'cover oneself' may be ineffective: since the practice decisions made *today* only become problems in the *future*, risks can never really be forestalled. The dilemma is that even though staff may come to appreciate this, they *still* feel compelled to do all that they can to colonise the future in order to protect themselves. Since protective strategies can themselves provoke problems a vicious circle is set in train. Herein lies the irony, for the panic culture that emerges, and the negative backlash that it effects, is itself a product of the consumerism and new managerialism that seeks, in fact, to achieve the opposite; that is, to enhance rather than undermine the quality of care that is provided. [...]

The data

The data come from a study of legal accountability in nursing and midwifery that was conducted in 1994. They are drawn from two sources: a questionnaire survey of all trained nurses and midwives who were employed in one hospital trust in late 1994, and in-depth interviews with [19] nurses working on the neurology services of a different hospital trust.

[...]

A climate of risk

> You can't really put your finger on it, what it is. And it's like at the moment you feel you've got to watch your back all the time. That's the sort of atmosphere it is. That you can't...if you're talking to somebody you've got to be careful. That's the feeling; the openness has gone. (Sister)

> I think nursing *is* stressful, but as far as accountability is concerned...you see it's something you think about *all* the time. It's not here in front of your head, it's in the *background* and I think until something comes up, a mistake has been made, then you're made aware of it; that's when you start thinking about it. (Staff nurse)

As these comments reveal, risk surrounds practice, it is in the *background*, there is an *atmosphere*: it is always there. As one staff nurse explained, it is 'always on your mind that you may be held responsible in a legal dispute for actions or words'. Or, as one sister more graphically put it, 'litigation is the "bogey man" that stands behind my shoulder as I practice as a midwife'. This atmosphere engenders a feeling of vulnerability, a fear that you may do the 'wrong thing' or, more worryingly, that whatever you do may not be 'right'. [...] Feelings of vulnerability, the sense that the future haunts actions in the present, can create a fair degree of stress. Indeed, only 23 percent of the survey sample reported that concerns with legal accountability did not cause them 'any stress at all', while 60 percent said it caused them a 'little' and 17 percent a 'great deal' of stress. General fears of either making a mistake, experiencing a complaint or being sued, and a general fear of the nurses or midwives' actions being used against them, were identified as the source of this stress by just over 40 percent [...]

It could be argued that these concerns are intrinsic and long-standing to medical and nursing work. [...] Yet, the nurses in the survey and interview samples felt almost without exception that the concerns that they identified were of *recent* origin. Over 55 percent of the survey sample felt that legal accountability had become a concern over the last 3 years, and 37 percent over the last 5 years. The sample was

Table 1   Reasons for increased concern about legal accountability (those answering 'yes')

	Number	Percent
Patients/relatives more aware of their rights	298	98
Increased concern from professional bodies	235	76
Professionalisation of nursing	156	50
Hospital trusts/management more concerned	185	60
Other	38	12

asked to indicate (yes/no) whether *each* of the factors listed in Table 1 was a reason for increased concern about legal accountability. [...]

It is also interesting to note that 87 percent of the survey sample felt that legal accountability would become even *more* of a concern over the next 5 years (10 percent were *not sure* and 3 percent felt that it would *not*). [...]

Consumers as risk generators

The phrase 'patients are more aware of their rights' was a constant refrain in both the nurse interviews and survey data. This *awareness* seemed to be an omnipresent cloud hanging over daily practice. Although consumerism need not be viewed negatively, it was often taken to be a new and rather malevolent presence which was resented by staff,

Staff nurse: The introduction of the Patient's Charter gets Joe Public to go to bat. It's quoted considerably in the hospital, people quote it to you. So there's an emphasis on 'my granny needs to see a surgeon', you get quite a bit of that. You got it even *before* the Patient's Charter came out, when it was a White Paper.
Int: You mentioned talk about the White Paper around the hospital?
Staff nurse: By patients and relatives. And in the community. People are more aware of what they're entitled to and expect standards to be higher than they used to be. Whether it's through the media, I don't know. But I've found that; they're very articulate.
Int: What about?
Staff nurse: Nursing care, waiting lists: 'My mother's not been seen.'

[...] They know more, want and expect more information,

> Before, I think people used to sit back and say Oh, they're in hospital and, you know, 'let the doctors and nurses get on with it, they know what they're doing.' But with erm, there's so much hype, so much information from the media, they tend to question things because they're more aware of the things that *could* go wrong. (Staff nurse)

The consumerist attitudes that are expressed in a desire for information can become particularly hard to take when they also involve a desire to blame someone for a 'bad outcome'. This is something that was particularly to the forefront of midwives' concerns:

People generally have high, unrealistic expectations and think pregnancy, birth and newborns should be planned and perfect in line with their ideals. When it doesn't, they sue the pants off professionals. (Sister)

[...]But since patients' awareness is an awareness of nurses' and midwives' practice, it can also be experienced as a form of threat and a lack of trust:

Although at the time you feel you have done the right thing, often people, mainly relatives, interfere and question if you have given the right treatment in an attempt to intimidate you by suggesting they will take further action. (Staff midwife)

The concerns that we have seen expressed by nurses and midwives bear witness to the shift in relations of authority from producer to consumer that many commentators have deemed characteristic of late modern society (cf. Abercrombie, 1994). According to Giddens (1994), Beck (1992, 1994) and others, this shift is bound up with the inherently reflexive character of contemporary life. Reflexivity, which involves a process of self-monitoring as well as the monitoring of others, takes place against the backdrop of an implosion of information systems. In the context of health and illness individuals are effectively *forced* to confront the vast array of different 'knowledges' about 'health and lifestyle' and therapies which are displayed in the media. Health-related knowledge has become more visibly contested as the risks of applied science in the form of medical and nursing practice are paraded in newspapers, TV soaps, and documentaries. The reassuring face of medicine of yester-year has been replaced by visions of institutional risk. Financial cut-backs, bungled operations and incompetent practice are now at the heart of television medical dramas and news reports. This new knowledge can bear down heavily on the individual health care 'consumer' creating a sense of anxiety and the felt need to question and challenge.

[...]

[...] There is, [...] a sense in which the new consumerism may be more apparent than real. Perhaps, in line with findings for physicians in the US (Ennis & Vincent, 1994), nurses and midwives overestimate the *true* risk of experiencing a complaint or a malpractice suit. However, it is important to appreciate that 'it is what people *take* to be real that has real consequences' (Dingwall, 1994: 51, my emphasis). It is in these terms that patients can generate concern, as suggested in the following dialogue.

Staff nurse: ... I've not really had any *problems* though. I can't really give you anything to say that there was a problem. But, erm, I'd say that it's from the media.
Int: I'm just wondering how you know that patients are aware [of their rights] then?
Staff nurse: Yes. I don't know! (laughs). Yes, a good question. Excellent question! But erm, I just ... [long pause].
Int: Sense it?
Staff nurse: Maybe I do. I don't know, maybe people have *said* a few things and ... [long pause]. I don't really know *where* I get it from. Though I'm sure ... maybe it's because *I'm* more aware and it's rubbing off, I don't know! (laughs).

Int: That's interesting because other people I've spoken to have said there's this awareness and then can't think of examples.
Staff nurse: No, I *can't . . .*
Int: That's interesting.
Staff nurse: It *is*. It is, but I can't think of anything.
Int: Yes.
Staff nurse: I'll probably think afterwards of – yes, there's this.

[. . .]

Working in the new NHS

The radical changes set in train by the NHS and Community Care Act of 1990 (DoH, 1989) have gained so much momentum that the formal structure of health care now bears little resemblance to that which existed even a decade before. These changes were premised on the vision of a costly and inefficient service marked by stultifying bureaucracy and driven more by the needs of professionals than the provision of quality care to patients. The internal market has sought to introduce accountability into the system at every level, making clinical and financial decision-making more visible through contracting, standard setting and audit mechanisms. In line with broader changes in the economy, this shift has been accompanied by new '"leaner and flatter" managerial structures, decentralised cost centres, devolved budgets, the use of performance indicators and output measurement, localised bargaining, performance-related pay, and customer-oriented quality service' (Pinch, 1994: 207). On the face of it, this new organisational context would seem to cohere well with nursing's professionalising strategy. Yet devolved authority 'does not in itself guarantee that the staff who are "close to the customer" will gain greater control over decision-making' (Walby *et al.*, 1994: 16). As the following discussion will demonstrate, nurses feel that they have responsibility, but sometimes little control. In this context individual accountability can be experienced more as downward pressure than personal autonomy,

> I feel there is less support from management. More putting the blame on individuals. (Staff nurse)

> I'm concerned because management won't back you up, and someone is always singled out to take the blame. What if someone sues me? (Staff nurse)

[. . .] The fact that many nurses and midwives may conceive of individual accountability as a management tool, does little to lessen its impact on their day-to-day experience.

Int: Thinking about accountability in general then, do you think it's something that nurses on the ward are concerned about?
Sister: Very much so.
Int: Is it something that they talk about?
Sister: They don't actually use the word accountability, but on a day to day basis you have people doing things like, 'God, I hope I've done everything before I go.'

There's even one child – one young nurse – who was coming in on days off on a *pretence* that she was visiting, just to make sure that she'd done everything and that she wasn't in trouble. And people are just very *aware* that they can be hauled up. I don't feel that accountability *seems* to be taught to them in a way of telling them, or illustrating to them, that they *have* independence, that they have some *autonomy*; that ... this is balanced with accountability. The impression that I get from them is that their job is on the line, and *their* head's on the block. That is the bit that they've picked up.

[...] Some nurses made a direct link between what they saw as the hospital trust's fear of the costs of litigation and downward pressure on them as individuals. For example,

> Trusts will shift blame onto individuals so as not to incur heavy claims for damages. (Sister).

This may be bound up with the fear of actually losing one's job or professional registration,

Staff nurse: In the present climate, I think everyone wants to keep their job. And everyone is so aware that jobs that were once secure now aren't. And I think that's the one thing that frightens most nurses more than anything.
Int: Why has that changed?
Staff nurse: Because of the economic climate of the Health Service and because ... you know, *no one* in my group who I qualified with has got a permanent contract. So it's a matter of keeping your nose clean, otherwise you don't get your contract extended. And it's the same with a lot of the other staff as well; they *can* be replaced. There are so many nurses out there.

The problem for many of the respondents was that in their opinion management expected them to assume responsibility as individuals, but failed to consistently provide a safe environment in which they could work. Ironically, in the minds of a number of nurses, this only served to increase the likelihood that mistakes would occur. [...] Individually, changes in the NHS and consumerism can generate a sense of unease, but the real feeling of vulnerability comes from their *combined effect* on nurses' work experience. Patients' 'awareness of their rights' and higher expectations can particularly take their toll when they exist side-by-side with the new business culture of the NHS, lack of resources, devolved responsibility and the new roles that nurses are expected to take on (this latter aspect of nurses' work is discussed in more detail below). Nurses and midwives said they were concerned because

> lack of resources; equipment, manpower, time and finance, are taking their toll on the sort of service we can provide. People are given wonderful choices and they are disappointed when they are let down – they complain, quite rightly so. But we don't have the resources to back up the choices they are told they are entitled to. (Sister)

[...] It is in these terms that staff can experience a degree of ambivalence about the patients that they care for.

Consumerism and ambivalence about patients

Nurses and midwives can have mixed feelings about patient consumerism. On the one hand they appreciate why patients want to know more and question more, but at the same time they can also experience the informed patient as a threat. This sense of ambivalence can be seen in the quite different ways in which some nurses talked about their patients over the course of an interview. A senior sister remarked that yes, nurses on her ward *did* feel that patients are more aware of their rights, more aware of what they are entitled to. But, then, she said, we give them a lot of information anyway, particularly in terms of helping to explain what the doctor has said. Care plans are at the bottom of the bed, and the hand over between shifts takes place on a 'walk-round' of the beds on the ward, 'so we've got nothing to hide.' Relatives, in particular, will

> come up and ask you and erm, you know, they're entitled to know about it, which is right. I mean, I'm not saying that's wrong. What I'm saying is it's a feeling you get that they are aware much more of what they are entitled to.

But, she went on to say, patient awareness does

> make you aware of, you have to be aware of what you are doing and you have to make, you have to justify what you are doing to people more than anything else.

In her eyes society was changing, litigation in general, she felt, is on the increase because people 'are just out for what they can get for themselves', forgetting that 'what is good for *them* may not be good for somebody else'. When she first began nursing, many years ago, 'if things went wrong, you'd done your best. People are only human and you'd done your best, and that's that.' Whereas now, 'your best isn't good enough anymore and you need to know what went wrong and why it went wrong, I think.' There is, she felt, an attitude of 'I'm going to make you pay.' These comments suggest that there appears to be an 'openness' with patients and a respect for their wishes to know more and have more input, but simultaneously a wariness, a need to 'watch your back all the time', to be careful what you say to people in case they use it against you at a future date. In some instances, staff may even feel that patients are *seeking* to catch them out. When asked how you could tell if this was likely to happen, the same sister remarked,

> It's just a manner that they approach you with and they try, I suppose they try and pin you down. You're trying to be evasive because that's the way you deal with something you're not quite sure of, but they are sort of ferreting away at it and they're ferreting away at you and they're just waiting for a little something to go wrong, and they've got you.

This sister's comments suggest that it may not just be nurses' and midwives' *perceptions* of their patients that are affected by consumerism, but also their work practice. That is, the care that they provide to patients.

Risk culture and nursing practice

[...] The discussion so far has concentrated on feelings and perceptions, rather than behaviours. The questions that we must now address are: how do nurses and midwives *cope* with the risks that they confront? Are these strategies successful in reducing risk? And, what effects do they have upon patient care?[...]

[...] Nurses and midwives in the current research were asked to respond to the following very general question – 'Concern about legal accountability may influence nurses' and midwives' day to day work in both positive and negative ways. Do you feel that it affects any of the following aspects of your work': documentation, giving drugs, communicating with colleagues (doctors and nurses), and communicating with patients/relatives (see Table 2).

[...] These figures [...] suggest a strong connection of some kind between a general concern with personal accountability and practice. Interestingly, there is also a significant association between the amount of *stress* that concern about accountability causes nurses and midwives in their work ('quite a lot' for 23 percent, 'a little' for 59 percent and, 'non at all' for 17 percent) and the aspects of practice that are listed in Table 2. Specifically, those who reported higher levels of stress were significantly more likely to say that concern about legal accountability influenced the giving of drugs ($p < .02$), communication with colleagues ($p < .01$) and communication with patients/relatives ($p < .01$).[1]

[...] Risks, then, 'essentially express a future component', they have 'something to do with anticipation, with destruction that has not happened but is threatening' (Beck, 1992: 33). Beck's contention that risk consciousness lies not in the present, but in the future, aptly characterises the experiences and, as we will see, the risk-reduction strategies of nurses and midwives. He writes,

> the centre of risk consciousness lies not in the present, but *in the future*. In the risk society, the past loses the power to determine the present. Its place is taken by the future, thus, something non-existent, inventive, fictive is the 'cause' of current experience and action. We become active today in order to prevent, alleviate or take precautions against the problems and crises of tomorrow and the day after tomorrow... (Beck, 1992: 34)

[...]

[...]If actions are likely to 'come back on them' in the future, they feel that they must try to forestall them in the present. A number of practical strategies emerge to cope with this sense of risk.

Table 2 Does legal accountability influence practice?

Percent	Yes		No		Not sure	
	Number	Percent	Number	Percent	Number	[Percent]
Giving drugs	253	81	42	13	17	5
Communicating colleagues	175	63	57	20	48	17
Communicating patients	263	83	32	10	22	7
Documentation	304	95	5	2	9	3

Coping with risk

The most general way that respondents cope is by engaging in a constant process of *checking*, and re-checking what they do and say. Checking and covering are defensive strategies that may have both positive and negative effects on the care that patients receive. They are also more or less successful as risk reduction strategies. As we have seen, nurses and midwives feel quite strongly that concern about legal accountability influences their practice in terms of how they document material in patients' records; how they communicate with patients and their relatives, and with colleagues; and their experience of administering drugs.

One of the most noticeable effects was a heightened concern with accuracy. This was highlighted by 49 percent of the survey sample in reference to documentation. Comments like, 'everything must be written clearly leaving no room for misinterpretation', 'concern ensures accurate and thorough documentation' were made frequently. Patient records are an important resource for the different members of staff who are involved in caring for the patient over the course of the day. Their accuracy, therefore, should contribute significantly to information exchange and, through this, to quality of care. But, there is no doubt that the quest for accuracy is also bound up with covering oneself,

> You feel pressured to document minor irrelevant detail to 'cover yourself'. (Sister)

> You are more personally responsible *now*. Everything needs to be documented, however trivial – at the end of the day it falls back on *you*. (Enrolled nurse)

These respondents suggest that nurses and midwives might write too much, much of it trivial, in the process of covering themselves. Documenting 'everything' is a defence strategy: since they never know what may come back on them at a future date, they feel that they must write it all down 'just in case'. Thus there is a feeling that they must write things down to prove that they have done such diverse things as given a drug, noted and told others about a change in the patient's condition, discussed the patient's condition with his or her relatives, noted a complaint or even just the possibility of a complaint,

> You find yourself documenting everything i.e. a conversation you had with relatives, for instance, if you get the slightest feeling that somebody is not happy. (Staff nurse)

Respondents were well aware that medical and nursing records are legal documents that can be used in a court of law. Contemporaneous records offer a sense of security since they can be evoked as 'proof' of action at a future time when memories have faded. Thus records become simultaneously a crutch and a site of risk in their own right; as one staff nurse put it, they can be 'your saviour or your downfall'. Quite simply, respondents questioned how sure they could ever be that they had covered themselves adequately. The following interview extract illustrates the way in which documenting creates both security and insecurity for nurses and midwives precisely because they can never totally predict which actions or aspects of a patient's care may be defined as a problem at a future date,

Sister: We're very careful about documentation to ensure it's thorough and complete (. . .)
Int: So is that a positive thing?
Sister: Yes, it's a good instrument for the nurses, to protect themselves.
Int: Some people have said [in interview] that they feel anxious about documenting (. . .). Is that something that concerns you?
Sister: . . . I'm very *aware* about documentation. I'm very aware how much *time* it takes. Erm, it doesn't make me *anxious* particularly, I'm getting *fast* to the stage of thinking no matter *how* much you write, you never seem to write exactly what would be needed if, you know, there was a complaint. Erm, sometimes you just miss the one vital thing that you can't imagine that would come back at you. So I think all you can do is just be as precise and concise as you *can* be, *hope* you've covered what you need to cover (. . .).
Int: (. . .) Are you aware of the legal side when you *are* documenting?
Sister: Oh definitely.
Int: Is it in the *back* of your mind?
Sister: Yes, yes it's *constantly* there, and *especially* so if you've had a difficult patient or difficult relatives. You know, you can sit and write a thesis almost trying to cover every aspect that may come back at you. And, as I say, very often it's the *one* thing that you felt was *far* too trivial to document that *does* come back at you (. . .).
Int: Obviously you're documenting on any one day on a number of patients. You've just mentioned a *difficult* patient, how do you know you've got a difficult patient, is it intuitive?
Sister: Yes, you already know your patients that are complaining, or your relatives that are complaining about things, and just discontented patients. You know the type of patient and you need to be as *absolutely* thorough as you can be with them. Obviously, people are encouraged to be thorough with *every* patient, but there are particular patients that you just *need* to ensure that absolutely *everything* is documented. Obviously you do get patients who complain who you *didn't* think would complain and *have*, but you know documentation should be thorough for *every* patient. But sometimes you just need to be that little bit more careful.

Even though documenting is a way for nurses and midwives to protect themselves against patients, the principle protection strategy of 'writing everything down' does not seem to be to the patient's detriment, except insofar as it takes time away from direct patient care. As several respondents implied, it is not really possible to separate out the extent to which the extra (in the minds of some, excessive) documentation that now takes place is for the purposes of good patient care and the extent to which it is done to cover oneself.

   The same is broadly true when we consider the risks that nurses and midwives face when administering drugs. Undoubtedly, staff have *always been* concerned to make sure that patients receive the right drug, at the right dose, at the correct time. But this concern is heightened as a litigious climate has made trust management increasingly concerned about drug errors. The fact that many wards now have single nurse administration of drugs, means that the come-back is squarely on the individual who has signed for the drug,

> For oral drugs, it's one nurse administration, therefore, one nurse accountability. (Sister)

But, of course, even though they *feel* individually accountable, nurses do not work independently. Health care work is inherently collective which means that any one individual's work is invested with the (correct and incorrect) actions of others. Hence an important source of vulnerability is the opening up of the nurse or midwife's work to scrutiny by others who are fearful that other people's actions will bounce back onto them. As one nurse put it,

> It's as if every move and decision is being watched and pulled to pieces making me less confident. (Staff nurse)

Simultaneously, stress also occurs because respondents' own actions may be compromised by the actions of others who are less vigilant or aware. As with written documentation, the need to communicate verbally with colleagues is both a means of 'covering oneself' *and* of enhancing quality of care. In all, 43 percent of the survey sample said that more effective communication occurred as a result of concern about legal accountability. For example,

> Unclear communication could potentially lead to errors in patient care. Each practitioner – doctor and nurse – has a responsibility to their patients to ensure communication is clear and unambiguous. (Staff nurse)

At the same time better communication covers one's own actions,

> There is much more contact with doctors to ensure that anything is passed on that is needed straight away in order to cover oneself. (Staff nurse)

Communicating to cover oneself was referred to by 21 percent of the survey sample. One of the reasons why they felt the need to do this is because of culpability for others' bad practices or mistakes.

Staff nurse: you're careful, you always think twice before doing something. If you're not sure you always check and re-check. You tend to check what other nurses and doctors do as well.
Int: So, you always *check* things?
Staff nurse: You can't trust anybody. Everyone makes mistakes and you've got to check and re-check everything.
Int: Check other people's work?
Staff nurse: It depends if it involves you or not. For example, if it was a doctor's prescription, you check with a doctor.

Many respondents felt a particular need to cover themselves in interactions with doctors, relating that it can be difficult to get them to do things like re-writing drugs or setting up the first dose of an intravenous drug,

Staff nurse: I tend to write everything down. If I've called a doctor, I write down when I've called him; I write down what I've told him; I write down what I've said to him. Especially if I realise that the situation is serious, then I would go back to the records and say 'doctor said he would come up', document the time and put 'he didn't come' and 'bleeped again', 'said he would be up', 'bleeped again' and *then* I would go on and go further up [the medical hierarchy]. I would do that because they won't cover you if you were held accountable.

[...]

The overriding concern of respondents in the current study was to resist being pressured by doctors and by managers to undertake tasks that they either did not feel competent, or were not certified, to do:

Charge nurse: ...going back to drugs, you've got to be careful and make sure you've given the correct things, at the correct time and, if you're giving IV drugs you've got to be aware of whether you can give them or *not*. You know, that's been tried on with me.
Int: Doctors have asked you to do things?
Charge nurse: Well, you've got to realise what you're supposed to do and what you're not supposed to do because, for example, we don't take blood off patients and we don't do arterial blood gasses. It's the simplest thing in the world, but it's not our role, at the *moment*. We're hoping to get it changed. So you've got to be very aware of all that. If anything happened then if you did it, then it's down to you.

As with communication with colleagues, the risk of complaints or being held to account for their actions can improve the quality of nurses' and midwives' communication with patients and their relatives. Almost a third of the survey sample said that concern about legal accountability helped to ensure that the correct information was communicated and/or that patients were fully informed.[...] Respondents referred to the risk of giving out the wrong information and/or giving out information that may be against the patient's wishes leading to caution since 'things that you say could be misinterpreted or you could be accused of saying something that you didn't'. Thus, while they made more references to the generally positive effects that personal accountability and 'patients' awareness of their rights' had on communication, they did also report a worrying need to be more guarded in the information that they did communicate. One senior sister spoke at length about the way that her practice had changed,

Int: What about communication with patients and relatives, has that been affected in either a positive or negative way by concerns about accountability?
Sister: Yes. The role of the nurse is changing, the culture of health care is changing. And there's the Patient's Charter factor. This sounds dreadful, but being a ward sister is a privileged position – you can have a big influence on a patient's recovery. We're dealing with degenerative diseases, death and rehabilitation and there are times when you take a risk if you care enough. It's a job where you become involved, nurses are with patients round the clock and feel the effects of illness on the family, and there are times when senior people take a risk, and you need to be careful and trusting in the patients to do that (...) you may feel you can take a

risk to provoke a step for rehabilitation which could be misunderstood by the patient and the family as harsh and not what nurses do...and I would say there are times, for example, if a patient has chronic MS and you're a skilled person who knows the patient and they're depressed, they've been coming in for years, well you will mentally jolt them. It's being cruel to be kind, which works in rehabilitation occasionally. And even if I know that intuitively that is right, now I would be very careful.

Int: Why is that exactly?

Sister: Because it may be misinterpreted by others. So this may compromise patient care, make you work within the limits of the job, not according to its potential. We had a difficult relative who appalled staff and they were very aware of what they did and what they wrote and this behaviour could be adverse for the patient.

Int: So these concerns could affect patients?

Sister: Yes. For example, as ward sister if I felt someone had an excessive number of visitors and the other patient in the room had a migraine, I'd feel that I must say that it's not fair. But people could challenge that now and complain. And nurses could now steer away from that responsibility when really it's good for the welfare of all patients. But people think and think again now before they take that on. So it definitely affects practice.

Int: Is that more the case recently?

Sister: Yes, definitely in the last couple of years.

As Freidson (1994: 21) writes, if the customer is always right, 'then professionals are no longer able to exercise the authoritative discretion, guided by their independent perspective on what work is appropriate for their craft.' The quality of the nurse or midwife's *own* experience can also be compromised. Several respondents referred to having to sit back and take informal complaints or just niggling remarks from patients. As one staff nurse remarked, 'sometimes you feel like an air hostess. You have to keep a smile on your face when you might feel more like shouting at them'. Thus nurses and midwives engage in on-stage performative work; 'the smile on the flight attendant's face, the pleasantness of the manner of the waiter, the sympathy in the eyes of the nurse' that is indicative of the service ethos (Lash and Urry, 1994: 202).

Concluding discussion

The provision of health care is in considerable flux at the present time. In an environment of apparently constant change the boundaries of individual responsibility and accountability need to be attended to on a continuing basis. The nurses and midwives in the current study reported the need to be almost constantly vigilant; 'looking over their shoulders', 'watching their backs' and 'covering themselves' in light of the risks of practice today that could come back on them in the future. In many instances the defensive coping strategies that they developed appear to contribute simultaneously to good practice (in terms of quality of care to patients) and to their self-protection. For example, taking extra care to write detailed notes in patient records and to pass on information clearly, would seem to benefit both the nurse or midwife *and* the patient. Yet, these practices can also have a backlash effect. Thus respondents reported that excessive documentation took precious time away from direct patient care, and that 'patients' awareness of their rights' could generate caution and restraint in communication. More generally, the need to be wary and 'covering oneself' all the time could generate stress.

[...]

The risks that confront nurses and midwives in their day-to-day work are closely bound up with broader changes in the conceptualisation of citizenship. As Walsh (1994: 192) relates, a new model has emerged in which 'the market is the most effective means of enabling citizenship to be maintained, and the citizen is best seen as a customer.' In these terms, better and more cost efficient care is to be achieved through the individual acting in a simulated market. The environment in which nurses and midwives work is certainly marked by the individualistic ethos of the market and, ultimately, it is this ethos that fosters the sense of risk that surrounds practice. Although the patient as consumer is undoubtedly valued and cared for, he or she is also viewed as someone who *generates* risk. There is a strong ideology of 'partnership with patients', a sense of developing a unique knowledge where the 'nurse's role is seen partly as that of teacher or facilitator, enabling patients to marshal their own healing resources; involving patients as partners in care' and thereby increasing their knowledge and control of their health (Salvage, 1992: 13). But the likelihood of this approach being put into practice seems remote, when patients are simultaneously seen as risk generators.

[...]

Acknowledgement

The author acknowledges the support of the Economic & Social Research Council's Risk and Human Behaviour Programme. An earlier version of this paper was presented at the ESRC's 'Risk in Organisational Settings' Conference in May 1995.

Note

1   The very skewed distribution in response to the effects on documentation rules out the possibility of looking at associations with stress for this variable.

References

Abercrombie, N. (1994), 'Authority and consumer society', in *The Authority of the Consumer*, R. Keat, N. Whitley, and N. Abercrombie, (eds), London: Routledge, 43–57.
Beck, U. (1992), *The Risk Society*, London: Sage.
Beck, U. (1994), 'The reinvention of politics: towards a theory of reflexive modernization', in *Reflexive Modernization*, U. Beck, A. Giddens and S. Lash, Cambridge: Polity, 1–55.
DoH (Department of Health) (1989), *Working for Patients*, London: HMSO.

Dingwall, R. (1994), 'Litigation and the threat to medicine' in *Challenging Medicine*, J. Gabe, D. Kelleher and G. Williams (eds), London: Routledge, 46–64.

Ennis, M., and Vincent, C. (1994), 'The effects of medical accidents and litigation on doctors and patients', *Law and Social Policy*, 16 (2): 97–121.

Freidson, E. (1994), *Professionalism Reborn*, Cambridge: Polity.

Giddens, A. (1994), 'Living in a post-traditional society', in *Reflexive Modernization*, U. Beck, A. Giddens and S. Lash, Cambridge: Polity, 56–109.

Lash, S. (1994), 'Reflexivity and its doubles: structure, aesthetics, community', in *Reflexive Modernization*, U. Beck, A. Giddens and S. Lash, Cambridge: Polity, 110–73.

Lash, S. and Urry, J. (1994), *Economies of Signs and Space*, London: Sage.

Pinch, S. (1994), 'Labour flexibility and the changing welfare state: is there a post-Fordist model?', in *Towards a Post-Fordist Welfare State?*, R. Burrows and B. Loader (eds), London: Routledge, 203–222.

Salvage, J., (1992) 'The new nursing: empowering patients or empowering nurses?', in *Policy Issues in Nursing*, J. Robinson, A. Gray, and E. Elkan (eds), Milton Keynes: Open University Press.

Walby, S. and J. Greenwell, with L. Mackay and K. Soothill (1994), *Medicine and Nursing*, London: Sage.

Walsh, K. (1994), 'Citizens, charters and contracts', in *The Authority of the Consumer*, R. Keat, N. Whitley and N. Abercrombie (eds), London: Routledge, 189–206.

27

Consumerism, Reflexivity and the Medical Encounter

Deborah Lupton

Introduction

When the highly paid specialist said the decision to have a fancy medical test was up to me, I knew 'empowerment' had gone too far. I was paying him to make the decisions. But he was acting like the junior partner in my health care. I might have yelled 'Power to the People' in some demo 20 years ago when he was clawing his way into the Macquarie Street medical establishment, but I didn't actually mean power to me over every technical decision that would crop up in my life. I didn't seek to be 'empowered' in matters that bored me, like tax, or that totally baffled me, like expensive tests. I long for the old doctor-as-God, for the expert who would tell me what to do rather than lay out the odds (Horin, 1995).

[...]

[...] According to the classical economic theory of expected utility, consumers are rational economic decision-makers who have complete sovereignty over the choice of how to use their resources to their best advantage, or to their 'maximum utility' (Fine, 1995). The archetype that is generally set up in opposition to this model of the idealized patient/consumer is that of the 'passive' or 'dependent' patient. This subject position is viewed as undesirable because of the implications of dependency and unquestioning compliance to an authoritative Other. Such compliance deviates from current dominant and privileged notions in Western societies about the importance of the autonomous self, the self who governs personal behaviour via reason rather than emotion.

[...]

The 'consumerist' subject also fits the sociological notion of the 'reflexive project of the self'. This draws upon the assumption that in late modern Western societies individuals constantly seek to reflect upon the practices constituting the self and the body and to maximize, in an entrepreneurial fashion, the benefits for the self (see, for example, Giddens, 1992, 1994). Life, in this formulation, is carried out as an enterprise, demanding a continual search for knowledge to engage in self-improvement. Instead of simply accepting the 'way things are', individuals must continually make decisions from a variety of options as part of everyday life. It is argued, therefore, that individuals experience self, the body and the social and physical worlds with a high degree of reflection, questioning, evaluation and uncertainty. Consonant with this concept of contemporary subjectivity is the contention that expert knowledges, such as medicine and science, are no longer simply accepted on face value. Rather, it is asserted that these knowledges are now open to scepticism and to challenge on the part of lay people due to an increasing public awareness of their uncertainties (Beck, 1994).

There is, therefore, a congruence between the notions of the 'consumerist' patient and the 'reflexive' actor. Both are understood as actively calculating, assessing and, if necessary, countering expert knowledge and autonomy with the objective of maximizing the value of services such as health care. Both tend to portray a type of subject that is non-differentiated; for example, there is little discussion of how gender, sexual identity, age, ethnicity, social class and personal biography or life experiences affect the taking up of 'consumerist' or 'reflexive' positions. Further, neither approach tends to take into account the role played by cultural, psychodynamic and affective processes in individuals' everyday life choices, decisions and actions. [...]

[...] The study presented here was an attempt to explore these issues with Australians; more specifically, using in-depth individual interviews with 60 lay people living in Sydney eliciting their responses to general issues around the role played by medical practitioners in their lives and their opinions of medicine and the medical profession.

The changing role and status of doctors

When the participants were asked whether they thought the social status of medical practitioners in Australian society had changed over time, nearly everyone agreed that it had. A common observation put forward by the participants was that while doctors may still be generally respected in Australia, they are now subject to more criticism. In doing so, regardless of their age, the participants routinely drew comparisons between the medical practitioners they remembered from their childhood, and those they had dealings with today. An almost mythological account was given of a kindly (almost invariably middle-aged, white male) doctor, the traditional archetype of the 'family doctor' who had visited the house and given close and caring attention to them as children:

> [The family doctor] would come to the bed of the child who was ill with my mother. He would take blood pressure, temperature, generally, you know, a gentle hands on approach, and he was actually very comforting. His nature was a very comforting nature. I suppose we all revered him in a way because it was the general feeling in that period that the family doctor was someone you really listened to and respected. (Carol, part-time counsellor and postgraduate student, age 41)[1]

These days, it was often contended, this ideal figure of the 'family doctor' had been challenged by increasing publicity around medical negligence or mistakes, sexual harassment or assault of patients by doctors, medical fraud and so on. There was no general agreement, however, about the extent to which doctors' status had fallen in recent years. The participants were extremely variable in their negative comments about the medical profession. In the interviews they tended to oscillate back and forth between expounding their support of medicine and doctors and criticizing them. Some participants were vehement in their opinion that the image of medical practitioners had been severely damaged:

> I think [doctors] are perceived as money hungry, as incompetent, often not being able to diagnose properly. And you often hear conversations about or participate in conversations about things that have gone wrong with you, and the doctor has given completely the wrong thing or they have prescribed something for the sake of prescribing something without really knowing what they are doing. And I think the community perception of doctors is a poor one. (Graham, pensioner on sickness benefits, 41)

Others, however, were less adamant about the change in doctors' social position and authority, arguing that doctors are still highly respected by members of the general public and that people tend not to challenge them. Even those people who expressed a strong dislike of doctors, contending that they avoided going to see them if at all possible, would often then go on to mention times when doctors had helped themselves or a family member, and the gratitude they felt for this help.

The major emphasis of the criticism of the medical profession articulated in the interviews was not the extent to which medicine had gained power, but rather the proficiency with which individual doctors used their medical knowledge and dealt on a personal level with their patients. The participants tended to be highly aware of the way doctors interacted with them and to judge them harshly if they felt they had been badly treated. This was particularly the case if the doctor had responded to them in what they considered to be an 'uncaring' or abrupt manner, appearing to be insensitive to their feelings or not wanting to take the time to listen. Such doctors, it was contended, could not be trusted with one's health. Such 'atrocity stories' relating to the doctor's personal manner have been identified in other qualitative research studies with lay people (for example, Meredith, 1993).

However, even when people felt that their trust had been violated by their doctor, they said that it can be difficult to confront or challenge the doctor due to his or her institutional power. Grace, a 21-year-old Chinese–Singaporean woman in Australia to study at university, recounted an experience she had had when seeking attention from a doctor in Australia for a wound on her heel. The doctor started rubbing her thigh, and told her that she was 'the most beautiful girl that I have ever seen from Singapore'. Grace said that while she was shocked and angry at this behaviour, 'at the time I felt like I don't have the power to say anything because he was a doctor...I mean like, I mean like I'm a patient. I mean, I guess, who would believe me?' [...]

Despite recounting these stories, most of the participants also referred to a particular doctor they had consulted who demonstrated all the characteristics they considered to be the qualities of a 'good' doctor, including an ability to listen and communicate well, demonstrating empathy and providing comfort when appropriate (see Lupton, 1996). The participants were very certain about how they would distinguish between 'good' and 'bad' doctors. Medical expertise was also valued, but this meant different things for different participants. For Julia, 32 years old, herself a trained nurse, a good doctor 'is someone whose work, and that, is right up to date with all the current research', while for Dolly, a 78-year-old retired bus driver, a good doctor 'knows his onions, so to speak – and if he doesn't know, he refers you to another'. Others mentioned the importance of diagnostic skills and doctors being familiar with the latest technology. Some participants said that it was important that doctors should be able to be willing to countenance the possibility of alternative treatments: 'a good doctor has to be someone that can give people that alternative and say, "Hey, there is another way of doing things"' (Saskia, mother and homemaker of Dutch ethnicity, age 24). Good doctors should also be able to produce results: 'a good doctor is one who operates on you and it is successful and everything is fine – that is what I would call a good doctor' (Joe, fisherman, age 66).

That is not to say that all participants expressed a desire to have a close, friendly relationship with their doctors. For some, the maintenance of a kind of 'professional distance' was seen as important. For example, one man, who had had extensive interaction with doctors over recent years because he had developed multiple sclerosis, asserted that he prefers a more distant relationship:

> that is just the way it is for me with doctors, I prefer that slight distance or to see them as a figure of authority and I will sit there and take instruction from them [laughter], if you know what I mean. (Tom, Anglo–Celtic–Jewish, professional musician, age 42)

[...]

Biomedicine vs alternative therapies

There is evidence that people in Western societies, including Australia, are seeking the help of alternative therapists in greater numbers (Lloyd *et al.*, 1993; Saks, 1994). Some commentators have suggested that this represents a greater cynicism on the part of lay people towards the claims and expertise of biomedicine. The findings of the present study, however, suggest that faith in biomedicine remains strong. Most participants, when asked if they believed in medical science as a good remedy for illness and disease, agreed that they did. Several participants expressed the opinion that medical science itself, while not necessarily possessing the cure for every ill, is continually progressing and will eventually discover a solution. Indeed, for many people, the developments in medical knowledge could only be described as beneficial for society, by dealing with illnesses and diseases that previously were not easily treatable. As Jason, a 16-year-old school student, commented:

> Well, I mean you look at the transplants, heart transplants, livers, kidneys, lungs, cancer – the latest cure for cancer is slowly getting better and improving with new methods and treatments. And so I think the medical system, whether it be the research teams, the development teams, whatever, they deserve some respect for the job that they're doing, the work they're accomplishing.

[...] Despite this general expression of faith in medical science, several of the participants had sought alternative therapies for illnesses or conditions they thought had not been adequately treated by biomedicine. This did not mean that they had avoided medical treatment, however. Typically they had sought alternative therapy after orthodox medicine had first been tried. In some cases, alternative therapies were combined simultaneously with biomedical treatment. For example, Julia, who was receiving treatment for breast cancer at the time of her interview, as a nurse is herself trained in orthodox medicine. Despite her background, she has tried herbalism and naturopathy for her condition. Nonetheless, she commented that orthodox medicine

> ...will be my first line of defence. Like when I went and saw the herbalist a couple of weeks back, he said, 'Oh, if you really want to take my advice, don't have the chemotherapy and we will go from there.' And I just said, 'No, I have just got to have' – what is the word I am looking for – 'conventional treatment and then I will back it up with all the herbs and things.'

For some people, alternative therapies offer the empathetic interaction with a health provider they feel many doctors lack the time or inclination to provide. Rochelle, 23 years old and unemployed, who had had chemotherapy treatment for a brain tumour, said she found the experience extremely alienating:

> At times you just felt like you were just another like animal coming in for the check-in station and getting, you know, they'd measure the size of it, they'd put your skull on that, get out like the callipers and like, a couple of words said here and there but just like a job more than anything. They were going through the motions.

By contrast, Rochelle commented, the naturopath she now sees twice a year for more minor health problems is far more interested in her as an individual. She thinks that compared to naturopaths, many doctors are not as interested in people's emotional states and personal relationships and how they affect health:

> ...when you go and see a naturopath, sure you might pay a bit extra, but I would rather pay the 50 dollars to see my naturopath at the holistic medical centre where I get to see her for an hour or an hour and a half. She goes through everything, from what I've eaten in the last month that I can remember, to mood swings, to the effect that the weather plays on people, to everything – pollution, I mean, you know, being in the city...Doctors don't think of it like that. They're just willing to hand out the drugs without actually thinking that there could be another problem.

These comments underline the importance that most people tend to place upon the affective aspects of health care. If patients think that doctors cannot provide the emotional support and personal interest they feel they need, then they may seek treatment from other kinds of practitioners. Nevertheless, the authority and expertise that attend biomedicine and those who are medically trained still carry much weight, and no participants had completely rejected biomedicine in favour of alternative therapies.

Differences among participants: the influence of age and social class

Previous research (Blaxter and Paterson, 1982; Calnan, 1988; Donaldson *et al.*, 1991) has suggested that older people are more deferential than are younger people towards the medical profession, and that people who are university educated and in professional occupations themselves are more likely to challenge the authority of doctors and seek detailed information on their medical condition. These differences were also evident in the present study. The participants who were aged in their 70s or 80s were more likely to express extremely positive and grateful attitudes about doctors and to state that they had never had a bad experience with a doctor compared with younger participants, who tended to express somewhat more cynical views. Some of the older people had been seeing the same doctor for 30 or more years, growing old with her or him. The older participants were also much less likely than the younger participants to say that they had sought treatment from alternative therapists.

[...]

Discussion

[...] The data here presented suggest that for many people the discourse of consumerism and the reflexive subject position are important parts of the contemporary medical encounter. All participants expressed strong opinions about how they would characterize and distinguish between a 'good' and a 'bad' doctor, and some told 'atrocity stories' involving cases of medical negligence and sexual harassment. Factors such as social class and age or generation group appear to continue to shape the ways that lay people approach the medical encounter, while other factors such as gender and ethnicity seem not to be as influential.

Despite a general agreement that the medical profession is subject to more criticism than in previous times, most people still articulated respect for doctors and faith in medical science. Even those people who had appeared to support and adopt the discourse of consumerism suggested that at least on some occasions they would be willing to invest their trust and faith in a particular doctor, should that doctor earn this trust. This suggests the importance of acknowledging the personal experiences of individuals, including the embodied and affective dimension of illness, and how their interaction with experts is part of their ceaseless construction and reconstruction of subjectivity.

[...] Health care [...] incorporates the use of several kinds of tangible and quite prosaic consumables: drugs, vaccines, lotions, bandages, ointments and so on. The major component of health care, however, is more intangible, involving body work and affective exchanges and outcomes. Thus, for example, the physical examination involves the doctor looking at and touching the patient, using her or his knowledge to search for signs of illness to make a diagnosis. The touch of the doctor and the way she or he interacts with the patient, the doctor's tone of voice, the manner, the words chosen, are all central to the 'consumption' experience, as is how the patient 'feels' during and after the encounter.

It has often been pointed out by critics of the consumerist approach to health care that lay people simply lack the specialized knowledge that medical professionals possess, and this is regarded as a major barrier to consumerism. Over and above this 'asymmetry of knowledge', however, is the almost unique nature of the medical encounter in relation to embodiment and emotional features. Dependency is a central feature of the illness experience and the medical encounter and serves to work against the full taking up of a consumer approach. Illness, disease, pain, disability and impending death are all highly emotional states, and they all tend to encourage a need on the part of the suffering person for dependency upon another (Stein, 1985; de Swaan, 1990; Cassell, 1991). As noted earlier, the late modern notion of reflexivity presented by writers such as Giddens and Beck tends to privilege, above all, a conscious and rational state, involving continual monitoring and criticism based on a challenging approach that is itself reliant on knowledge. The privileged representation of the patient as the reflexive, autonomous consumer simply fails to recognize the often unconscious, unarticulated dependence that patients may have on doctors. This representation also tends to take up the mind/body separation in its valorizing of rational thought over affective and embodied response. It is as if 'the consumer' lacks the physically vulnerable, desiring, all-too-human body which is the primary object of medical care.

A more nuanced interpretation of reflexivity may be to acknowledge the ways that knowledges are constructed via embodied and affective experiences which are both accumulative and dynamic over a person's lifetime. This approach can accommodate the notion of subjectivity itself as fragmented and subject to ambivalence and pulls between the conscious and unconscious levels of experience and feeling (see Henriques et al., 1984). It may be difficult to adopt the ideal-type consumer subject position, to think clearly and to calculate costs and benefits, if one is suffering from pain, distress and illness and the attendant emotions of fear and anxiety. Some people may respond to such situations in which loss of control seems imminent by adopting the consumerist position; others prefer to allow an authoritative figure to 'take over'. Both subject positions may be viewed as 'rational' responses to a distressing and frightening situation. Neither of these subject positions, however, is unproblematic; each is often fraught with ambivalence (Stein, 1985). In a sociocultural context in which autonomy and rationality are highly privileged and dependency upon others is largely viewed as evidence of weakness and irrationality, lay people may feel a continual tension between wanting to behave in a consumerist manner and avoid dependency on doctors and other health care workers, and their equally strongly felt desire at other times to take on the 'passive patient' role and invest their trust and faith in these professionals.

One of the major sociologists of reflexivity, Ulrich Beck, claims that doubt and uncertainty in relation to expert knowledges, or what he terms a 'new modesty' in relation to their claims, may be beneficial, engendering greater curiosity, openness and 'tolerance that is based in the ultimate final certainty of error' (Beck, 1994, p. 33). In the context of medical knowledge, however, such doubt is untenable for most people who are faced with chronic pain, a failing body, severe disability or possible death. It is here that the consumerist approach may be counterproductive, undermining the very trust and faith that is central to the healing and comfort that very ill people desperately seek in the medical encounter. We need doctors to provide us not only with medical expertise and knowledge, but with emotional comfort, concern and empathy towards our suffering and personalized care. 'Satisfaction' with doctors' services could indeed spring from indulging a desire for dependence upon a paternalistic doctor, even as this confounds expectations around 'consumerism' (Williams, 1994, p. 513).

To conclude, there seems little reason to attempt to position one particular kind of response to bodily or psychic distress or pain as more appropriate than the other, for example, by urging people to adopt the 'active consumer' rather than the 'dependent patient' approach. Calls for the increased and continual undermining of professional claims to medical expertise and authority, as advocated by the proponents of consumerism and as supported by the sociological concept of reflexivity, threaten to undermine the beneficial aspects of the doctor–patient relationship, particularly in a context in which uncertainty is inevitable (Katz, 1984). If we cannot invest our trust and faith in the expertise of at least some of the medical practitioners to whom we have access, relying on embodied and affective experience and judgement as guides, the alternative may be paralysis and distress in the face of conflicting options.

Acknowledgements

Thanks are due to the Australian Research Council for funding this research by awarding a large grant for 1994–1995, to the project's research assistant, Jane McLean, for her expertise in arranging and carrying out the interviews, and to the participants themselves.

Note

1   All names are pseudonyms. Unless otherwise stated, individual participants referred to in this article are of Anglo–Celtic ethnicity.

References

Beck, U. (1994) The reinvention of politics: towards a theory of reflexive modernization. In *Reflexive Modernization: Politics, Tradition and Aesthetics in the Modern Social Order*, eds U. Beck, A. Giddens and S. Lash, pp. 1–55. Polity, Cambridge.

Blaxter, M. and Paterson, E. (1982) *Mothers and Daughters: A Three Generational Study of Health Attitudes and Behaviour*. Heinemann, London.

Calnan, M. (1988) Lay evaluation of medicine and medical practice: report of a pilot study. *International Journal of Health Services* 18 (2), 311–22.

Cassell, E. (1991) *The Nature of Suffering and the Goals of Medicine*. Oxford University Press, New York.

Donaldson, C., Lloyd, P. and Lupton, D. (1991) Primary health care amongst elderly Sydney-siders. *Age and Ageing* 20, 280–6.

Fine B. (1995) From political economy to consumption. In *Acknowledging Consumption: A Review of New Studies*, ed. D. Miller, pp. 127–64. Routledge, London.

Giddens, A. (1992) *The Transformation of Intimacy: Sexuality, Love and Eroticism in Modern Societies*. Polity, Cambridge.

Giddens, A. (1994) Living in a post-traditional society. In *Reflexive Modernization: Politics, Tradition and Aesthetics in the Modern Social Order*, eds. U. Beck, A. Giddens and S. Lash, pp. 56–109. Polity, Cambridge.

Henriques, J., Hollway, W., Urwin, C., Venn, C. and Walkerdine, V. (1984) Theorizing subjectivity. In *Changing the Subject: Psychology, Social Regulation and Subjectivity*, eds. J. Henriques, W. Hollway, C. Urwin, C. Venn and V. Walkerdine, pp. 203–26. Methuen, London.

Horin, A. (1995) It's the price we pay for empowerment. *Sydney Morning Herald*, 7 October, p. 21.

Katz, J. (1984) Why doctors don't disclose uncertainty. *The Hastings Center Report* February, 35–44.

Lloyd, P. Lupton, D., Wiesner, D. and Hasleton, S. (1993) Socio-demographic characteristics and reasons for choosing natural therapy: an exploratory study of patients resident in Sydney. *Australian Journal of Public Health* 17 (2), 135–44.

Lupton, D. (1996) 'Your life in their hands': trust in the medical encounter. In *Health and the Sociology of Emotion*, Sociology of Health and Illness Monograph Series, eds. J. Gabe and V. James, pp. 158–72. Blackwell, Oxford.

Meredith, P. (1993) Patient satisfaction with communication in general surgery: problems of measurement and improvement. *Social Science & Medicine* 37 (5), 591–602.

Saks, M. (1994) The alternatives to medicine. In *Challenging Medicine*, eds. J. Gabe, D. Kelleher and G. Williams, pp. 84–103. Routledge, London.

Stein, H. (1985) *The Psychodynamics of Medical Practice: Unconscious Factors in Patient Care*. University of California Press, Berkeley.

de Swaan, A. (1990) *The Management of Normality: Critical Essays in Health and Welfare*. Routledge, London.

Williams, B. (1994) Patient satisfaction: a valid concept? *Social Science & Medicine* 38 (4), 509–16.

Index